The Primary ICT and E-learning Co-ordinator's Manual

Book 2: A guide for experienced leaders and managers

The Primary ICT and E-learning Co-ordinator's Manual

Book 2: A guide for experienced leaders and managers

James Wright

SAGE Publications

Los Angeles • London • New Delhi • Singapore

SAGE Publications Ltd
1 Oliver's Yard
55 City Road
London EC1Y 1SP

SAGE Publications Inc.
2455 Teller Road
Thousand Oaks, California 91320

SAGE Publications India Pvt Ltd
B 1/I 1 Mohan Cooperative Industrial Area
Mathura Road
New Delhi 110 044

SAGE Publications Asia-Pacific Pte Ltd
33 Pekin Street #02-01
Far East Square
Singapore 048763

Library of Congress Control Number: 2007933694

British Library Cataloguing in Publication data

A catalogue record for this book is available from the British
Library

ISBN 0 978-1-4129-3560-9
ISBN 0 978-1-4129-3561-6 (pbk)

Typeset by Pantek Arts Ltd, Maidstone
Printed in Great Britain by the Cromwell Press, Trowbridge,
Wiltshire
Printed on paper from sustainable resources

Contents

Ofsted material is Crown Copyright and reproduced under the terms of HMSO Guidance Note 5.

Qualifications and Curriculum Authority copyright material is reproduced under the terms of HMSO Guidance Note 8.

Preface

In recent years the traditional position of ICT co-ordinator within the primary school setting has expanded and evolved beyond recognition. No longer is it simply a matter of organizing appropriate software and timetabling access to a suite of computers to deliver a discrete curriculum. As ICT has demonstrated its impact upon all areas of the curriculum, school networks need to be effectively managed and resourced, staff needs to be trained, pupils need to be guaranteed a technological entitlement. Concurrently the expansion of the Internet has brought with it a host of E-safety concerns that schools need to address such that all ICT and E-learning co-ordinators must possess or develop a long-term strategic view that can steer them through this complex process.

The Primary ICT and E-learning Co-ordinator's Manual is a two-volume work that covers all areas of this demanding brief in the form of two distinct 'manuals'. Book 1, 'A guide for new subject leaders', is directed primarily at new subject leaders and details a 33-task schedule of activities spread carefully over the co-ordinator's first year. As with Book 2, the first manual guides ICT co-ordinators term by term covering the following aspects of the subject leader's brief:

TERM 1 – in which co-ordinators will audit existing school systems to provide a clear overview of current hardware and software provision and to establish a manageable model for the development of the E-learning community. In particular the co-ordinator will be guided through a strategic self-review using the British Educational Communications and Technology Agency (BECTA) online matrix and will take an initial view of the manner in which ICT is delivered as a discrete subject area.

TERM 2 – in which co-ordinators will review and revise the school policy for ICT including an initial review of safe Internet practice. They will complete a review of the manner in which ICT is used as a teaching and learning tool across other subject areas fulfilling statutory requirements and spend reading time researching the position of ICT within the National Primary Strategy. On a practical level, co-ordinators will examine methods for the management of technical support services and consider the implications of various print strategies.

TERM 3 – in which co-ordinators will focus upon establishing a clear overview of standards in ICT. Including a review of assessment procedures, moderating work, monitoring teaching and learning and creating E-portfolios. Co-ordinators will ensure that the National Digital Curriculum has been effectively adopted. In addition co-ordinators will complete a staff skills audit and review CPD provision for all staff.

Book 2, 'A guide for experienced leaders and managers', develops the co-ordinator's journey into the second year, but may also be a useful starting point for more experienced leaders and school managers seeking a revised strategic E-learning overview. In particular, this second text deals more specifically with issues that lie at the heart of school improvement and connects each E-learning initiative with the school's central self-evaluation procedures. The manual's activities, and the dialogue that accompanies them, will challenge school leaders to question current pedagogical thinking surrounding the adoption of new technologies and invite them to reflect upon the implications and consequences of failing to embed ICT within their own school curriculum.

Each book follows a group of virtual co-ordinators from various school settings as they are mentored through a systematic series of activities that guide them through the school year. During weblog discussions we witness their distinctive interactions and evolution as effective leaders attempting to integrate the book's 33 guided tasks and ultimately to produce a sustainable strategy for E-learning.

Whilst the characters within the weblog are fictional they are based in the author's real experience of working with hundreds of primary co-ordinators and headteachers in his advisory work across two local authorities. As Senior Adviser for ICT with Warrington Children's Services, with strategic responsibility for schools ICT, James worked with a wide range of schools in order to develop the strategic leadership of ICT before moving to Lancashire Education Authority where he currently works as a School Improvement Partner and Primary Adviser. He has written and developed a wide range of training materials for headteacher and subject-leader seminars including 'School Self Evaluation for ICT', 'Assessing Standards in ICT' and 'E-safety and Every Child Matters'.

Readers may contact James directly via his companion website at www.james-wright.org through which co-ordinators may join live blogs supporting the implementation of both manuals.

Book 1 of the series, *The Primary ICT and E-learning Co-ordinator's Manual – Book 1: A guide for new subject leaders*, covers the following subject areas.

Blogging
Chapter 1 September
- Fact Finding Audit, the Subject Leader File
- A Vision for E-learning
- A Model of Leadership

Chapter 2 October
- Auditing Hardware
- A Review of Technical Support
- Strategic Audit and Self-Review, Part 1

Chapter 3 November
- Strategic Audit and Self-Review, Part 2
- Completing a Network Software Audit
- Provision for the Discrete ICT Curriculum

Chapter 4 December
- Strategic Audit and Self-Review, Part 3
- Reviewing Software Licence Agreements
- Understanding Attainment in ICT

Chapter 5 January
- Writing a Policy for ICT, Part 1
- Using ICT across the Curriculum – Statutory Requirements
- An Initial Review of Internet Safety Arrangements

Chapter 6 February
- Writing a Policy for ICT, Part 2
- Defining a Print Strategy
- Using ICT across the Curriculum – an Autumn Term Macro Plan

Chapter 7 March
- Using ICT across the Curriculum – Spring and Summer Macro Plans
- Creating a Policy for ICT, Part 3
- Managing Breakdowns

Chapter 8 April
- Creating a Policy for ICT, Part 4
- ICT in the Primary Strategy – Literacy
- ICT in the Primary Strategy – Mathematics

Blogging

17th August

Toby

Posts:

Where does one begin? Well as way of introduction, my name's Toby and I have been the assistant headteacher at a large primary school in Swindon for around 6 months now. We have 540 children currently on role. I am the school's E-learning co-ordinator and have been asked by Gambo to act as a kind of chairperson for this series of blog entries following on from my participation in the first manual, 'A guide for new subject leaders'. I feel as though my position has now moved on and I'm looking to strategically embed sustainable E-learning structures across our school. I also like cutting-edge technology and want to put interactive E-learning at the heart of every school initiative, Gambo, you may need to rein me in from time to time.

This is a big year for me following my promotion on to the Leadership team last year and I hope to complete ICT Mark accreditation by the end of the summer. It is of course more of Gambo's blog than mine but I have agreed in principal to stick at it throughout the year. Okay, Gambo? Over to you.

Quote

Gambo

Posts:

Hi, Toby, I trust you had a good summer and thanks for taking over at the hub, so to speak. Alex, who chaired the blog last year and indeed initiated the whole programme, has a new job in Stafford and won't be joining us on this board; she decided to consolidate last year's protocols within her new setting this year. To reintroduce myself to new contributors, I am an ICT Adviser and have supported hundreds of primary co-ordinators and school leaders in developing the strategic role of ICT within schools. That is the core function of my 'manuals' they deal with the decisions at the heart of school management that have a sustained long-term impact upon learning and teaching. I remind colleagues of the importance of a long-term strategic plan and intend through this web log to deal directly with school leaders who have a vision for twenty-first century education and wish to use this forum to try out ideas.

19th August

#1

Sue

Posts:

Hi, guys, I am so excited about getting access to this blog and chatting to the mysterious 'Gambo'. Followed the first manual very closely, and obviously found it useful or I wouldn't be here. This sounds like just the type of support group that I need. I am a headteacher by the way, have been for seven years at a very small four-class school in Norfolk. As such I have to be master of many trades and so co-ordinate ICT along with science and geography. I cover PPA time for the other teaching staff but have no class commitment myself. I love technology! We videoconference locally and I want to know how this can take off; any ideas will be most gratefully received and I hope that I can offer suggestions of support to colleagues.

Quote

#2

Toby

Posts:

Welcome, Sue, it's good to have a headteacher on board.

Quote

#3

Colonel

Posts:

Just had to say hello, guys.

Quote

#4

Toby

Posts:

Going to say anything else, Colonel?

Quote

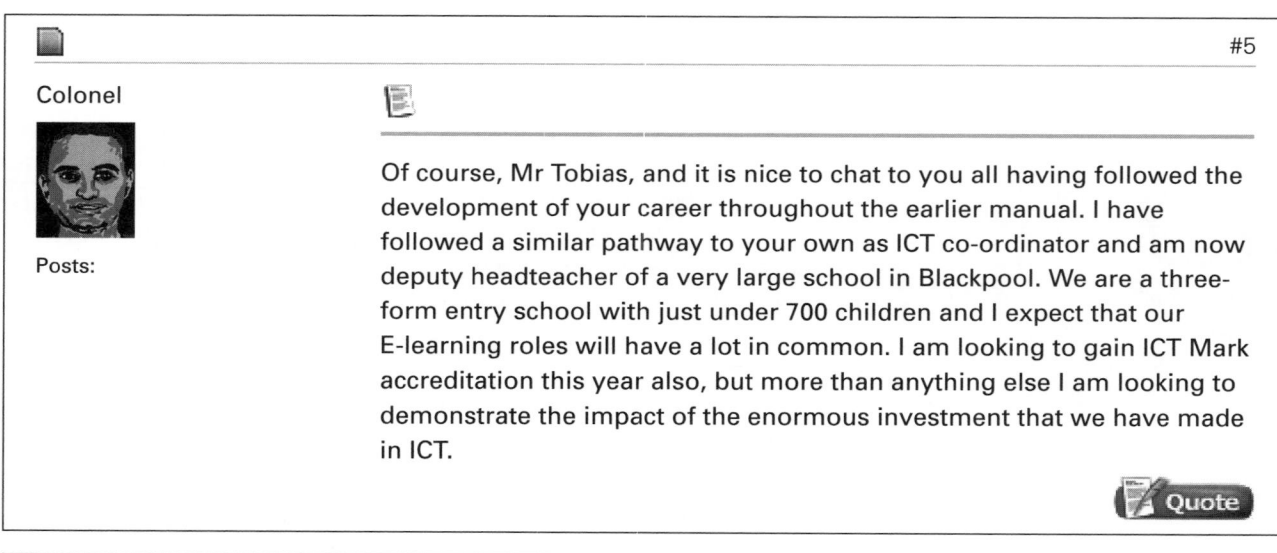

Colonel

Posts:

#5

Of course, Mr Tobias, and it is nice to chat to you all having followed the development of your career throughout the earlier manual. I have followed a similar pathway to your own as ICT co-ordinator and am now deputy headteacher of a very large school in Blackpool. We are a three-form entry school with just under 700 children and I expect that our E-learning roles will have a lot in common. I am looking to gain ICT Mark accreditation this year also, but more than anything else I am looking to demonstrate the impact of the enormous investment that we have made in ICT.

Quote

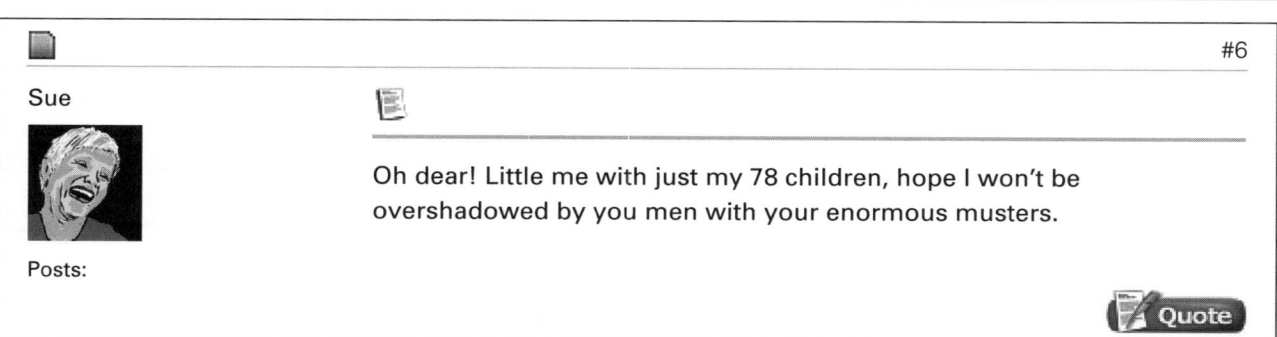

Sue

Posts:

#6

Oh dear! Little me with just my 78 children, hope I won't be overshadowed by you men with your enormous musters.

Quote

24th August

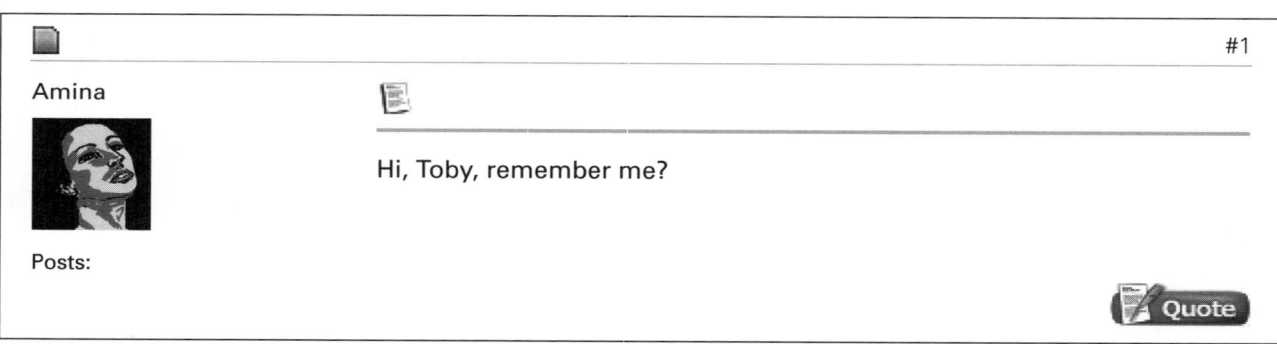

Amina

Posts:

#1

Hi, Toby, remember me?

Quote

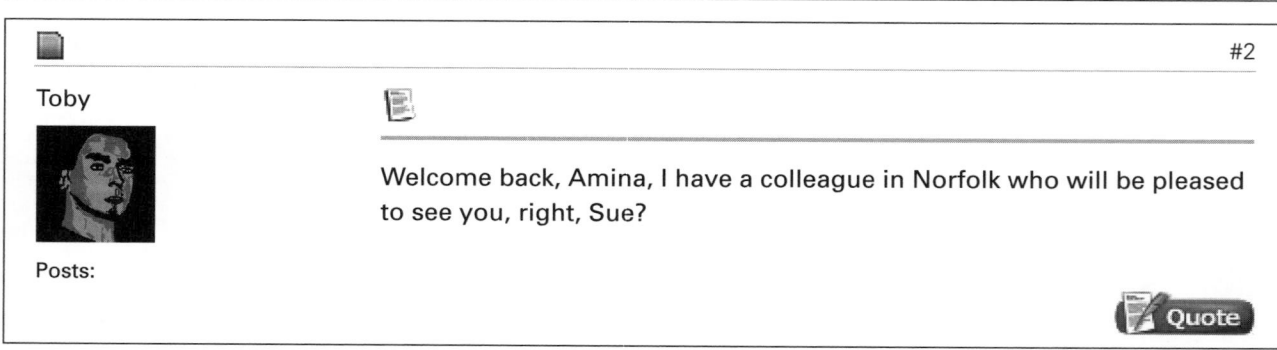

Toby

Posts:

#2

Welcome back, Amina, I have a colleague in Norfolk who will be pleased to see you, right, Sue?

Quote

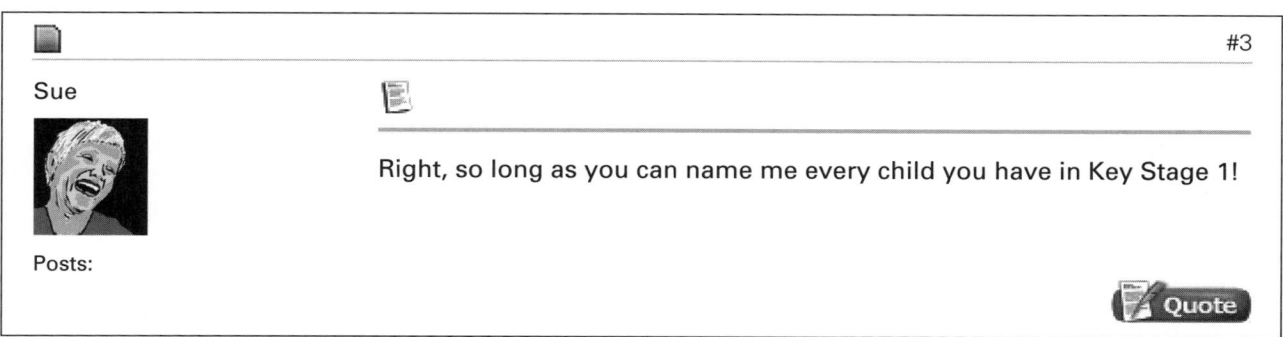

Sue

Posts:

#3

Right, so long as you can name me every child you have in Key Stage 1!

Quote

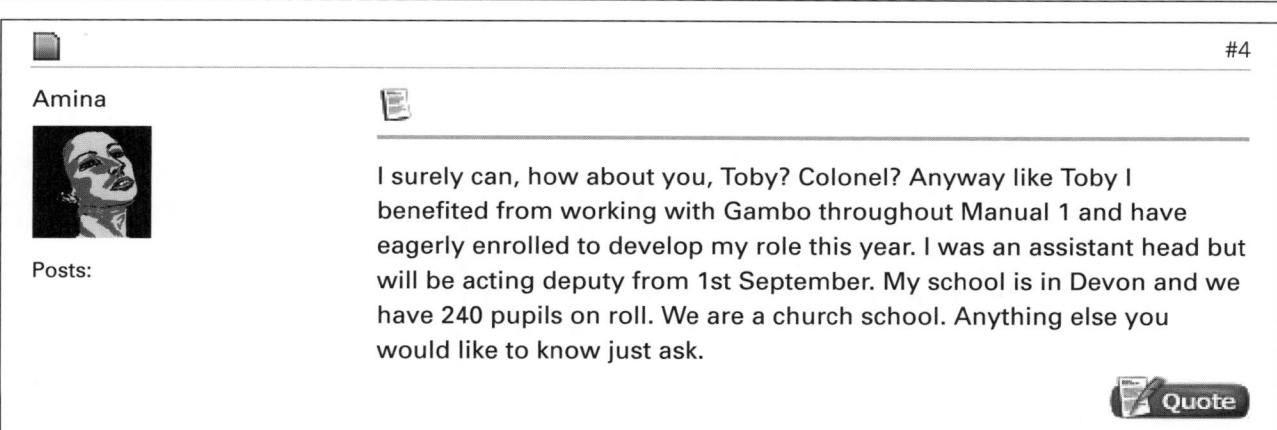

Amina

Posts:

#4

I surely can, how about you, Toby? Colonel? Anyway like Toby I benefited from working with Gambo throughout Manual 1 and have eagerly enrolled to develop my role this year. I was an assistant head but will be acting deputy from 1st September. My school is in Devon and we have 240 pupils on roll. We are a church school. Anything else you would like to know just ask.

Quote

27th August

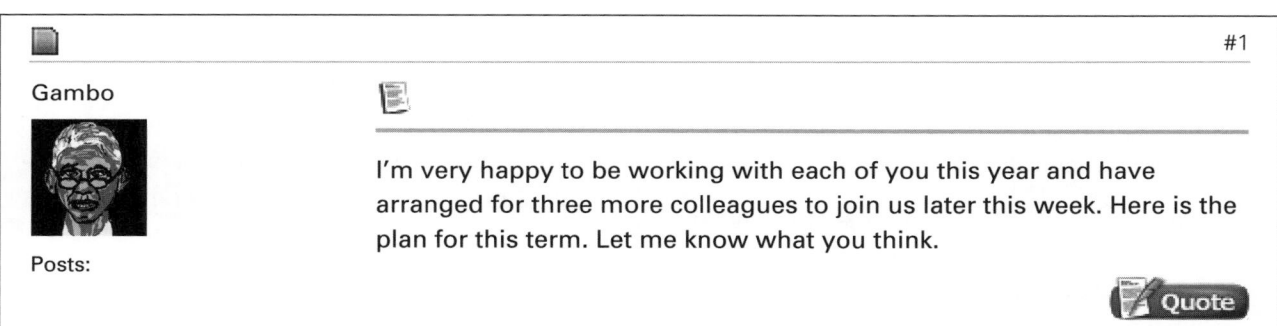

Gambo

Posts:

#1

I'm very happy to be working with each of you this year and have arranged for three more colleagues to join us later this week. Here is the plan for this term. Let me know what you think.

Quote

Table 1.1 Autumn term plan

AUTUMN TERM			
SEPTEMBER	OCTOBER	NOVEMBER	DECEMBER
Barriers to Success – Evolving Vision and Leadership. A two-part process review of self-reflection to identify the key characteristics of leaders capable of creating and sustaining high-impact technological initiatives		**Funding**	
		A Sustainable Funding Model Consider funding models in order to plan for ICT developments with due regard to the total cost of ownership	**Understanding ICT Funding Streams** A historical overview of national investment in ICT and E-learning
Preparing an E-learning Narrative	**Effective Team Evaluations**		
E-SAFETY In which co-ordinators will undertake a complete review of E-safety procedures in the light of the Every Child Matters agenda			
Raising Staff Awareness	**Policy and Procedures**	**Teaching Internet Safety**	**Home–School Links**
Effective Self-Evaluation for ICT			**Network Security** Securing ICT equipment within a school network. A review of strategies and priorities and identification of key issues
Revising the Self-Review Framework A return to the BECTA SRF to determine progress since the initial audit was undertaken	**From Self-Review to a Strategic Plan for ICT** A broader ICT action planning review to embed a revised E-learning vision through a series of long-term sustainable actions	**Establishing ICT Priorities within a Whole-School Context** Combining the findings from the E-learning narrative with the SRF review to create clear unambiguous priorities for development	

Available on the net at http://www.james-wright.org

29th August

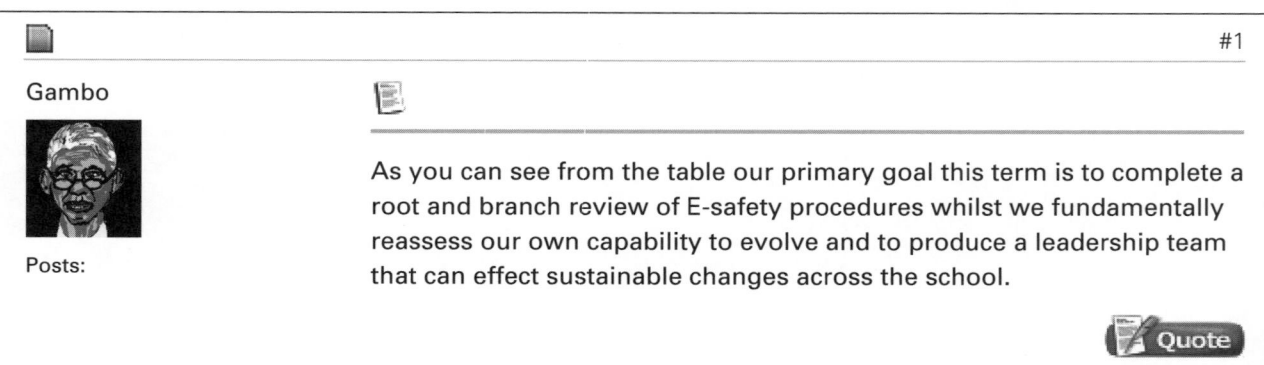

#1

Gambo

Posts:

As you can see from the table our primary goal this term is to complete a root and branch review of E-safety procedures whilst we fundamentally reassess our own capability to evolve and to produce a leadership team that can effect sustainable changes across the school.

Quote

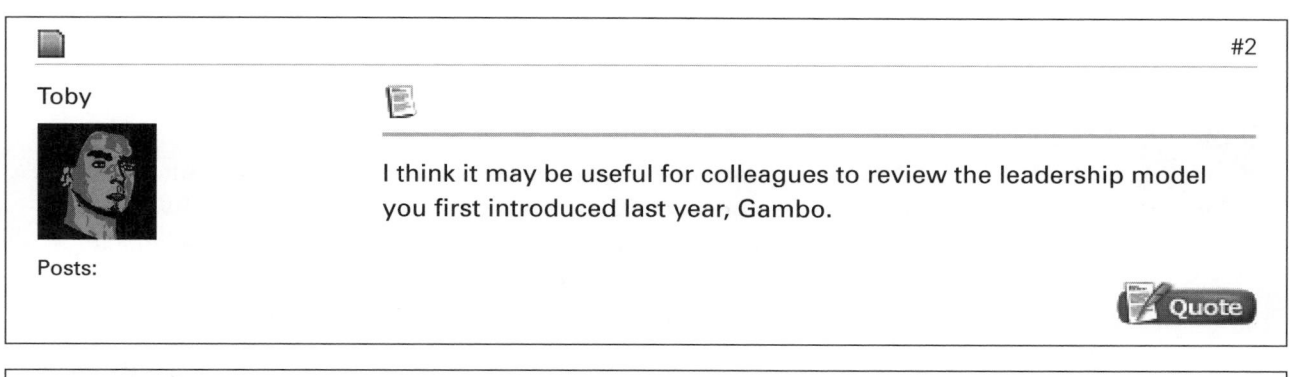

Toby

Posts:

I think it may be useful for colleagues to review the leadership model you first introduced last year, Gambo.

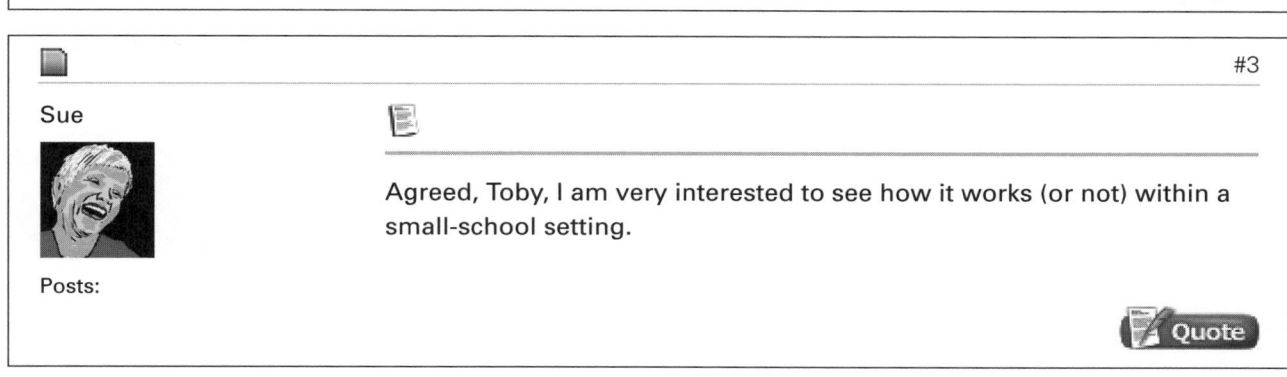

Sue

Posts:

Agreed, Toby, I am very interested to see how it works (or not) within a small-school setting.

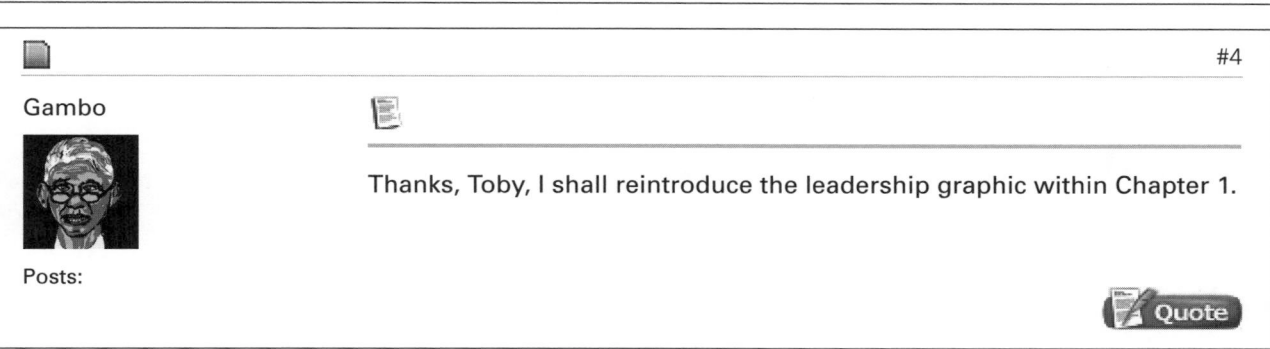

Gambo

Posts:

Thanks, Toby, I shall reintroduce the leadership graphic within Chapter 1.

30th August

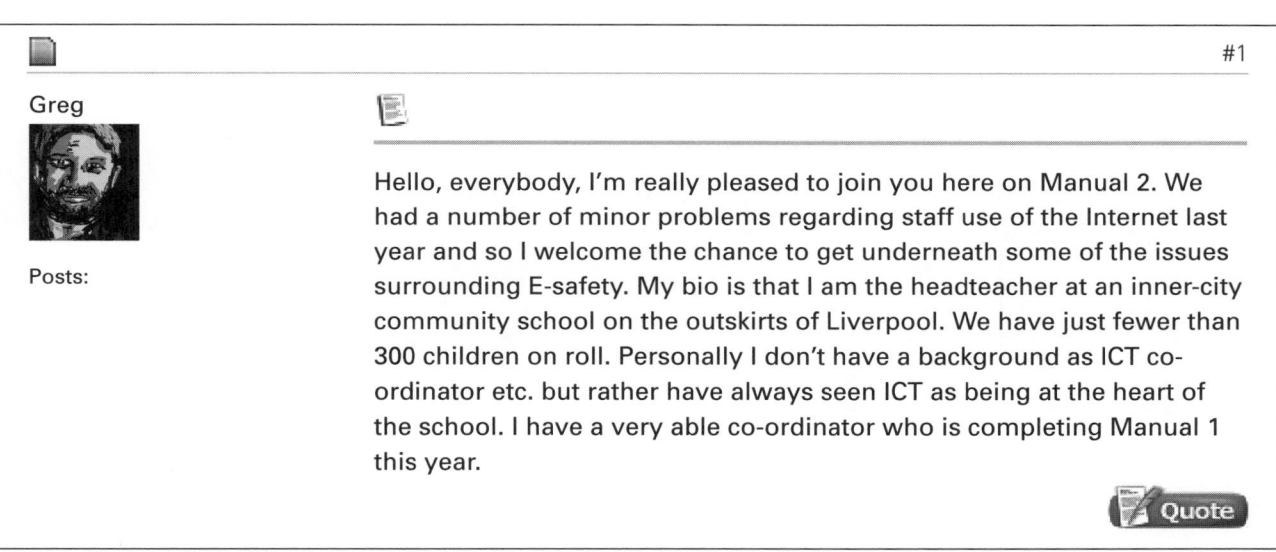

Greg

Posts:

Hello, everybody, I'm really pleased to join you here on Manual 2. We had a number of minor problems regarding staff use of the Internet last year and so I welcome the chance to get underneath some of the issues surrounding E-safety. My bio is that I am the headteacher at an inner-city community school on the outskirts of Liverpool. We have just fewer than 300 children on roll. Personally I don't have a background as ICT co-ordinator etc. but rather have always seen ICT as being at the heart of the school. I have a very able co-ordinator who is completing Manual 1 this year.

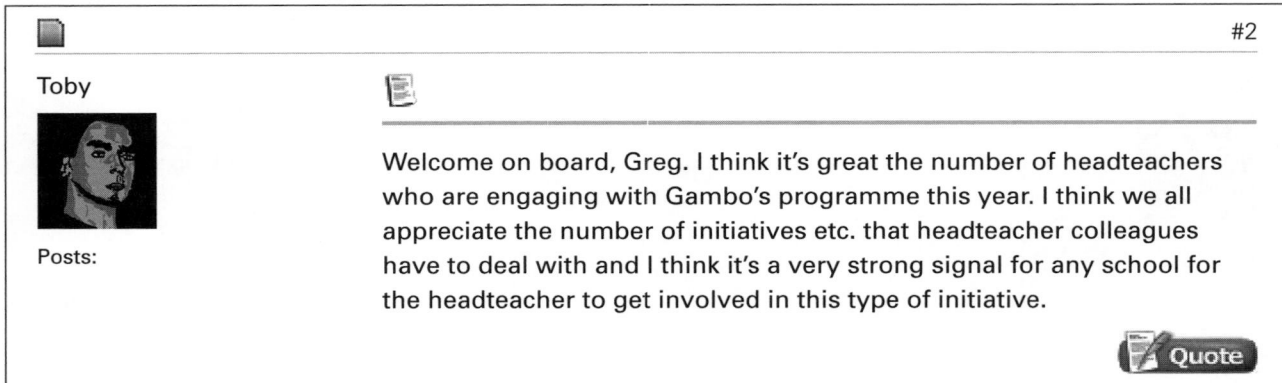

Toby

Posts:

Welcome on board, Greg. I think it's great the number of headteachers who are engaging with Gambo's programme this year. I think we all appreciate the number of initiatives etc. that headteacher colleagues have to deal with and I think it's a very strong signal for any school for the headteacher to get involved in this type of initiative.

Quote

Chapter 1 • *September*

3rd September

Week 1, Task 1 – Barriers to Success – Preparing an E-learning Narrative

This second manual in the series is written for school leaders who wish to capture and to understand the essence of that which connects all E-confident schools – Schools in which the use and promotion of information technologies is embedded across all aspects of the school. It is leadership that takes schools forward as with other key indicators of school improvement and it is the vision and effectiveness of the leadership group that will separate technologically progressive schools from those who falter or who regard ICT merely as a burden.

In recent years I have adopted a process model of work with schools that seeks to identify and to deconstruct the barriers that get in the way of technological developments. My aim is to empower school leaders both to recognize these barriers and to identify where changes need to be made, even when these changes lie within themselves. Typically, opposition and resistance at a variety of levels is the core reason why schools fail in their efforts to embed E-learning.

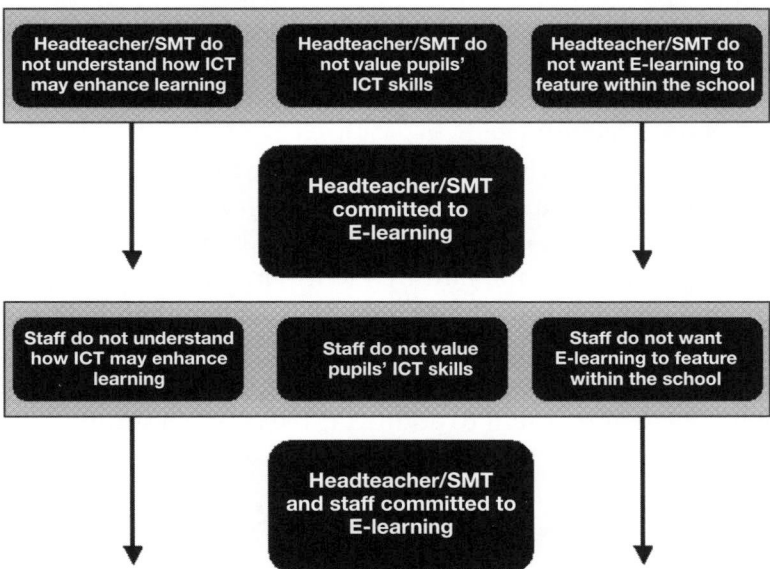

Figure 1.1 Barriers to embedding E-learning
Available on the net at http://www.james-wright.org

Figure 1.1 paints a simple and somewhat damning picture in terms of a school's inability to get its E-learning dimension to function correctly, invariably as a result of the ambivalent position of senior managers within the school. It is imperative, therefore, that anyone leading E-learning within a school understands the human landscape that lies behind such initiatives and has the full support and confidence of the broader leadership group.

By definition, most of the leaders studying this blog will have moved beyond the first layer of the figure and will be considering and developing strategies to challenge staff. Now is the time to formulate a clear vision for ICT that is shared and distributed to everyone involved, and through which the school's leaders may challenge resistance and 'sell' the vision in all that they say and do.

In *Beyond Entrepreneurship* (1992: 7) James Collins captures this focus within his discussion of authenticity through the context of organizational leadership. Being authentic relates to the manner in which a leader's actions validate their spoken beliefs and the means by which staff identify the core values of the organization.

> *'Just speaking authentically isn't enough; you also have to act authentically. Each decision and action should dovetail with your philosophy, being in itself a statement of your core values.'*

Leaders set the agenda for change and must be the role models for this philosophy. Therefore this is the point at which I invite colleagues to review the school's collective attitude towards E-learning. Over the coming weeks, whilst colleagues continue to develop their school's E-learning strategy and to implement its operations, I should like to propose a greater challenge. That of creating a powerful and united ICT leadership team that fulfils Collins's criteria for authenticity. There are no half measures here and to be successful you must be clear about the sort of team that will transform learning within your school. There should be no passengers and no 'union of the unwilling'. Time invested at this early stage in creating this partnership will pay back many times over by identifying and removing the key barriers that prevent schools from attaining E-confidence – barriers that are sometimes pedagogical but more often characterized through different human agendas. Be clear and confident about the team that you have built. Over the coming weeks each member of the ICT team will be challenged to scrutinize their own contribution, beginning with yourself in your lead role as E-learning co-ordinator. Your first task therefore is to review your perception of the E-learning journey that you have embarked upon, with particular regard to your own personal development and that of the school. Working with a trusted colleague or partner, you will describe your journey in order to understand the bigger picture, to clarify its direction and to identify its destination. Often it may be useful to work with an external consultant at this stage to challenge your thinking about the core issues facing the school, but it may be undertaken as a self-reflection exercise.

As a model for your reflection and self-analysis I suggest that you adopt procedures often used outside schools, in business and caring services, to develop organizational and individual change. In his work, *The Skilled Helper* (1998), Gerard Egan described a three-stage model or framework for support, which aims to move a client forward by identifying key actions that will lead directly to his or her chosen outcomes. Egan's Model B process helps clients to see themselves and others in new ways and provides a framework for conceptualizing the helping process. Central to the adoption of this method is an emphasis upon empowering the client by making their agenda central to the process and ultimately enabling them to address three core questions:

'What is going on?'
'What do I want instead?'
'How might I get to what I want?'

Egan's is a three-stage model useful in helping individuals and organizations to solve problems and to identify opportunities, with an emphasis upon empowerment. It provides a map often used within mentoring and applied flexibly to identify opportunities for change. Clearly this model has potential value in supporting your self-review at the present time by providing a framework for managing change within the E-learning leadership group.

Stage 1 – What is going on?
Egan's stage 1 provides a safe place for the speaker to tell their story in their own way. It gives an opportunity for each person to hear and understand their story whilst the listener attempts to reflect back the broader picture as it unfolds, identifying others' perspectives of these same events. In its first expansive phase, the helper listens actively to explore the tale, and summarizes what is said, in order to make sense of the journey. They may question the speaker's feelings at various points in the narrative and seek further explanation.

Your first activity is to create and reflect upon your own E-learning narrative forged out of two parallel and interconnected pathways – the school's and your own. Consider the school's E-learning journey over the past five years, where it has come from, its current direction and the highs and lows. Alongside this describe your own journey from an E-learning ICT perspective. What role has it played within your own career as a leader, as a teacher and as a learner?

You need to articulate these interconnected stories in order to be clear about the next steps for yourself and the school. Ideally you should aim to share this story, perhaps with a peer from another school, or the schools adviser or a linked consultant. You want someone who can listen objectively yet be able to challenge you to define any blind spots. If you cannot gain external support then be your own inquisitor, starting with a mind map that includes all the pertinent events and personalities within each journey.

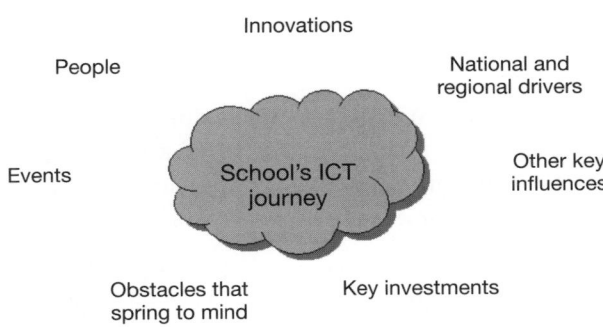

Figure 1.2 School's ICT journey
Available on the net at http://www.james-wright.org

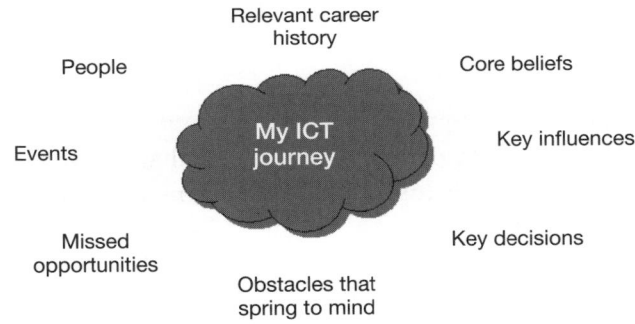

Figure 1.3 My ICT journey
Available on the net at http://www.james-wright.org

Figures 1.2 and 1.3 provide potential start points for the mind-mapping activity including appropriate prompts that may be useful to you. Having reflected upon the current scenario it is useful to identify blind spots that may be pertinent in bringing together your own journey and that of the school. Egan notes that it can be difficult for individuals to see their own situation clearly or from different angles. An objective listener may help you to uncover gaps in perceptions of the situation. It is my intention when we move on to the team element of this exercise to ask you to work in pairs with a colleague in the presentation and feedback of your narrative. For now, having created the concept maps, you should attempt in one sitting, taking no more than an hour, to bring the two sets of events together in the form of an honest written narrative that describes a combined history and provides you with a baseline for the coming months.

4th September

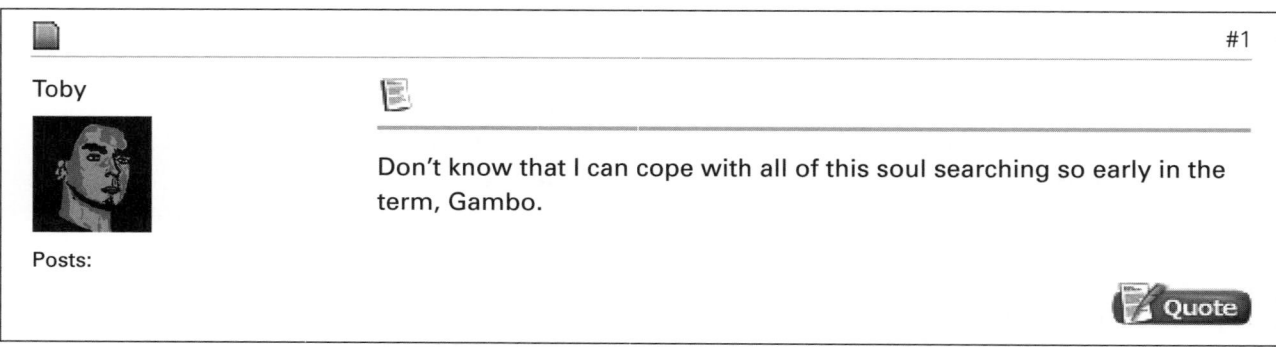

Toby

Posts:

#1

Don't know that I can cope with all of this soul searching so early in the term, Gambo.

Quote

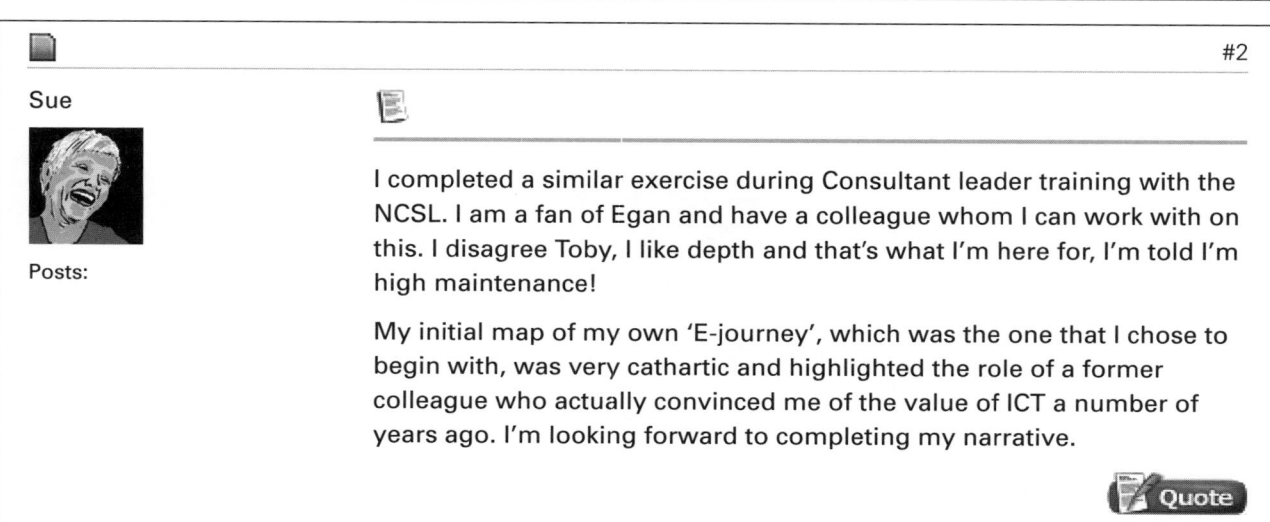

Sue

Posts:

#2

I completed a similar exercise during Consultant leader training with the NCSL. I am a fan of Egan and have a colleague whom I can work with on this. I disagree Toby, I like depth and that's what I'm here for, I'm told I'm high maintenance!

My initial map of my own 'E-journey', which was the one that I chose to begin with, was very cathartic and highlighted the role of a former colleague who actually convinced me of the value of ICT a number of years ago. I'm looking forward to completing my narrative.

Quote

4th September

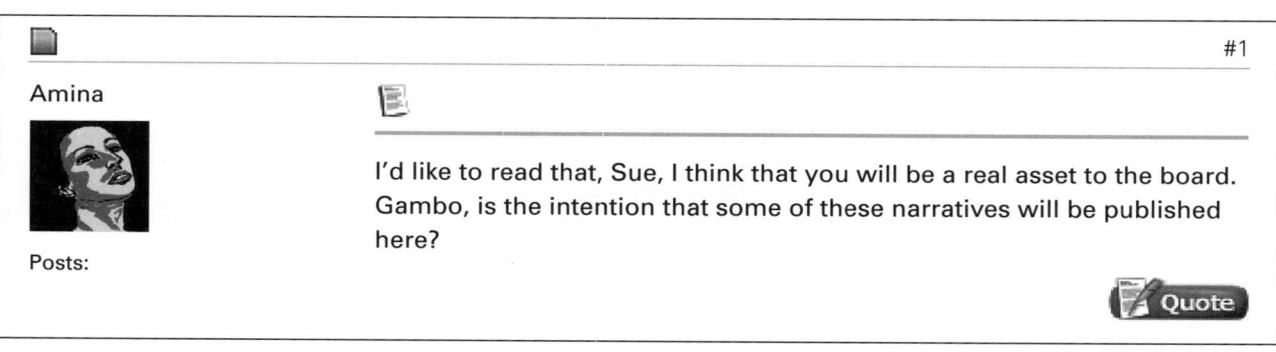

Amina

Posts:

#1

I'd like to read that, Sue, I think that you will be a real asset to the board. Gambo, is the intention that some of these narratives will be published here?

Quote

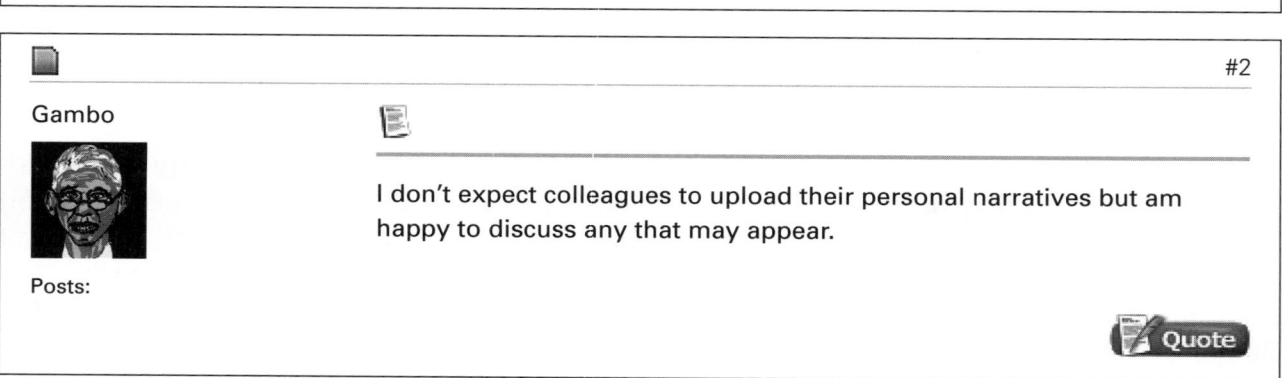

Gambo

Posts:

#2

I don't expect colleagues to upload their personal narratives but am happy to discuss any that may appear.

Quote

5th September

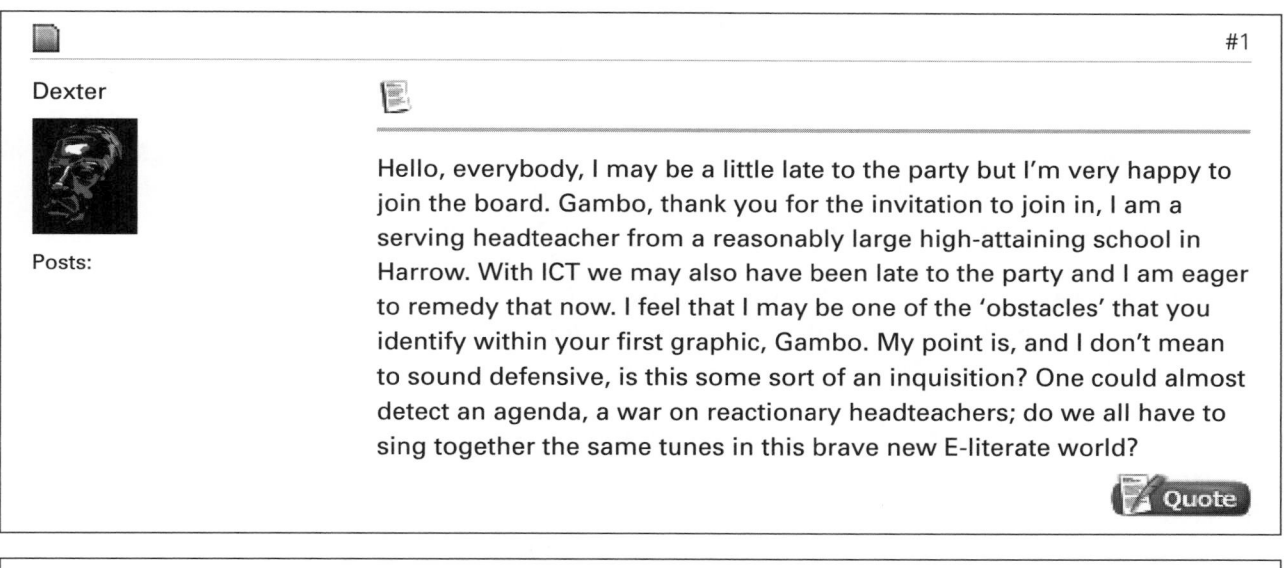

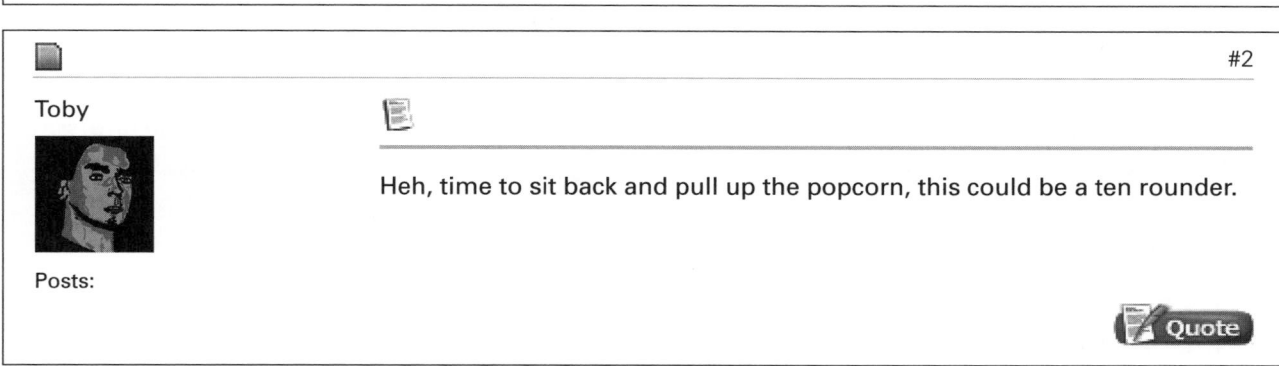

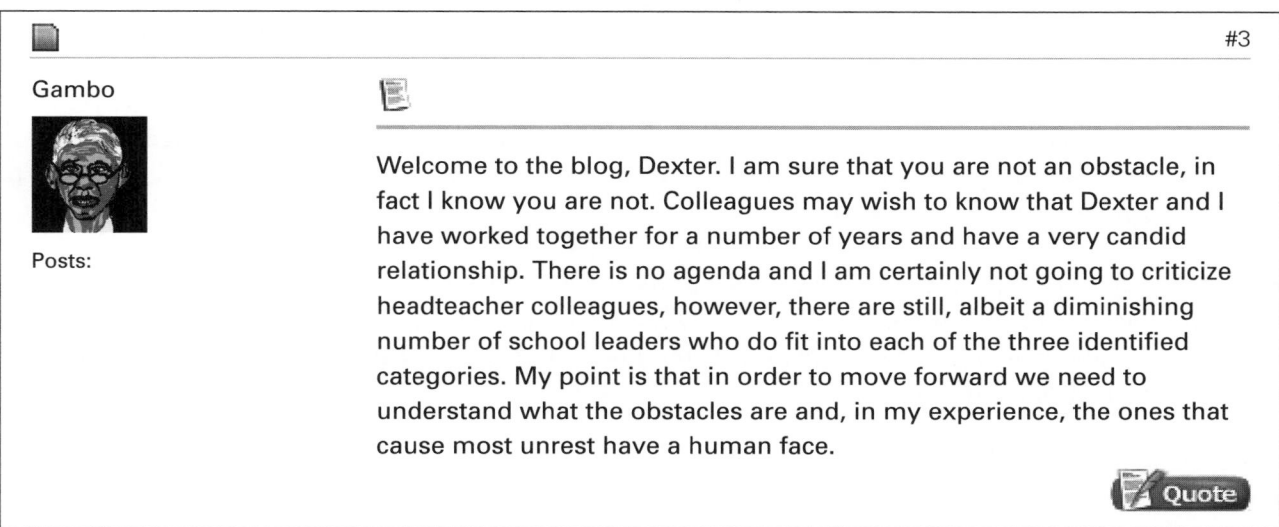

7th September

It may be helpful to take a look at the sample narrative below, which is an extract from a consultation I gave recently. I hope that the subject of this work will join the blog next month to develop the procedure into its second and third phases.

School's ICT journey

Reflecting upon my school's ICT journey it is self-evident that there were a number of key events that served as critical moments.

The effective introduction of an ICT suite complete with a managed service seemed revolutionary at the time and fundamentally added something to the curriculum. What had gone before, the single classroom PC now seemed token and piecemeal in comparison. The suite provided a clearer and richer focus for the scheme of work and also connected together activities across the school in a clear coherent form.

The second key event I think was the investment in networked classrooms. Once again this stands out as a watershed period that caught everybody's attention. The Internet in particular totally enriched the cross-curricular work that the class PC was doing at that time

The next stepping stone is identified as the point when the ICT co-ordinator who was outstanding, bright and extremely good at reassuring staff, giving them courage to try things out, took a promotion elsewhere which left a huge gap at the time and we all feared stagnation. The school was put in a position of requiring a critical appointment and we realized that in order to maintain the momentum that the previous co-ordinator had generated a significant allowance would have to be attached to the post. This had implications for the existing management structure and a few feathers were ruffled as the post was advertised. At interview we were incredibly disappointed with the calibre of candidate whose ICT credentials were immaculate but who had no understanding of broader teaching and learning considerations ...

Personal ICT journey

My own E-learning journey began many years earlier, in fact long before I entered teaching. It was at a time when computers, largely databases, were first beginning to appear in commercial environments and it seemed so logical to me that they could save the company that I was working for back then enormous amounts of time and money if they would invest to replace paper-based systems.

Several years later I was teaching in Manchester and in very challenging circumstances as the first Windows PCs filtered into schools. It was obvious the potential that the machines had for reaching out to disconnected pupils. To me at that time the computer was simply another tool that had the potential to enrich the primary learning environment.

From that point onwards ICT was always part of my repertoire so to speak but I never thought anything particular about it. I had invested in a decent PC myself and soon realized its value and I suppose championed to colleagues how the insane amount of planning we were expected to do at this point in time could be greatly reduced through using the PC.

My next challenge really came as the two narratives draw together. Following the unsuccessful attempt to replace the school's previous outstanding ICT co-ordinator (I was DH [deputy headteacher] by this stage) my HT [headteacher] asked if I was prepared to take on the role ...

To conclude this first activity you should complete a review text that you can work on with colleagues next month. In addition, identify each member of your ICT team and ask him or her to complete the same task in preparation for next month's work when we will develop Egan's model to identify appropriate ways for the team to move forward.

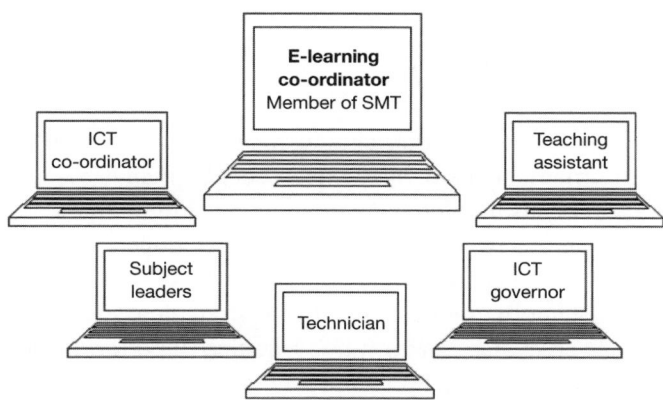

Figure 1.4 ICT team leadership model

Available on the net at http://www.james-wright.org

Figure 1.4 is a reminder of the roles that need to be fulfilled. We shall discuss this in greater detail in November.

10th September

Week 2, Task 2 – Revising the Self-Review Framework

I want to spend the next two weeks following up last year's work on the self-review framework (SRF) but realize that some colleagues may not have actually completed the matrix. This presents us with something of an impasse, as this is an essential strategic audit with which all schools should engage.

Therefore if you have not already completed the BECTA self-review matrix then this must be a strategic priority for the school. A detailed approach to the task was developed in Book 1 of this series, Chapters 2–4. Alternatively BECTA guidelines and support materials are available through their DVD and publication, *Ways to Use the Self-Review Framework* ref: BEC1-15446, available for download or to order from BECTA Publications at http://becta.org.uk/corporate/publications/index.cfm.

I strongly recommend that if colleagues need to do so, they address this area now. Also those who completed the review last year, either following Book 1 or independently using the online BECTA matrix, should return to the BECTA site to update the plan and, in so doing, identify action areas that will need to be addressed this year in order to gain ICT Mark accreditation. This is your second activity for this term. It may be useful to look at the BECTA materials available to support self-evaluation against the eight key elements within the matrix at: http://matrix.becta.org.uk, paying particular attention to the action plan that you completed last year (if appropriate) and the extent to which these actions have been followed through.

13th September

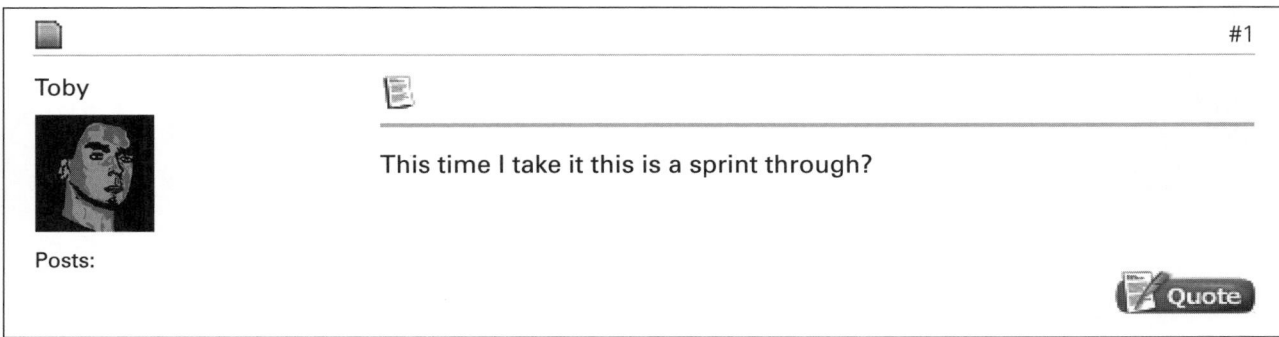

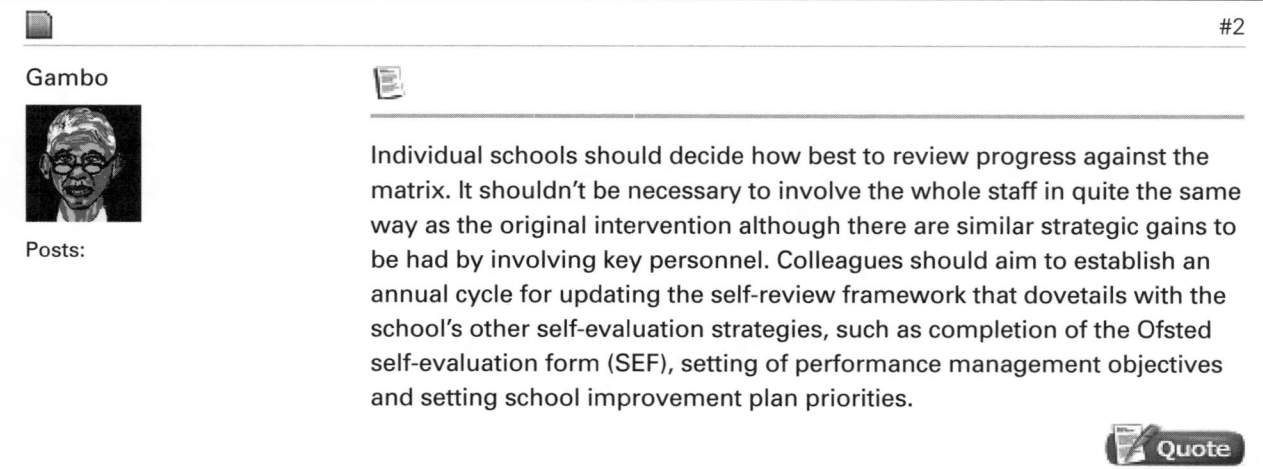

#2

Gambo

Posts:

Individual schools should decide how best to review progress against the matrix. It shouldn't be necessary to involve the whole staff in quite the same way as the original intervention although there are similar strategic gains to be had by involving key personnel. Colleagues should aim to establish an annual cycle for updating the self-review framework that dovetails with the school's other self-evaluation strategies, such as completion of the Ofsted self-evaluation form (SEF), setting of performance management objectives and setting school improvement plan priorities.

Quote

16th September

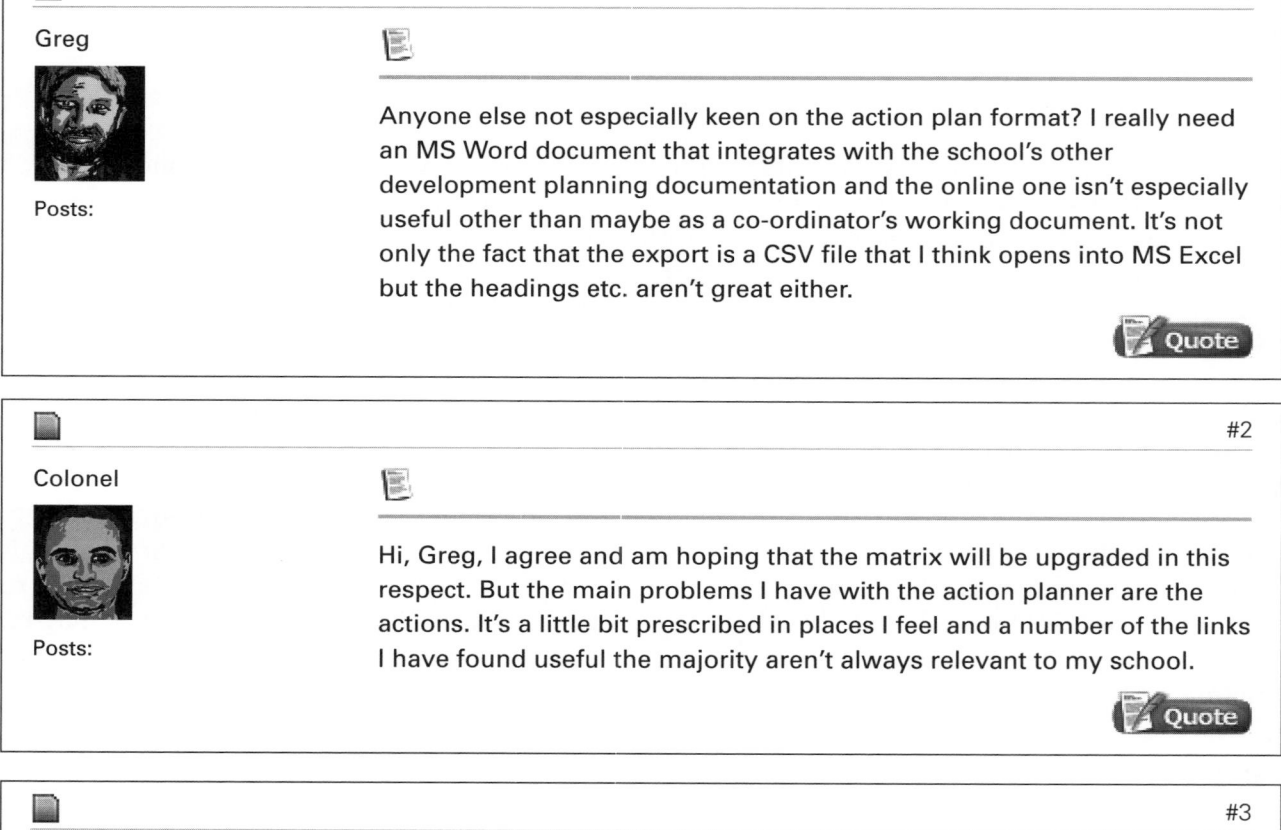

#1

Greg

Posts:

Anyone else not especially keen on the action plan format? I really need an MS Word document that integrates with the school's other development planning documentation and the online one isn't especially useful other than maybe as a co-ordinator's working document. It's not only the fact that the export is a CSV file that I think opens into MS Excel but the headings etc. aren't great either.

Quote

#2

Colonel

Posts:

Hi, Greg, I agree and am hoping that the matrix will be upgraded in this respect. But the main problems I have with the action planner are the actions. It's a little bit prescribed in places I feel and a number of the links I have found useful the majority aren't always relevant to my school.

Quote

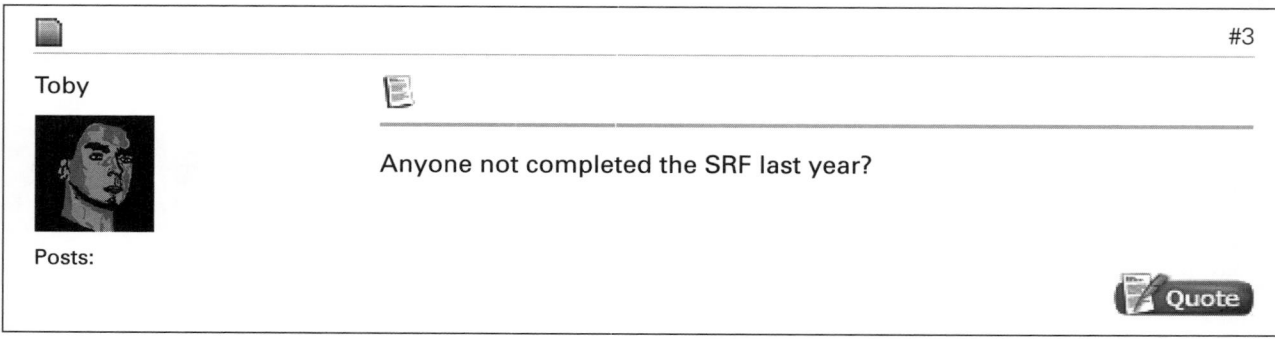

#3

Toby

Posts:

Anyone not completed the SRF last year?

Quote

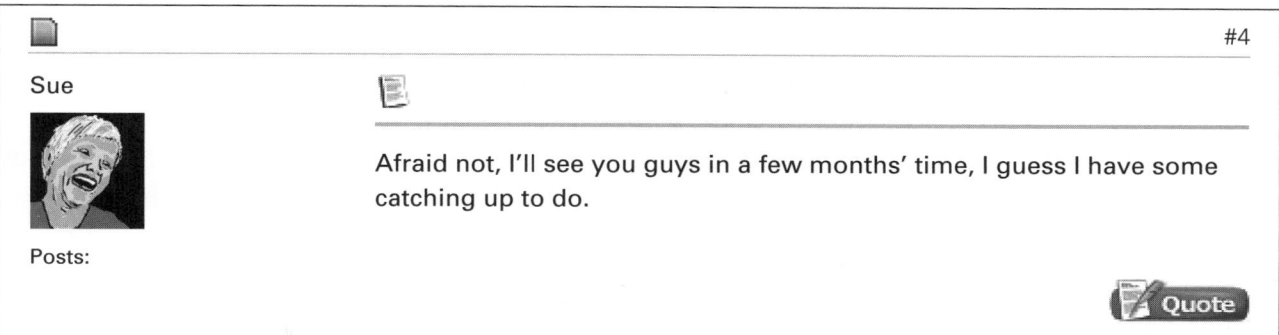

18th September

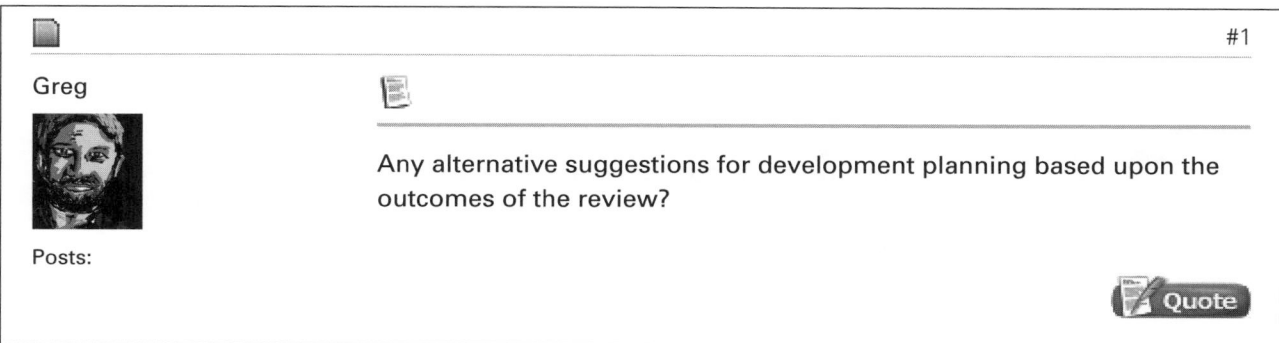

20th September

Having updated the framework colleagues should be able to produce a plan such as the one depicted in Figure 1.5.

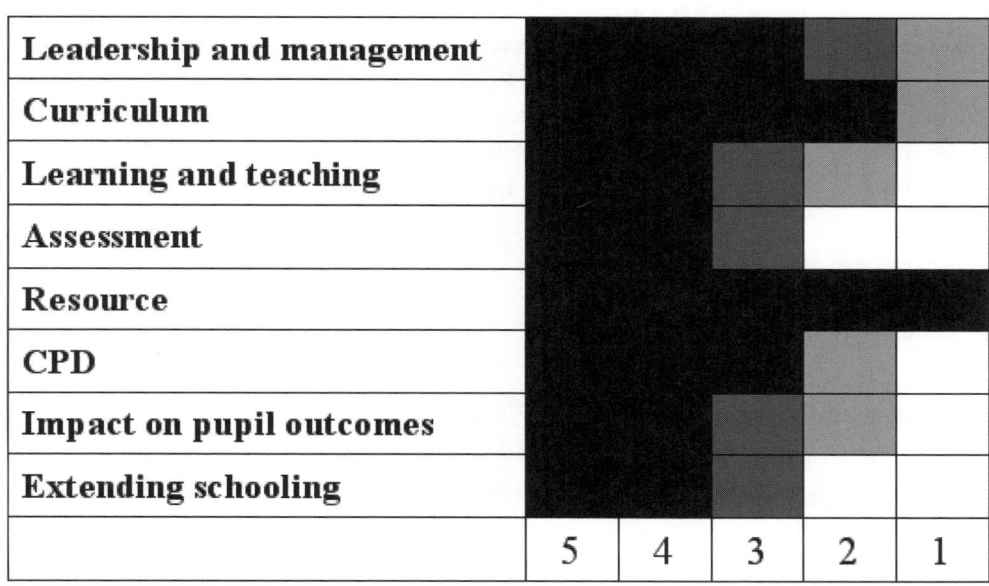

	5	4	3	2	1
Leadership and management					
Curriculum					
Learning and teaching					
Assessment					
Resource					
CPD					
Impact on pupil outcomes					
Extending schooling					

Figure 1.5 BECTA SRF Progress

Available on the net at http://www.james-wright.org

This provides an overview of developments across three evaluation points and demonstrates clear progress within these areas. It is noteworthy that this provides very useful self-evaluation evidence for cross-reference into the Ofsted SEF document, as schools will wish to incorporate the outcomes of the SRF process into their broader self-evaluation cycle. In particular try to identify key short-term priorities that will feature within this year's school improvement plan. Colleagues may also wish to integrate the broader SRF action plan, or their own bespoke derivative within a three-year development plan. Next month I shall work through the given example to model how this can work in practice by transferring the SRF outcomes into a model ICT development plan and use this to prioritize issues that will need to be addressed throughout the year in order to position the school for ICT Mark accreditation.

22nd September

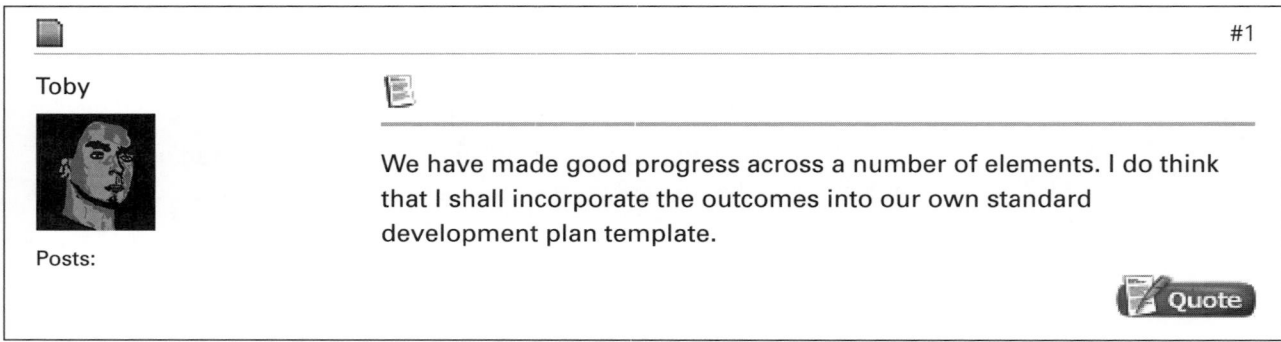

24th September

Week 3, Task 3 – E-safety – Raising Staff Awareness

Last spring we completed an initial audit of Internet safety arrangements in the light of the Every Child Matters Education Act with a view to completing a root-and-branch review this year. As noted in the first E-learning manual, Outcome 2, 'Staying Safe' places specific requirements upon schools to ensure that children are provided with a safe E-learning environment. From an ICT perspective this means that the security of the school network is one of its highest priorities and that self-evaluation of school systems must be robust and their outcome visible within the school's SEF. In this, the first part of this major strategic review, we are going to address the issue of raising staff awareness of E-safety within the primary school. Colleagues would be well advised to take E-safety issues extremely seriously, not least for the fact that many of your pupils will be using the Internet freely without supervision at home and need to become intelligent and informed users.

Schools should be able to answer the following questions:

Are we all aware of potential E-safety dangers?
Have we kept pace with developments?
Are we teaching E-safety?

It is likely that your local authority has resources, documentation and workshops available for you or your ICT co-ordinator to disseminate to staff. I think that you should at the very least designate a full staff meeting to the issue at this stage, possibly supported by local authority staff, at which you aim to address many of the core issues outlined within BECTA (2005) guidance (Ref: 15327 *E-safety*, *Developing a Whole-School Approach to Internet Safety*).

Staff need to be aware that all who work in schools, not only teaching staff, are bound by a duty of care to ensure that children and young people are able to use the Internet and related technologies appropriately and safely. Therefore it is essential that regular updates be provided regarding school policy and practice. Too often colleagues may slip into complacency regarding E-safety because the school operates an effective Internet filter. Witness the frequency of unstructured and unsupervised web searches, or acceptable use codes that are not widely displayed alongside Internet accessing computers. Latest research demonstrates that children and young people are vulnerable when using the Internet and other technologies, and one of your core aims at this stage is to highlight potential dangers to staff whilst not fuelling the fears of those who would gladly disconnect the computers altogether.

Provide all staff with an overview of the risks involved. In effect these fall into five main categories: exposure to inappropriate materials; copyright infringement; inappropriate or illegal behaviour; threat of physical danger; and staff misuse.

Table 1.2 E-safety, an overview of risk

E-SAFETY – An Overview of Risk		
Exposure to inappropriate materials	**Despite filtering pupils may still stumble across websites containing**	
	Pornography	Racist materials
	Hate – Violence	Sexist materials
	Age-inappropriate or biased sites	Negative self-image/self-harm sites
	Extreme political sites	
Inappropriate/Illegal Behaviour	**Anonymous cyberlinks allow bullies to torment victims at any time of day or night using email, chat or text messages**	
	Online bullying	Cyber stalking
	Involvement in identity theft	Buying and selling of stolen goods.
	Access to online gambling	Suicide sites
	Sites for the sale of weapons	Hacking sites
	Sites providing recipes for drug or bomb making	Participation in hate or cult websites
Copyright infringement	**Copyright law applies on the Internet, but is ignored by many young people**	
	Download and swap music files	Download and trade DVD – media
	Network used to trade media files	Trade files using media storage devices
	Cut and paste homework assignments	Purchase whole assignments from online cheat sites
Threat of physical danger	**Adults, who use the Internet, particularly chat rooms to make contact with young people, to establish and develop relationships with the sole purpose of persuading them into sexual activity**	
Staff misuse	Staff should discuss the appropriate use of school technologies and identify what is meant by 'professional discretion'	
	What is the acceptable use of the Internet inside and outside of school hours?	
	How should digital images be stored?	
	When should you use personal photo/film equipment?	
	Should images be transferred to and from home?	
	How does the school ensure that its laptops remain secure?	
	Viewing or circulating inappropriate material via email	
	Viewing, possessing, making or distributing indecent and/or pornographic images	

Source: BECTA *E-safety*, 'Developing a Whole-school Approach to Internet Safety (2005)
Available on the net at http://www.james-wright.org

Table 1.2 provides a comprehensive overview of many of the issues that schools now face with regard to child protection, its computer network and online E-learning environment. These should be introduced and discussed with staff as part of this initial awareness-raising event. In particular having highlighted many of the dangers faced by pupils, time should then be directed towards dealing specifically with matters arising from the review of staff misuse of resources. I also think it may be useful to address these issues via the blog as questions raised by colleagues here are likely to replicate those you meet back in the staff room.

25th September

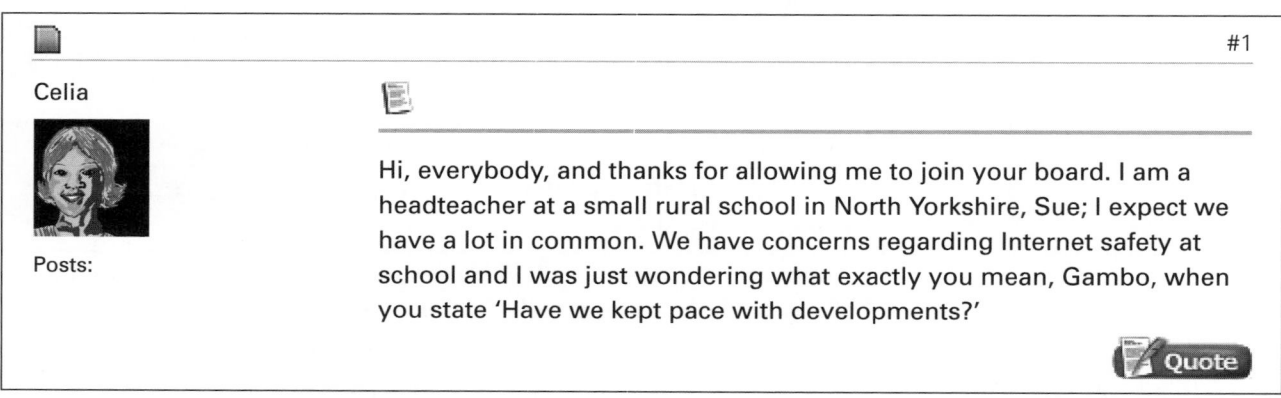

#1

Celia

Posts:

Hi, everybody, and thanks for allowing me to join your board. I am a headteacher at a small rural school in North Yorkshire, Sue; I expect we have a lot in common. We have concerns regarding Internet safety at school and I was just wondering what exactly you mean, Gambo, when you state 'Have we kept pace with developments?'

Quote

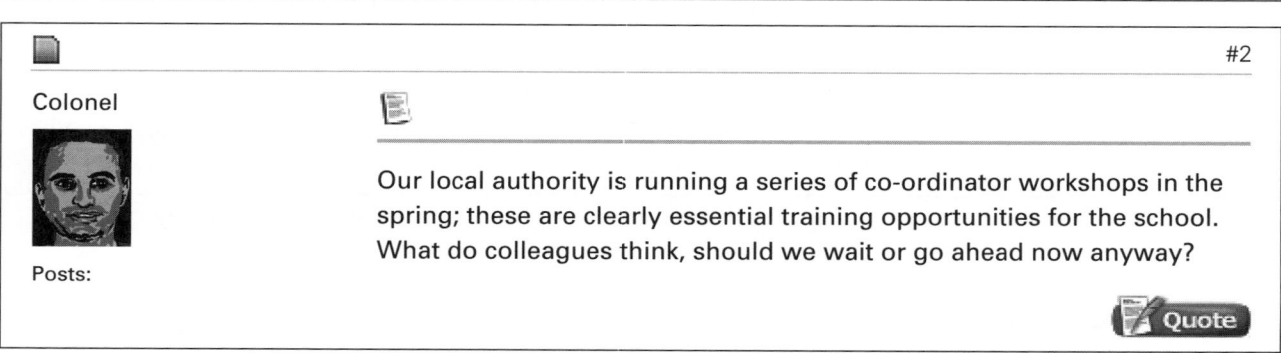

#2

Colonel

Posts:

Our local authority is running a series of co-ordinator workshops in the spring; these are clearly essential training opportunities for the school. What do colleagues think, should we wait or go ahead now anyway?

Quote

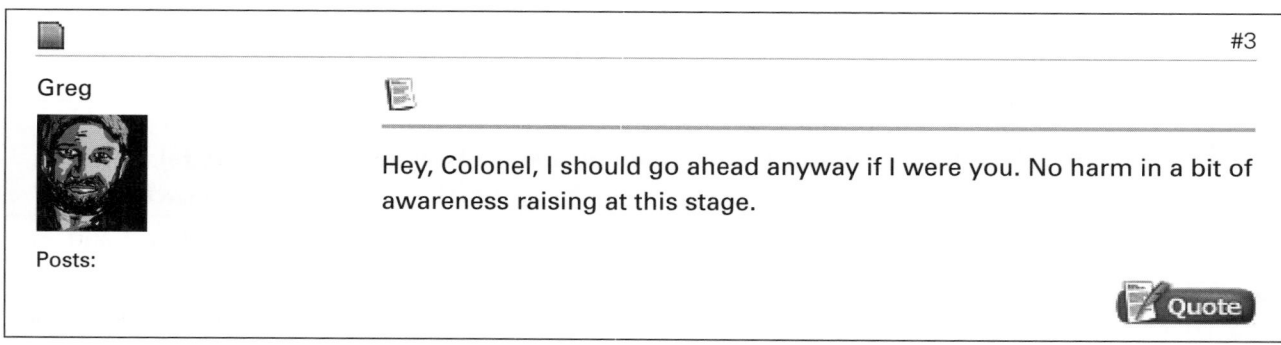

#3

Greg

Posts:

Hey, Colonel, I should go ahead anyway if I were you. No harm in a bit of awareness raising at this stage.

Quote

#4

Gambo

Posts:

I agree with Greg, you should take advantage of any guidance and support that your local authority is offering. Also, keep abreast of developments with regard to your Local Safeguarding Children Board. It is their role to co-ordinate safeguarding and to promote the welfare of children in your area, E-safety falls centrally within their brief. There is an up-to-date record of the local chair of each board (usually the council Chief Executive or Director of Children's Services) available from the Every Child Matters website: www.everychildmatters.gov.uk/lscb.

Hello, Celia, you are the final permanent member of this group and are very welcome to the boards. With regard to developments I am really referring to the need for policy to move beyond Internet acceptable use protocols in order to respond to the demands of networking and the introduction of wireless and Bluetooth technologies that have raised levels of risk in schools. In a more general sense though this also serves to remind colleagues that there really is little room for complacency in the field of E-safety.

26th September

#1

Toby

Posts:

Hi, Gambo, can you explain what exactly is meant by 'professional discretion'?

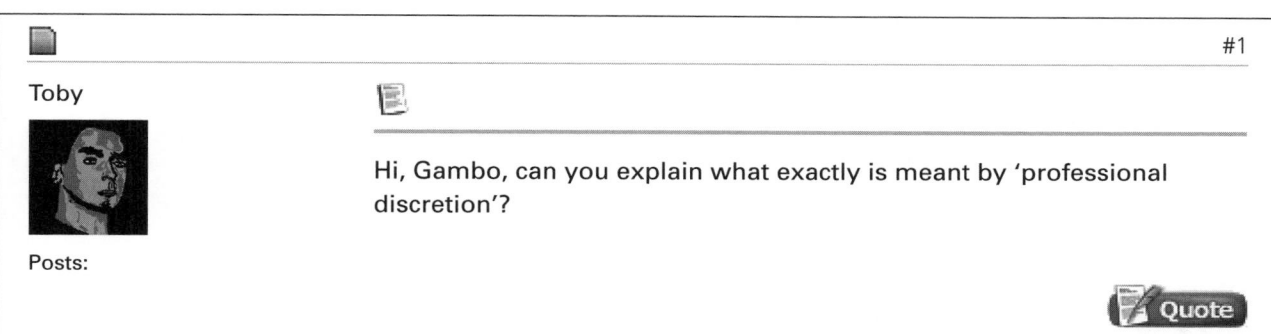

#2

Gambo

Posts:

This is a term widely incorporated within traditional Internet acceptable use policies to remind colleagues of their responsibilities when using the Internet. Schools have made very different interpretations of this however and whilst it remains a useful term to include within protocols staff do need to know exactly what is meant. For example, many schools that I have worked with are very comfortable allowing staff to use the Internet out of hours if, for example, they are staying late after school to support a production. Other schools will not permit any use of the network that is not directly related to school business no matter what time of day etc. it takes place. I don't know of any schools that would be happy for a member of staff to be privately surfing the web during lesson times. As the senior manager responsible for E-safety you should lead on developing where the line lies at your school. This should be addressed during this initial staff meeting.

27th September

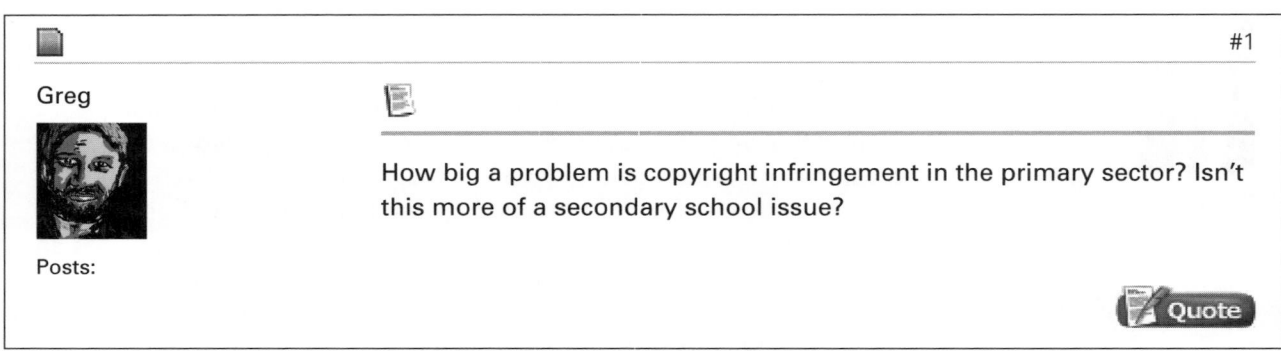

#1

Greg

Posts:

How big a problem is copyright infringement in the primary sector? Isn't this more of a secondary school issue?

Quote

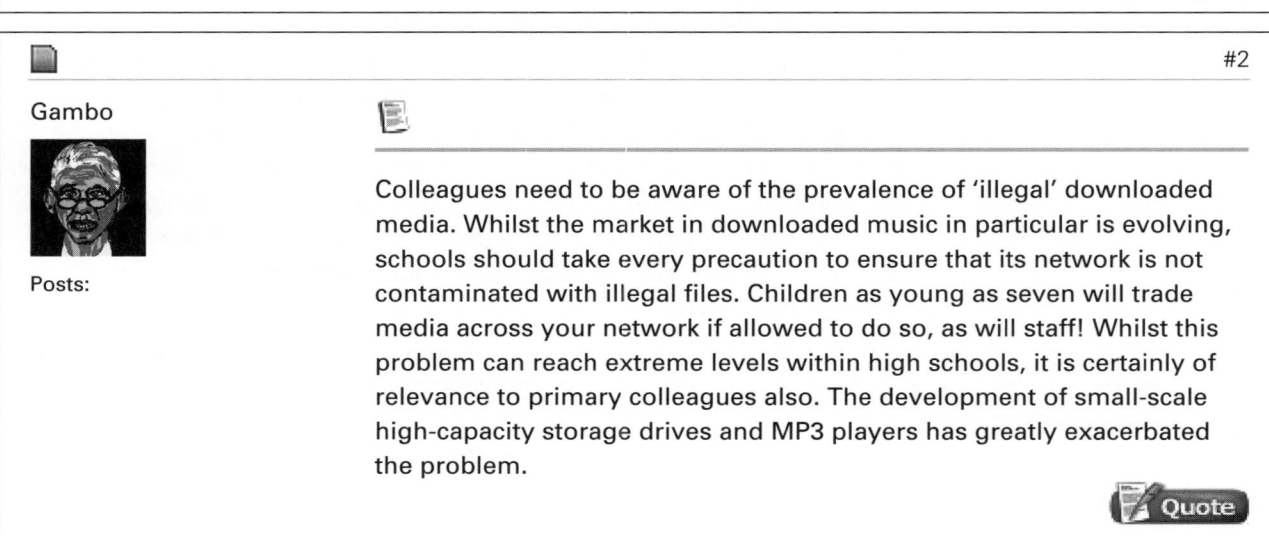

#2

Gambo

Posts:

Colleagues need to be aware of the prevalence of 'illegal' downloaded media. Whilst the market in downloaded music in particular is evolving, schools should take every precaution to ensure that its network is not contaminated with illegal files. Children as young as seven will trade media across your network if allowed to do so, as will staff! Whilst this problem can reach extreme levels within high schools, it is certainly of relevance to primary colleagues also. The development of small-scale high-capacity storage drives and MP3 players has greatly exacerbated the problem.

Quote

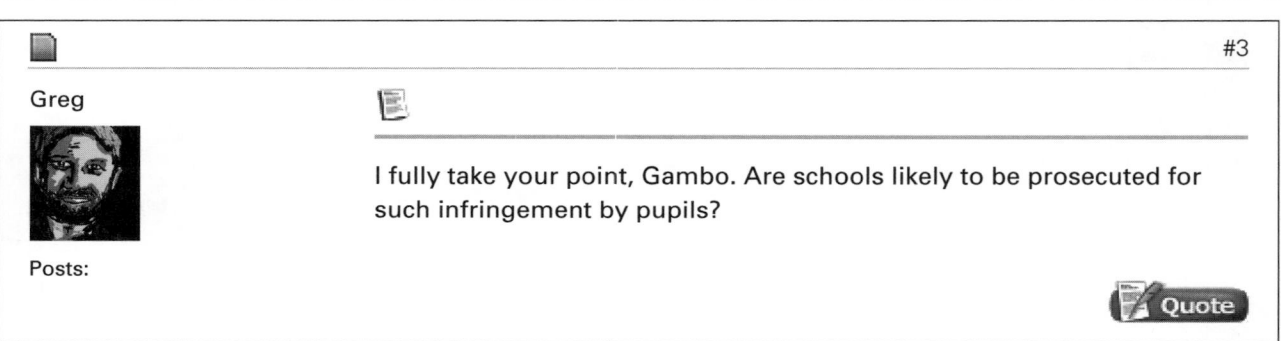

#3

Greg

Posts:

I fully take your point, Gambo. Are schools likely to be prosecuted for such infringement by pupils?

Quote

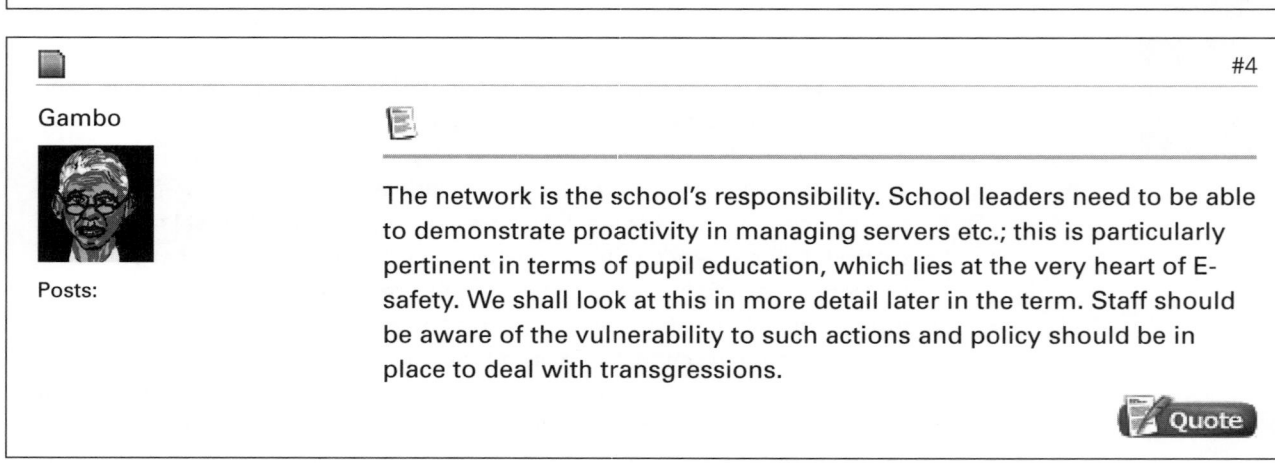

#4

Gambo

Posts:

The network is the school's responsibility. School leaders need to be able to demonstrate proactivity in managing servers etc.; this is particularly pertinent in terms of pupil education, which lies at the very heart of E-safety. We shall look at this in more detail later in the term. Staff should be aware of the vulnerability to such actions and policy should be in place to deal with transgressions.

Quote

29th September

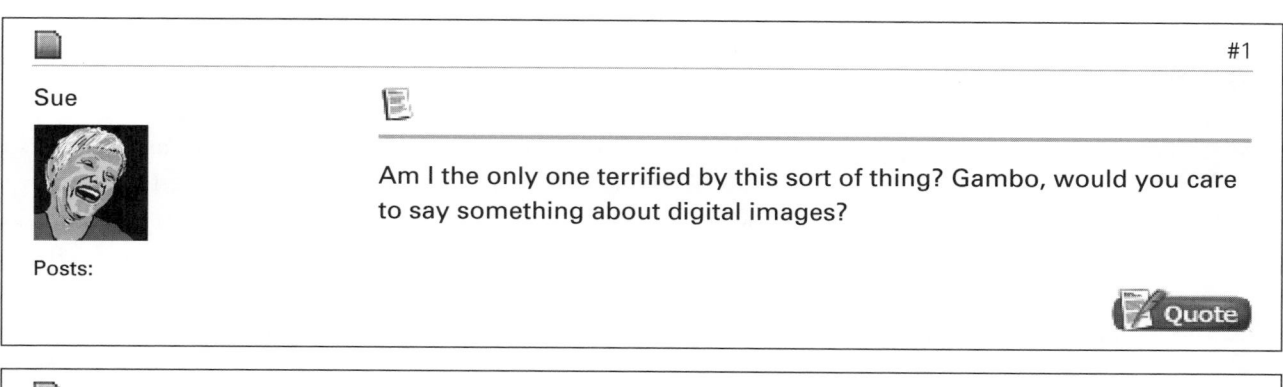

Sue

Posts:

#1

Am I the only one terrified by this sort of thing? Gambo, would you care to say something about digital images?

Quote

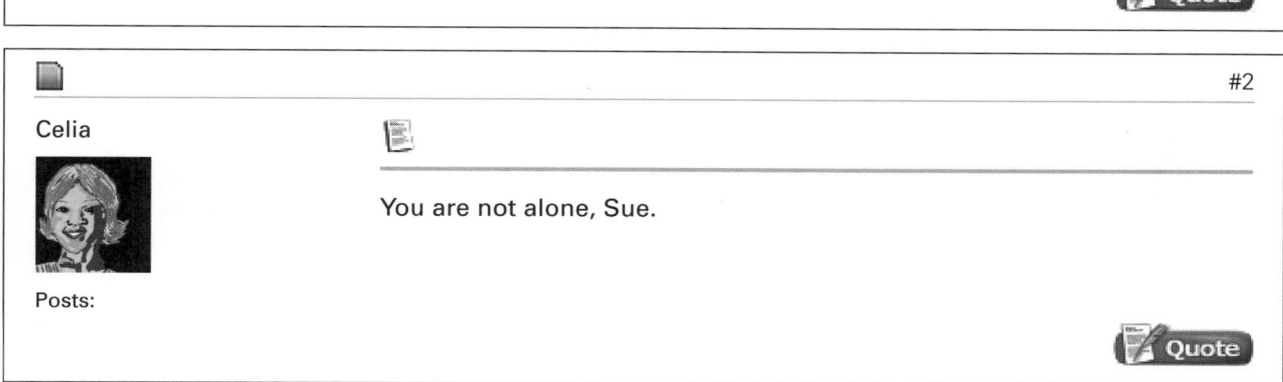

Celia

Posts:

#2

You are not alone, Sue.

Quote

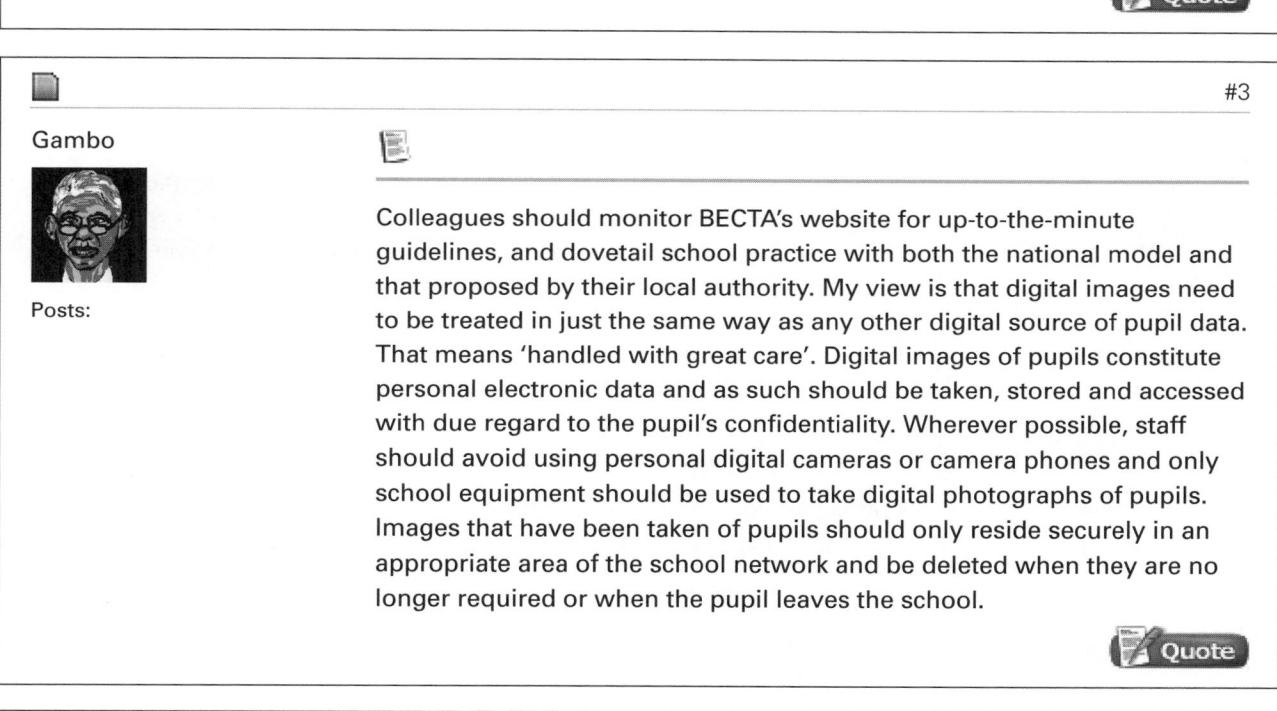

Gambo

Posts:

#3

Colleagues should monitor BECTA's website for up-to-the-minute guidelines, and dovetail school practice with both the national model and that proposed by their local authority. My view is that digital images need to be treated in just the same way as any other digital source of pupil data. That means 'handled with great care'. Digital images of pupils constitute personal electronic data and as such should be taken, stored and accessed with due regard to the pupil's confidentiality. Wherever possible, staff should avoid using personal digital cameras or camera phones and only school equipment should be used to take digital photographs of pupils. Images that have been taken of pupils should only reside securely in an appropriate area of the school network and be deleted when they are no longer required or when the pupil leaves the school.

Quote

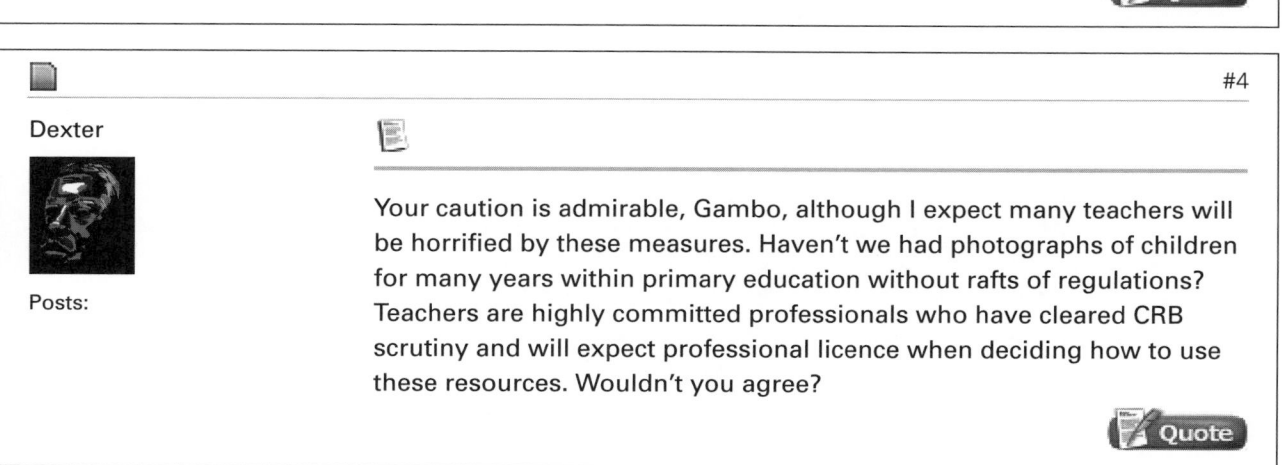

Dexter

Posts:

#4

Your caution is admirable, Gambo, although I expect many teachers will be horrified by these measures. Haven't we had photographs of children for many years within primary education without rafts of regulations? Teachers are highly committed professionals who have cleared CRB scrutiny and will expect professional licence when deciding how to use these resources. Wouldn't you agree?

Quote

	#5

Colonel

Posts:

I don't think that you can get too much comfort from old school photography, Dexter, digitization of images has moved the goalposts due to the ease with which images can be copied and distorted then reproduced across the web.

	#6

Celia

Posts:

Imagine a picture of a pupil taken by a staff member on a field trip that later turns up on the Internet in some grotesque pose. It really is alarming!

	#7

Gambo

Posts:

And the school leader's role is to allay such alarm and to protect staff through sensible discussion and agreed procedures. Schools will vary in their response and this returns to professional discretion again. Specifically, Dexter, I don't think there is any issue with professional staff who have been cleared using these images within school, indeed I should be surprised if they weren't. It is really the transfer of the images off the school network which makes staff vulnerable, and it is this area that I believe that schools have to provide very clear guidelines in order to take away that vulnerability.

I hope that your staff meetings go well. Next month we shall continue with our E-safety focus when we look more closely at policy and procedures.

Chapter 2 • *October*

2nd October

October's priorities are:

1 Complete the E-learning narrative to incorporate a review of the ICT leadership team and development of a shared vision for embedding E-learning at the school.
2 Identify school improvement priorities for ICT and E-learning from the revised self-review framework.

We shall also continue with the E-safety review looking specifically at policy and procedures.

Week 5, Task 4 – Barriers to Success – Effective Team Evaluation

Stage Two – Articulating a preferred scenario

Following on from last month's E-learning narratives, your work now needs to evolve in two directions. First, your own version of events, your story, should be challenged in order to identify any blind spots that may need to be addressed. This process aims to uncover potential gaps within your perception of given situations and relates to the second aspect of Egan's Model B. It is based upon the premise that since you actively engaged in the situation, it can be difficult to see it clearly or from a different perspective. Through considered challenges any gaps within your assessment of the situation and the impact of your behaviour may be highlighted. Therefore your aim is to identify key factors within your narrative, possibly personal characteristics, traits, experiences or events, that will be of particular value to the team and provide leverage for future strategic developments.

2nd October

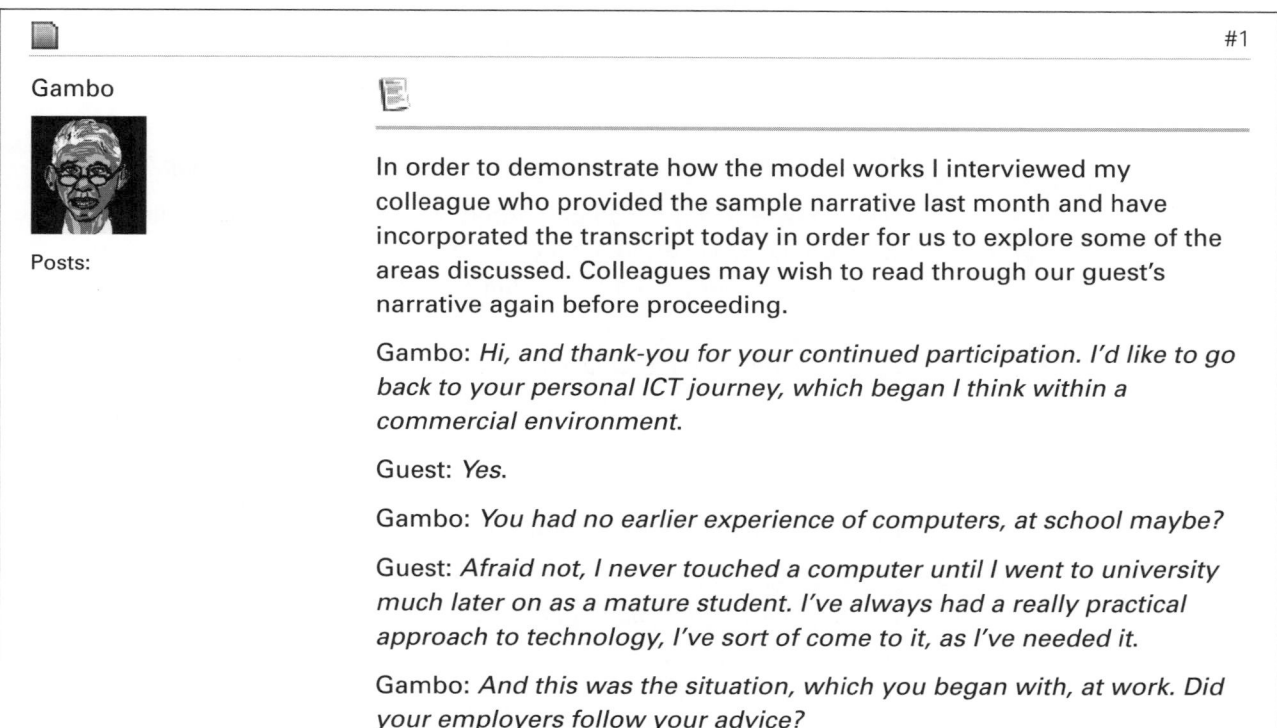

		#1

Gambo

Posts:

In order to demonstrate how the model works I interviewed my colleague who provided the sample narrative last month and have incorporated the transcript today in order for us to explore some of the areas discussed. Colleagues may wish to read through our guest's narrative again before proceeding.

Gambo: *Hi, and thank-you for your continued participation. I'd like to go back to your personal ICT journey, which began I think within a commercial environment.*

Guest: *Yes.*

Gambo: *You had no earlier experience of computers, at school maybe?*

Guest: *Afraid not, I never touched a computer until I went to university much later on as a mature student. I've always had a really practical approach to technology, I've sort of come to it, as I've needed it.*

Gambo: *And this was the situation, which you began with, at work. Did your employers follow your advice?*

Guest: *No, afraid not.*

Gambo: *Why was that?*

Guest: *I guess they felt it was all a bit 'pie in the sky' at that time. Not a sound investment.*

Gambo: *Was it?*

Guest: *Maybe to some extent. It wasn't thought through I suppose, not a proposition as such just an idea. I wouldn't have spent my own money on it at the time either.*

Gambo: Colleagues may wish to note that all I am really trying to do at this stage is to paraphrase what is being said, to fill in the gaps and to explore areas. I really want to discuss the quite fascinating events at the school when our guest took over as ICT co-ordinator but want her to have the opportunity to reflect upon the journey. It really is an empowering and pleasurable experience to be listened to quite intently whilst one examines something powerful from one's own past.

Gambo: *Within your description of the school's journey you highlighted the period immediately after the very talented ICT co-ordinator left the school. You spoke about the 'huge gap' that was left at the time. You said that 'We all feared stagnation'. Could you say a little more about this, maybe identify whom you mean when you say 'we'?*

Guest: *It just stands out in my mind as, well, almost shocking at the time when Phil left. All of us really felt that he had done so much and couldn't see how the clubs and the training and so on would now go on unless we appointed someone similar, but teachers like Phil are a rare commodity. When the candidates for the post were shown around it was a bit awkward. They were offered three management points at the time. I think Phil had worked for one and they were only really second, maybe third year qualified.*

Gambo: *You were the deputy headteacher?*

Guest: *Yes. I was very worried; I felt that the whole ethos of the school, its direction was about to change. I didn't recognize the school the guys who came for the post were describing.*

Gambo: *What were they saying exactly that was so disturbing?*

Guest: *It was just mechanics, hardware, networks as though the technology was everything and that all we needed to do was to pop on some headphones, plug in the children and sit back and enjoy.*

Gambo: *It is difficult for colleagues to appreciate the silence that now lies between us but it feels appropriate.*

Guest: *It's quite an uncomfortable silence, Gambo. I find I'm thinking carefully about what I have just said. I am quite exasperated, almost upset angry.*

Gambo: *Silence is very meaningful colleagues shouldn't be afraid to let it hang for a moment.*

Guest: *Anyway they didn't get the job either of them.*

Gambo: *No appointment was made?*

> Guest: *No. We were devastated, ICT was very highly valued in the school but it seemed obvious now that Phil was largely irreplaceable. Because he had been an NQT at the school our ethos was reflected so strongly in his work.*
>
> Gambo: *Which ethos?*
>
> Guest: *That learning is about discovery and that each child is unique. We aimed to create powerful learning experiences that would encourage children to develop their own knowledge and understanding of the world. Whether it is through literature, art and music or indeed through the intelligent use of technology.*
>
> Gambo: *So you were asked to take over. Inspirational! Your headteacher was clearly very perceptive.*
>
> We'll finish there. Thank you.

Clearly it is advantageous if you can work with a skilled helper in order fully to explore this process. If no external support is available rely upon a trusted colleague to provide the necessary feedback. Parallel to this task you should aim to consolidate and strengthen the ICT team by you yourself conducting interviews with each team member that will not only serve to challenge their own personal narratives but will also focus each member upon their own E-learning role and build in an individual commitment from each team member to the ultimate success of the project. At this stage I encourage colleagues to establish a leadership ethos that will disseminate across the school. To do so look again at the model of leadership that was first postulated within Book 1 and revisited in Chapter 1 of this manual (Figure 1.4). Over the coming weeks it is suggested that, having identified the make-up of the school's leadership team for ICT, you spend some time with each individual member working to define their role and to provide an opportunity for that colleague to describe their perspective of the school's E-learning journey. The object of this exercise is not only for you to gain a real understanding of the team and the perceptions of the individuals within it, but also to give colleagues the opportunity to fully commit to the journey that you are on.

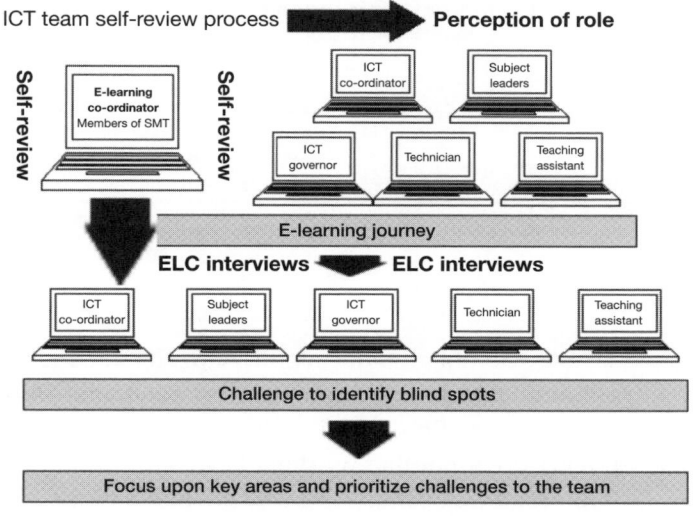

Figure 2.1 ICT team self-review process
Available on the net at http://www.james-wright.org

You will need to receive feedback upon your own self-review and subsequent narrative prior to interviewing colleagues, as indicated in Figure 2.1. Then schedule professional discussions with each member of your ICT team following the same structure as your own. I shall describe these interviews in slighter greater detail later this week following feedback from the weblog.

5th October

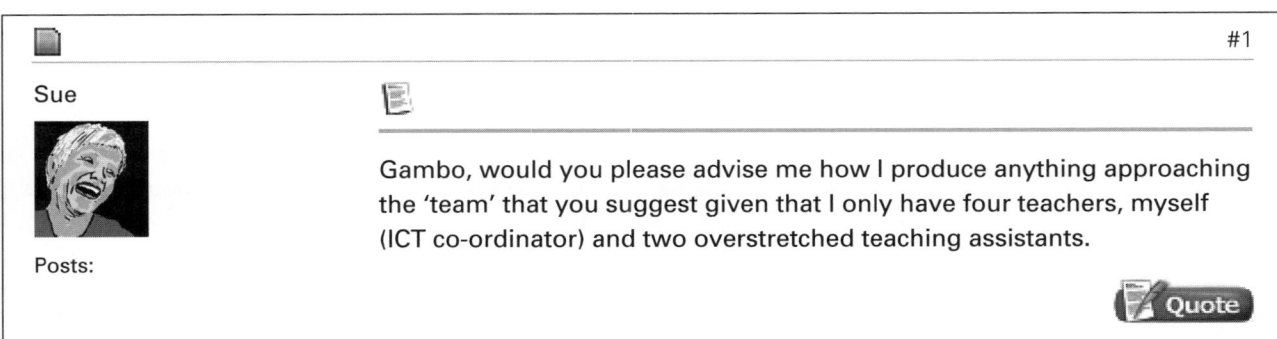

Sue

Posts:

#1

Gambo, would you please advise me how I produce anything approaching the 'team' that you suggest given that I only have four teachers, myself (ICT co-ordinator) and two overstretched teaching assistants.

Quote

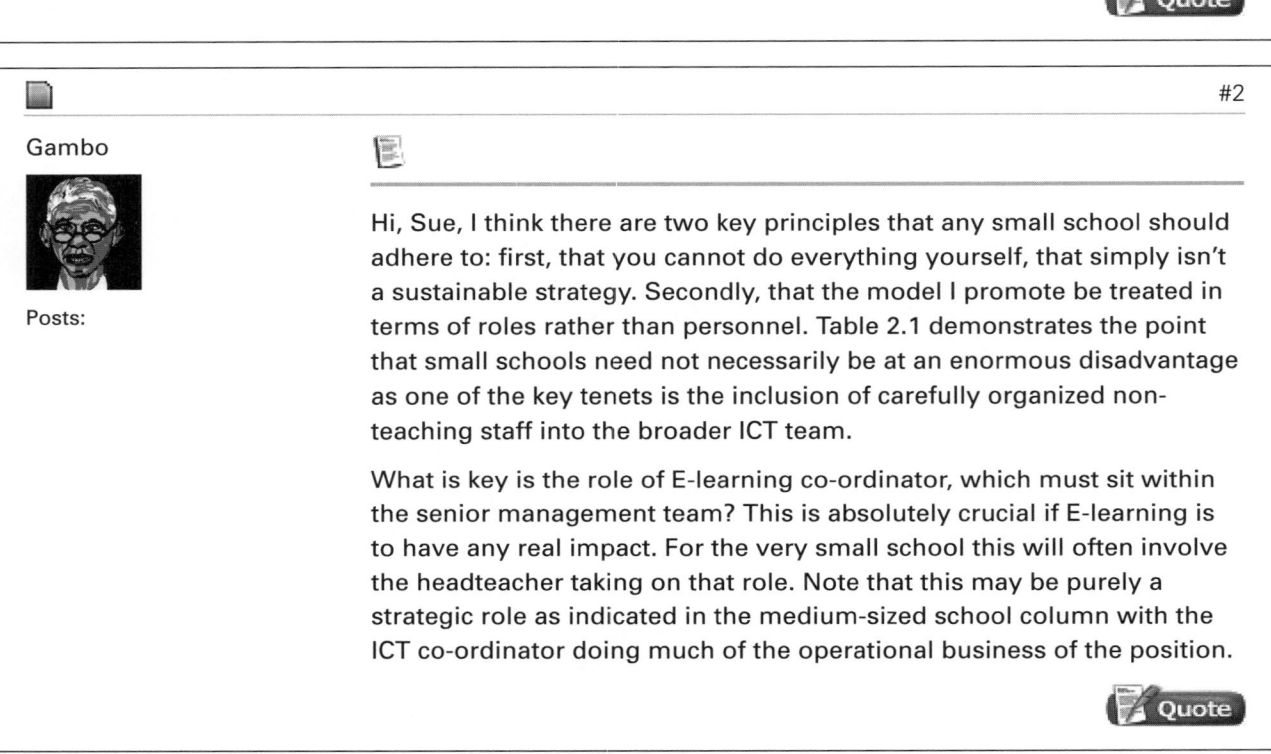

Gambo

Posts:

#2

Hi, Sue, I think there are two key principles that any small school should adhere to: first, that you cannot do everything yourself, that simply isn't a sustainable strategy. Secondly, that the model I promote be treated in terms of roles rather than personnel. Table 2.1 demonstrates the point that small schools need not necessarily be at an enormous disadvantage as one of the key tenets is the inclusion of carefully organized non-teaching staff into the broader ICT team.

What is key is the role of E-learning co-ordinator, which must sit within the senior management team? This is absolutely crucial if E-learning is to have any real impact. For the very small school this will often involve the headteacher taking on that role. Note that this may be purely a strategic role as indicated in the medium-sized school column with the ICT co-ordinator doing much of the operational business of the position.

Quote

6th October

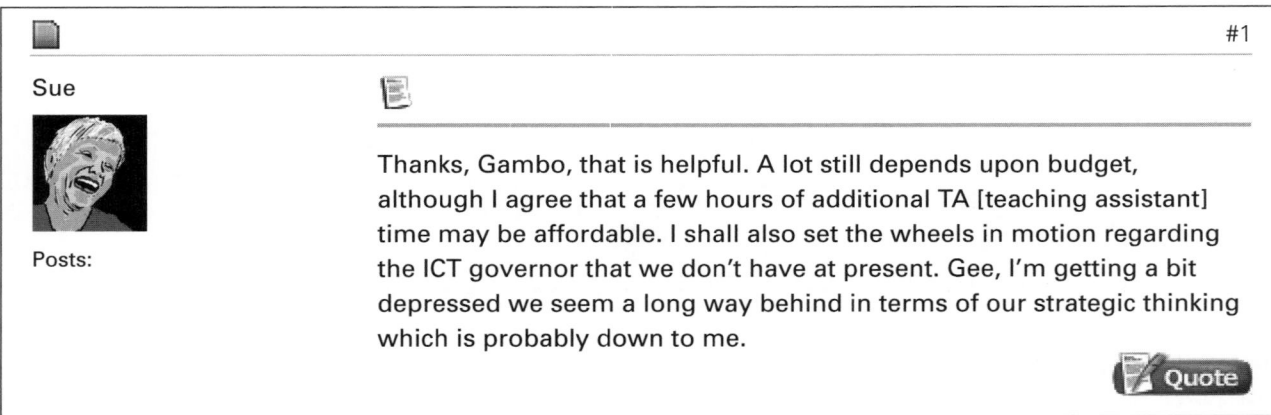

Sue

Posts:

#1

Thanks, Gambo, that is helpful. A lot still depends upon budget, although I agree that a few hours of additional TA [teaching assistant] time may be affordable. I shall also set the wheels in motion regarding the ICT governor that we don't have at present. Gee, I'm getting a bit depressed we seem a long way behind in terms of our strategic thinking which is probably down to me.

Quote

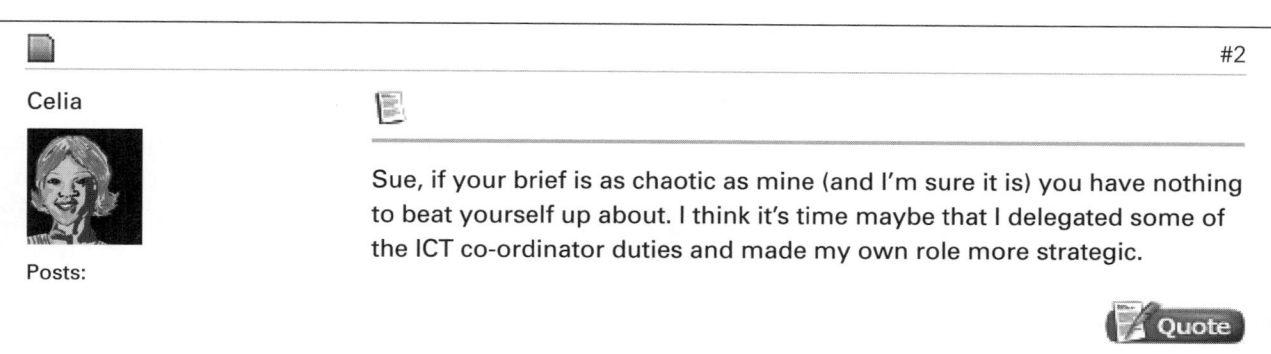

Table 2.1 ICT leadership team comparative models

Role	Large school 500 + pupils	Average school 200 + pupils	Small school 100 + pupils	Very small school 50 + pupils
Headteacher				E-learning co-ordinator and ICT co-ordinator
Deputy headteacher		E-learning co-ordinator (strategic)	E-learning co-ordinator and ICT co-ordinator	
Assistant headteacher	E-learning co-ordinator	Subject leaders	Subject leaders	
Assistant headteacher				
Teacher	ICT co-ordinator	ICT co-ordinator	Shadow ICT co-ordinator	Subject leaders
Teacher	Subject leaders	Subject leaders	Subject leaders	Subject leaders
Teacher	Subject leaders	Subject leaders	Subject leaders	
Teacher	Subject leaders			
Teacher	Subject Leaders			
Teaching assistant	Identified TA (0.1–0.5)	Identified TA (0.1–0.5)		Identified TA (0.1–0.5)
ICT technician	External contract	External contract	External contract	
Governor	Identified governor	Identified governor	Identified governor	Identified governor

Available on the net at http://www.james-wright.org

9th October

If you have managed to forge ahead with this, you will have completed your one to one with regard to your own narrative and timetabled professional discussions with the appropriate colleagues. Initially your primary function is that of active listener, encouraging the speaker to tell their story and helping them to explore the narrative. In order to get the most out of the interview use paraphrasing carefully to check that you have fully understood each person's perspective and summarize what they have said, being prepared to challenge. Given that there may be power dynamics involved in the situation, do tread carefully and under no circumstances should the review become adversarial or threatening to colleagues. Listen for negative self-talk, discrepancies and examples where the speaker's awareness of a situation is clearly incomplete. Remember that the conversation should incorporate their role within the ICT team, their contribution and ambitions both for themselves and the broader project. Then, as with your own narrative, help them to identify an area that they may wish to develop that would result in clear benefits both for themselves and the school. Once completed you will have collected a massive amount of qualitative data about your E-learning team and potentially made substantial advances in terms of the team's capacity for developing E-learning, highlighting where the core strengths lie and opportunities for development exist. Your colleagues should feel empowered by the whole experience and their commitment to the project will have been invigorated, ultimately enabling the team to energize the school in terms of its E-learning development.

13th October

#1

Amina

Posts:

I thought I'd share a little from my experience with the team-building activities. My situation is typically that outlined for the mid-sized school in the examples given. I am the deputy head with quite a lot of previous experience as an ICT co-ordinator although my role now is largely strategic. I have an ICT co-ordinator with whom I work closely. Within the school we have cross-subject thematic working groups such as communication, language and literacy, art and humanities, mathematics and science technologies, which would generally have an input within the E-learning agenda, although I felt it was not necessary or appropriate to incorporate them within the narrative work at this time. More appropriate maybe if this was a whole-school venture similar to that in which we engaged last year with regard to the SRF. We have appointed a part-time teaching assistant to provide some technical support alongside the external contract. We have an ICT governor. Consequently I held four interviews last week and was amazed by the work that colleagues had put into preparing their personal narratives and how candid the conversation was that we enjoyed. It has highlighted for me the depth of experience and talent available within the school and I can't wait to bring together a meeting so that this can be properly shared. The best aspect was my meeting with Cara, my governor, who is a real gem and I think welcomed the opportunity more than anyone else to share her experience and to feel needed. The most difficult aspect was the leverage at the end of each meeting which almost felt a little superficial, identifying elements which stood out was often contrived, although I can see the benefits from a practical sense of moving the whole team forward in the long run. Hope the experience was equally rewarding for colleagues. Thanks, Gambo.

16th October

Week 6, Task 5 – E-safety – Policy and Procedures

Last month you hosted a staff meeting aimed at raising awareness to the range of serious issues surrounding E-safety as highlighted within Table 1.2, 'E-safety, an overview of risk'. This will provide a strong context for the revision of the existing policy to be amended this month and delivered to staff, senior management and the governor's curriculum committee at the earliest possible time.

Your task for this week is to produce a revised E-safety policy that you as a group are happy to take to staff.

Familiarize yourself with BECTA's revised 2006 E-safety document *E-safety, Developing Whole-School Policies to Support Effective Practice* (BECTA, 2006a). Consider carefully BECTA advice regarding the role of the Internet safety co-ordinator who has core responsibility not only for overseeing the production of policy but of managing all issues related to E-safety and providing a central point of contact. Clearly this role needs to be fulfilled by a senior manager at the school, whom according to our leadership model shall be the E-learning co-ordinator. In addition to overseeing policy development you will have a pivotal role in implementing and policing school procedures as well as reporting breaches of policy to the headteacher. You may wish to begin with your existing Internet acceptable use policy and update this document to ensure that it covers the breadth of advice recommended within the 2006 BECTA guidance. Principally you should aim to address the following sections within the revised document:

The role of the Internet
Providing a secure online learning environment
Managing pupils' network and Internet access
Use of chat rooms and instant messaging services
Use of email
Use of emerging technologies
Managing staff network and Internet access
Laptops for teachers
Use of digital images
Managing the school website
Monitoring use of the school network and Internet
Managing community access to the school network
Complaints.

Table 2.2 E-safety key policy guidelines

1. The role of the Internet	An essential element in 21st Century life	Schools have a duty to provide students and staff with a secure online learning environment
2. Providing a secure online learning environment	Children are vulnerable when using the Internet and other technologies	Includes a range of technological tools
	An infrastructure of whole-school awareness	Designated responsibilities
	Comprehensive Internet safety education programme	Internet safety co-ordinator role
	Local filter provision	Headteacher to ensure Internet policy is implemented and compliance monitored

3. Managing pupils' network and internet access	Internet responsible use statement, posted by all PCs	Precautions to ensure that users access only appropriate material
	No filtering system alone is 100% effective	Purposeful Internet usage planned to enrich and extend learning activities
	Develop parameters of acceptable online behaviour	Appropriate search engine usage
	Image searches should not be 'live' within a classroom setting	Taught understanding of the Internet as a vast public forum
	Awareness of risk	Statements relating to defamatory references, illegal activity, viruses, hacking, copyright materials
	Cross-reference to appropriate legislation	
4. Use of chat rooms and instant messaging services	No access to public or unregulated chat rooms	Explain instant messaging services and inherent dangers within such systems
	IMS systems not available in school unless a specific initiative identified	Reference to school's anti-bullying policy
5. Use of email	Pupils' approved email accounts restricted to educational purposes	Pupil email addresses will not disclose personal pupil information
	Pupils must not reveal details of themselves or others	Access to external, personal email accounts will be blocked
	Guidance re cyber bullying	
6. Use of emerging technologies	Risk assessment for all new technologies	Use of mobile phones by pupils
	Personal digital devices will not be used for alternative Internet access	Abusive or inappropriate text messages are forbidden
	Portable media monitored as potential sources of computer virus	Virtual school communities monitored
7. Managing staff network and Internet access	Staff must accept responsible Internet use code before using the Internet	Training statement regarding acceptable behaviour
	Internet traffic will be monitored Senior management will supervise such procedure	Accidental access to inappropriate materials
	Professional discretion	Defamatory references
	Downloading of offensive or explicit material	Illegal behaviour by a staff member
8. Laptops for teachers	Laptop remains the property of the school	Appropriate usage with regard to Internet access, data protection and use of software

9. Use of digital images	Digital images of pupils constitute personal electronic data	Pupil confidentiality
	Personal digital cameras or camera phones should be avoided	Images must be held securely in an appropriate area of the school network
10. Managing the school website	Website photographs will not enable individual pupils to be identified	Pupils' full names will not be used
	Written permission from parents	Overall editorial responsibility rests with the school
11. Monitoring use of the school network and Internet	Explain school's duty to monitor	Data protection principles
	Up-to-date record of all staff and pupils who are granted Internet access	Files checked to ensure network is not compromised
	ICT systems will be protected against virus and malware	Monitoring procedures overseen by the Internet safety co-ordinator and a log of such monitoring maintained
12. Managing community access to the school network	Out of hours users of the school ICT network to sign the acceptable use policy	Usage to comply with E-safety procedures
13. Complaints	Incidents delegated to the Internet safety co-ordinator	Any complaint about staff misuse will be referred to the headteacher
	A partnership approach with parents	Complaints of a child protection nature trigger child protection procedures

Source: BECTA (2006a) *E-safety, Developing Whole-school Policies to Support Effective Practice*
Available on the net at http://www.james-wright.org

Table 2.2 provides a section-by-section overview of the key areas to be covered within each section of the policy. The detail of each paragraph will have been developed during your earlier staff awareness discussions. A full template of the E-safety policy is available from the accompanying website at www.james-wright.org. Do be aware of the need to keep staff abreast of changes that will arise in this area, in particular through the continuing development of wireless and Bluetooth devices, which may compromise the integrity of school networks and the development of virtual learning communities.

18th October

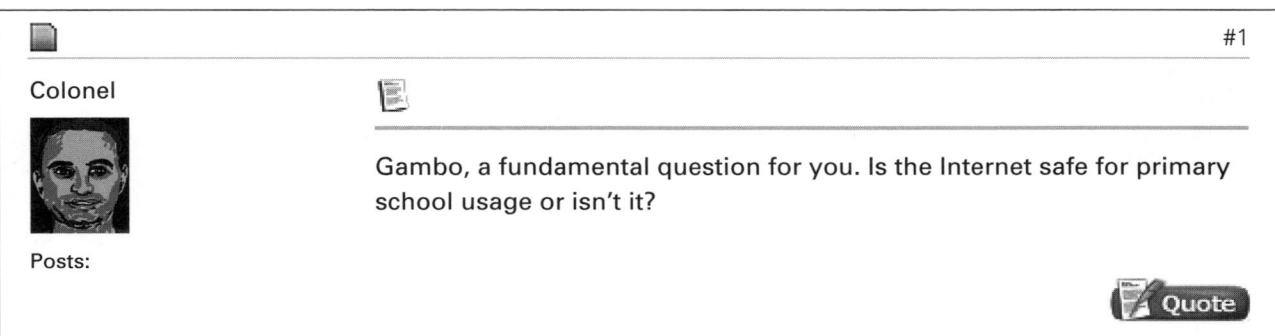

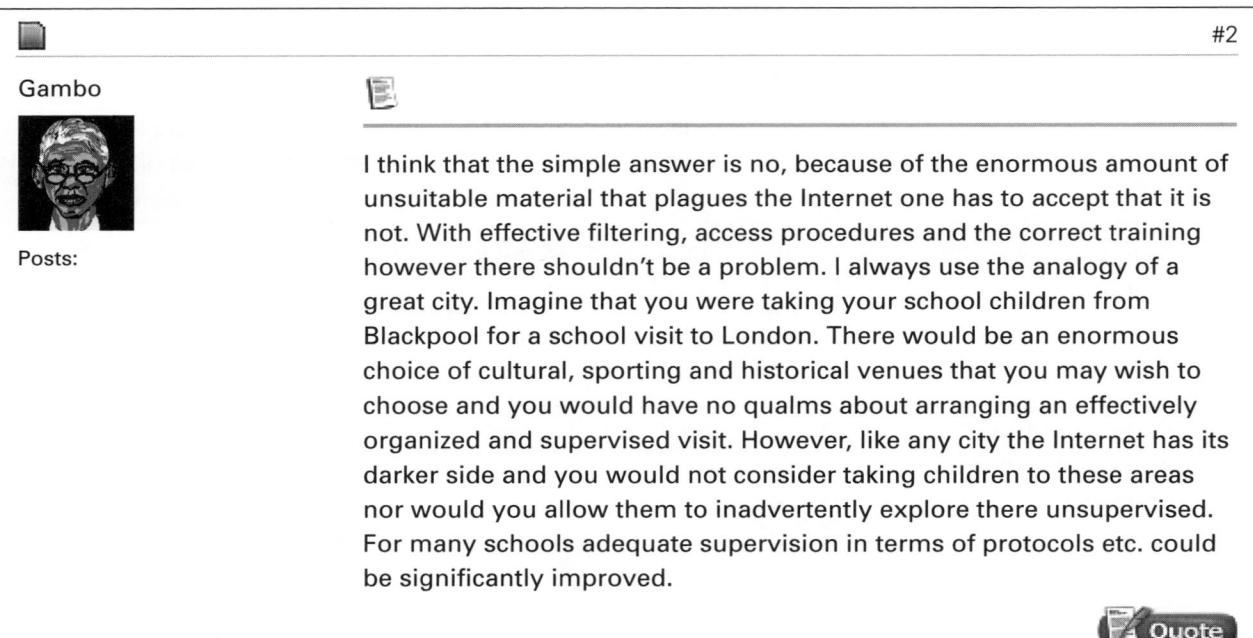

Gambo

Posts:

I think that the simple answer is no, because of the enormous amount of unsuitable material that plagues the Internet one has to accept that it is not. With effective filtering, access procedures and the correct training however there shouldn't be a problem. I always use the analogy of a great city. Imagine that you were taking your school children from Blackpool for a school visit to London. There would be an enormous choice of cultural, sporting and historical venues that you may wish to choose and you would have no qualms about arranging an effectively organized and supervised visit. However, like any city the Internet has its darker side and you would not consider taking children to these areas nor would you allow them to inadvertently explore there unsupervised. For many schools adequate supervision in terms of protocols etc. could be significantly improved.

19th October

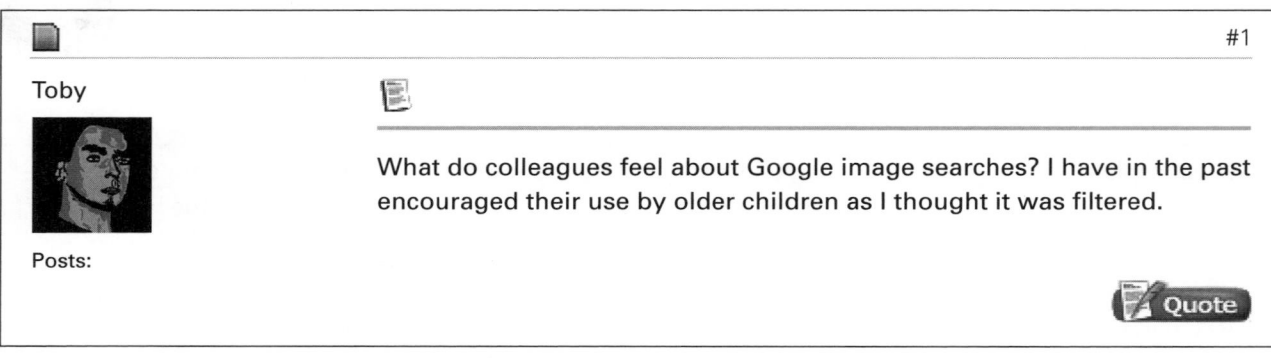

Toby

Posts:

What do colleagues feel about Google image searches? I have in the past encouraged their use by older children as I thought it was filtered.

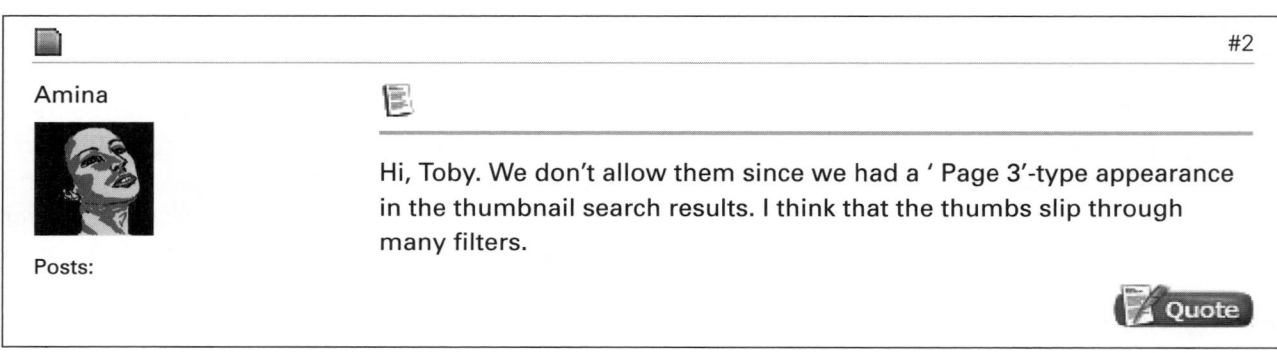

Amina

Posts:

Hi, Toby. We don't allow them since we had a ' Page 3'-type appearance in the thumbnail search results. I think that the thumbs slip through many filters.

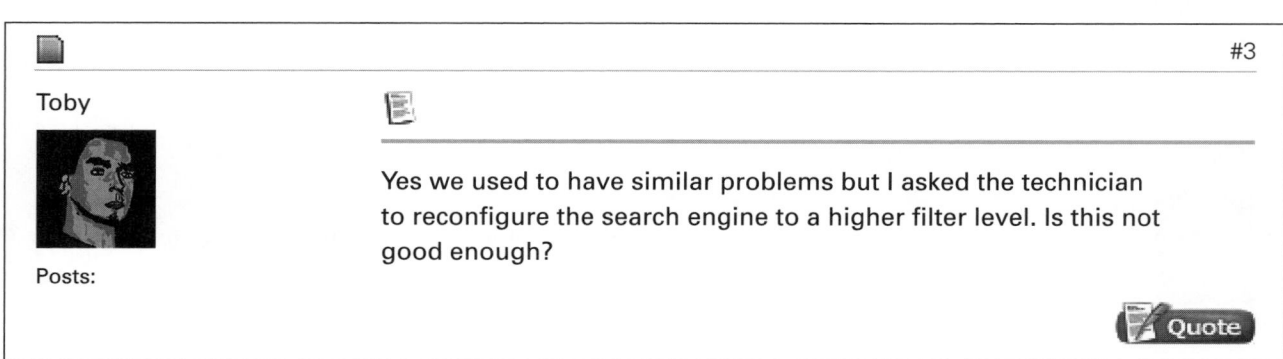

Toby

Posts:

Yes we used to have similar problems but I asked the technician to reconfigure the search engine to a higher filter level. Is this not good enough?

#4

Dexter

Posts:

I think that the decision rests with the school. You may well have provided an adequate solution, although personally I should restrict this activity to Year 6 children. I generally find that most children carrying out blanket searches either for images or text can be a complete waste of time.

#5

Amina

Posts:

I sort of agree with Dexter. I think you have to get the procedures tight. I am very concerned about our children being sent to the library PCs to carry out searches and had to address this with one or two staff last year. It is really about the purposefulness of the task.

#6

Greg

Posts:

I am very nervous about the children using email. I don't feel that I have any control over it. Didn't I hear that the government was now only recommending whole-class email addresses for primary age children?

#7

Gambo

Posts:

There is no specific recommendation that group email should be used, although it is seen as a solution to the identification of individual pupils from email addresses thereby reducing the risk of unsolicited attention. Schools should consider the range of activity that it is intended to use email for. The minimum one might expect is the completion of the QCA [Qualifications and Curriculum Authority] ICT Unit 3E in which children are taught how to use email to send and receive messages. Many schools will have developed a much richer and broader use of this medium and will require individual email functionality. I think that for primary children you do need to have some system by which the email is monitored and that there is some editorial control over what is sent out and received. This can be time-consuming but I think provides an essential layer of security along the lines that Greg requires. Online systems such as that employed by ePALS (www.epals.com) are ideally suited for primary schools and operate on the basis that all messages are approved by the teacher prior to passing between the sender and recipient.

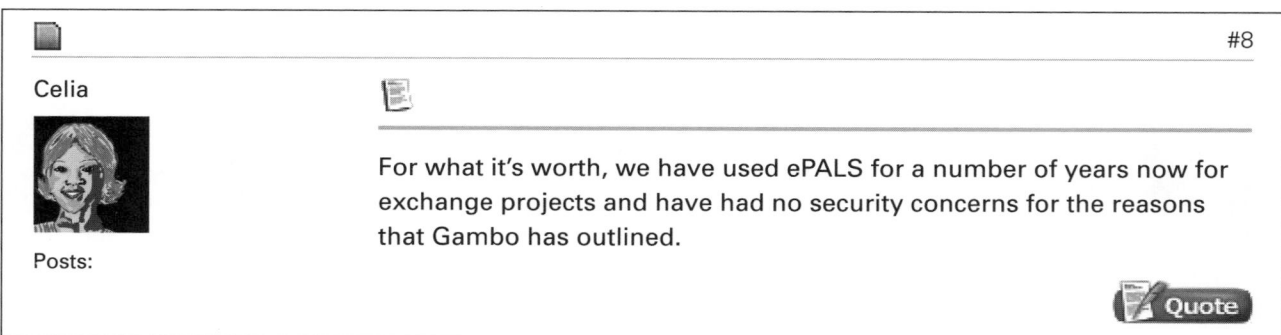

#8

Celia

Posts:

For what it's worth, we have used ePALS for a number of years now for exchange projects and have had no security concerns for the reasons that Gambo has outlined.

Quote

20th October

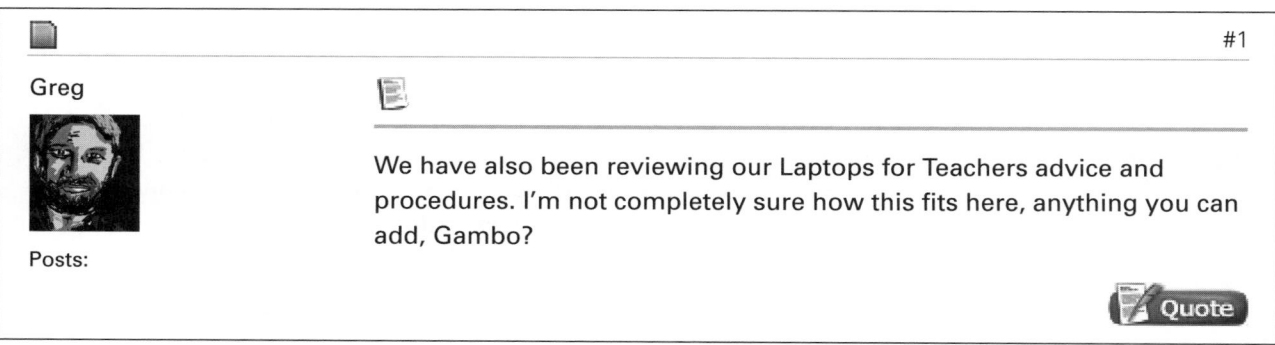

#1

Greg

Posts:

We have also been reviewing our Laptops for Teachers advice and procedures. I'm not completely sure how this fits here, anything you can add, Gambo?

Quote

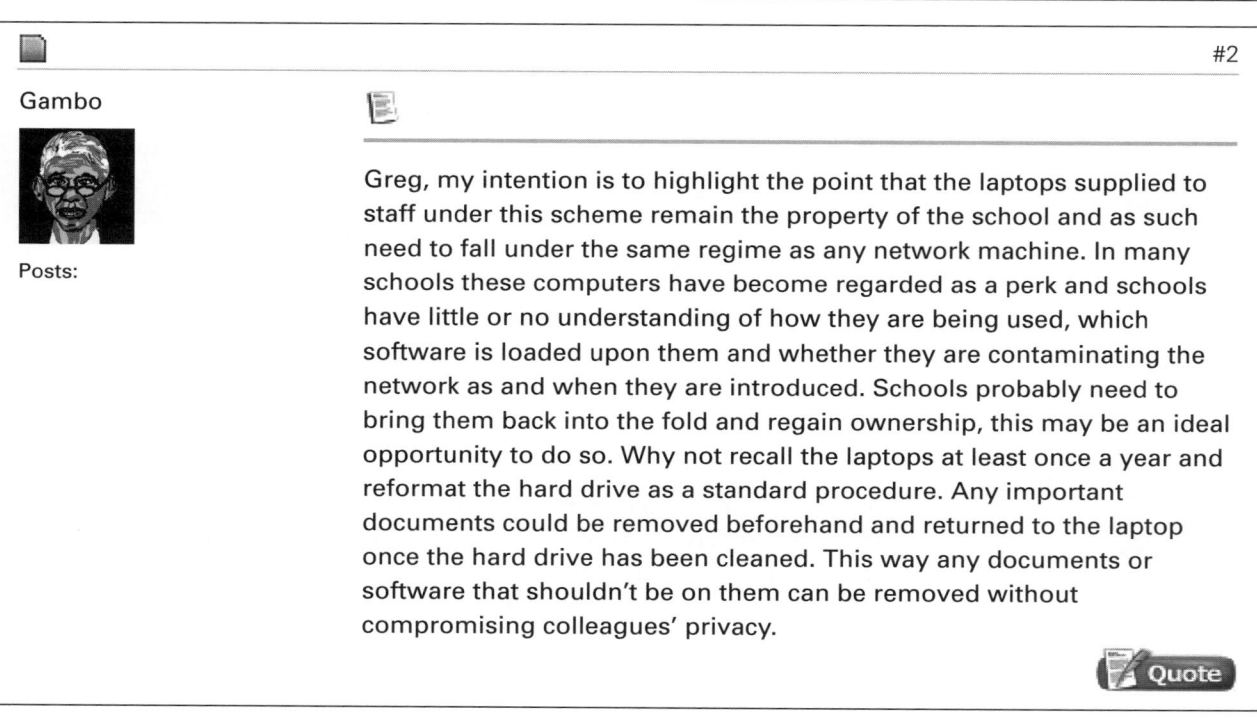

#2

Gambo

Posts:

Greg, my intention is to highlight the point that the laptops supplied to staff under this scheme remain the property of the school and as such need to fall under the same regime as any network machine. In many schools these computers have become regarded as a perk and schools have little or no understanding of how they are being used, which software is loaded upon them and whether they are contaminating the network as and when they are introduced. Schools probably need to bring them back into the fold and regain ownership, this may be an ideal opportunity to do so. Why not recall the laptops at least once a year and reformat the hard drive as a standard procedure. Any important documents could be removed beforehand and returned to the laptop once the hard drive has been cleaned. This way any documents or software that shouldn't be on them can be removed without compromising colleagues' privacy.

Quote

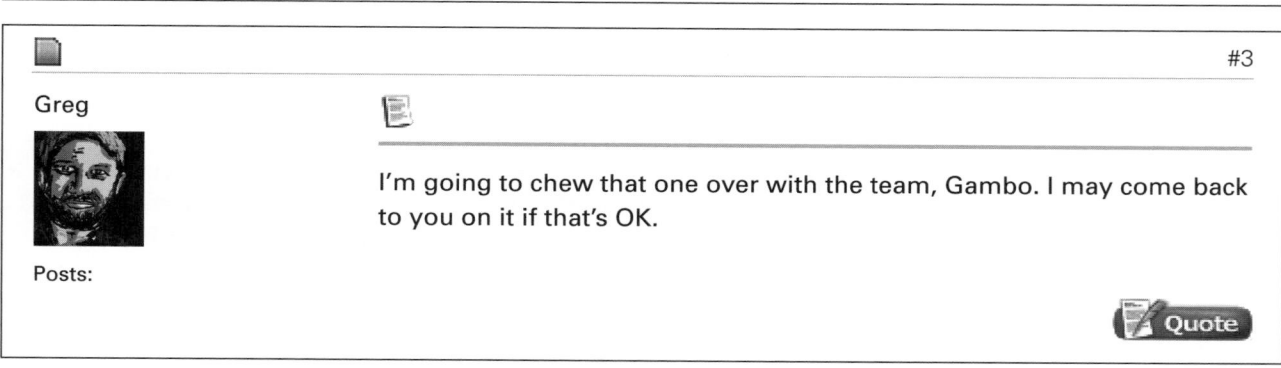

#3

Greg

Posts:

I'm going to chew that one over with the team, Gambo. I may come back to you on it if that's OK.

Quote

23rd October

Week 8, Task 6 – From Self-Review to a Strategic Plan for ICT

Following on from last month's update of the BECTA self-review framework we need quickly to move forward with priorities for action. In subsequent years it is important that this whole process is aligned with the school's broader development planning process so that the results of the review can feed into the school's annual improvement plan. It is good practice for the ICT co-ordinator to maintain a three-year development plan that sits beneath this top-level document. Many schools will be happy to use the plan produced from the SRF for this purpose, however colleagues have enquired about other integration options and it is a very simple process to cut and paste from the matrix into an MS [Microsoft] word template if this is your preferred planning documentation. Use the next step SRF level descriptions to form success criteria for your plan. Having established these you can then work on identifying appropriate actions to achieve the desired outcomes. To summarize therefore, this week you will either adopt the SRF online action plan and use this to identify your priorities or work through the example that I shall present based upon a traditional MS Word-based development plan. Next month we shall bring together the two leadership strands that we have now developed, that is, the leadership team activities formation with the self-review to identify specific actions matched to success criteria in order to achieve ICT Mark status by the year end. The starting point for this week's exercise is the benchmarking overview that was produced last month (Figure 1.5 'BECTA SRF progress'). In order to consider ICT Mark application this hypothetical school needs to develop its practice specifically in terms of Element 3 (learning and teaching), Element 4 (assessment), Element 7 (impact on pupil outcomes) and Element 8 (extended schooling.) More detailed consideration will also highlight individual strands from other elements that may require further action. For action planning purposes I am going to focus upon progress against Element 3, learning and teaching.

Figures 2.2, 2.3 and 2.4 provide a clear view of which individual aspects the school needs to progress set against the ICT Mark benchmark Level 2. If colleagues wish to attain accreditation this year, then actions should be set in place to address each of the outstanding aspects. This week's activity involves cutting and pasting success criteria from the matrix directly into your development plan template.

Element: Element 3. Learning and teaching

Strand: 3a. Teachers' planning, use and evaluation

Figure 2.2 SRF Benchmark for Element 3a (Reproduced with permission from BECTA)
Available on the net at http://www.james-wright.org

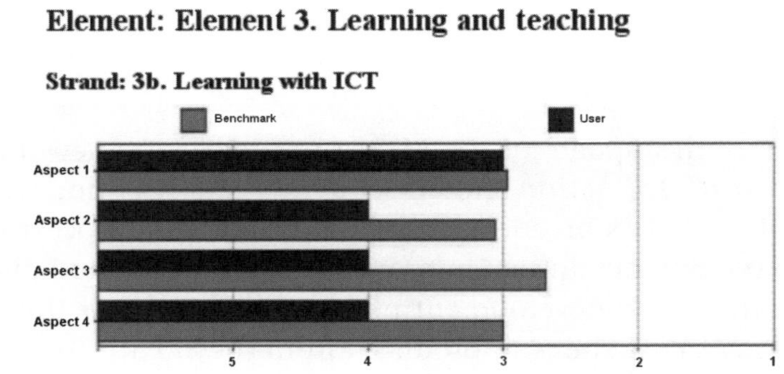
Element: Element 3. Learning and teaching
Strand: 3b. Learning with ICT
Benchmark
User
Aspect 1
Aspect 2
Aspect 3
Aspect 4
5
4
3
2
1

Figure 2.3 SRF Benchmark for Element 3b (Reproduced with permission from BECTA)
Available on the net at http://www.james-wright.org

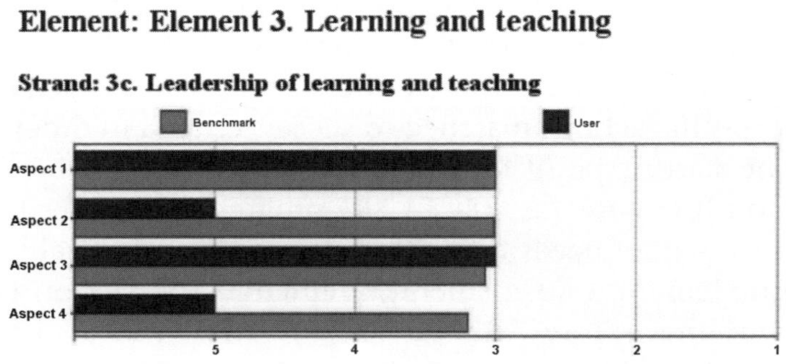
Element: Element 3. Learning and teaching
Strand: 3c. Leadership of learning and teaching
Benchmark
User
Aspect 1
Aspect 2
Aspect 3
Aspect 4
5
4
3
2
1

Figure 2.4 SRF Benchmark for Element 3c (Reproduced with permission from BECTA)
Available on the net at http://www.james-wright.org

Table 2.3 demonstrates how each of the aspects has been identified from the given sample. Because the aim is to achieve accreditation this year, each outstanding aspect has been given a number one priority. Colleagues may decide that accreditation is still perhaps two years away, in which case the number of actions required this year could be reduced. Colleagues using the site template should complete this for all aspects for which self-evaluation currently falls short of the ICT Mark level.

Next month the ICT team will compile appropriate actions and complete the plan as the final part of their team-building review.

Table 2.3 Development plan template, Element 3

Element 3. Learning and teaching				
Action point	**Resources**	**Responsibility and monitoring**	**Timescale**	**Success criteria/impact on pupil learning**
3a. Teachers' planning, use and evaluation				
3a-1 Planning for ICT in learning and teaching		CURRENT LEVEL 4		PRIORITY 1
				Many staff have the confidence to identify opportunities for the use of ICT and regularly build this into their planning.
				Nearly all staff know when, and when not, to use ICT and this leads to effective planning. A few staff go beyond this and can see new opportunities to extend learning and teaching.
3a-3 Building on prior learning		CURRENT LEVEL 5		PRIORITY 1
				Some account is taken of previous ICT learning when planning the use of ICT but many pupils have to repeat unnecessarily ICT learning or activities. Planning is sometimes informed by relevant assessment evidence.
				Most teachers' planning builds on pupils' experiences and relevant assessment evidence but some pupils are unchallenged by ICT work.
				Teachers routinely build on pupils' previous ICT experiences and relevant assessment evidence when planning learning experiences for pupils.
3a-5 Quality of use of ICT for learning and teaching		CURRENT LEVEL 4		PRIORITY 1
				Many staff use ICT to engage and motivate pupils in their learning through more varied approaches and resources, leading to more active and interactive learning experiences.

Action Point	Resources	Responsibility and monitoring	Timescale	Success criteria/impact on pupil learning
				Most staff use ICT to enhance teaching and learning experiences with approaches not readily accessible through more traditional methods.
3a-6 Ongoing critical evaluation		CURRENT LEVEL 3		PRIORITY 2
				Most staff are able to evaluate critically the way in which ICT has impacted on learning and teaching and share this with colleagues.
3b. Learning with ICT				
3b-2 Opportunities for pupils to choose to employ ICT		CURRENT LEVEL 4		PRIORITY 1
				Pupils make some decisions as to when to employ ICT but this is dependent on individual teachers rather than policy.
				In most curriculum areas/classes pupils are able to identify, select and employ ICT appropriately.
3b-3 Digital literacy skills		CURRENT LEVEL 4		PRIORITY 1
				Many pupils have some skills and understanding that enable them to access and use web-based information and learning resources. Many are not aware of how to effectively use these resources to support their learning.
				Most pupils have a good range of skills that enable them to access and use web-based resources to support their learning. They are fully aware of key issues for using web based information and resources.

3b-4 Pupils' responses	CURRENT LEVEL 4	PRIORITY 1
		Pupils are beginning to reflect on how ICT impacts on their learning. Some can discuss elements of this when prompted, and sometimes use examples drawn from their own experience.
		Pupils have a good understanding of how their use of ICT improves learning. They are able to explain, with examples, how they use ICT and how it impacts on their achievements.

3c. Leadership of learning and teaching

3c-1 Leadership of learning and teaching with ICT	CURRENT LEVEL 3	PRIORITY 2
		There is an agreed whole-school approach to the use of ICT in teaching and learning. This is led strategically by senior management, promoted by all subject leaders and consistently implemented.
		Transfer and transition arrangements between years, phases, key stages and schools pays little attention to pupils' ICT learning.

3c-2 Transfer and transition	CURRENT LEVEL 5	PRIORITY 1
		Some effort is made to share information about ICT experiences at transfer and transition between years, phases, key stages and schools, but little practical use is made of this information.
		The school has a policy that underpins and ensures continuity of ICT learning at transfer and transition between years, phases, key stages and schools and partners.

Action Point	Resources	Responsibility and monitoring	Timescale	Success criteria/impact on pupil learning
3c-4 Evaluation of the impact of ICT on the quality of learning and teaching		CURRENT LEVEL 5		PRIORITY 1
				Some ad hoc evaluations have taken place but these have not been systematic or contributed to a whole-school picture. These have generally been informative but have not led to improved practice.
				Evaluation occurs as part of the whole-school strategy, but does not involve all staff at all levels. Evaluation has had some identifiable impact on improving practice but not systematically across the whole school.
				There is regular and systematic evaluation of the impact of ICT on learning and teaching at all levels. The results of this feed back into the identification of areas for development.

Available on the net at http://www.james-wright.org

Chapter 3 • November

1st November

As we enter November you will already have plotted your strategic priorities for the coming year and established an embedded team structure that will help to develop these priorities.

This month we shall build upon October's work in order to:

1 Complete the team activities by incorporating the final stage of the self-review analysis and finalizing activities for the coming year.
2 Continue our E-safety review to include a carefully planned programme of teaching units that develop pupil awareness of how to use the Internet and associated technologies safely.
3 Begin a review of the school's long-term financial strategy and funding model for ICT in order to plan for developments with regard to total cost of ownership.

Week 9, Task 7 – Establishing ICT Priorities within a Whole-School Context

This week try to host your initial strategy group meeting with the revised ICT team emphasizing to colleagues the importance of attendance. Every effort should be made to get the school-based team together with your governor and technician.

Consider using the following agenda.

AGENDA
Individual feedback upon E-learning narratives
Summary of team strengths and foci from E-learning co-ordinator
Reprise development plan objectives identified via SRF (Table 2.4)
Identify ideal scenarios for each outstanding aspect
Identify activities that will achieve the desired outcomes (Pairs brainstorm)
Individual feedback and agreed next steps
Allocation of specific areas for completion

2nd November

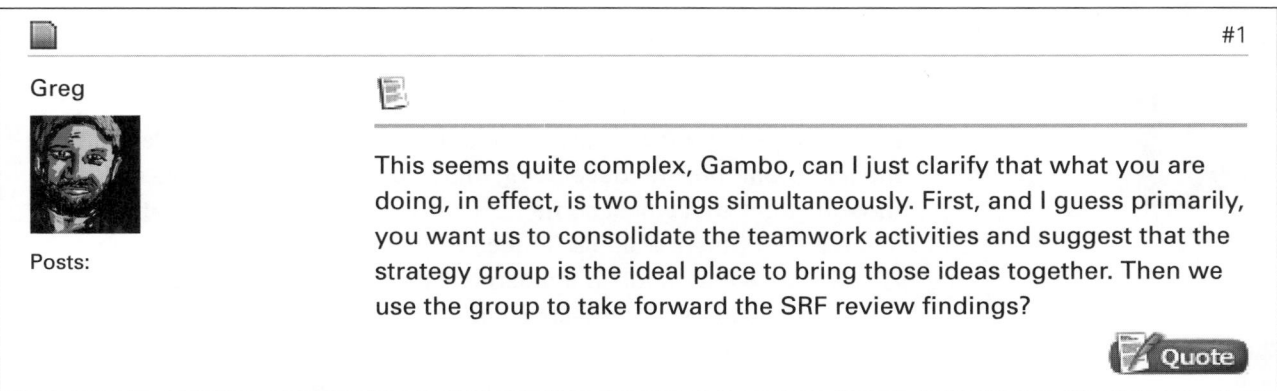

	#1
Greg	
Posts:	This seems quite complex, Gambo, can I just clarify that what you are doing, in effect, is two things simultaneously. First, and I guess primarily, you want us to consolidate the teamwork activities and suggest that the strategy group is the ideal place to bring those ideas together. Then we use the group to take forward the SRF review findings?

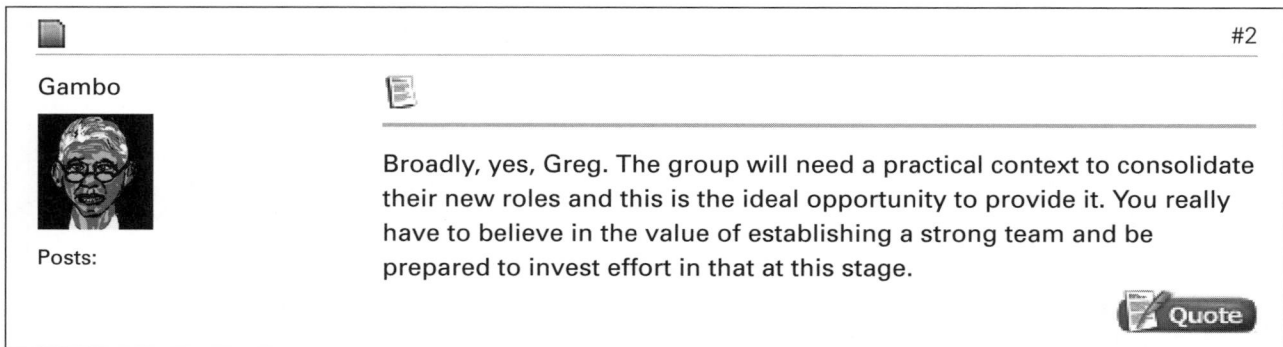

Gambo

Posts:

> Broadly, yes, Greg. The group will need a practical context to consolidate their new roles and this is the ideal opportunity to provide it. You really have to believe in the value of establishing a strong team and be prepared to invest effort in that at this stage.

With regard to the team-building dimension of this meeting, take time to consider the preferred outcomes that will support a strong ICT team with a clear sense of purpose and direction. As the team leader you will want to use this first group meeting since the individual self-analyses to reinforce each person's role within the team, to demonstrate the value that the school places upon each role and to ensure that the expertise identified during the individual narratives is utilized to serve the school. Be mindful of these outcomes as you open the meeting and invite each individual to offer feedback on their own narrative, including the key factors that arose from your paired work. Prepare in advance any points that you feel should be shared across the group and prompt colleagues accordingly, being mindful of any inherent sensitivity that may have arisen during your initial paired work.

Clarify in advance how you wish this part of the meeting to unfold and be mindful of time constraints. As soon as every team member has had an opportunity to contribute, summarize what you now see as the team's strengths and each individual's focus for the coming months. You can then move on to the development planning part of the meeting, using this to provide a practical focused task for the team to work on together and so consolidate the new dynamic that has been created.

Last month key targets from BECTA's self-review framework were synthesized within your ICT development plan in order to produce a series of success criteria and key priorities for this year. The core task for you and your team now is to identify attainable actions matched against those success criteria. It may be practical for the team to split into pairs to work on each section of the plan using the template that was produced last month from Table 2.3, allocating sections of the document to colleagues, as you feel most appropriate. Be aware of any links between potential activities, as each criterion will not necessarily require a unique action for it to be achieved and this will avoid colleagues duplicating their work.

3rd November

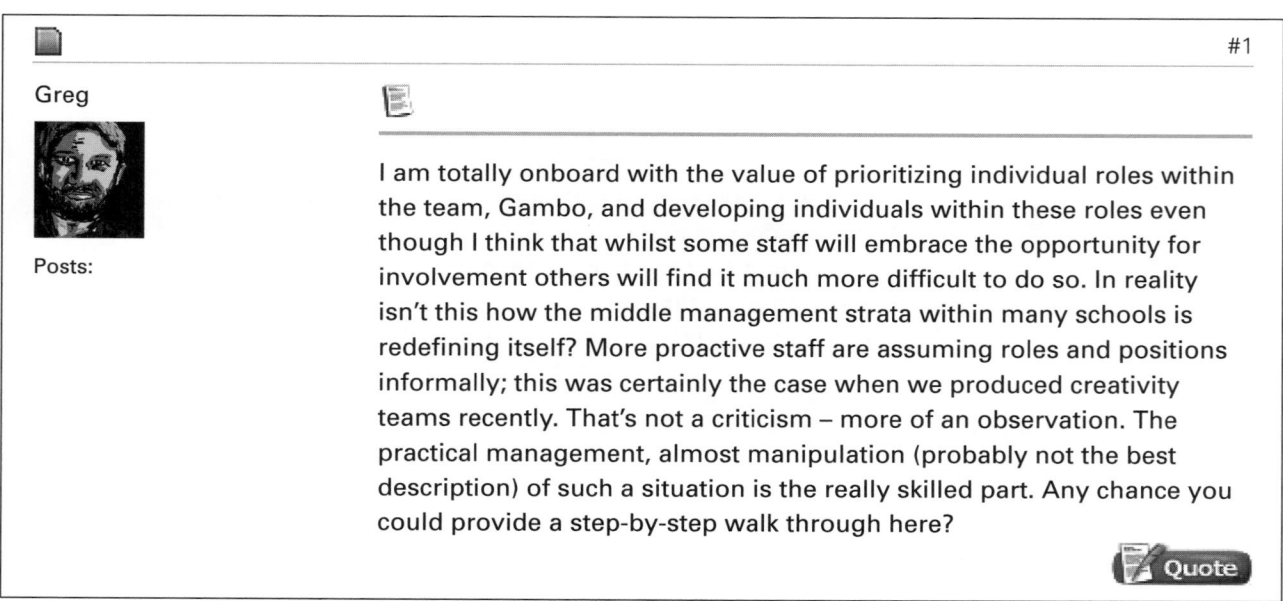

Greg

Posts:

> I am totally onboard with the value of prioritizing individual roles within the team, Gambo, and developing individuals within these roles even though I think that whilst some staff will embrace the opportunity for involvement others will find it much more difficult to do so. In reality isn't this how the middle management strata within many schools is redefining itself? More proactive staff are assuming roles and positions informally; this was certainly the case when we produced creativity teams recently. That's not a criticism – more of an observation. The practical management, almost manipulation (probably not the best description) of such a situation is the really skilled part. Any chance you could provide a step-by-step walk through here?

Table 3.1 Element 3.1 action points

Action point	Resources	Responsibility and monitoring	Timescale	Success criteria/impact on pupil learning
Element 3. Learning and teaching				
3a. Teachers' planning, use and evaluation				
3a-1 Planning for ICT in learning and teaching		CURRENT LEVEL 4		PRIORITY 1
				Many staff have the confidence to identify opportunities for the use of ICT and regularly build this into their planning.
				Nearly all staff know when, and when not, **to use ICT** and this leads to **effective planning**. A few staff go beyond this and can see new opportunities **to extend learning and teaching.**
3a-3 Building on prior learning		CURRENT LEVEL 5		PRIORITY 1
				Some account is taken of previous ICT learning when planning the use of ICT but many pupils have to repeat unnecessarily ICT learning or activities. Planning is sometimes informed by relevant assessment evidence.
				Most teachers' planning builds on pupils' experiences and relevant assessment evidence but some pupils are unchallenged by ICT work.
				Teachers routinely **build on** pupils' previous ICT experiences and **relevant assessment evidence** when planning learning experiences for pupils.
3a-5 Quality of use of ICT for learning and teaching		CURRENT LEVEL 4		PRIORITY 1
				Many staff use ICT to engage and motivate pupils in their learning through more varied approaches and resources, leading to more active and interactive learning experiences.
				Most staff use ICT to enhance teaching and learning experiences with **approaches not readily accessible through more traditional methods.**
3a-6 Ongoing critical evaluation		CURRENT LEVEL 3		PRIORITY 2
				Most staff are able to **evaluate critically** the way in which ICT has **impacted** on learning and teaching and share this with colleagues.

Available on the net at http://www.james-wright.org

Let us examine how colleagues might identify ideal scenarios against each outstanding aspect. For this example we shall assume that you and a colleague are working upon Strand 3a 'Teachers' planning, use and evaluation' and therefore have eight criteria to meet

Within the example shown in Table 3.1, colleagues felt that Level 2 (L2) of the framework was attainable for each aspect and therefore decided that actions aimed at meeting the higher level (L2) were most appropriate incorporating the lower-level activities in the process. In addition they highlighted the following key outcomes:

- 3a-1 Effective planning to use ICT to extend learning and teaching
- 3a-3 Build on relevant assessment evidence
- 3a-5 Approaches not readily accessible through more traditional methods
- 3a-6 Critically evaluate impact.

Figure 3.1 demonstrates the next phase of the operation in which discussion identified core areas that would help to achieve each objective.

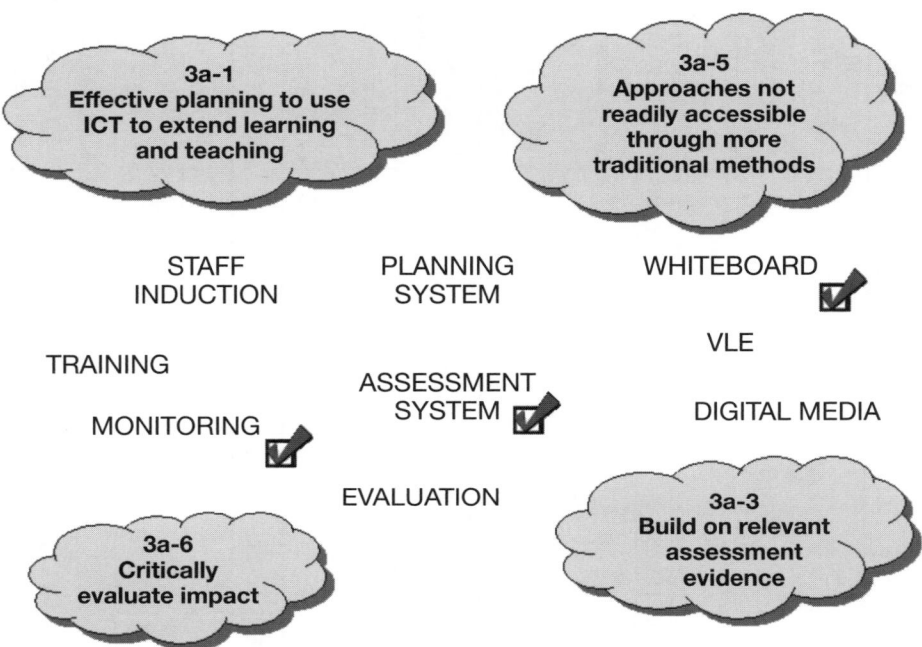

Figure 3.1 Paired activity map
Available on the net at http://www.james-wright.org

Processes already under way with regard to the assessment of ICT, interactive whiteboard training and revised monitoring procedures would successfully meet the requirements for some of these aspects, whilst fresh activities were required specifically to address other core training issues including induction, planning and evaluation systems. Bespoke activities would be needed to advance the virtual learning environment and further use of digital media.

Colleagues should select specific actions that have direct relevance to school before disseminating the outcomes of this session to the rest of the group. When the team reassembles, the E-learning co-ordinator should again chair discussions inviting each pairing to provide feedback. In the given example, it is likely that some duplication may arise with regard to existing initiatives, such as assessment and the virtual learning and digital media initiatives. It is equally likely that new actions regarding staff training and planning procedures would need to be developed. In order for progress against the matrix to be achieved these actions will need to be projected as whole-school priorities and next-steps procedures identified and delegated.

Colleagues wishing to complete the plan individually will need to ensure that the overall identified priorities are acknowledged and included within the school improvement plan at the earliest convenient point in the planning cycle, so that sufficient resources are attracted to ensure their work has the desired impact. The completed development plan will now provide clear unambiguous tasks and success criteria that will dovetail directly with the school improvement plan, if necessary, and provide a direct route to the desired accreditation should they be effectively completed this year.

7th November

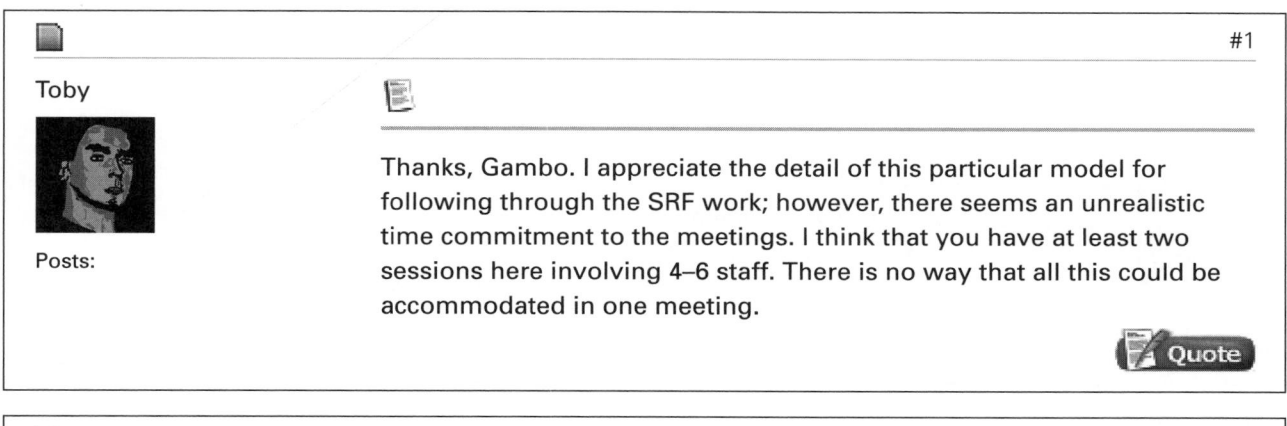

#1

Toby

Posts:

Thanks, Gambo. I appreciate the detail of this particular model for following through the SRF work; however, there seems an unrealistic time commitment to the meetings. I think that you have at least two sessions here involving 4–6 staff. There is no way that all this could be accommodated in one meeting.

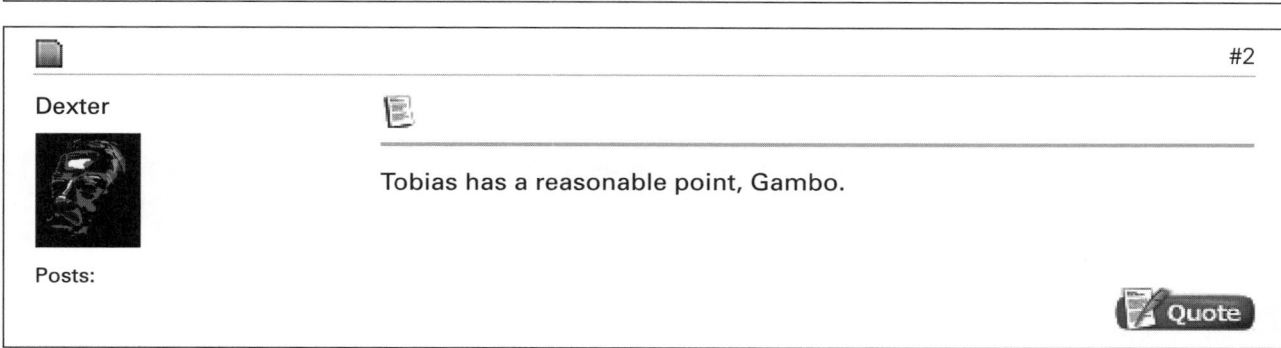

#2

Dexter

Posts:

Tobias has a reasonable point, Gambo.

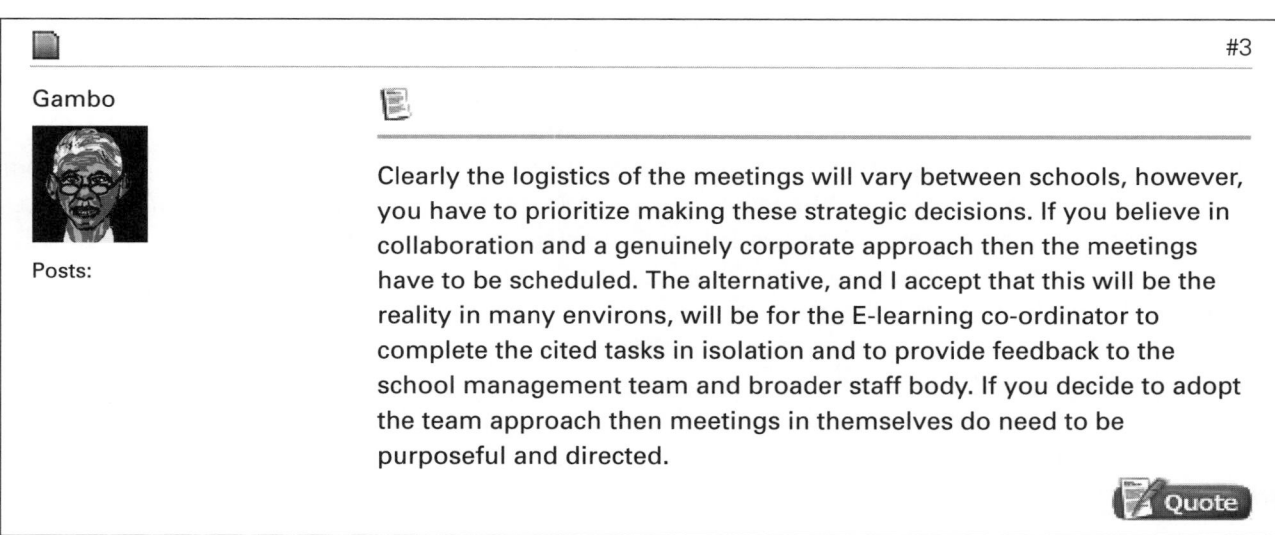

#3

Gambo

Posts:

Clearly the logistics of the meetings will vary between schools, however, you have to prioritize making these strategic decisions. If you believe in collaboration and a genuinely corporate approach then the meetings have to be scheduled. The alternative, and I accept that this will be the reality in many environs, will be for the E-learning co-ordinator to complete the cited tasks in isolation and to provide feedback to the school management team and broader staff body. If you decide to adopt the team approach then meetings in themselves do need to be purposeful and directed.

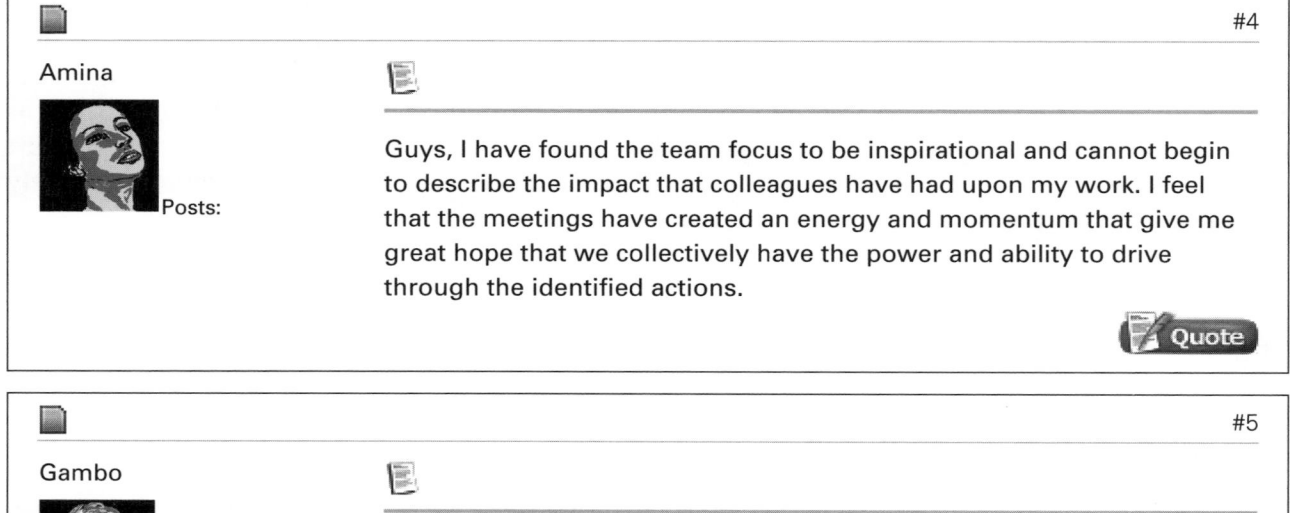

8th November

Week 11, Task 8 – E-safety – Teaching Internet Safety

You may recall that at the beginning of this term we identified three core outcomes from our E-safety review:

Are we all aware of potential E-safety dangers?
Have we kept pace with developments?
Are we teaching E-safety?

Over the next two weeks you are going to evaluate the extent to which E-safety is taught at your school. Governments both at home and abroad are identifying this as the third pillar of effective E-safety strategy, together with technological web filtering solutions and effective school policies.

Education is essential in helping children to understand how to behave on the Internet and how to protect themselves online when without the benefit of a firewall. Consequently, as part of your school self-evaluation, specifically 'the extent to which learners adopt safe and responsible practices in using new technologies, including the Internet' (Ofsted SEF Section 4b) schools should consider and report exactly how children are taught to use these resources safely. How can we teach children without frightening them and distorting their view of these incredibly valuable resources?

There are a series of options for schools wishing to develop a cross-curricular approach to E-safety, particularly with regard to the broader citizenship and PSHE agenda. There are clear correlations with the schools' broader 'care' initiatives, road safety and stranger-danger campaigns, and each school will wish the project to integrate within this context. Try to establish what your children's needs are because these will vary. If your school uses the Internet with Key

Stage 1 pupils then clearly they need to be included within your teaching programme, especially if audit data indicates that significant numbers of infants access the Internet from home. Other key anchor points may be for example the Year 3 QCA Email Unit of Study or alternatively adoption of email for delivery of the revised National Literacy Framework. Schools that deliver the ICT core curriculum based on the QCA Scheme of Work for ICT will need to consider carefully its implications upon their broader E-safety curriculum.

12th November

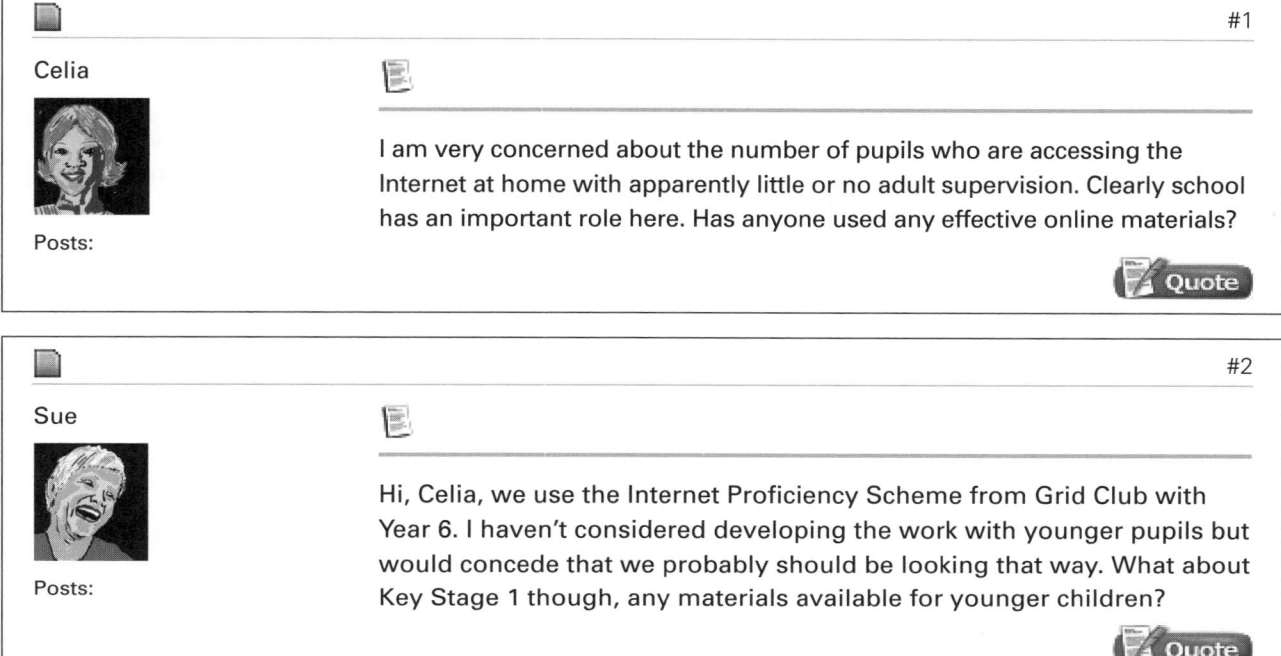

#1

Celia

Posts:

I am very concerned about the number of pupils who are accessing the Internet at home with apparently little or no adult supervision. Clearly school has an important role here. Has anyone used any effective online materials?

Quote

#2

Sue

Posts:

Hi, Celia, we use the Internet Proficiency Scheme from Grid Club with Year 6. I haven't considered developing the work with younger pupils but would concede that we probably should be looking that way. What about Key Stage 1 though, any materials available for younger children?

Quote

14th November

Table 3.2 provides a matrix of activities that could be planned across the school based on a two-tier model of support. An annual reminder session of the school's policies and procedures delivered to all children and differentiated by outcome and support exists with online materials based on interactive PC-based activities. The school input is a real opportunity to build into the system procedures that not only provide an annual reminder to each class about the school's rules but also ensures that staff are kept abreast of changes, providing a common frame of reference for all users of the school's resources. The class teacher may deliver such sessions or, if more appropriate, the E-learning co-ordinator might choose to do so if release time is available. Please note that the E-learning co-ordinator should not simply release the class teacher for this to take place, as that may give the impression that this is an issue that does not affect them when clearly it does.

Table 3.2 E-safety planning matrix

Autumn term	Spring term	Summer term
YEAR R	YEAR R	YEAR R
YEAR 1	YEAR 1 School Acceptable Internet Use Agreement	YEAR 1 Netty's World 'Exploring the Net'
YEAR 2 School Acceptable Internet Use Agreement	YEAR 2 Hector's World 'Online Privacy'	YEAR 2 Internet Proficiency Scheme Lesson 1 – 'Using technology to to communicate'
YEAR 3 School Acceptable Internet Use Agreement	YEAR 3 Internet Proficiency Scheme Lesson 2 – 'Introducing the Cybercafé web site'	YEAR 3 Internet Proficiency Scheme Lesson 4 – 'Using email safely'
YEAR 4 School Acceptable Internet Use Agreement	YEAR 4 Internet Proficiency Scheme Lesson 3 – 'Communication and Information'	YEAR 4 Surfswell Island
YEAR 5 School Acceptable Internet Use Agreement	YEAR 5 Internet Proficiency Scheme Lesson 5 – 'Responsible use of the Internet'	YEAR 5 Internet Proficiency Scheme Lesson 6 – 'Chatting with care'
YEAR 6 School Acceptable Internet Use Agreement	YEAR 6 Internet Proficiency Scheme Lesson 7 – 'Using text and picture messaging' Lesson 6 – 'Behaving responsibly'	YEAR 6 Cyberquoll

Available on the net at http://www.james-wright.org

17th November

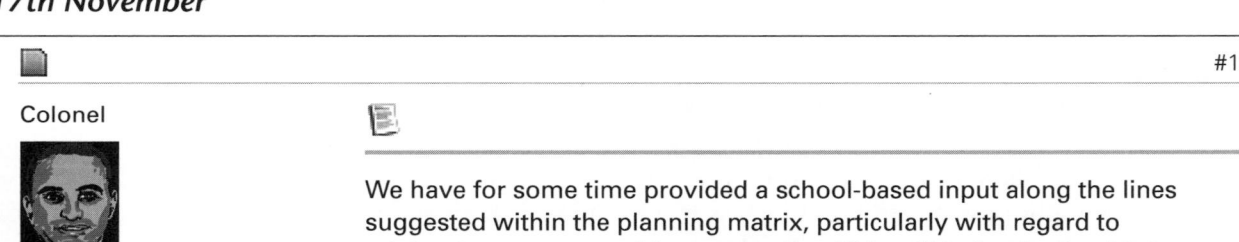

	#1
Colonel	

Posts:

We have for some time provided a school-based input along the lines suggested within the planning matrix, particularly with regard to reinforcing our acceptable usage policy. This will in fact be the third year in which we have run such a programme and I feel we have learnt that the essential early focus is to discuss what the Internet really is. Most young children don't understand that the Internet is a worldwide collection of computer networks; they tend to regard it as a single entity a bit like the BBC or something. It's only with this understanding that you can begin to demonstrate that each separate computer can be seen as representing an individual person, a stranger in fact operating that computer. This is the basis of our E-safety strategy and provides a context for the work within the broader stranger-danger initiatives leading to an acceptance and understanding of the school's rules that links directly to the Acceptable Internet Use Agreement. Clearly the lessons are adapted slightly to suit the age of the pupils but are broadly repeated each year as a necessary reminder, only updated to account for technology changes.

Quote

18th November

Individual schools may have sound reasons to introduce the scheme within Reception although I do not advocate this, as it is a priority for Foundation Stage children. The plan provides a simple school-based introduction during Year 1 followed by some early years online support materials. There remains a dearth of materials available for Key Stage 1, the best of which are provided by southern hemisphere government sites – Netty's World being an example provided by Net Alert, the Australian Internet Safety Advisory Body (www.nettysworld.com.au). The Year 2 resource, 'Hector's World' is a New Zealand resource based around a bottlenose dolphin and provided by Netsafe, New Zealand's Internet Safety Group (www.hectorsworld.com). Colleagues may also wish to use the innovative Hector Protector Safety Button, which provides young children with the option to quickly launch a Hector screensaver that may instantly cover the screen should they stumble across inappropriate materials. Viewing the resources available from these services may help inform colleagues' decisions regarding the adoption of E-safety materials with Key Stage 1 children.

The core Key Stage 2 programme advocated is based around the UK's Grid Club Internet Proficiency Scheme and its associated cybercafé website available at www.gridclub.com/freearea/tasters/cybercafe/base.htm.

Figure 3.2 Grid Club cybercafé (The Cybercafé @ Crown copyright. Reproduced with permission)
Source: Crown copyright. Reproduced with permission.
Available on the net at http://www.james-wright.org

BECTA, the Department for Education and Skills (DfES) and the QCA developed the scheme and all lessons are accompanied by a comprehensive free teacher's pack that can be downloaded from Grid Club at (www.gridclub.com/teachers/t_internet_safety.html).

Grid Club Activities

Lesson 1 – Using technology to communicate
Lesson 2 – Introducing the Cybercafé web site
Lesson 3 – Communication and information
Lesson 4 – Using email safely
Lesson 5 – Responsible use of the Internet

Lesson 6 – Chatting with care
Lesson 7 – Using text and picture messaging
Lesson 8 – Behaving responsibly

Source: The Internet Proficiency Scheme @Crown Copyright. Reproduced with Permission.

Note that the email support unit (Lesson 4) has been placed within Year 3 to match the QCA Unit of Work. In addition to the Grid Club core activities I have recommended provision from Surfswell for Year 4 and Cyberquoll in Year 6. These are fun reinforcement activities provided by the Disney Group (www.disney.go.com/surfswell) and Netalert (www.cyberquoll.com.au) respectively. Together I believe that this provides a comprehensive E-safety programme that will enable all schools to support their pupils and meet their core goals in terms of E-safety provision.

20th November

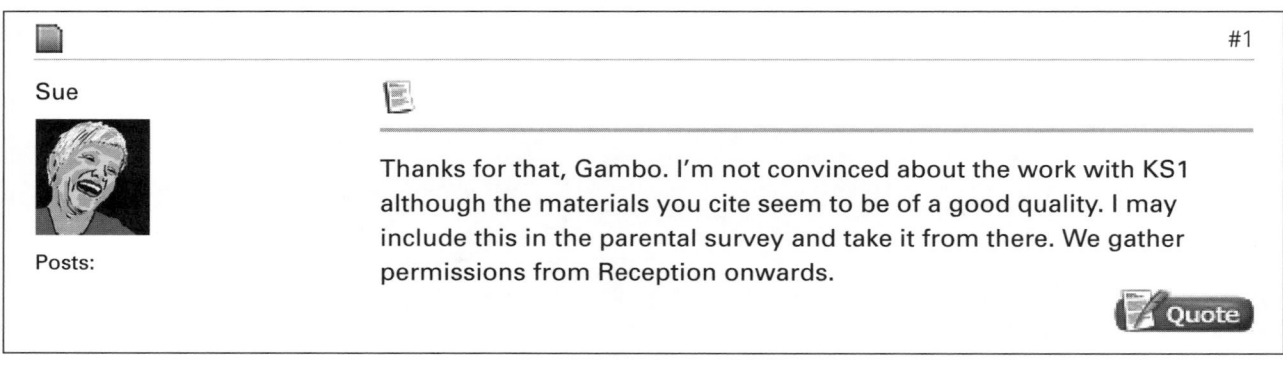

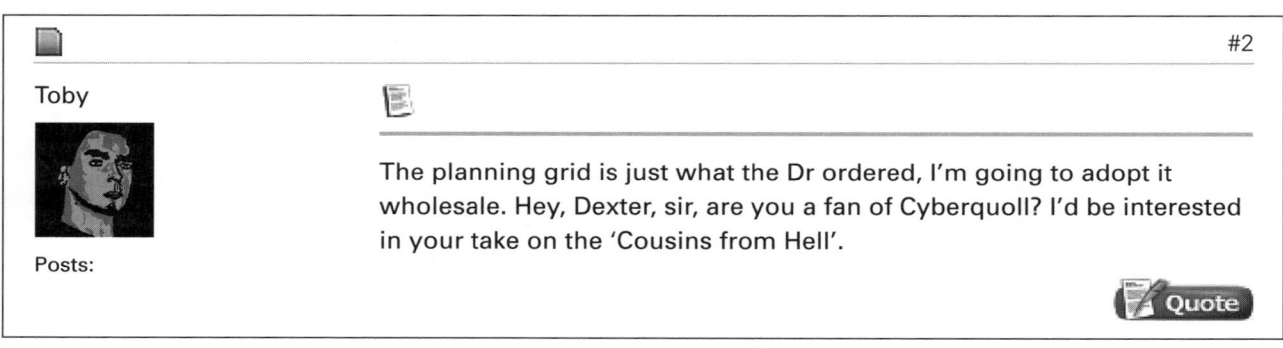

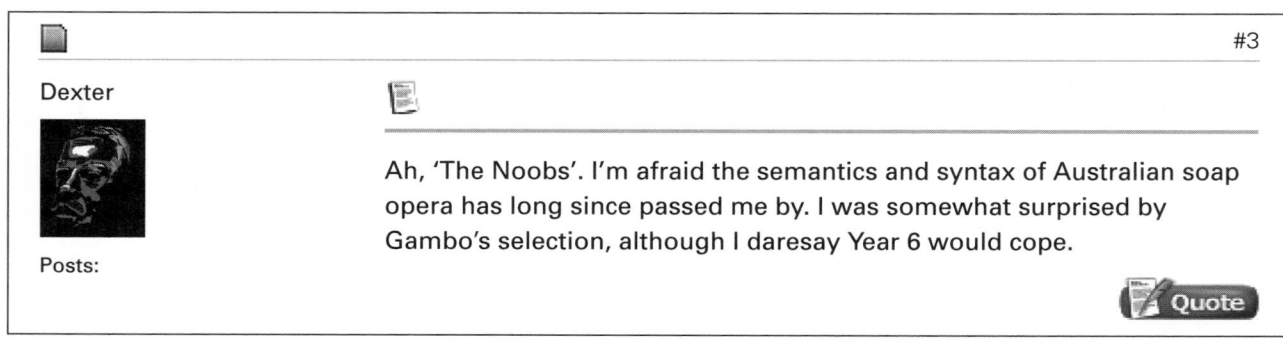

22nd November

Week 12, Task 9 – A Sustainable Funding Model

Spend some time this week reflecting on the financial context to your ICT and E-learning initiatives. In particular aim to produce a three-year spending plan that will help you to direct priorities with due regard to their full funding implications. Of course ICT costs, like revenue, will vary from school to school based upon individual circumstances, however, there are also certain inbuilt givens which are common across all schools and which you will need to account for within your plans. As the person responsible for managing the budget for ICT and E-learning there are certain strategic decisions that you need to be able to accurately steer based on a sound understanding of your funding streams, the cost of maintaining your ICT network requirements and projections of how much these costs will increase in the coming years. Only through an accurate understanding of cost as the true consequence of your strategic decisions will you be able to plan developments and extensions to the network in a realistic and efficient manner.

Central to planning is the ability to understand the concepts behind what is generally termed 'Total cost of ownership' (TCO). In very simple terms this is a reminder that the initial cost of any hardware purchase is only a small part of financing the effective management of that equipment. The TCO provides a realistic financial estimate of all costs, direct and indirect, related to a purchase. These would normally incorporate maintenance support including training charges plus hidden costs that lie behind the headline figure when buying a PC. Your task this week is to complete a TCO analysis that will not only provide costings to support your network over the next three years but also directly inform colleagues with regard to future spending decisions regarding quality specifications and so on.

Table 3.3 is a completed exemplar budget planner that incorporates all of the key elements required for a TCO analysis. A blank template form is available from the companion website (www.james-wright.org). It may be useful to reflect upon the example as we go through the various inherent elements.

Table 3.3 ICT budget planner

A = < 1 year, B = 1–2 year C = 2–3 year, D = >3 year		Unit value	Assets	Cost	Year 1	Cost	Year 2	Cost	Year 3	Cost
Desktop PC	A	£400	8	0	12	4,800	15	6,000	20	8,000
	B	0	20	0	8	0	12	0	15	0
	C	0	15	0	20	0	8	0	12	0
	D	0	6	0	15	0	20	0	8	0
Totals			49		55	4,800	55	6,000	55	8,000
Laptops	A	£600	4	0	6	3,600	11	6,600	15	9,000
	B	0	15	0	4	0	6	0	11	0
	C	0	5	0	15	0	4	0	6	0
	D	0	0	0	5	0	15	0	4	0
Totals			24		30	3,600	36	6,600	36	9,000
Network laser printer	A	£600	1	0	0	0	1	600	0	0
	B	0	0	0	1	0	0	0	1	0
	C	0	0	0	0	0	1	0	0	0
	D	0	1	0	1	0	0	0	1	0
Totals			2		2	0	2	600	2	0
Classroom inkjet printers	A	£100	2	0	0	0	2	200	4	400
	B	0	8	0	2	0	0	0	2	0
	C	0	3	0	8	0	2	0	0	0
	D	0	0	0	3	0	8	0	6	0
Totals			15		13	0	12	200	12	400

A = < 1 year, B = 1–2 year C = 2–3 year, D = > 3 year		Unit value	Assets	Cost	Year 1	Cost	Year 2	Cost	Year 3	Cost
Interactive whiteboard	A	£1,200	2	0	0	0	0	0	2	2,400
	B	0	5	0	2	0	0	0	0	0
	C	0	2	0	5	0	2	0	0	0
	D	0	0	0	2	0	7	0	7	0
Totals			9		9	0	9	0	9	2,400
Data projectors	A	£600	2	0	0	0	0	0	3	1,800
	B	0	5	0	2	0	0	0	0	0
	C	0	4	0	5	0	2	0	0	0
	D	0	1	0	4	0	8	0	7	0
Totals			12		11	0	10	0	10	1,800
Digital video cameras	A	£300	0	0	1	300	0	0	0	0
	B	0	1	0	0	0	1	0	0	0
	C	0	0	0	1	0	0	0	1	0
	D	0	0	0	0	0	1	0	1	0
Totals			2		2	300	2	0	2	0
Digital cameras	A	£150	0	0	2	300	2	300	0	0
	B	0	0	0	0	0	2	0	2	0
	C	0	5	0	0	0	0	0	2	0
	D	0	2	0	7	0	5	0	5	0
Totals			7		9	300	9	300	9	0
Servers	A	£3,000	0	0	0	0	0	0	0	0
	B	0	0	0	0	0	0	0	0	0
	C	0	1	0	0	0	0	0	0	0
	D	0	0	0	1	0	1	0	1	0
Totals			1		1		1		1	0
Cache server	A	£1,000	1	1,000	0	0	0	0	0	0
	B	0	0	0	1	0	0	0	0	0
	C	0	0	0	0	0	1	0	0	0
	D	0	0	0	0	0	0	0	1	0
Totals			1	1,000	1		1		1	0
	A									
	B									
	C									
	D									
Totals										
	A									
	B									
	C									
	D									
Totals										

Software curriculum	Eng	200	200	200	100
	Math	400	0	0	100
	Sci	200	200	0	0
	ICT	1,000	0	0	200
	DT	0	0	100	0
	Hist	150	0	100	100
	Geog	150	0	100	100
	Mus	200	0	0	0
	Art	0	200	0	0
	MFL	0	0	200	0
	Oth	200	900	300	400
Totals		2,500	1,500	1,000	1,000
Software operational	Op Sys	1,200	1,200	1,200	1,200
	Office	0	0	0	0
	MIS	200	200	200	200
	Other	100	100	100	100
Totals		1,500	1,500	1,500	1,500
SEN budget		500	500	500	500
Consumables		300	300	300	300
Professional devlopment	Co-ord	1,000	1,000	1,000	1,000
	Teach	750	750	450	450
	TA	300	300	300	300
	Admin	250	250	250	250
Total		2,300	2,300	2,000	2,000
Connectivity	A	1,500	1,500	1,500	1,500
Technical support budget	Int	0	1,000	1,000	1,000
	Ext	1,500	1,500	1,500	1,500
Total		1,500	2,500	2,500	2,500
BUDGET			£19,100	£23,000	£30,900

Available on the net at http://www.james-wright.org

23rd November

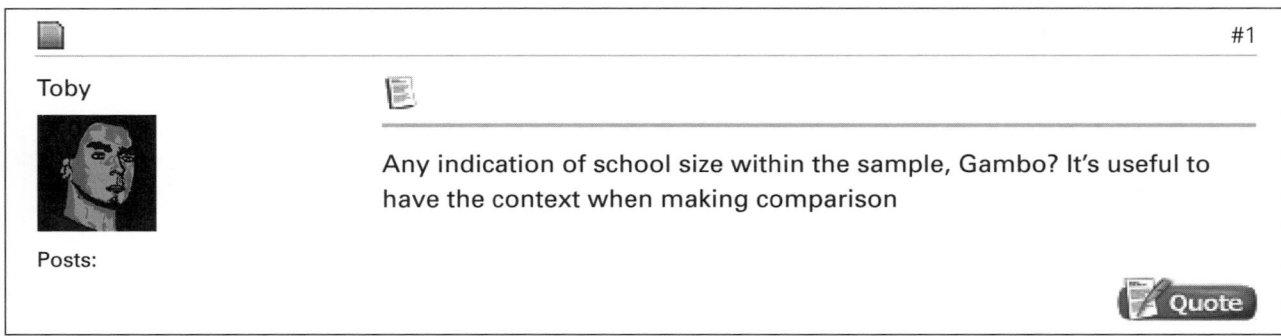

#1

Toby

Posts:

Any indication of school size within the sample, Gambo? It's useful to have the context when making comparison

Quote

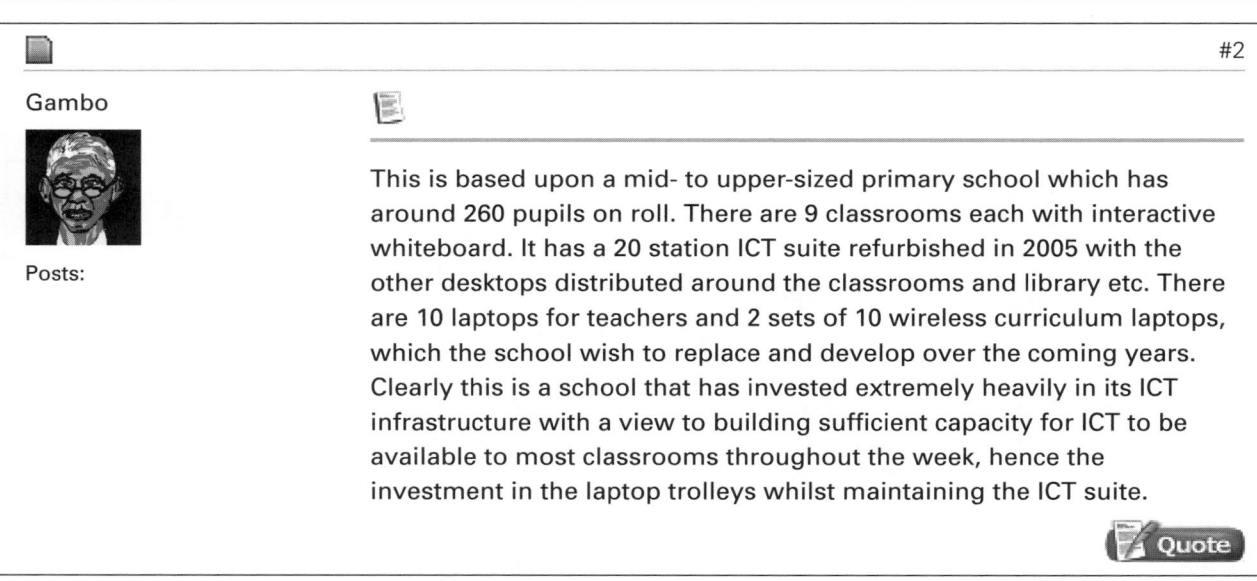

#2

Gambo

Posts:

This is based upon a mid- to upper-sized primary school which has around 260 pupils on roll. There are 9 classrooms each with interactive whiteboard. It has a 20 station ICT suite refurbished in 2005 with the other desktops distributed around the classrooms and library etc. There are 10 laptops for teachers and 2 sets of 10 wireless curriculum laptops, which the school wish to replace and develop over the coming years. Clearly this is a school that has invested extremely heavily in its ICT infrastructure with a view to building sufficient capacity for ICT to be available to most classrooms throughout the week, hence the investment in the laptop trolleys whilst maintaining the ICT suite.

Quote

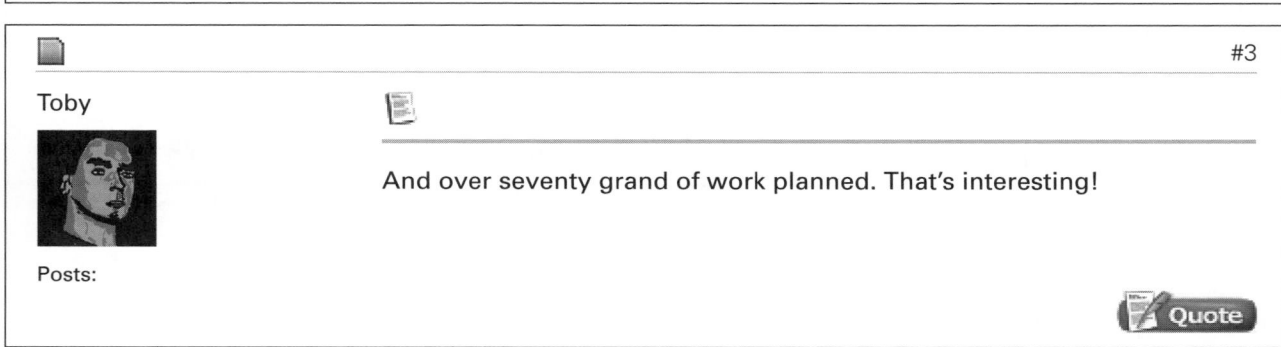

#3

Toby

Posts:

And over seventy grand of work planned. That's interesting!

Quote

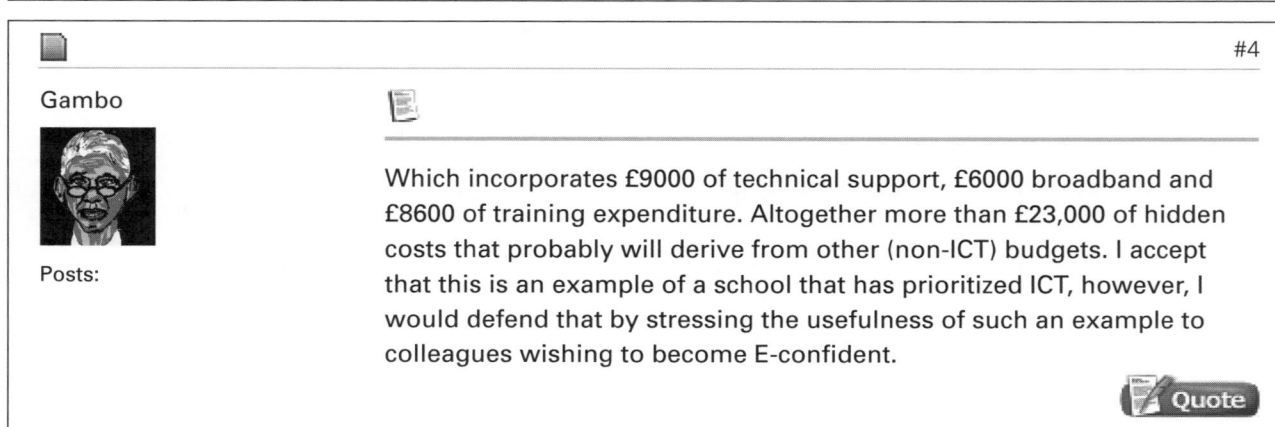

#4

Gambo

Posts:

Which incorporates £9000 of technical support, £6000 broadband and £8600 of training expenditure. Altogether more than £23,000 of hidden costs that probably will derive from other (non-ICT) budgets. I accept that this is an example of a school that has prioritized ICT, however, I would defend that by stressing the usefulness of such an example to colleagues wishing to become E-confident.

Quote

25th November

Replacement costs

Colleagues will not need to be reminded that computers do not last forever. Most equipment will have a conventional life cycle of between three and five years, and every school must decide upon its own replacement strategy. If a school has the finances to do so, it should adopt a three-year rolling replacement programme, which will effectively future-proof investments and may also lend itself favourably to leasing agreements. This is ideal if the budget can afford to absorb computer replacements after three years, removing concerns about supporting ageing and obsolete equipment. If equipment is needed to operate within front-line classroom environments for longer periods, then years four and five may be regarded as 'free' years economically only if one fails to factor in associated maintenance costs. Therefore it is sensible for any school to buy new computers on a three- to five-year cycle based upon its known financial capacity and to replace them on the same cycle. Older machines may be recycled but do be aware of the incrementally greater cost of supporting such items as the hardware deteriorates and inevitably conflicts with more modern systems that may ultimately lead to additional costs in the areas of support and maintenance. The major section of Table 3.3 allows colleagues to assess the condition of current assets through the age-related bandings A, B, C and D.

Table 3.3 allows schools to plot equipment degradation across the chart and to plan for replacement. Note that the school in the example is operating a standard four-year replacement budget, therefore realizing the need to invest in new desktop computers in years two and three of the cycle. Because this currently clashes with plans to extend the laptop provision, it faces major investment in both of those years. The interactive whiteboards are expected to remain current for six to eight years so there is a less aggressive replacement principal. Also of note is the ageing server, which may become problematic by the third year of the cycle. This problem of planning ahead for ICT replacement can be compounded by the difficulty that many schools experience when setting finance plans in advance for large co-ordinated purchases of computers and associated equipment at any one time. Schools are actively discouraged from saving money to make such a purchase in subsequent years, therefore effective financial planning is crucial.

Table 3.3 had additional space for schools to enter peripheral equipment costs, however, as discussed at the beginning of this section, equipment purchase is only part of the story.

25th November

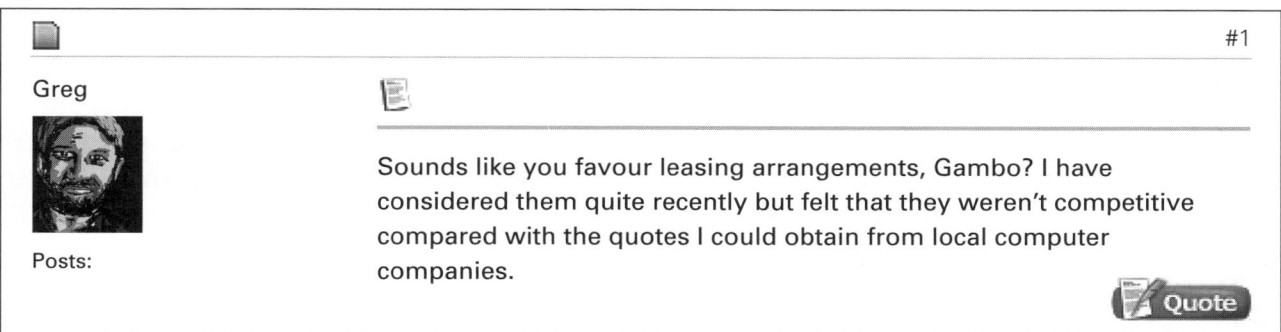

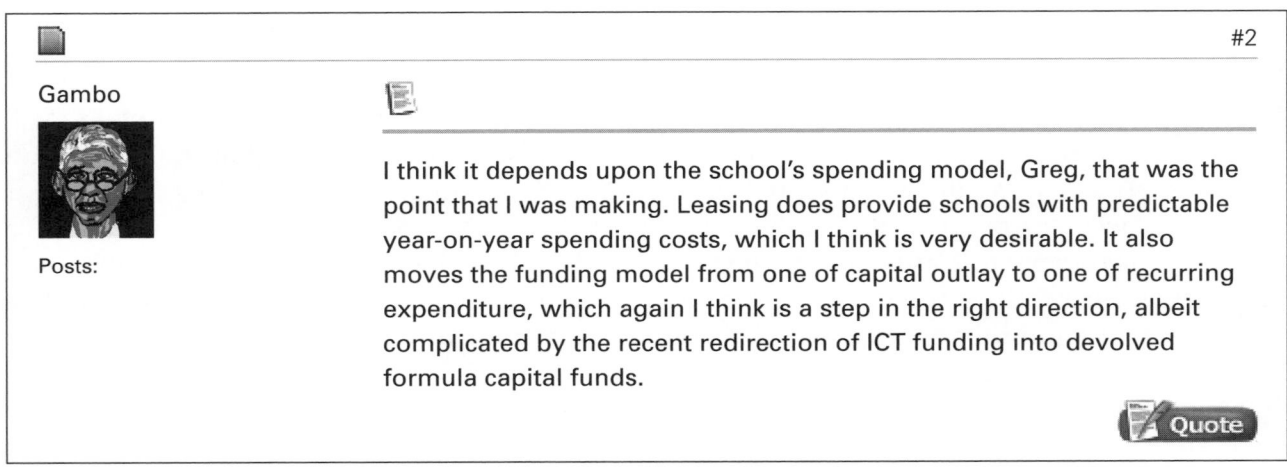

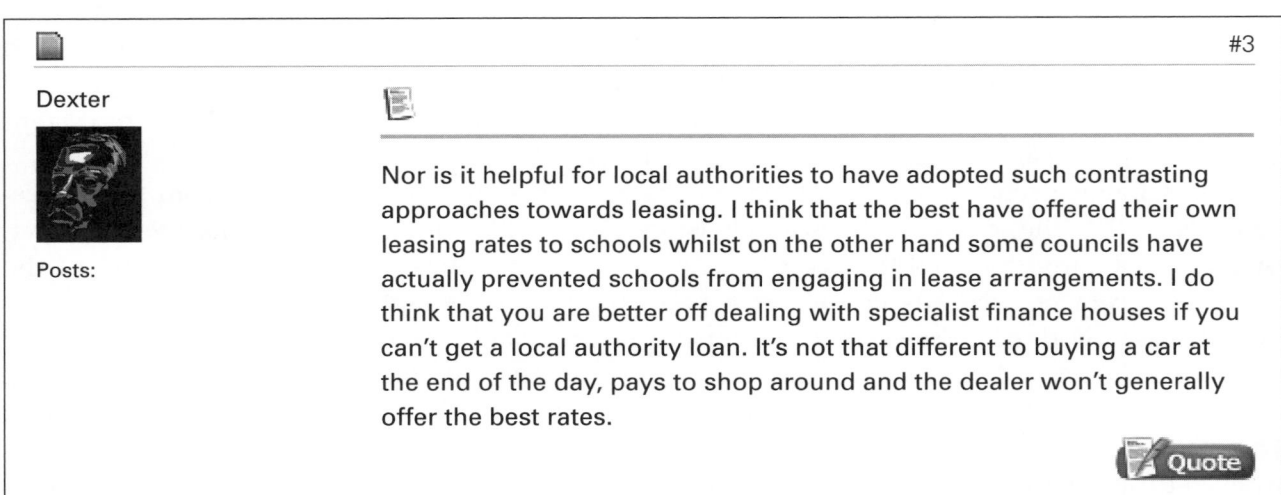

27th November

Software

Often the cost of software can equal or outweigh the cost of hardware. Since 2003, UK schools have received over £450 million of ring-fenced funding (E-learning credits) to support the development of innovative curriculum content, however this funding stream is unlikely to be repeated and schools need to review future expenditure with regard to curriculum content. Likewise this funding has never been eligible for operational, office, management or network software, which will also need to be planned for. The first manual (Book 1) provided a detailed overview of licensing issues, which colleagues may wish to refer to again (Chapter 4, Task 11). In the example provided, the school invites bids from subject leaders within an overall curriculum software budget that is declining. Operational software is bought via a Microsoft Agreement that will also need to be maintained over the coming years.

Professional development

However you budget for professional development (remember that as with any training budget you need to incorporate supply cover costs of around £150 per day if taken during the school day), it is an essential and inevitable prerequisite whenever introducing new technologies. If teachers and other staff members do not understand how to use equipment or software or how to incorporate them into the classroom then the investment will have no impact. Inadequate staff training will lead to underutilization of computers and a loss of return on investment. Within the example provided (Table 3.3) the school has allowed a significant budget for co-ordinator release time and whilst these figures may look quite high much of the cost may be offset against existing supply budgets and training will not specifically be ICT based. Primary Strategy training and funding may also cover and offset some of these costs.

Technical support

I do not intend deconstructing technical support here as again it was covered extensively within the first manual (Book 1, Chapter 2 Task 5; Chapter 7, Task 21) and I also included a projected costing there, which you should now incorporate into your TCO calculations. Remember, it is a false economy to have your co-ordinator or other teacher act as your technical support provider; simply apply the £150 a day supply figure to realize how much this actually costs. A complete lack of support will again undermine the ICT in Schools initiative and produce ill feeling and stress amongst teachers and pupils struggling with failing kit. Lengthy equipment downtime means reduced access for teachers and learners, and ultimately will discourage them from using the equipment at all.

Connectivity

The costs of connecting to the Internet are a relatively small yet significant proportion of the total costs of ICT. Most schools contribute an annual sum to their local authority for connection onto the regional broadband network. Such costs may be higher for rural schools, although these are often aggregated out across an authority. Be wary if your connection is 'free'; it is almost certainly chargeable at some point and may be taken from your school's funding at source.

BECTA has produced comprehensive guidance on the total cost of operating school networks and a useful downloadable investment planning tool is available that will provide colleagues with projections for future spending: http://schools.becta.org.uk/downloads/ICT%20Investment%20 Planner%20%20v.1.04.xls

Complete a valuation of your current infrastructure this week including any invisible costs for support staff, peripherals, consumables, and so on. This valuation will include the grading of equipment in order to reflect its anticipated replacement status. The hardware audit completed during Book 1 using Table 2.1 from that manual should assist in this task. Use Table 3.3 in this book to project costs for the next three years and to align these to any planned priorities in order to ensure that there is adequate funding securely in place.

28th November

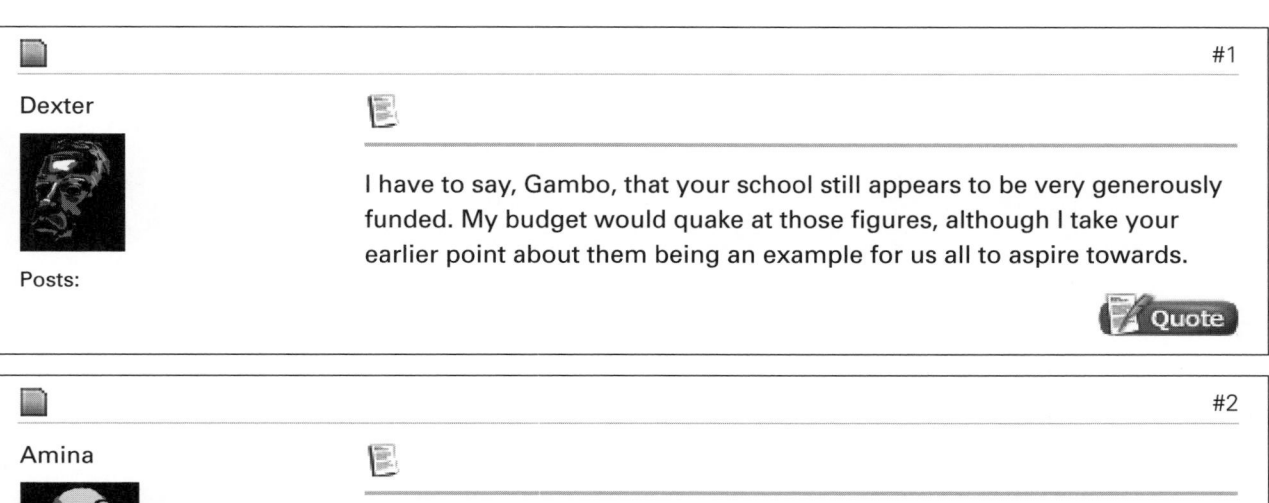

Dexter

Posts:

> I have to say, Gambo, that your school still appears to be very generously funded. My budget would quake at those figures, although I take your earlier point about them being an example for us all to aspire towards.

Quote #1

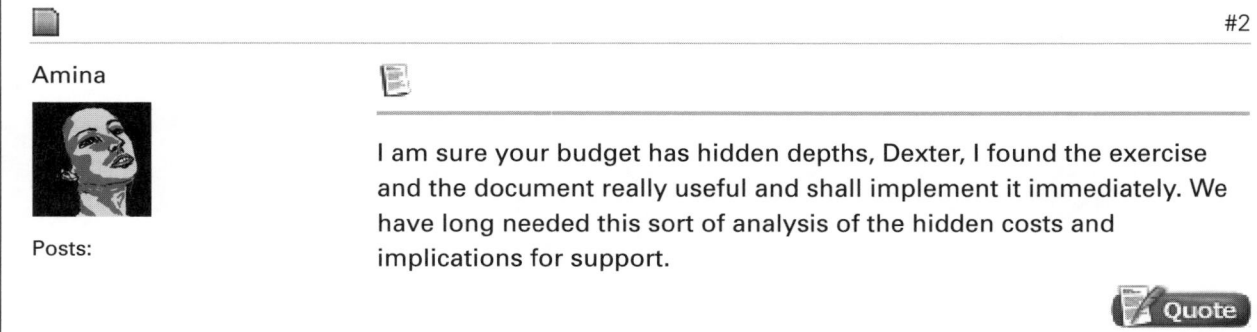

Amina

Posts:

> I am sure your budget has hidden depths, Dexter, I found the exercise and the document really useful and shall implement it immediately. We have long needed this sort of analysis of the hidden costs and implications for support.

Quote #2

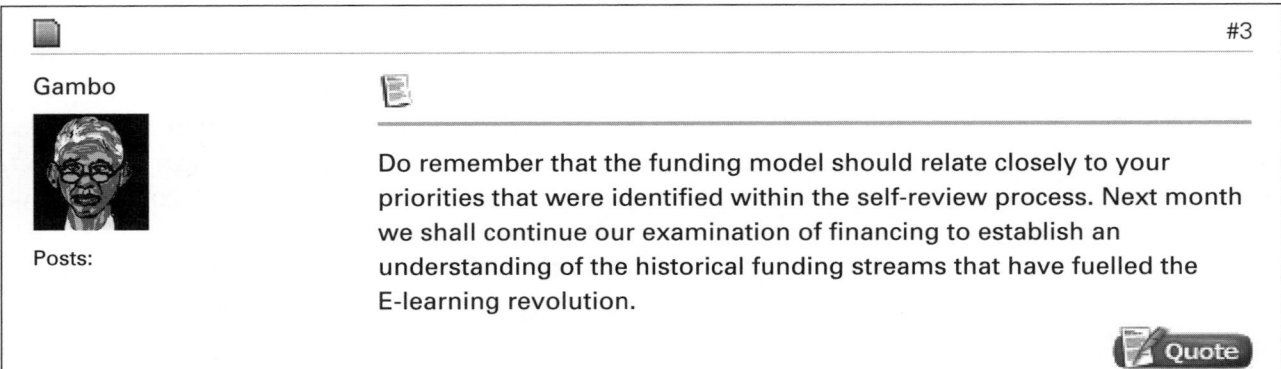

Gambo

Posts:

Do remember that the funding model should relate closely to your priorities that were identified within the self-review process. Next month we shall continue our examination of financing to establish an understanding of the historical funding streams that have fuelled the E-learning revolution.

Chapter 4 • *December*

3rd December

Colleagues who followed the first programme within Book 1 will know that I aim to lighten the workload at this time of year and am aware that the seasonal demands are probably more intense upon senior managers than other staff. This is a time to draw together the work from the term and in particular to conclude our major overview of E-safety. I also want to encourage you to consider some of the ICT related security issues that face the twenty-first-century primary school before concluding the term by recommending some reading for the holiday aimed at developing understanding of ICT financing.

Week 13, Task 10 – E-safety – Home–School Links

So far in our discussion of E-safety we have looked at raising staff awareness of the core issues, developing policy and providing an effective and appropriate education programme. In this chapter I aim to reflect upon how schools can mobilize the support of parents in order to provide a united and integrated approach to E-safety that will protect children both in school and at home when they are most vulnerable. The task is to consider your school's approach to working with parents with regard to E-safety and to plan the outline of a parents' evening or event, part of which will focus upon providing information about Internet safety.

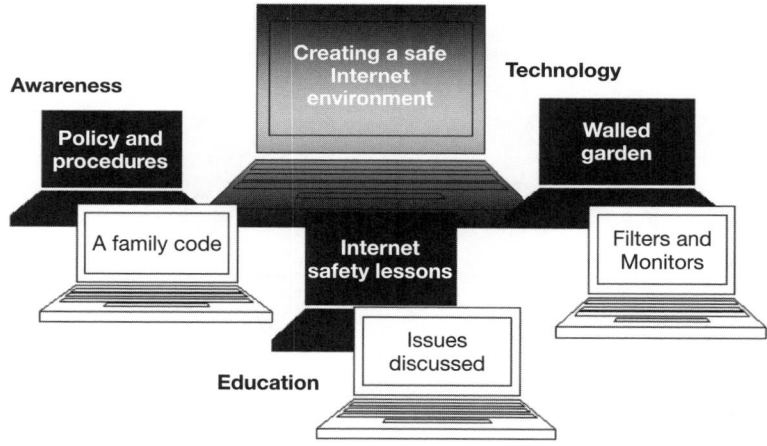

Figure 4.1 Home support for E-safety measures
Available on the net at http://www.james-wright.org

Figure 4.1 demonstrates how home support for E-safety measures should closely mirror school measures in terms of our original triad of raising awareness of the issues involved, employing appropriate technology with which to support pupils and providing the right information about how to use the Internet safely. Therefore our objectives when working with parents are not only to inform them in a reassuring manner of the systems and processes in place within school, but also to contribute meaningful advice and support as to what parents could and should do to ensure that their home Internet experience is a good one.

Parents may be encouraged to establish a family code for home Internet use and to talk with their children openly about the potential dangers. Schools may also wish to broker software deals for filter programs or simply to advise parents of measures that are available for home use filter systems.

Innovative E-confident schools will produce an Internet family code and send it home as advisory information, encouraging parents to go through this with their children, ensure that it will be written down and that everyone in the house will agree to stick to it. Internet-connected computers should be placed in shared areas of the house with the screen facing inward so that parents can see what is going on. Simple rules such as all personal information being kept secret should be agreed and children should know not to disclose any indication of their age or gender within a personal email address.

Much of this information can be shared with parents during an Internet safety evening and I should challenge colleagues to host such an event, invite a local authority representative to attend and to provide an input potentially as part of a wider ICT evening. As well as reassuring parents of the processes going on in school it would be an opportunity to provide specific advice with regard to the use of filters, child-friendly search engines and the setting up of security measures within their home systems that will support parents in monitoring their children's Internet usage.

5th December

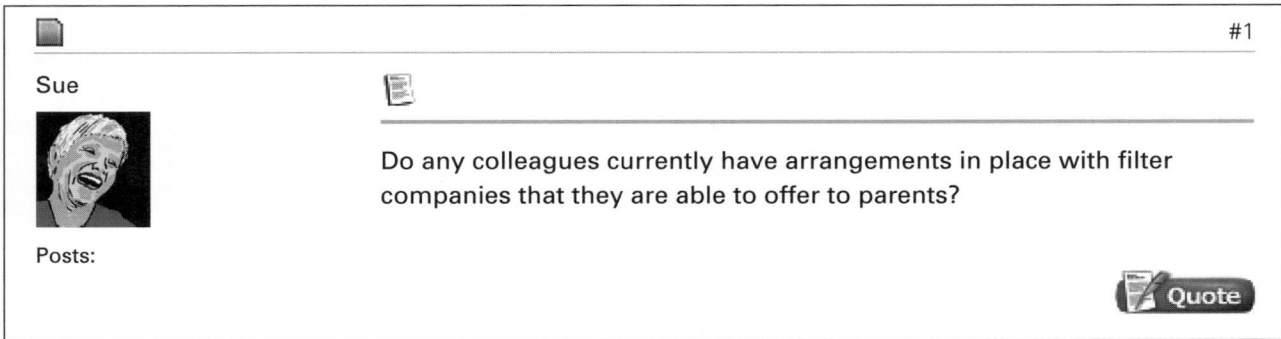

Sue

Posts:

#1

Do any colleagues currently have arrangements in place with filter companies that they are able to offer to parents?

Quote

7th December

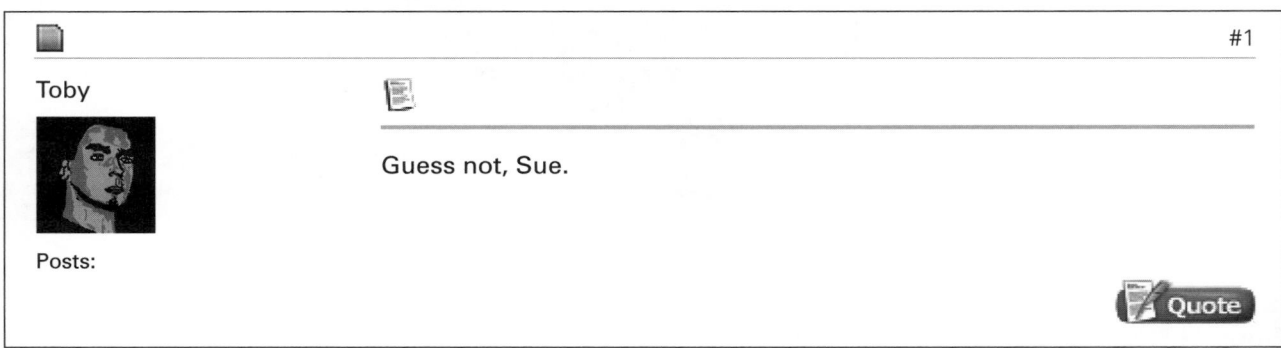

Toby

Posts:

#1

Guess not, Sue.

Quote

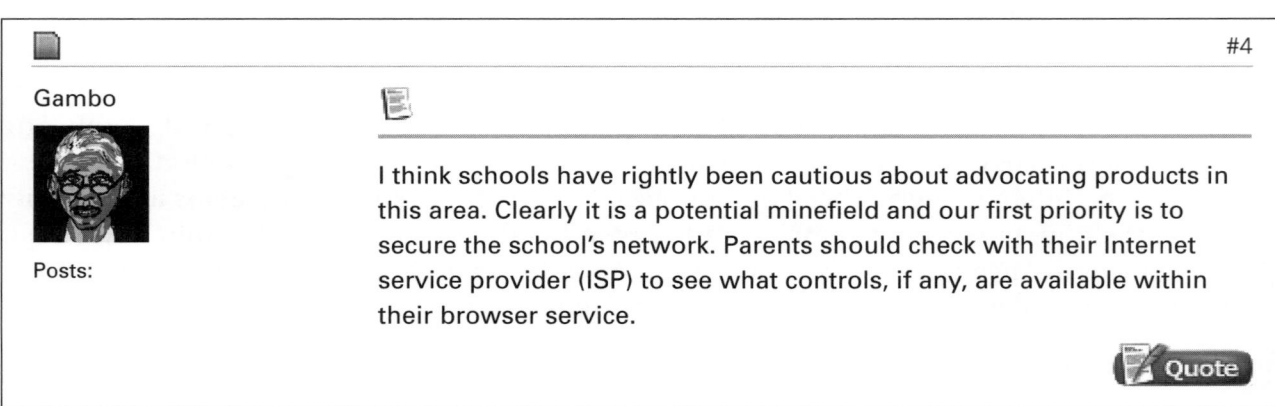

Gambo

Posts:

#4

I think schools have rightly been cautious about advocating products in this area. Clearly it is a potential minefield and our first priority is to secure the school's network. Parents should check with their Internet service provider (ISP) to see what controls, if any, are available within their browser service.

Quote

8th December

Colleagues may wish to direct parents to a variety of home filter software products which should be assessed both in terms of their task efficiency and, in particular, their ease of use. Any home filter that in effect also disables legitimate adult use of the Internet is not going to be a welcome addition to the home network. A range of market-leading products might include:

- CYBERsitter (www.cybersitter.com)
- NetNanny (www.netnanny.com)
- Cyber Patrol (www.cyberpatrol.com)
- FilterPak (www.familyconnect.com)
- Cyber Sentinel (www.cybersentinel.com)
- McAfee Parental Controls (www.McAfee.co.uk)
- Norton Parental Controls (www.symantec.com)
- Child Safe (www.webroot.com).

Parents should at least be advised how to set up Internet Explorer's content advisor facility as a basic level of filter security.

Figure 4.2 Internet Explorer content adviser 1
Available on the net at http://www.james-wright.org

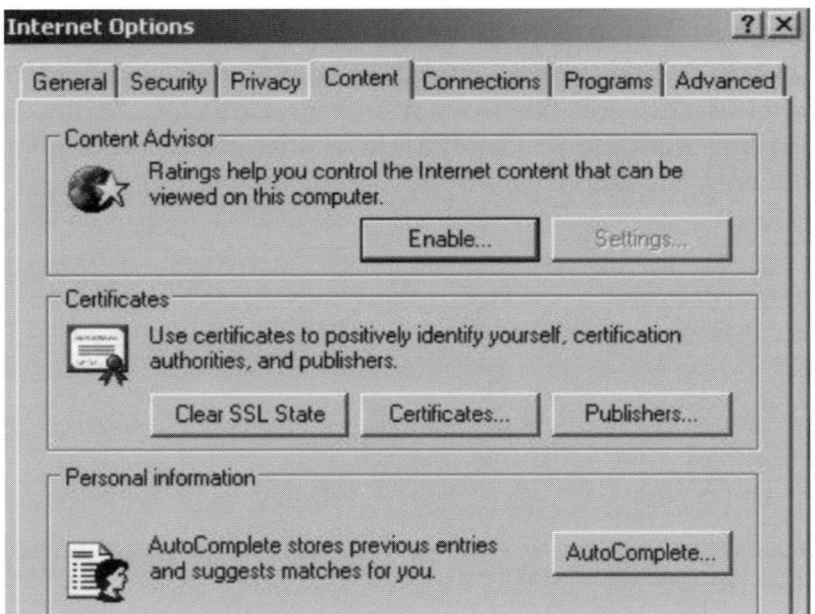

Figure 4.3 Internet Explorer content adviser 2

Available on the net at http://www.james-wright.org

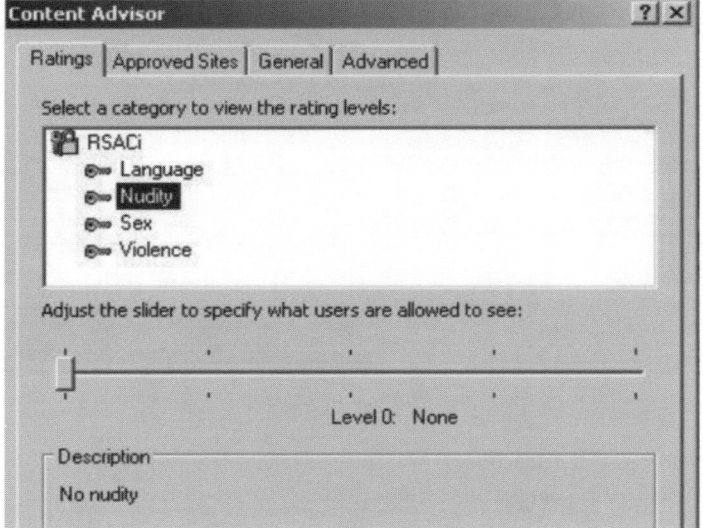

Figure 4.4 Internet Explorer content adviser 3

Available on the net at http://www.james-wright.org

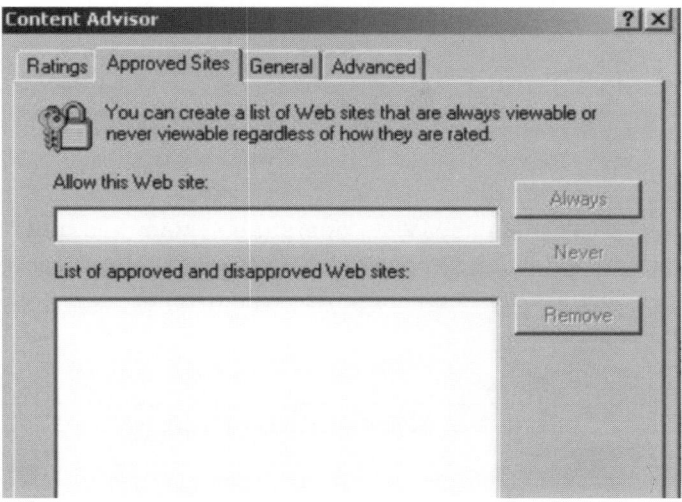

Figure 4.5 Internet Explorer content adviser 4
Available on the net at http://www.james-wright.org

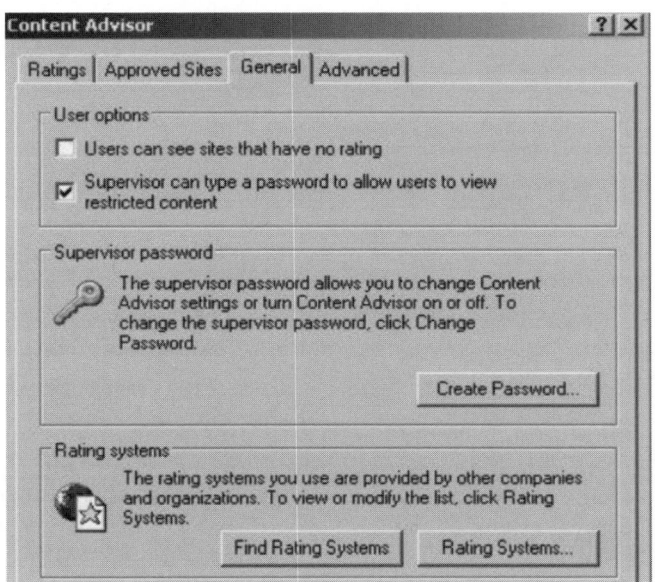

Figure 4.6 Internet Explorer content adviser 5
Available on the net at http://www.james-wright.org

Figures 4.2 to 4.6 provide a step-by-step demonstration of how parents may preset security levels using MS Internet Explorer upon a home computer for language, nudity, sex and violence. Likewise specific sites may be approved or disapproved and a superviser password may be set. This sort of advice should be incorporated within the school information event, together with opportunities for the E-learning co-ordinator to share school policy and procedures.

Primary-age children should be encouraged to use child-friendly search engines both at school and at home. Examples such as Yahooligans (www.yahooligans.yahoo.com) or Ask Jeeves for Kids (www.ajkids.com) provide an additional level of safety when children are online. Users of a shared family PC who prefer to use Google as their search engine may easily apply 'Safesearch Filtering' from the Google preferences page (www.google.co.uk/intl/en/help/customize) and either moderate or strict settings for text and image searches or for individual search items using the 'Advanced Search' option. Do be aware that if you regularly clear your computer cache of cookies and so on that your preference will be restored to its original setting each time that you return to the Google homepage.

9th December

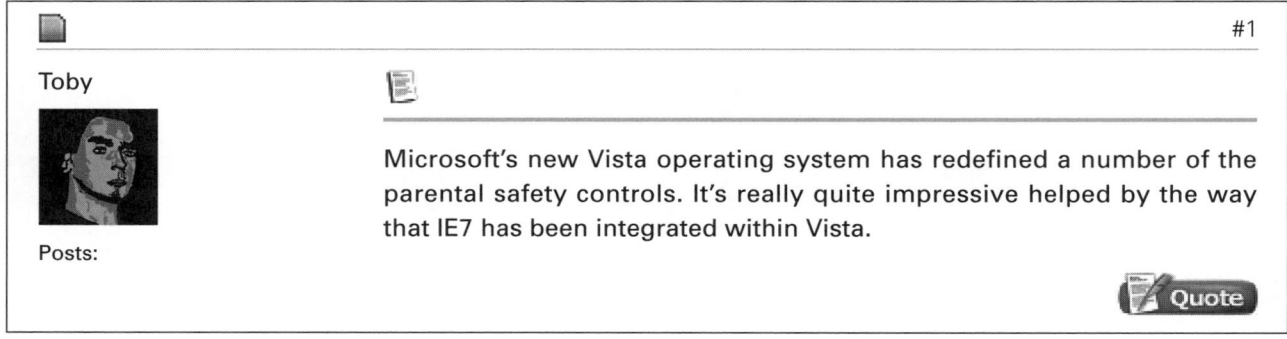

Toby

Posts:

> Microsoft's new Vista operating system has redefined a number of the parental safety controls. It's really quite impressive helped by the way that IE7 has been integrated within Vista.
>
> #1
>
> Quote

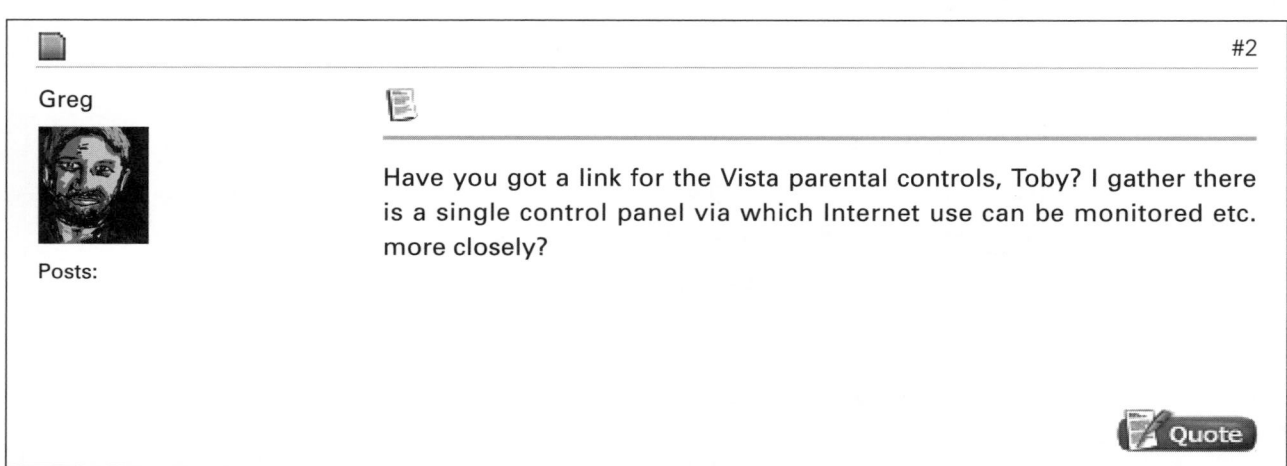

Greg

Posts:

> Have you got a link for the Vista parental controls, Toby? I gather there is a single control panel via which Internet use can be monitored etc. more closely?
>
> #2
>
> Quote

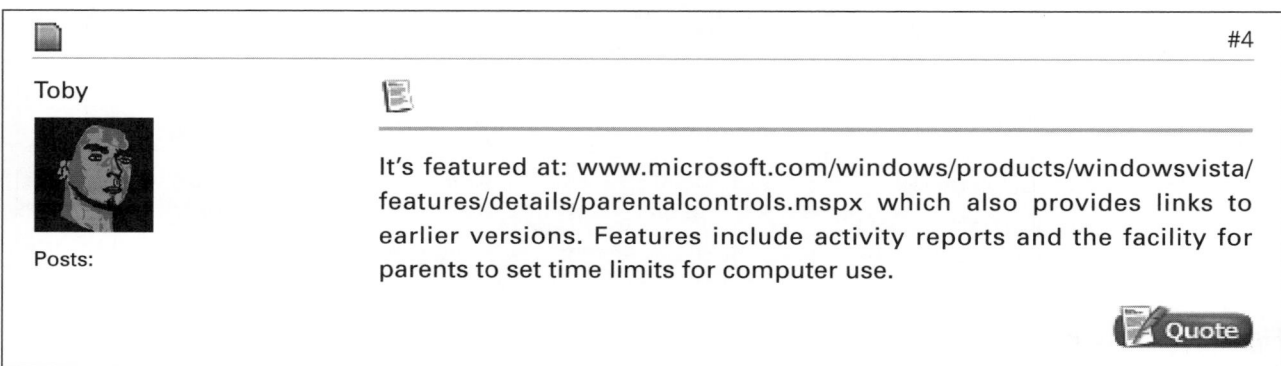

Toby

Posts:

> It's featured at: www.microsoft.com/windows/products/windowsvista/features/details/parentalcontrols.mspx which also provides links to earlier versions. Features include activity reports and the facility for parents to set time limits for computer use.
>
> #4
>
> Quote

10th December

Most frequently parents require strategies and advice for monitoring their children's use of the Internet. For example, all web browsers will have a history folder where website tracks may be viewed. Parents will have views about monitoring pupils' Internet habits and it is quite simple for pupils to cover their tracks; however, it is worth raising with parents that if the history cache is being emptied regularly by a child then a conversation may be needed as to what is being covered or hidden. Inevitably this raises issues of privacy and, ultimately, individual parents will have to decide where their comfort zone lies in this regard. Usually parents' concerns are most vivid when discussion moves towards chat rooms, online messenger services and virtual worlds such as Secondlife (www.secondlife.com) and Habbo Hotel (www.habbo.co.uk) among others where parents have expressed real concerns about their own lack of understanding of the underlying philosophy and technology. Colleagues should allow opportunities for such concerns to be aired and remind parents that public chat rooms are banned within school networks and should not be used at home by primary-aged children. Virtual worlds such as those mentioned are first and foremost commercial enterprises and parents should familiarize themselves and their children with the business model before they approve participation. Secondlife has a strict registration policy of persons aged 13 and over only being permitted to register, however, Habbo Hotel is marketed at children aged 11 and over, with players under 11 permitted to register with parental consent. Given that this is a place where teens 'hang out', I should encourage any parent whose child is desperate to join in to consider chaperoning them initially to form their own opinion of whether or not they are comfortable with these activities. Do point out that these virtual worlds, whilst moderated, will by definition replicate the social values and norms of the society and subculture that they serve.

Parents should be encouraged to take a very serious interest in their children's use of instant messenger services such as Windows MSN and Yahoo Messenger. Whilst such technology is very much part of young people's lives today, parents are rightly concerned that they do not really know what is happening when their son or daughter logs on to the service. How can they be sure what subjects they are discussing and with whom? Are they being exposed to obscenities and ideas that they would not allow in a conventional meeting with friends? Just how secure are the 'buddy' systems employed, especially when many children can 'collect' buddies as past generations used to collect football cards. Invariably parents do not know to whom their child is actually chatting and are often shocked at the level of conversation prevalent within such systems.

As part of an Internet safety meeting, colleagues may wish to encourage parents to discuss these issues with their children, exploring their use of instant messaging and asking who these contacts are and how they met. Children need to know what to do should they find themselves a victim of online bullying or cyber stalking.

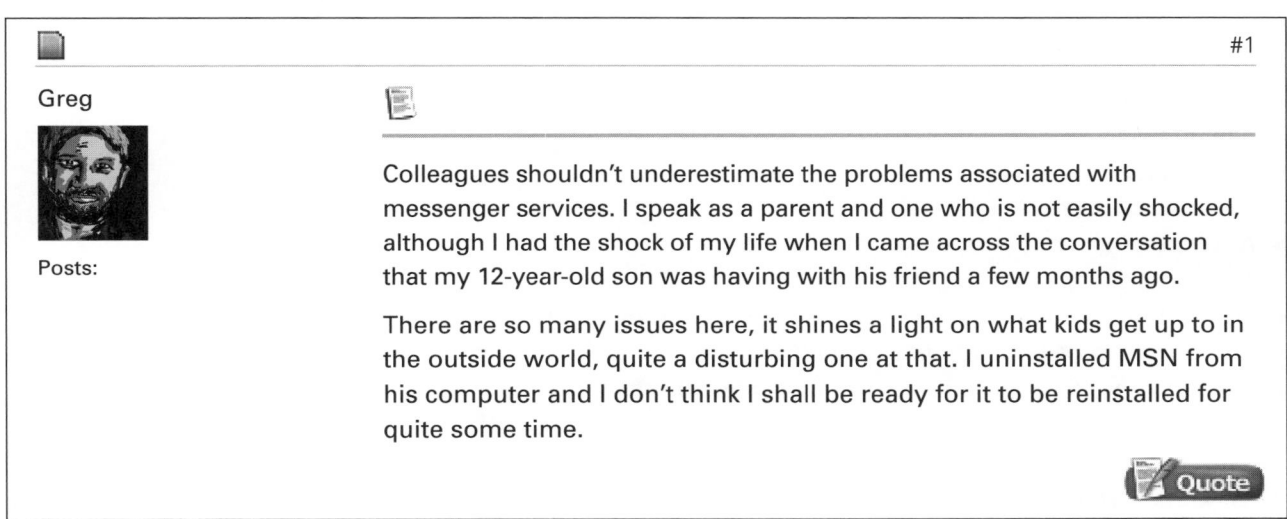

> #1
>
> **Greg**
>
> Posts:
>
> Colleagues shouldn't underestimate the problems associated with messenger services. I speak as a parent and one who is not easily shocked, although I had the shock of my life when I came across the conversation that my 12-year-old son was having with his friend a few months ago.
>
> There are so many issues here, it shines a light on what kids get up to in the outside world, quite a disturbing one at that. I uninstalled MSN from his computer and I don't think I shall be ready for it to be reinstalled for quite some time.
>
> Quote

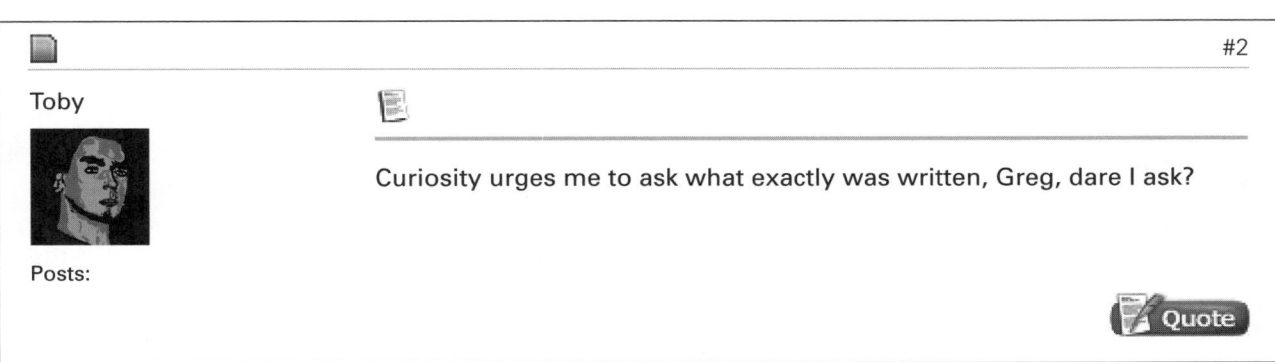

> #2
>
> **Toby**
>
> Posts:
>
> Curiosity urges me to ask what exactly was written, Greg, dare I ask?
>
> Quote

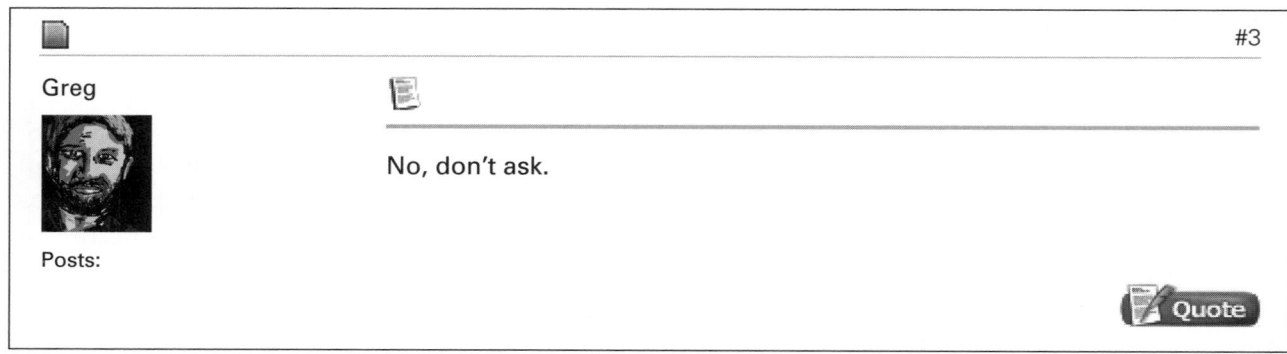

Bill Belsey (2004), founder of the Canadian cyberbullying website (www.cyberbullying.ca), defined this new phenomena as:

> 'Cyberbullying involves the use of information and communication technologies such as e-mail, cell phone and pager text messages, instant messaging, defamatory personal Web sites, and defamatory online personal polling Web sites, to support deliberate, repeated, and hostile behaviour by an individual or group, that is intended to harm others.'

His work has influenced many international organizations, including BECTA's approach to E-safety within the UK, and is largely behind the following code of conduct that might be agreed with parents that will inform them of what to do should their child experience online bullying.

How to Minimize Online Bullying
- *Keep personal information private*
- *Don't believe everything you read*
- *Use netiquette*
- *Never send messages when angry*
- *Never open a message from someone you don't know*
- *If it doesn't look or feel right, it probably isn't*
- *You don't have to be 'always on' – turn off, disconnect, unplug*
- *Don't reply to messages from cyberbullies*
- *Never arrange to meet someone you have met online*
- *Don't keep bullying to yourself.* (Belsey, 2004. Reproduced with permission)

11th December

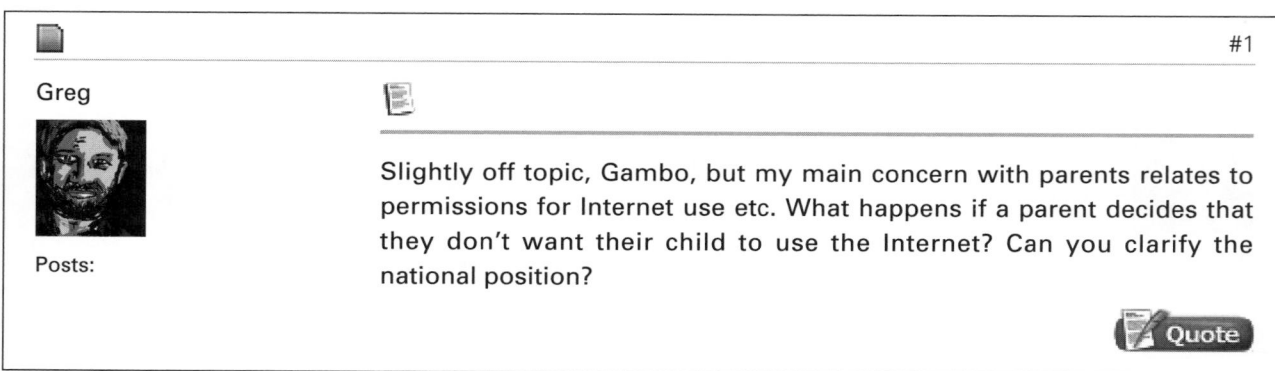

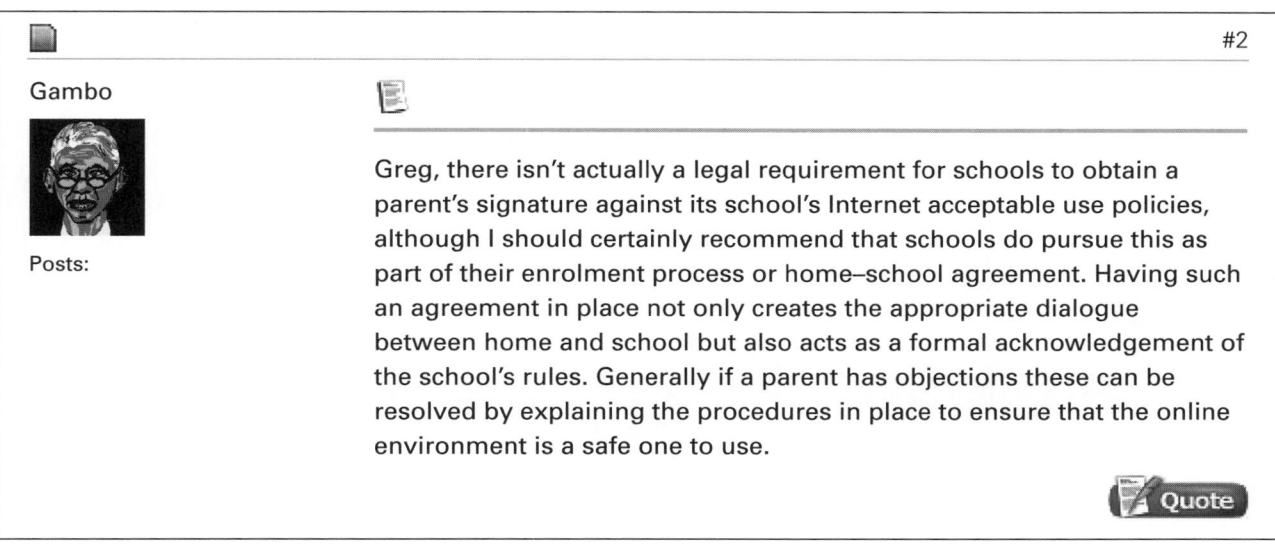

#2

Gambo

Posts:

Greg, there isn't actually a legal requirement for schools to obtain a parent's signature against its school's Internet acceptable use policies, although I should certainly recommend that schools do pursue this as part of their enrolment process or home–school agreement. Having such an agreement in place not only creates the appropriate dialogue between home and school but also acts as a formal acknowledgement of the school's rules. Generally if a parent has objections these can be resolved by explaining the procedures in place to ensure that the online environment is a safe one to use.

Quote

#3

Sue

Posts:

May I add to this. I had a parent who categorically refused to sign the standard consent form and was not remotely interested in listening to the school's procedures for ensuring a safe environment. It produced a very difficult situation for some time.

Quote

#4

Gambo

Posts:

I think this is quite common actually, Sue, and is part of the fabric of running a school. If a parent has specifically refused consent then separate provision should be made for the child and their teachers and support staff will need to be made aware of this. Usually if the matter is pursued and parents table specific objections that can be addressed that is the best way to resolve the problem. Also, if this can be introduced as part of each pupil's registration and induction in Reception that gives plenty of time for any issues to be resolved before the child is likely to go online. Not such a major issue these days now that the Internet is virtually omnipresent.

Quote

12th December

As part of the discussion that you host with parents you may wish to provide specific advice relating to recording conversations that children may have in Windows Messenger. With older primary children, Years 5 and 6, this will be a major concern for parents and demonstrating the capability to set history trails that will record their child's conversations is one way of giving back some semblance of control over the situation.

Figures 4.7, 4.8 and 4.9 demonstrate how Messenger may be configured to record each conversation strand into a designated folder where these may be viewed as necessary should a parent choose to do so. It is probably worth re-stating here that this is *not* something advocated as a school policy. Apart from the obvious issues regarding pupil privacy, Messenger services should not be accessible from a school network. This is a strategy that could be recommended for parental use.

An exemplar presentation for the parents event including step-by-step demonstration of the setting up of conversation trails is available for download from the author's website (www.James-Wright.org).

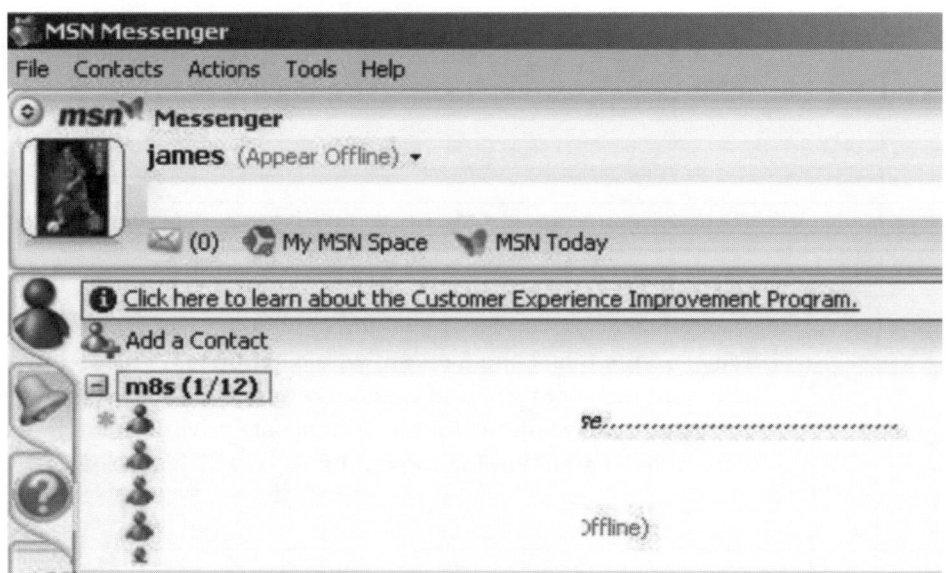

Figure 4.7 Messenger save history 7
Available on the net at http://www.james-wright.org

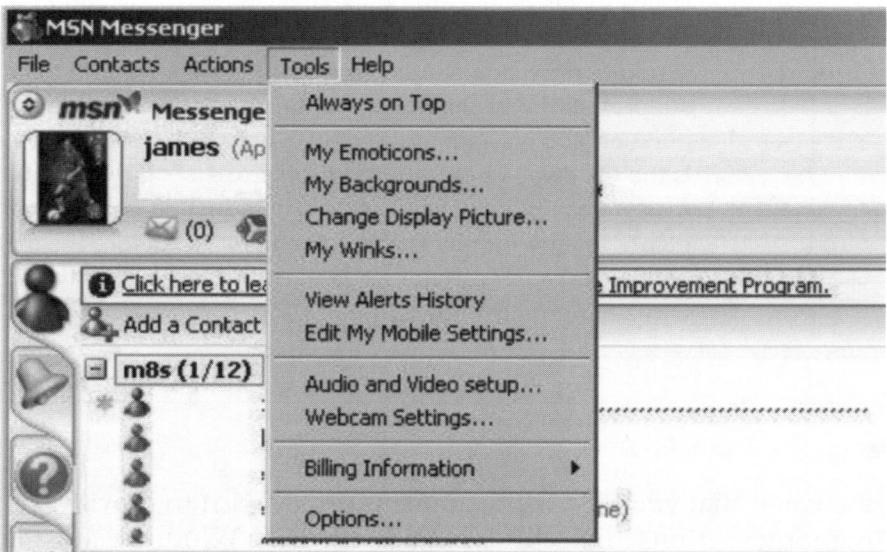

Figure 4.8 Messenger save history 8
Available on the net at http://www.james-wright.org

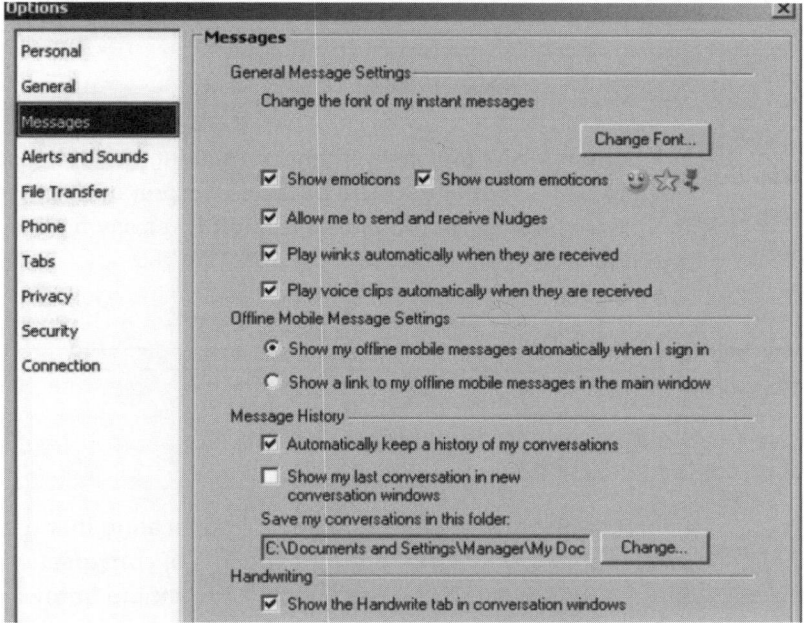

Figure 4.9 Messenger save history 9
Available on the net at http://www.james-wright.org

13th December

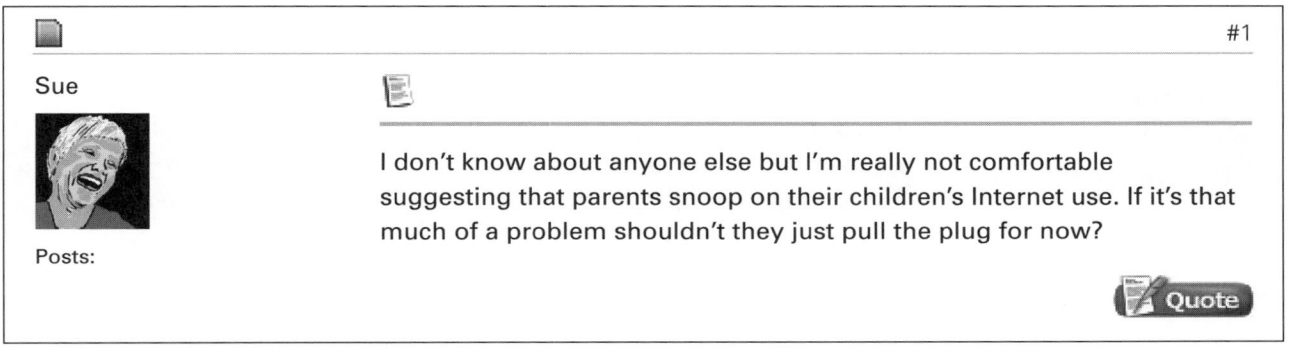

#1

Sue

Posts:

I don't know about anyone else but I'm really not comfortable suggesting that parents snoop on their children's Internet use. If it's that much of a problem shouldn't they just pull the plug for now?

Quote

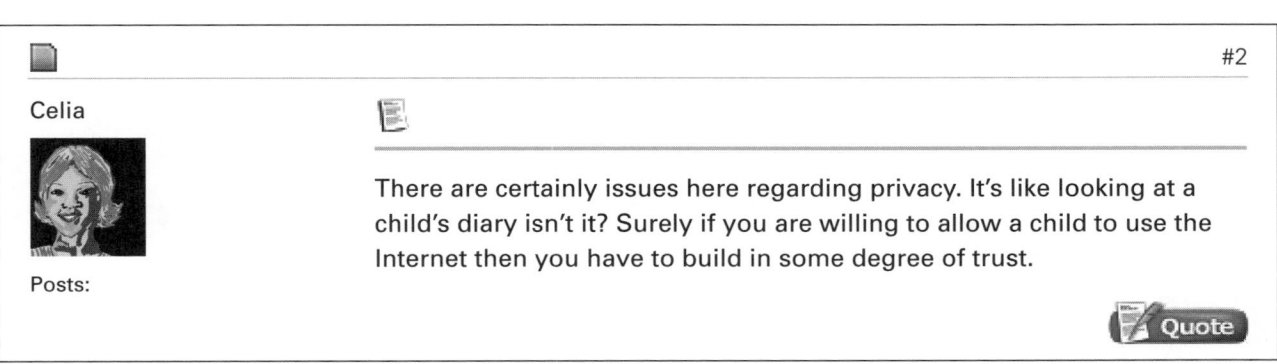

#2

Celia

Posts:

There are certainly issues here regarding privacy. It's like looking at a child's diary isn't it? Surely if you are willing to allow a child to use the Internet then you have to build in some degree of trust.

Quote

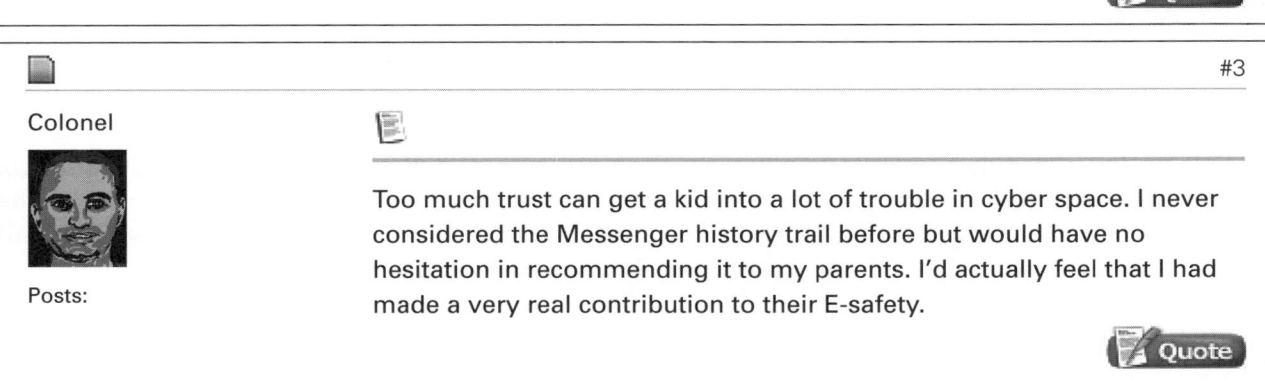

#3

Colonel

Posts:

Too much trust can get a kid into a lot of trouble in cyber space. I never considered the Messenger history trail before but would have no hesitation in recommending it to my parents. I'd actually feel that I had made a very real contribution to their E-safety.

Quote

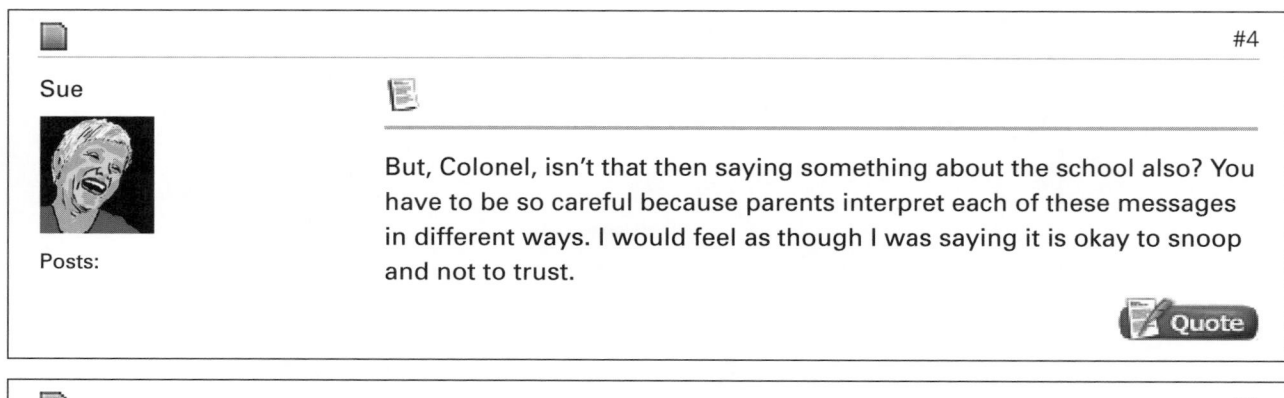

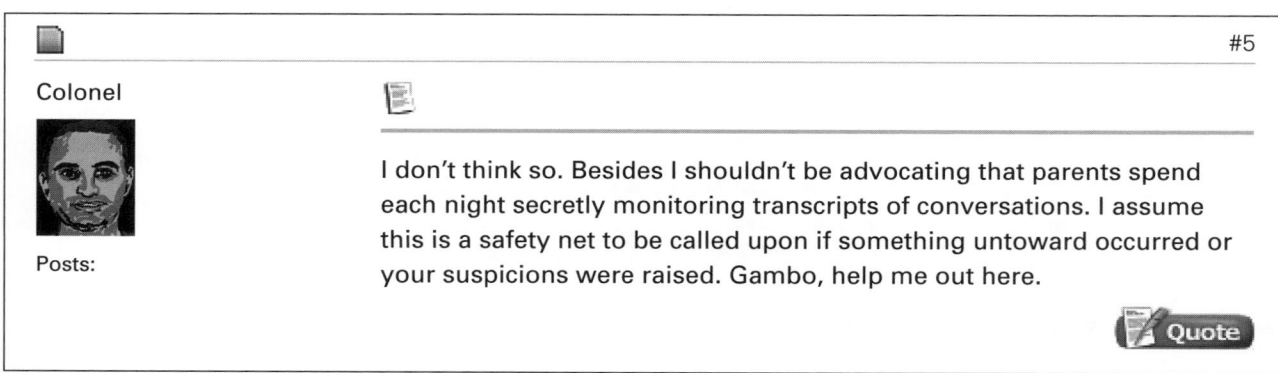

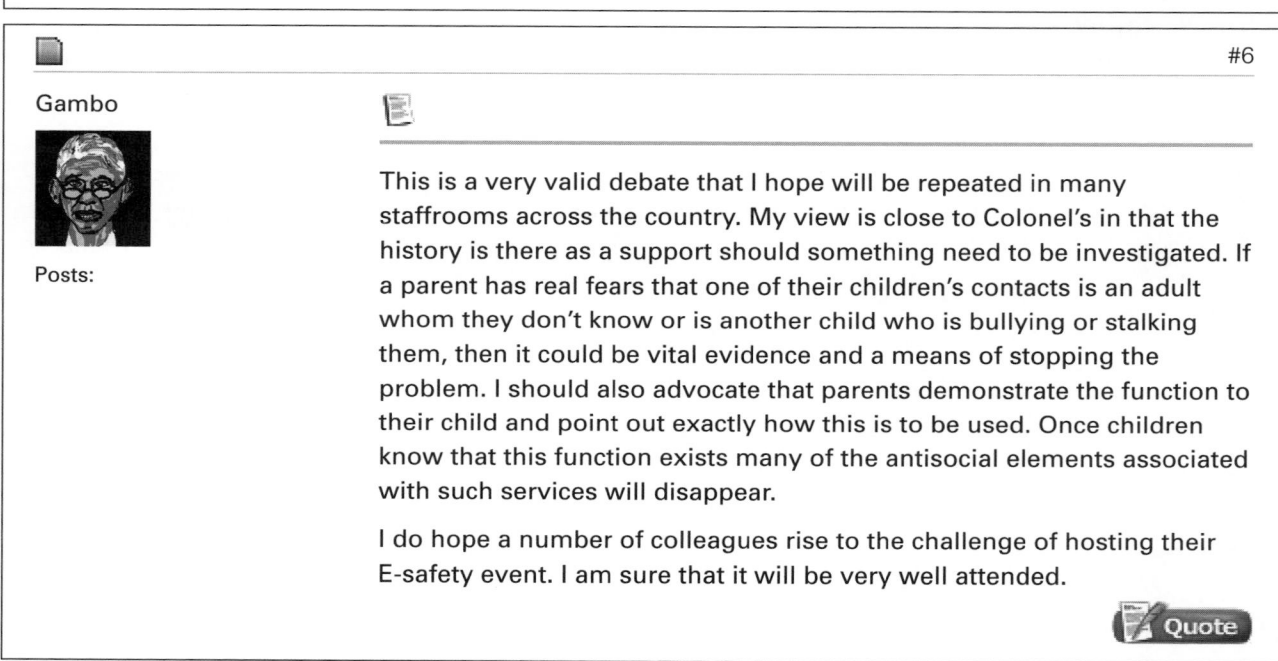

15th December

Week 14, Task 11 – Securing ICT Equipment

The penultimate task that I shall set this year is for colleagues to consider current strategies for securing ICT equipment and preventing debilitating break-ins. Theft of ICT equipment from UK schools drains huge amounts of revenue from the national ICT budget each year as well as forcing schools to spend weeks awaiting replacement equipment. The demoralizing inconvenience to the school and the disruption to the education of pupils, with the loss of records and schoolwork, and the possible negative impact such an incident would have on a school's good name cannot be underestimated. In 2004–05, the value of ICT equipment stolen from one English authority, North Yorkshire, was £33,582; a year later, it had risen to £187,265 (BBC News, 24 July 2006 : http://news.bbc.co.uk/2/hi/uk_news/england/west_yorkshire/5210888.stm).

Any E-learning co-ordinator needs to have in place proactive security measures that will prevent both future break-ins and walk-through thefts without developing a fortress mentality within a school.

If break-ins have been a factor in school life previously, then the school will undoubtedly already have in place a system of deterrents to prevent unauthorized access to buildings, such as perimeter fencing, closed-circuit television (CCTV), alarms and individual self-closure devices, suitable access control locks for ICT suites and classrooms and cages for data protectors. Colleagues need to balance security devices carefully in terms of their aesthetic and psychological impact upon the school environment.

This week I would encourage colleagues to review the variety of 'smart' ways by which equipment may be protected and, in particular, to consider the unspoken messages that the school sends out regarding its ICT assets.

Table 4.1 Comparative ICT security strategies

Equipment	Security measure or procedure	Consequence if stolen	Disadvantages
All	All equipment marked using a security marking code centrally registered	New owner would have to supply this code when purchasing replacement parts	Cost and logistics of setting up system
All	Physically marking your projector equipment with special pens or stickers	Difficult to resell goods	Can affect warranty
All	Sonic alarms can be fixed to equipment	When equipment is removed the alarm sounds	Cost
All	Fixed installations with locking boxes, ceiling mounts, etc.	Increases the physical difficult to remove	Additional damage
All	Pupil voice – educating the pupils as to the measures in place will reduce incidence of break-in	Reduced temptation, heightened risk	
All	Painted on anti-theft systems, a permanent, invisible label which assigns a unique DNA-style code to each school's equipment	May also be activated to spray thieves when they attempt to make off with goods	Cost Not a deterrent
All projectors	Customized splash screens during power-up, screen displays the school's name and logo	Alerts buyer as to who the real owner of the projector is	Set-up time Not a deterrent
Data projectors	Pre-programmed PIN code in data projectors	Code required at switch on rendering the projector useless	Cost and logistics of setting up system
Laptops	Secure overnight in locked storage cabinet	Increases the physical difficulty to remove	Daily set-up required causing inconvenience
Computers	Tracking software identifies the location of stolen equipment	Connection to the Internet sends a stealth email without alerting the current user	Cost and logistics of setting up system
Computers	Biometric finger print security replaces the user name and password	Stolen computers cannot be used without authentication	Cost and logistics of setting up system Logistics of managing the system
All	Visible personalization using stencils etc.	Difficult for thieves to sell on	

Available on the net at http://www.james-wright.org

Table 4.1 reviews a range of options colleagues may wish to pursue when protecting their ICT assets. Look again at the hardware audit that was produced during Chapter 2 of Book 1 as the basis of an audit and detail all equipment including serial numbers that will need to be available in the event of a theft.

15th December

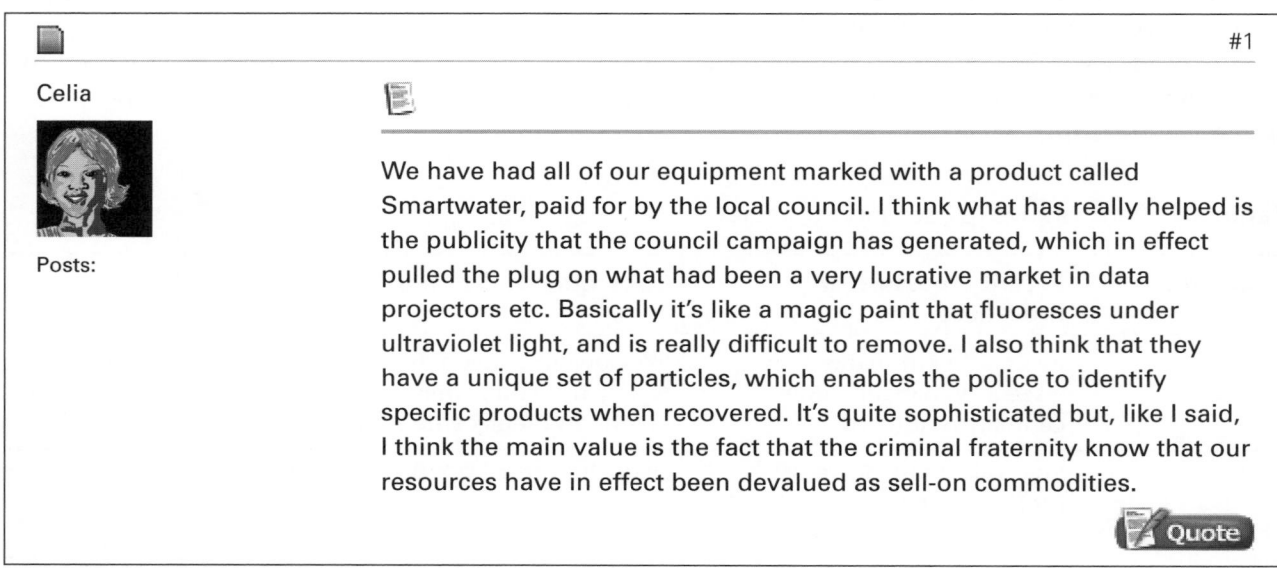

#1

Celia

Posts:

We have had all of our equipment marked with a product called Smartwater, paid for by the local council. I think what has really helped is the publicity that the council campaign has generated, which in effect pulled the plug on what had been a very lucrative market in data projectors etc. Basically it's like a magic paint that fluoresces under ultraviolet light, and is really difficult to remove. I also think that they have a unique set of particles, which enables the police to identify specific products when recovered. It's quite sophisticated but, like I said, I think the main value is the fact that the criminal fraternity know that our resources have in effect been devalued as sell-on commodities.

Quote

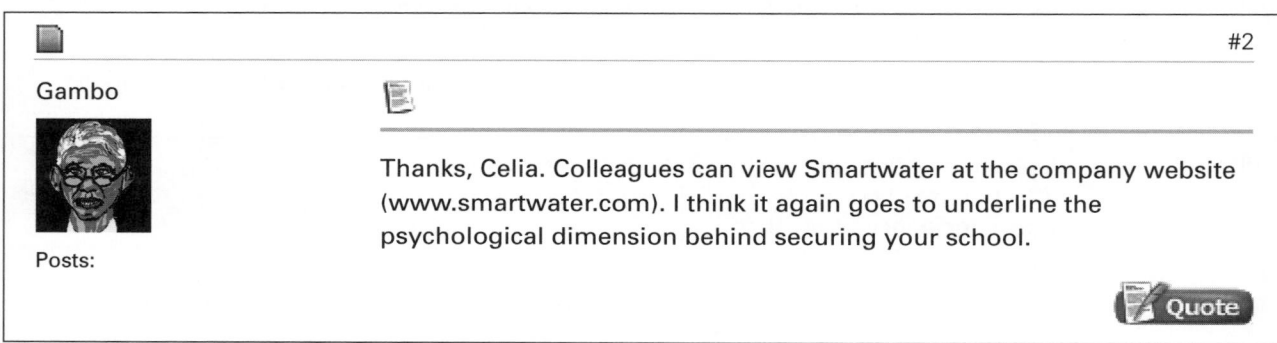

#2

Gambo

Posts:

Thanks, Celia. Colleagues can view Smartwater at the company website (www.smartwater.com). I think it again goes to underline the psychological dimension behind securing your school.

Quote

16th December

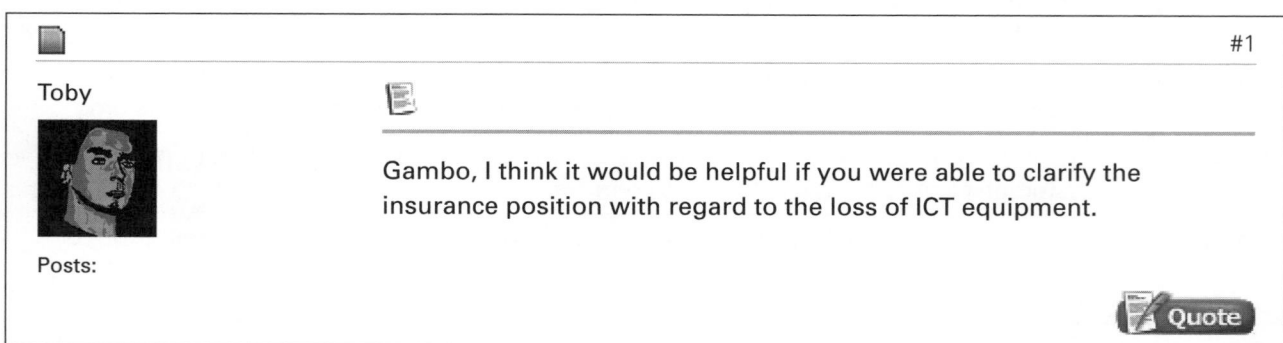

#1

Toby

Posts:

Gambo, I think it would be helpful if you were able to clarify the insurance position with regard to the loss of ICT equipment.

Quote

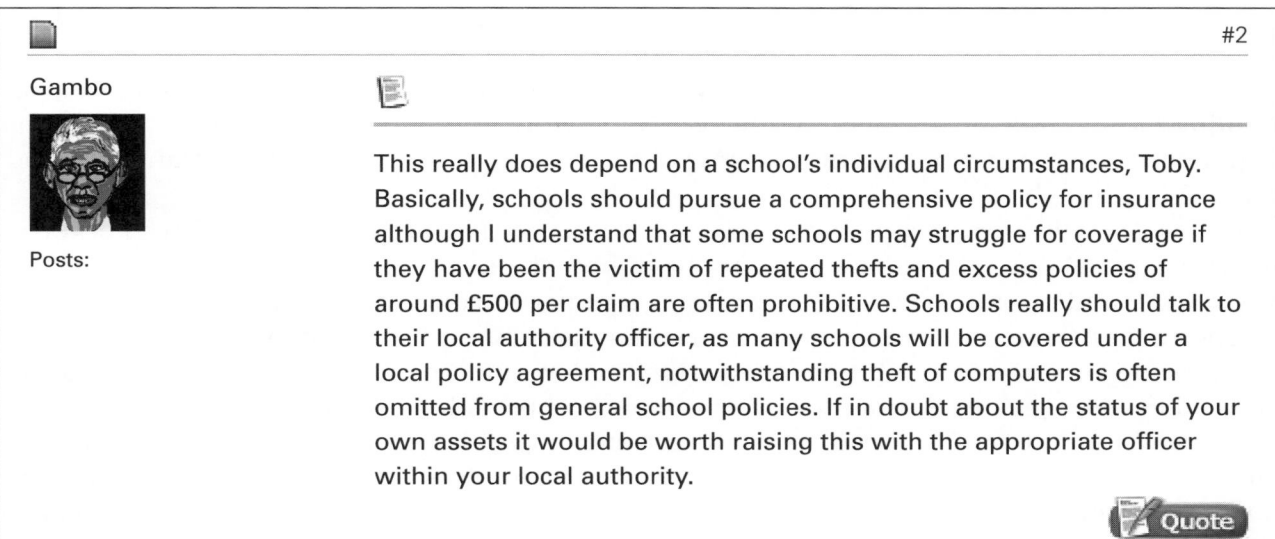

Gambo

Posts:

This really does depend on a school's individual circumstances, Toby. Basically, schools should pursue a comprehensive policy for insurance although I understand that some schools may struggle for coverage if they have been the victim of repeated thefts and excess policies of around £500 per claim are often prohibitive. Schools really should talk to their local authority officer, as many schools will be covered under a local policy agreement, notwithstanding theft of computers is often omitted from general school policies. If in doubt about the status of your own assets it would be worth raising this with the appropriate officer within your local authority.

Quote

20th December

I think whichever strategy you decide to implement security is going to be a major consideration for E-learning co-ordinators for many years to come and, whilst we are looking at future funding models and the total cost of ownership of ICT equipment, it is worth highlighting the various security solutions that companies can offer as key factors in product selection.

My apologies for the amount of material that you have had to cover again this term; however, I do believe that if you implement each of the activities then your school will be greatly empowered upon its journey towards becoming more E-confident.

To finish the term I'd like to take a second look at the financial model that underpins your long-term plans and strategy.

Week 15, Task 12 – Understanding ICT Funding Streams

Let us return to the subject of expenditure and more pertinently funding. It is very important that as the senior manager responsible for the strategic development of E-learning you are fully cognizant with the origins of this funding.

As mentioned in the previous chapter, the UK has enjoyed enormous national investment into its schools, ICT infrastructure as the digital E-strategy has evolved. All schools have had the opportunity to use traditionally ring-fenced funds to establish complex networks delivering state-of-the-art learning opportunities.

It has at times proved quite an art establishing exact amounts of funding allocated to individual schools, even when the majority of these monies came from ring-fenced standards funds. The removal of that protection from April 2006 onwards has made it increasingly difficult to quantify revenue sources, as schools have enjoyed ever greater flexibility in deciding amounts to invest in ICT. To give an example of the scale of funding enjoyed by schools, particularly with reference to the figures in the previous chapter (Table 3.3) which some colleagues felt were excessive: a large primary school such as Colonel's with up to 700 pupils, would have received around £45,000 for infrastructure in 2005–06 including around £7,000 from the Laptops for Teachers initiative and £10,000 of E-learning credits. In theory, a proportional amount of funding remains carried forward year on year, albeit now divided between the devolved formula capital grant (DFC) and the schools development grant (SDG). The E-learning credits remained ring-fenced, although significantly reduced and tailing off within Grant 122: ICT in Schools: E-learning Credits. Colleagues should also note that Laptops for Teachers funding ended in 2006 and, so, that proportion of the budget will have disappeared. Many schools reported a significant chill following the redirection of funds and removal of the ring fence. Traditionally, DFC funding is allocated in advance to offset numerous demands for buildings expenditure, and many local authorities report a significant fall in spending based upon buy-backs and so on.

Hopefully, the TCO exercise will have provided schools with a valid measure of your network funding means. Your final activity of the year is therefore to examine the manner in which this requirement will be met by regaining a sense of the funding streams, particularly standards funding within your school.

Table 4.2 is a very crude approximation of the streams of ICT funding that have been devolved to schools providing my own approximations of how these have been devolved for a variety of school sizes and so on. There will be significant regional variations with regard to local authority passporting of funds and arrangements for central purchase and so on, however, hopefully, this will provide a broad-brush estimate upon which to base funding models. The figures produced after 2006 when greater flexibility and autonomy was provided to schools with regard to how they spend funding means that there is no separately identifiable allocation for ICT within DFC and SDG. The figures produced are based upon a standard 60–40 per cent DFC–SDG split of the 2005–06 amounts minus the laptops for the teachers' stream that ended in 2006. This evident slippage in funding can be offset by a general increase in devolved capital particularly with regard to capital investments announced in 2006 up until 2010–11.

Your final task of the year, therefore, is to ensure that you understand the stream of revenues for ICT into your school and how they match to your network needs described in the previous chapter, concluding with how best you can ensure that the network is adequately funded and gains its fair share of budget now that it is no longer ring-fenced.

Table 4.2 Budget review 2003–08

Grant/initiative	NOR	2003/04	2004/05	2005/06	2006/07	2007/08
ICT Infrastructure Grants SF601 and SF31A	100	£6,500	£7,300	* #	£8,300	* #
	200	£8,700	£9,700	* #	£11,100	* #
	300	£10,300	£11,400	* #	£13,100	* #
	400	£11,800	£13,000	* #	£15,100	* #
	500	£14,300	£15,800	* #	£18,300	* #
Laptops for Teachers Grant 616	100	£800 1 provided*	£1,800 in SF31A*	£2,000 in SF31A		
	200	£800 1 provided*	£2,300 in SF31A*	£2,700 in SF31A		
	300	£1,600 2 provided*	£2,800 in SF31A*	£3,200 in SF31A		
	400	£2,400 3 provided*	£3,200 in SF31A*	£3,700 in SF31A		
	500	£3,200 4 provided*	£3,900 in SF31A*	£4,500 in SF31A		
Interactive Whiteboard Initiative Grant 37	100		£900			
	200		£900			
	300		£900			
	400		£900			
	500		£900			

Devolved Formula Capital Grant 201	100			Optional	£3,800	£3,800
	200			Optional	£5,000	£5,000
	300			Optional	£5,900	£5,900
	400			Optional	£6,800	£6,800
	500			Optional	£8,300	£8,300
Schools Development Grant Grant 101	100				£2,500	£2,500
	200				£3,400	£3,400
	300				£4,000	£4,000
	400				£4,600	£4,600
	500				£5,500	£5,500
E-learning Credits	100	£2,100	£2,100	£2,100	£1,600	£1,000
	200	£3,000	£3,000	£3,000	£2,300	£1,500
	300	£4,100	£4,100	£4,100	£3,100	£2,100
	400	£5,100	£5,100	£5,100	£3,800	£2,600
	500	£6,300	£6,300	£6,300	£4,700	£3,200
Total	100	£9,400	£10,300	£10,400	£7,900	£7,300
	200	£12,500	£13,600	£14,100	£10,700	£9,900
	300	£16,000	£16,400	£17,200	£13,000	£12,000
	400	£19,300	£19,000	£20,200	£15,200	£14,000
	500	£23,800	£23,000	£24,600	£18,500	£17,000

Available on the net at http://www.james-wright.org

21st December

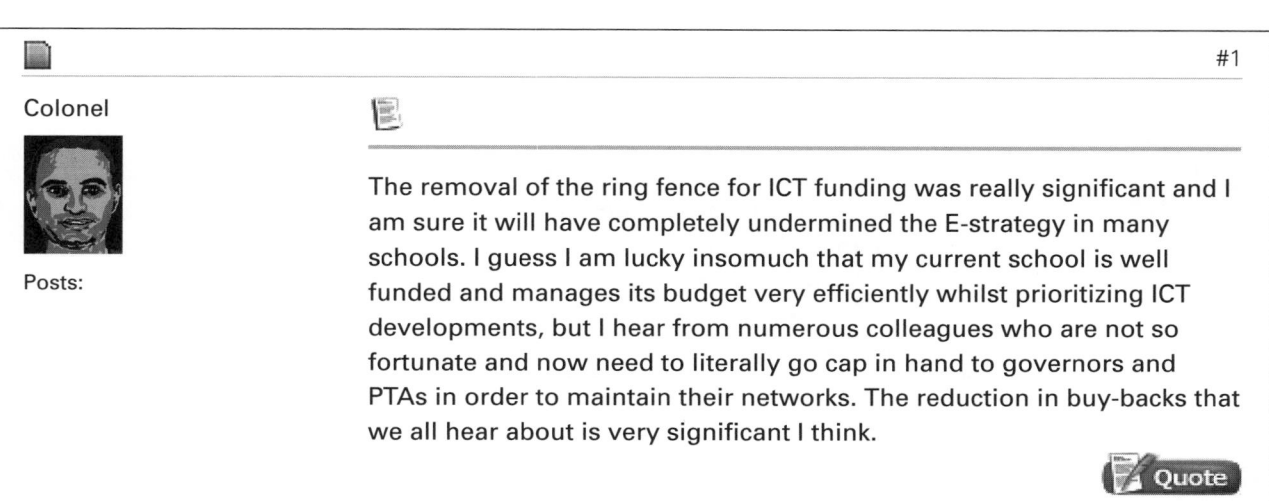

	#1
Colonel	

Posts:

The removal of the ring fence for ICT funding was really significant and I am sure it will have completely undermined the E-strategy in many schools. I guess I am lucky insomuch that my current school is well funded and manages its budget very efficiently whilst prioritizing ICT developments, but I hear from numerous colleagues who are not so fortunate and now need to literally go cap in hand to governors and PTAs in order to maintain their networks. The reduction in buy-backs that we all hear about is very significant I think.

Quote

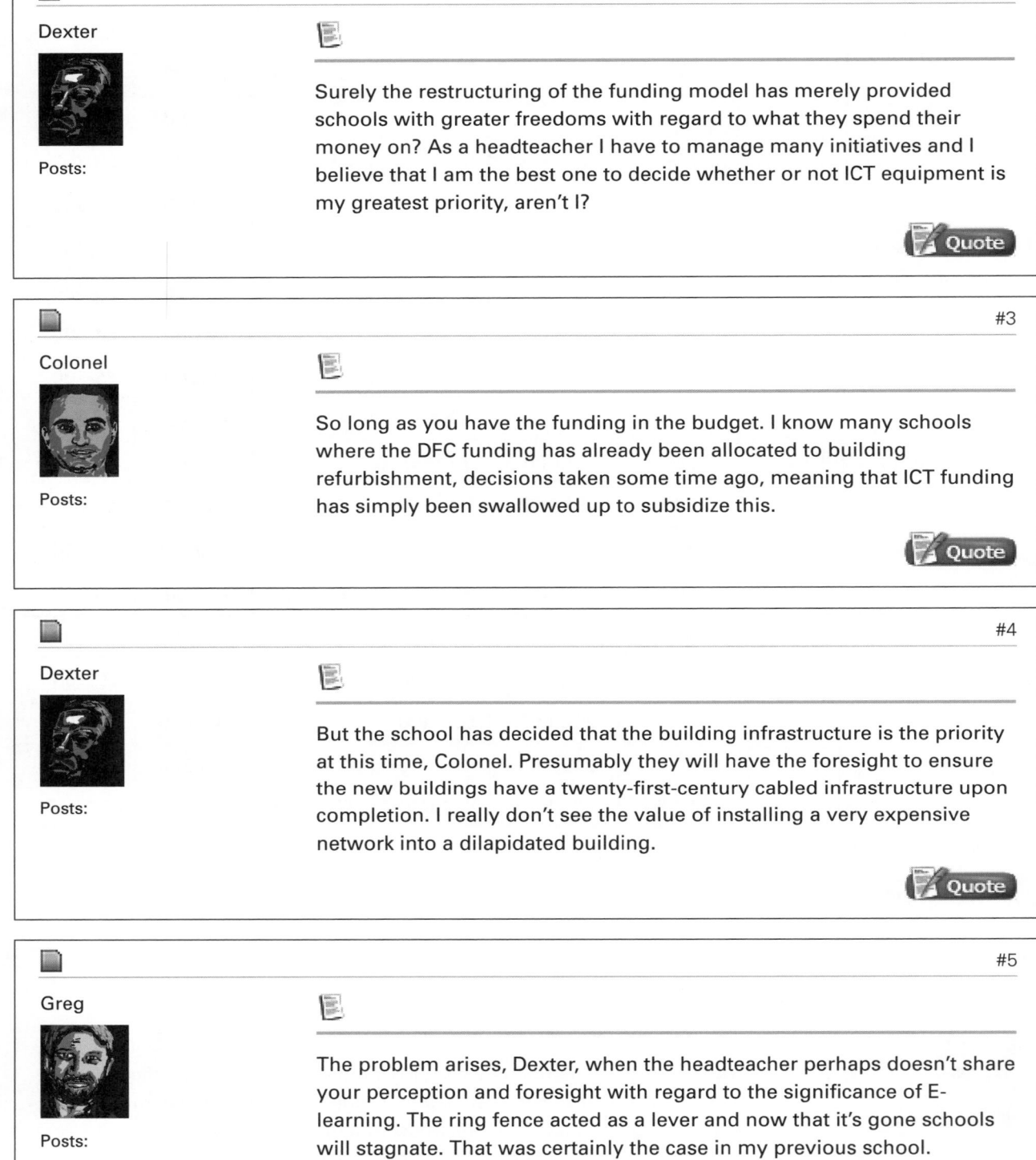

#2

Dexter

Posts:

Surely the restructuring of the funding model has merely provided schools with greater freedoms with regard to what they spend their money on? As a headteacher I have to manage many initiatives and I believe that I am the best one to decide whether or not ICT equipment is my greatest priority, aren't I?

Quote

#3

Colonel

Posts:

So long as you have the funding in the budget. I know many schools where the DFC funding has already been allocated to building refurbishment, decisions taken some time ago, meaning that ICT funding has simply been swallowed up to subsidize this.

Quote

#4

Dexter

Posts:

But the school has decided that the building infrastructure is the priority at this time, Colonel. Presumably they will have the foresight to ensure the new buildings have a twenty-first-century cabled infrastructure upon completion. I really don't see the value of installing a very expensive network into a dilapidated building.

Quote

#5

Greg

Posts:

The problem arises, Dexter, when the headteacher perhaps doesn't share your perception and foresight with regard to the significance of E-learning. The ring fence acted as a lever and now that it's gone schools will stagnate. That was certainly the case in my previous school.

Quote

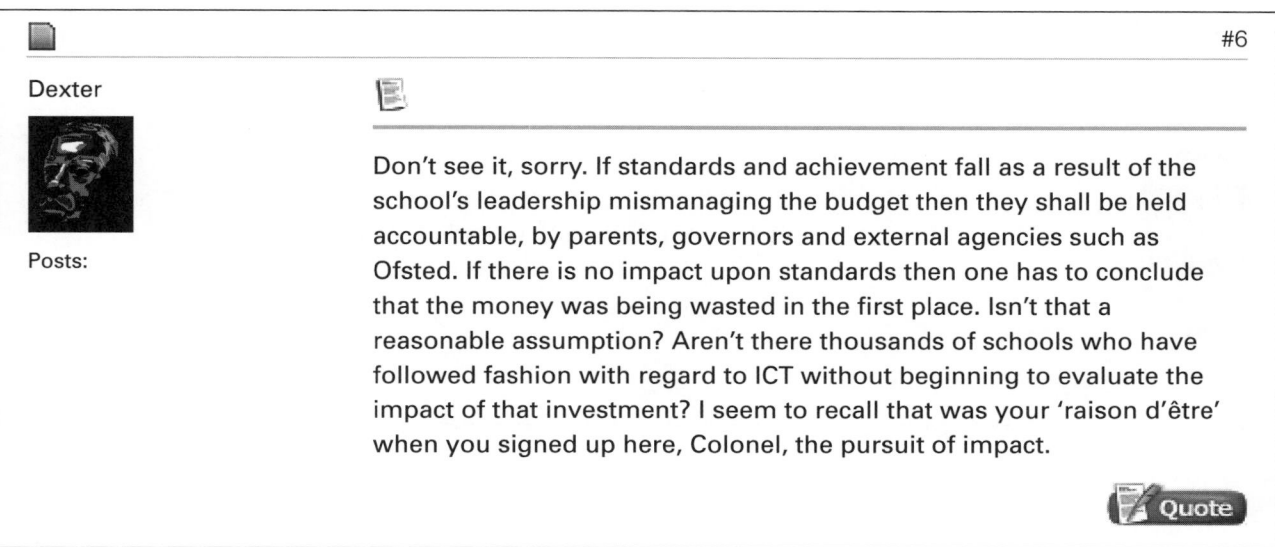

Dexter

Posts:

Don't see it, sorry. If standards and achievement fall as a result of the school's leadership mismanaging the budget then they shall be held accountable, by parents, governors and external agencies such as Ofsted. If there is no impact upon standards then one has to conclude that the money was being wasted in the first place. Isn't that a reasonable assumption? Aren't there thousands of schools who have followed fashion with regard to ICT without beginning to evaluate the impact of that investment? I seem to recall that was your 'raison d'être' when you signed up here, Colonel, the pursuit of impact.

#6

22nd December

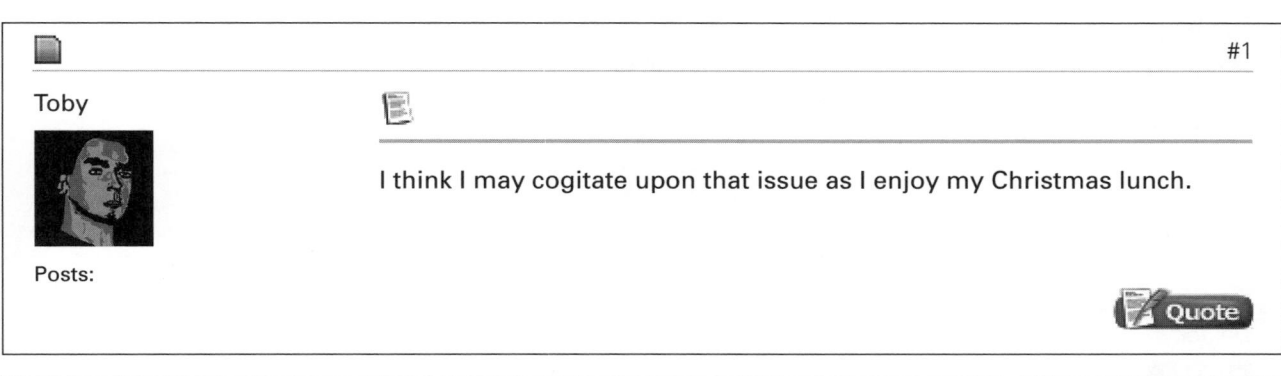

Toby

Posts:

I think I may cogitate upon that issue as I enjoy my Christmas lunch.

#1

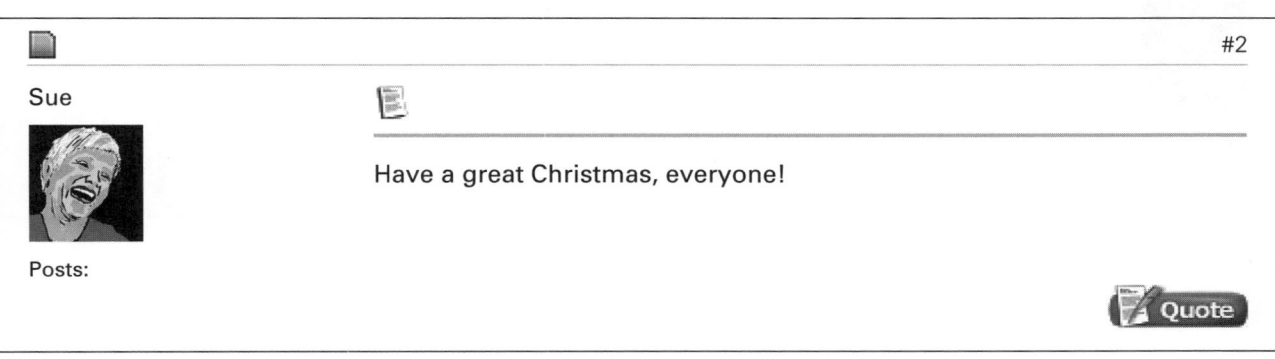

Sue

Posts:

Have a great Christmas, everyone!

#2

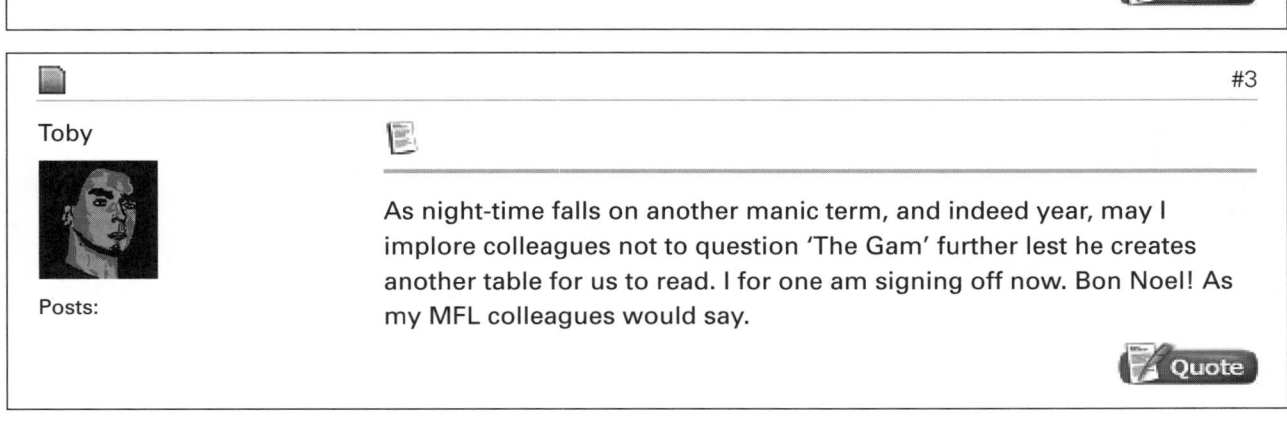

Toby

Posts:

As night-time falls on another manic term, and indeed year, may I implore colleagues not to question 'The Gam' further lest he creates another table for us to read. I for one am signing off now. Bon Noel! As my MFL colleagues would say.

#3

23rd December

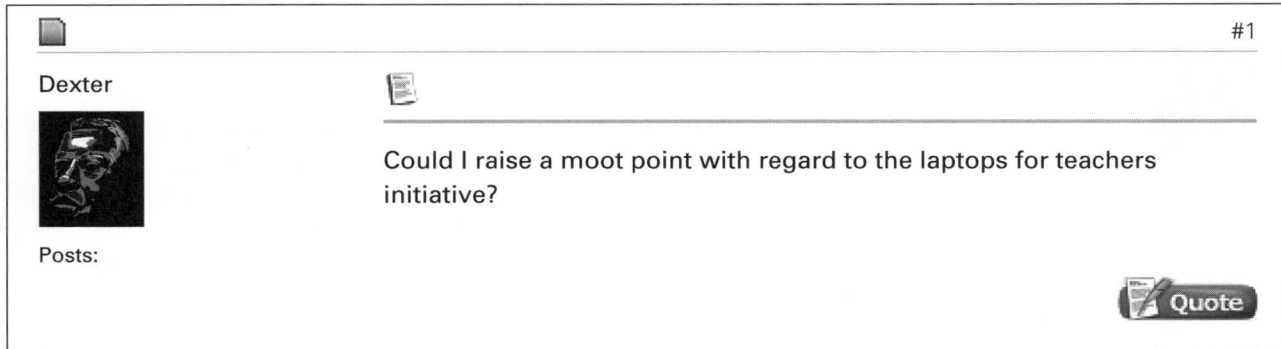

Dexter

Posts:

> Could I raise a moot point with regard to the laptops for teachers initiative?

#1

24th December

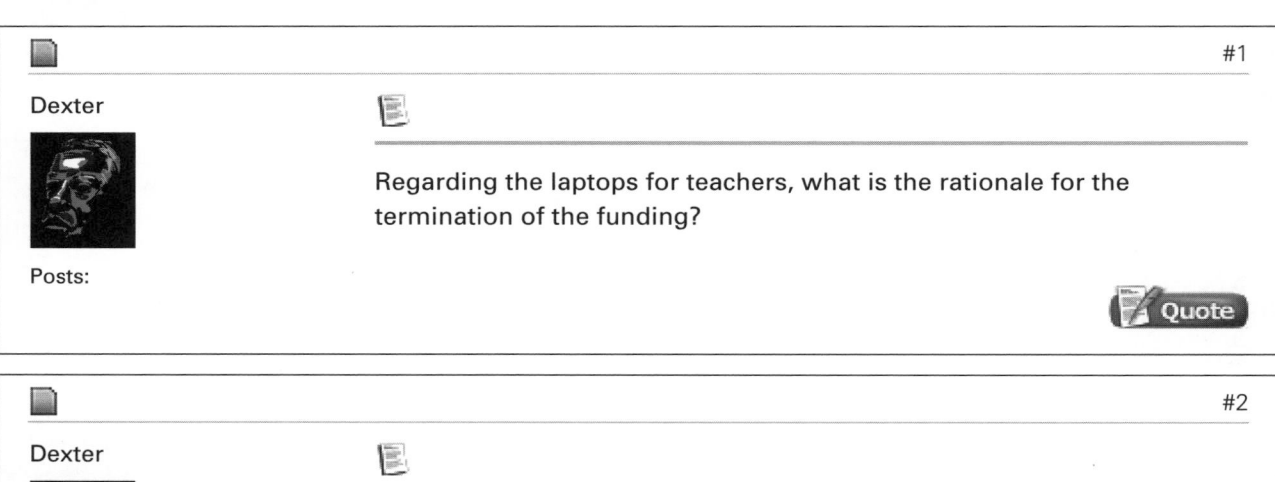

Dexter

Posts:

> Regarding the laptops for teachers, what is the rationale for the termination of the funding?

#1

Dexter

Posts:

> The laptops?

#2

25th December

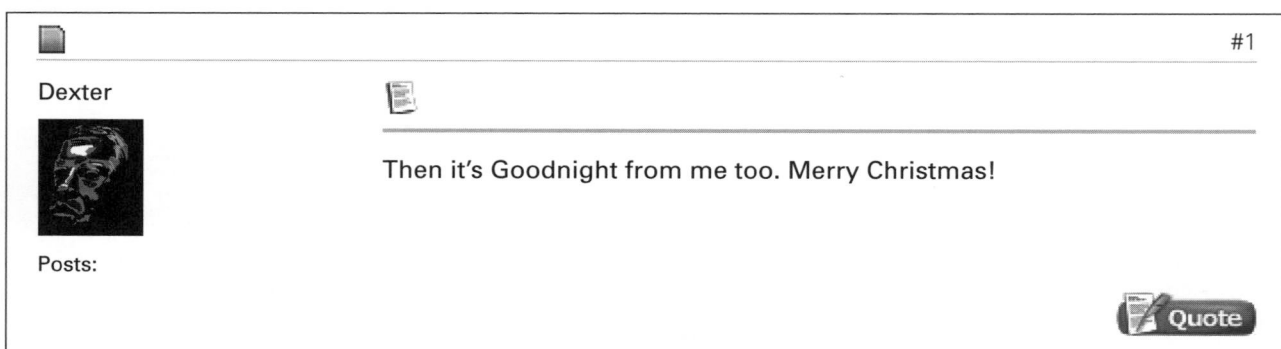

Dexter

Posts:

> Then it's Goodnight from me too. Merry Christmas!

#1

Chapter 5 • *January*

2nd January

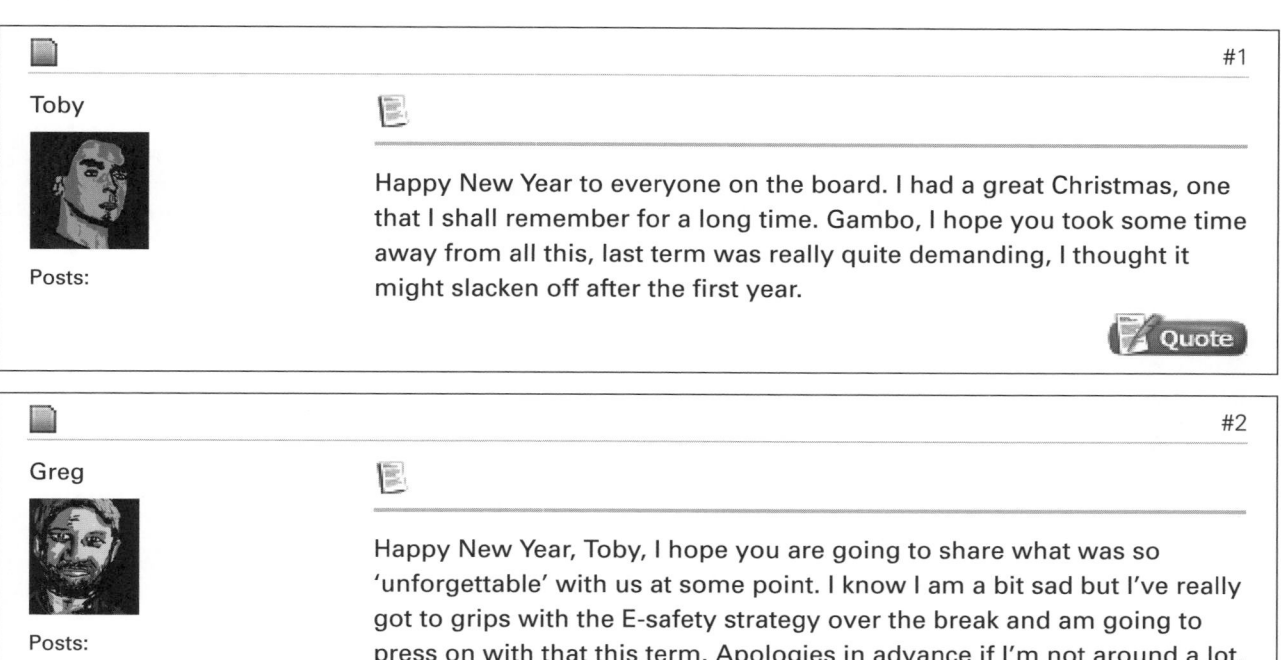

Toby

Posts:

#1

Happy New Year to everyone on the board. I had a great Christmas, one that I shall remember for a long time. Gambo, I hope you took some time away from all this, last term was really quite demanding, I thought it might slacken off after the first year.

Quote

Greg

Posts:

#2

Happy New Year, Toby, I hope you are going to share what was so 'unforgettable' with us at some point. I know I am a bit sad but I've really got to grips with the E-safety strategy over the break and am going to press on with that this term. Apologies in advance if I'm not around a lot.

Quote

4th January

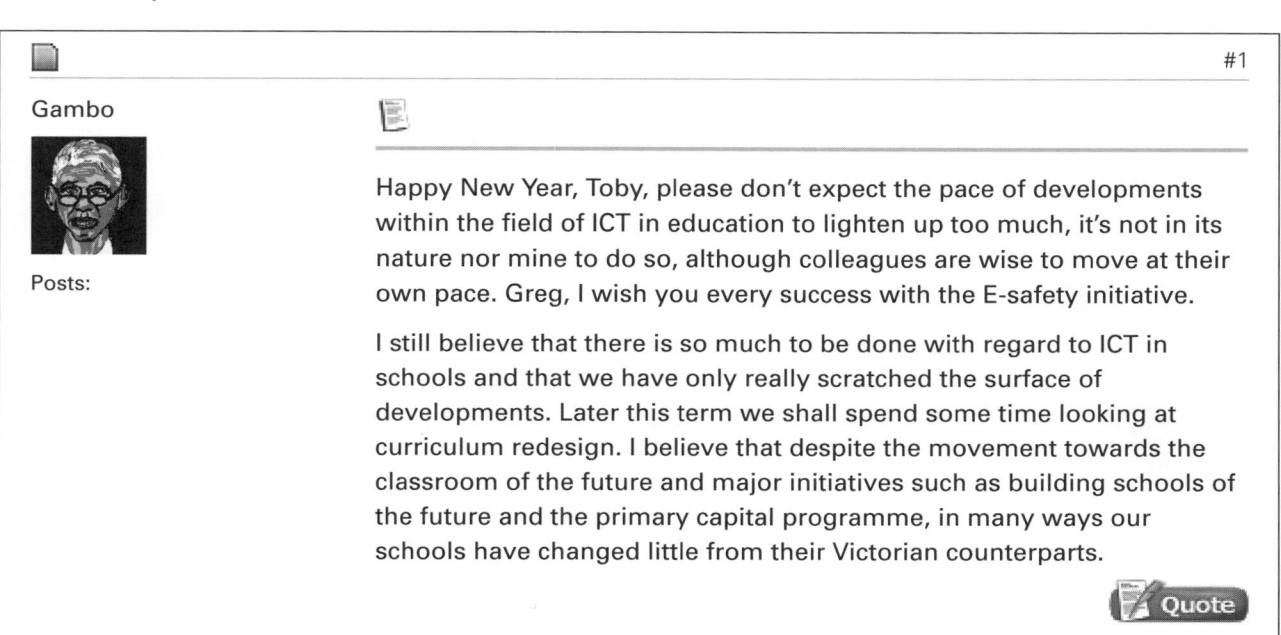

Gambo

Posts:

#1

Happy New Year, Toby, please don't expect the pace of developments within the field of ICT in education to lighten up too much, it's not in its nature nor mine to do so, although colleagues are wise to move at their own pace. Greg, I wish you every success with the E-safety initiative.

I still believe that there is so much to be done with regard to ICT in schools and that we have only really scratched the surface of developments. Later this term we shall spend some time looking at curriculum redesign. I believe that despite the movement towards the classroom of the future and major initiatives such as building schools of the future and the primary capital programme, in many ways our schools have changed little from their Victorian counterparts.

Quote

#2

Greg

Posts:

You are probably right, Gambo, in many ways the structure of the school day remains untouched by modern technology. My brother-in-law is a police inspector and technology has transformed the way that his service now operates. I strongly believe that in schools ICT predominantly still supports traditional means of teaching and learning. Time for a gear change maybe?

Quote

#3

Dexter

Posts:

Happy New Year gentlemen. As a traditionalist I am more than happy for the status quo to be maintained, long may it be so. I fear the extremes that your school of the future might offer, Gambo. I fear a depersonalized, overly sterilized antisocial learning environment, and am happy that we tread with great care down this pathway.

Quote

#4

Toby

Posts:

Sounds like that chapter may be particularly interactive.

Quote

#5

Gambo

Posts:

That's good, shall we save the debate until later?

Quote

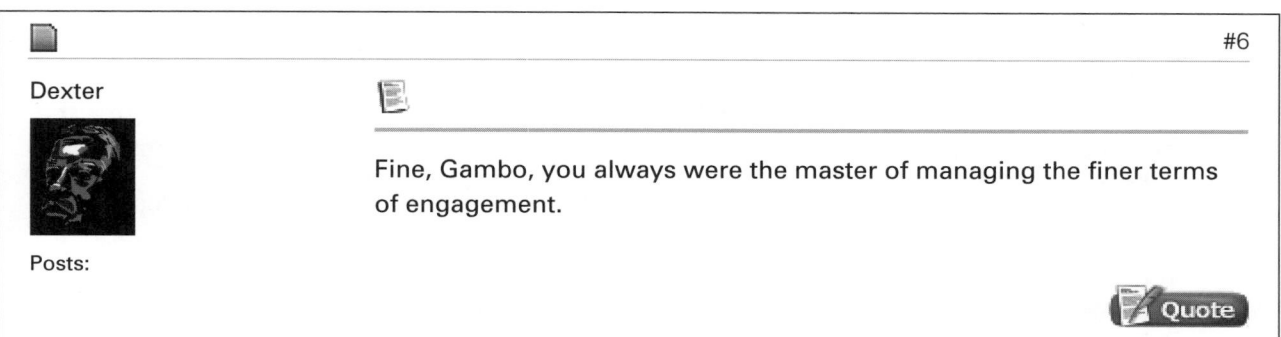

#6

Dexter

Posts:

Fine, Gambo, you always were the master of managing the finer terms of engagement.

6th January

Table 5.1 Spring term plan

SPRING TERM			
JANUARY	**FEBRUARY**	**MARCH**	**APRIL**
Online Learning Explores the evolution of primary learning platforms			**Curriculum review and Redesign**
The Digital Divide How does the school ensure that its online learning platform is inclusive and not divisive?	**Aspects of an Interactive School Website** Looks at the issues arising once an online learning platform is established to improve staff and parental interaction with the school's electronic resources	**Pupil access to Learning Resources** Review of the likely impact of pupil access to ICT resources out of school hours and discussion of some innovative and practical approaches	How will our school evolve to make the most use of the ICTs that we have embedded? Key questions are asked to challenge our current attitudes towards E-learning in the light of curricular evolution
Extended Learning Co-ordinators will consider how E-learning and the school's resources will evolve to meet the needs of the community that it serves			**Managing Information Systems (MIS)**
The Role of ICT in the Community What are the measures required to ensure that the school is adequately equipped to contribute to extended services?	**Extra Curricular Opportunities**		A Review of how ICT is supporting school management systems and which factors should be considered when formulating a medium-term strategy
	1. The first part of this discussion looks at the added value potential of simulation software and keyboard skills training	**2.** The second discussion reviews the adoption of CC4G resources and the creation of a digital arts studio	
Provision for Specific Groups of Children High-impact ICT should meet the every child's specific needs. A review of the use of ICT by a variety of pupil groupings			

JANUARY	FEBRUARY	MARCH	APRIL
The Role of ICT in the Foundation Stage Is ICT an appropriate learning tool for very young children? Co-ordinators get the opportunity to explore some of the key issues	**Able, Gifted and Talented**		**Provision across the Curriculum** Developing professional understanding of the ICT orders with regard to SEN and discussion of the different means in which ICT may impact in this area
	Provision for Children with Special Educational Needs Introduction to the identification of pupils whose special ability lies in the field of ICT	**Provision within ICT** Review of provision against the BECTA SRF inclusion strand and audit of how ICT facilitates able children working at their own pace through independent, personalized activities	

Available on the net at http://www.james-wright.org

The full agenda for this term is detailed within Table 5.1. As well as the 'debate' we anticipate surrounding curriculum redesign we shall examine the detail of our MIS strategy and how this may develop over the coming years. During two related studies we will prepare an outcome-based action plan for the development of online learning materials through the evolution of an interactive website and relate this to the school's expanding role with regard to the wider community through the extended learning initiative. Finally, and throughout the month, we shall undertake a number of separate yet related activities in which colleagues are encouraged to reflect upon the role of ICT with regard to specific groups of children.

Week 17, Task 13 – The Role of ICT in the Early Years Foundation Stage

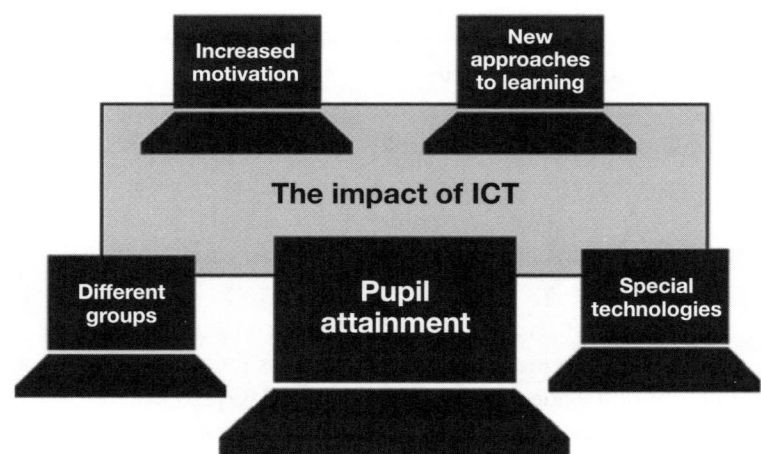

Figure 5.1 The impact of ICT
Available on the net at http://www.james-wright.org

Figure 5.1 reminds us that one of the five core areas in which ICT can impact upon learning is with particular regard to specific pupil populations. Throughout this term we shall take a look at different groups of children and assess the manner in which ICT might impact upon their specific learning outcomes. We begin this task by looking at the expanding role of ICT within the Early Years Foundation Stage (EYFS). In addressing this area E-learning co-ordinators should reflect carefully upon three core issues:

1 Is ICT an appropriate tool for the Foundation Stage at my school?
2 What are the specific curriculum requirements for ICT as set out within the six areas of learning and early learning goals?
3 What should ICT in the Foundation Stage look like within my school?

When I was leading ICT in school I had no great schema for the reception classes. The National Curriculum that dictated the requirements for ICT in schools did not really apply to reception-age children and I was and am very much committed to a broad sensory-rich, investigative learning experience for young children. The core ICTs of the time were all based around the computer suite and were not, I felt, appropriate for these groups who consequently remained outside of the broader E-learning agenda. I was, of course, aware of the excellent work that colleagues within these classes were developing using programmable toys and enhancements for the role-play areas and very much felt that this more than provided adequate exposure to information technology for very young children. As key practitioners in the development of E-learning today it is essential that you are aware of the debate about ICT usage within the Foundation Stage, the passionate position held by many educational colleagues and the need to safeguard children's health and development. Furthermore, your task for this week will be to articulate your own position within this debate, polarized as it is between those for whom computers are now a fundamental part of children's social and intellectual development and those who consider computers to be anathema for early years education and, at worst, a direct harm to children's health and learning.

In formulating your position in this respect, I recommend that colleagues ensure that they are abreast of recent thinking in the area and advocate reading, *ICT in Pre-school, a Benign Addition?* commissioned by Learning and Teaching Scotland (Stephen and Plowman, 2002) as a formative review of the literature in this field which will also provide an invaluable reference for many aspects of early years learning with regard to ICT that may challenge your present position in this respect. The review quotes Yelland (1999) and Haughland (2000) to highlight opposition to E-learning within the early years setting.

> *'The predominant view is that, as a screen-based medium, activities at the computer are not as effective as manipulatives in developing understanding and skills in the early years and that, as children learn through their bodies, computers are not developmentally appropriate.'* (Stephen and Plowman, 2002: 5)

There are a range of very real concerns to address with regard to the use of ICT in early years, and exponents of E-learning must develop a comprehensive rationale for any expansion of ICT applications within the Early Years Foundation Stage and an awareness of the associated continuing professional development (CPD) requirements for staff if this is to be a successful feature of the school.

9th January

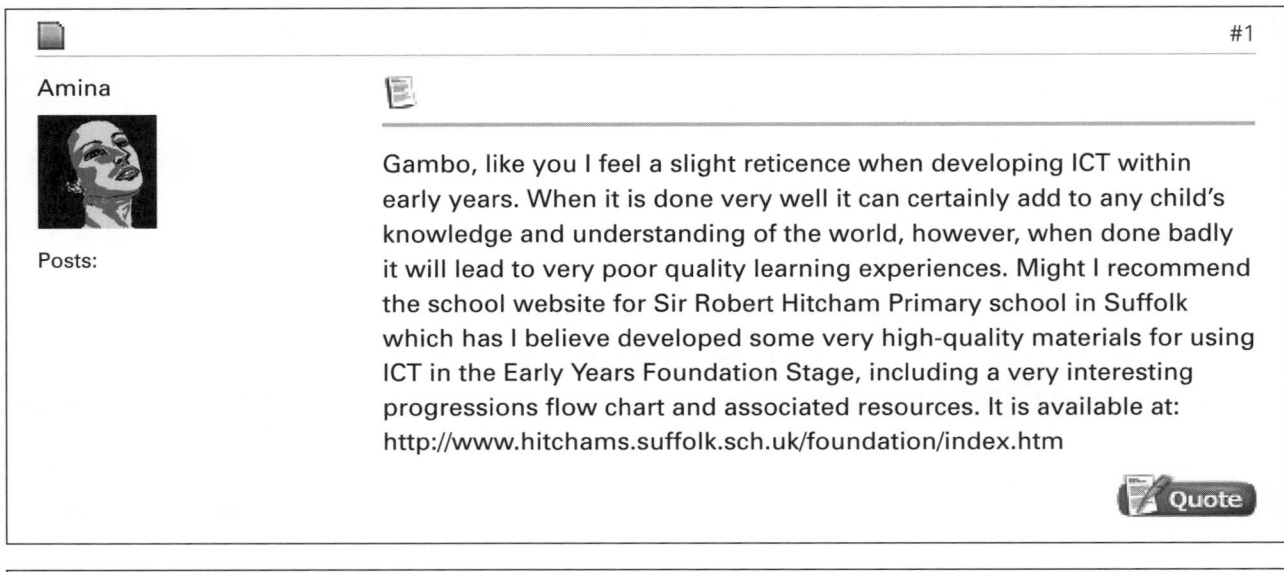

#1

Amina

Posts:

Gambo, like you I feel a slight reticence when developing ICT within early years. When it is done very well it can certainly add to any child's knowledge and understanding of the world, however, when done badly it will lead to very poor quality learning experiences. Might I recommend the school website for Sir Robert Hitcham Primary school in Suffolk which has I believe developed some very high-quality materials for using ICT in the Early Years Foundation Stage, including a very interesting progressions flow chart and associated resources. It is available at: http://www.hitchams.suffolk.sch.uk/foundation/index.htm

Quote

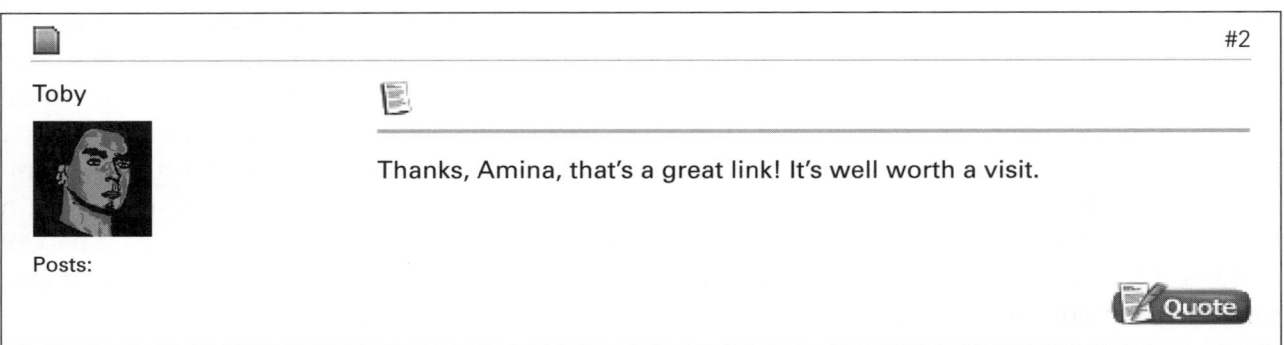

#2

Toby

Posts:

Thanks, Amina, that's a great link! It's well worth a visit.

Quote

14th January

Colleagues do need to understand the concerns regarding the overuse of ICT at an early age. Often this can be centred around fears regarding uncontrolled and excessive home use of gaming applications leading to an exposure to violent content that is then associated with aggressive anti-social behaviour. There is general unease surrounding apparently passive engagement with computers and anxiety regarding the addictive nature of the Internet and computer games, and the potential negative physical effects of prolonged exposure. Ultimately, many colleagues fear that computers may damage young children's development and see no place for such technologies in the early years learning environment. As a result of these fears it is essential that software available in pre-school settings must be free of unsuitable content and practitioners must ensure that they have a good understanding of each child's engagement with ICT through careful observations and recording of ICT activities. However as Stephen and Plowman (2003: 3) note:

> *'ICT is often narrowly construed as consisting mainly of desktop computers but the range of technologies available now and in the near future provides opportunities for a more radical transformation of teaching and learning relationships and activities.'*

Colleagues should consider auditing ICT provision within the early years classrooms beginning with reference to the Early Learning Goal for ICT, which states that children should find out about and identify the uses of technology in their everyday lives, and that children should use ICT and programmable toys to support their learning.

In particular colleagues may wish to review the 'developmental matters' identified within the EYFS towards achieving this goal, specifically relating to children from age 40 to 60 months who may:

Complete a simple programme on a computer.
Use ICT to perform simple functions, such as selecting a channel on a television remote control.
Use a mouse and keyboard to interact with age-appropriate computer software.

Colleagues should familiarize themselves with the progressions indicated within the EYFS with regards to ICT which replaced the three original ICT 'Stepping Stones', namely:

To show an interest in ICT (yellow).
To know how to operate simple equipment (blue).
To complete a simple program on a computer and/or perform simple functions on ICT apparatus (green).

Colleagues' second task therefore is to audit how provision is meeting these requirements within the 'Knowledge and understanding of the world' strand of the Early Years Foundation Stage curriculum as well as to review current opportunities to develop ICT within each separate area of learning. Co-ordinators may wish to ask colleagues to examine current provision for children to use construction equipment, to engage in role play, to observe and talk about the use of ICT in the environment, and to use ICT within investigation and design tasks.

17th January

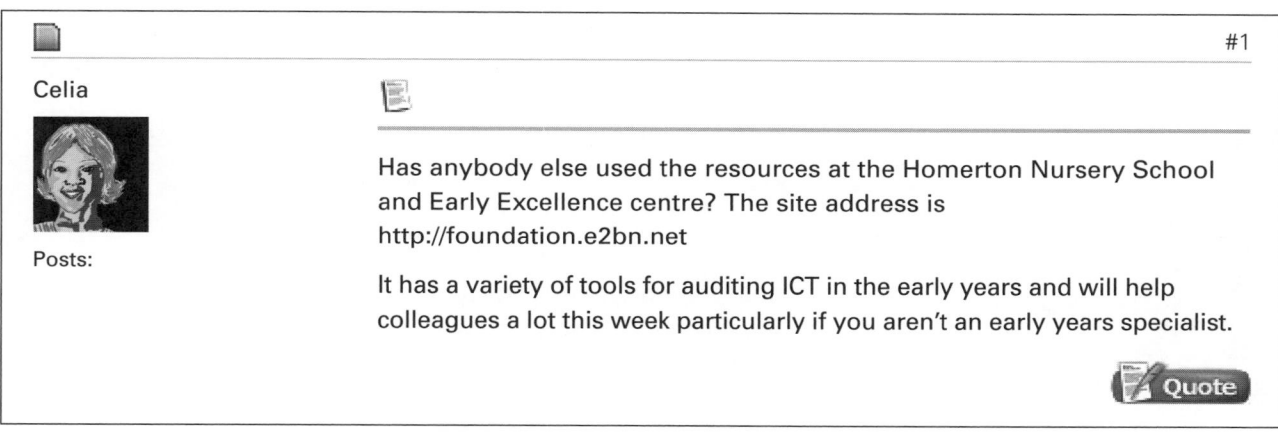

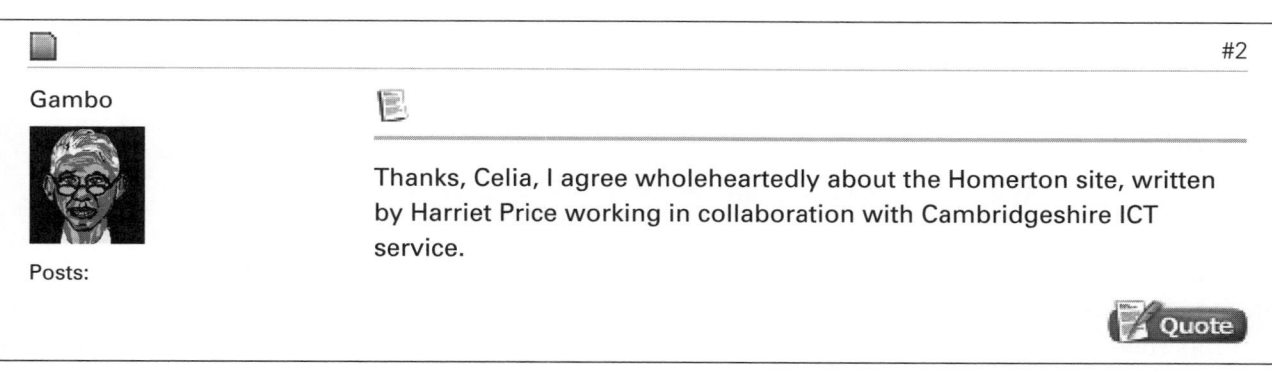

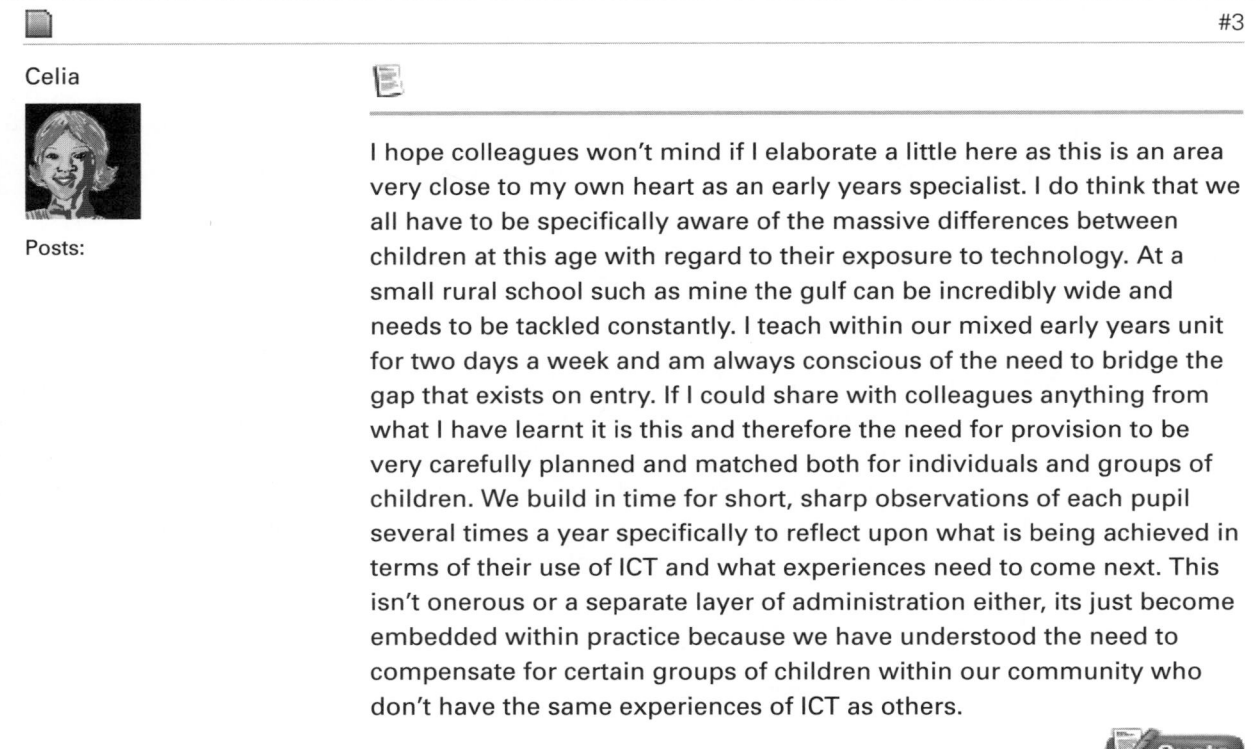

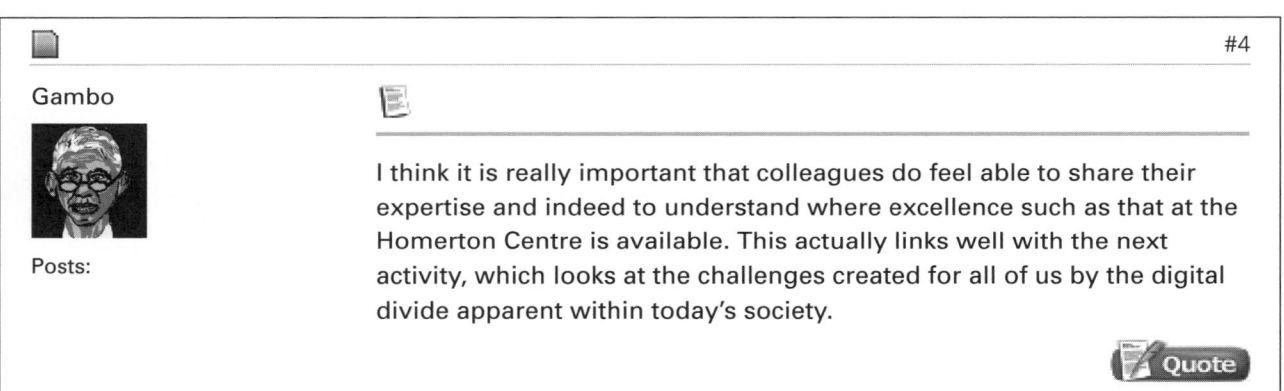

18th January

Week 19, Task 14 – Online Learning – the Digital Divide

Forward-thinking schools have for some time realized the importance of a dynamic online presence as a valuable secondary form of communication with parents both present and prospective. Schools have explored various options including free host solutions, LA brokered content management systems and innovative in-house options. Many have invested enormous amounts of time developing and sustaining websites, whilst others have ruefully watched their site diminish into an often poignant snapshot of a point in the school's history. The demands to maintain and develop a website often prove to be beyond the means of many schools, both in terms of time and cost. Additional concerns with regard to the E-safety perspectives, hosting of pupil images etc. have further delayed the development of effective interactive websites.

Primary schools by and large therefore approach with trepidation the arrival of virtual learning and the national E-learning vision as set out in section 10 of the national E-learning strategy (DfES, 2005a). This document, the DfES E-strategy, *Harnessing Technology: Transforming Learning and Children's Services*, sets out the government's targets for ensuring that better use is made of ICT in schools to improve standards, pupils' interest in learning and use of teachers' time. It aims to provide integrated online personal support for all learners, specifically identifying the need for all pupils to be able to access a personal online workspace, capable of supporting an e-portfolio by 2007–08.

'Pupils and students will be able to access online support when they need it ... learners should have a single point of access to all their course materials – a personal online learning space. They should be able to contact digital libraries, talk online to fellow students or gain online tutorial support when they are not in school.'

'We will make it easier for parents and carers to engage with and support their children's learning by opening up school based Internet systems, bridging the gap between school and home, making available secure access to pupil information, learning activities and email based communication.' (DfES, 2005a: 43)

Priority 2 of this section of the strategy sets the specific target to ensure integrated online personal support for learners by providing a personalized online learning space for every learner, which can encompass a personal portfolio. The specific identified milestone for such actions being a personalized learning space, with the potential to support e-portfolios available to every school by 2007–08. This is a quantum leap into the unknown for many primary schools.

In the next chapter we shall spend some time discussing the development of an interactive website; however, at this stage it is, I believe, more important that schools consider the strategic and pedagogical rationale that lies behind such a move. In particular, how may we best ensure that such a tool is an inclusive one that supports the breaking down of traditional educational barriers and does not merely reinforce and exaggerate any existing social and digital divide?

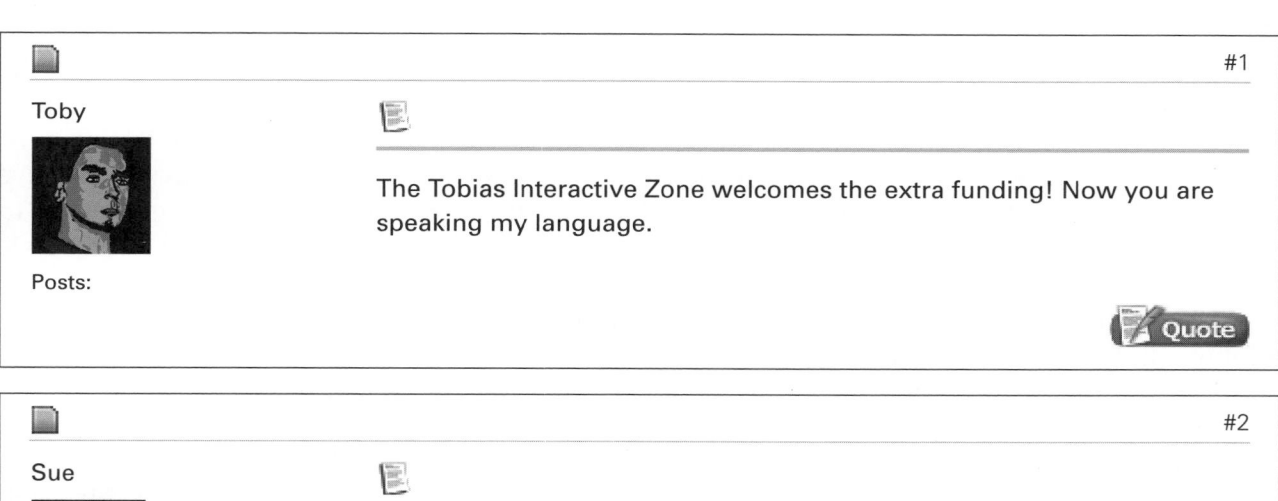

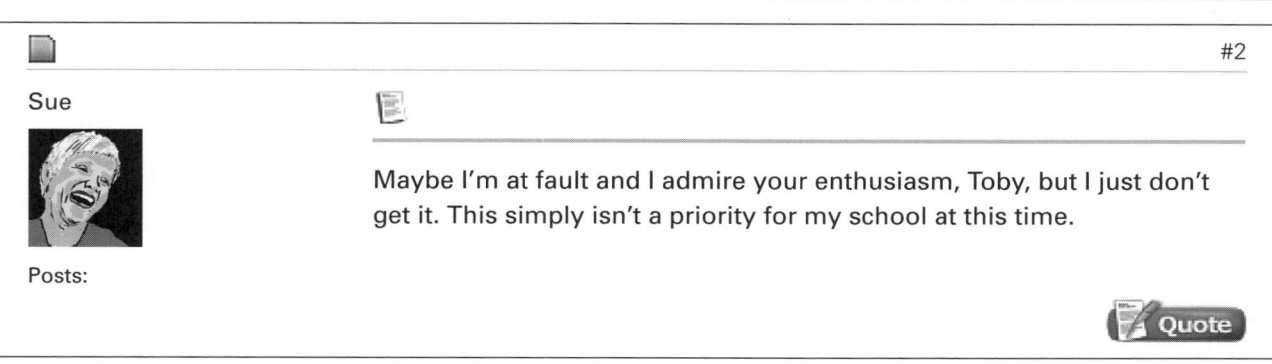

19th January

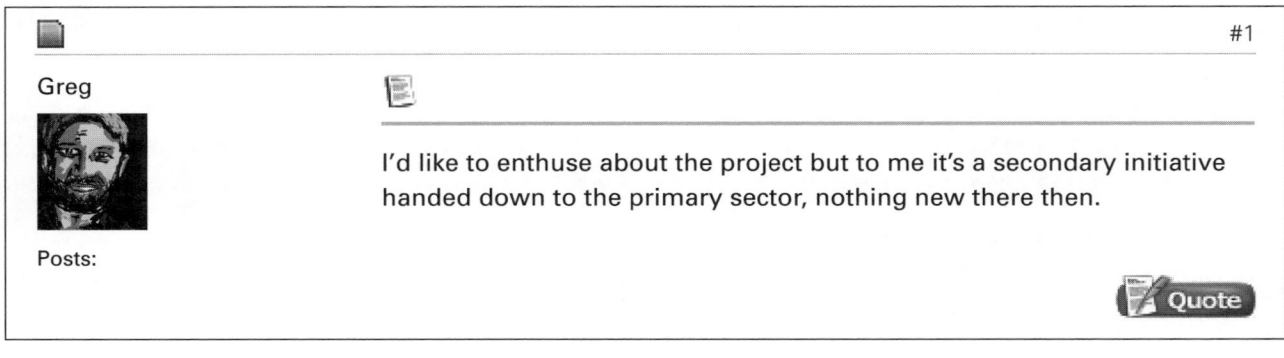

20th January

Local authorities were given the target of establishing the core provision referred to within the blog discussion by 2008 and there has been a lot of discussion as to what exactly this entails. BECTA were commissioned to produce functional requirements for any learning platform; however, I have to agree to some extent with the comments that this is largely a secondary initiative that primary colleagues have caught the tail of and, unless you are already really geared up to deliver out-of-hours learning and have a thoroughly embedded strategic approach to the whole initiative, it may be wiser to adopt a policy of wait and see.

What is important is that a primary model emerges and that colleagues are not tempted to simply emulate their secondary colleagues. Of course, there is validity in acquiring a system that supports transition into Year 7; however, interoperability is a key functional specification for any system and therefore the desire for smooth transition should not necessarily in itself dictate which provision is most appropriate for your school. We shall look in much greater detail at adopting and developing interactive online services within the next chapter. For now I think colleagues need to explore issues related to inclusion that will impact upon the success or otherwise of any such initiative.

In principle any interactivity within your website is designed to produce a virtual school that can parallel some of your 'real' school's key features. This will facilitate communication between school and staff, school and parent, and teacher and pupil. Initially, therefore, schools must ensure that they are able to exploit these opportunities, beginning with the renewed relationship between the school and staff. In order to be inclusive colleagues must ensure that all staff have access to the Internet and to email, and that any movement towards electronic communication does not place undue demands on staff. Be clear that many teachers will not welcome the introduction or extension of electronic messaging, briefings, and so on, even though this is now the norm in many sectors of the economy. In many ways school staff have been allowed to slip behind in terms of basic work skills. Schools should identify any critical skill gaps and plan to implement this aspect of the learning portal at a measured pace. Ultimately, be clear that email is the standard form of business messaging and staff who enjoy planning, preparation and assessment time off site must be prepared to have a staff email account open and 'live' at least during this period. Many schools now rely upon email to distribute staff briefings, reminders and memos, many of which will be hosted in the school portal. Think through in advance where the problems are going to arise and prepare a reasonable run in the period when parallel paper systems remain in place. Hopefully, this will not present too many challenges for colleagues. More problematic will be staff who have no access to the Internet from home, and schools will have to consider whether or not it is feasible to fund Internet connections or to provide alternate arrangements for the minority who will otherwise simply be unable to participate.

#1

Amina

Posts:

My desire to reduce my carbon footprint assures me that this is a positive move; however, haven't we all got at least one colleague who is going to be 'challenged' by this?

Quote

#2

Dexter

Posts:

Me?

Quote

#3

Sue

Posts:

This just isn't a priority at the moment. If it will genuinely help to simplify and streamline current systems then it will happen naturally. I already spend too much time out of school emailing my colleagues, some even respond!

Quote

#4

Toby

Posts:

Gambo, will we be discussing the obvious benefits of developing this aspect of the portal later? I think we need a full debate about this, it's easy to see the downside and we've all got colleagues who 'can't do'. I'm already ahead of the game in this respect and would be happy to share this but don't want to hijack the discussion at present with regards to inclusion.

Quote

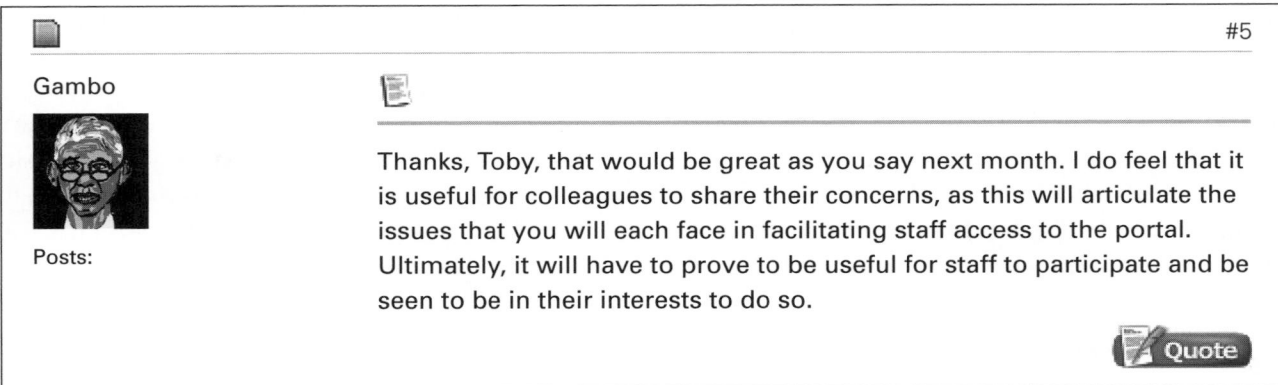

Thanks, Toby, that would be great as you say next month. I do feel that it is useful for colleagues to share their concerns, as this will articulate the issues that you will each face in facilitating staff access to the portal. Ultimately, it will have to prove to be useful for staff to participate and be seen to be in their interests to do so.

21st January

The second element to consider is how access to the school portal will transform ways in which the school may choose to communicate with its parental body. For now, again focus upon the inclusion aspects of this development. How will you ensure that families are not excluded? Certainly in the first instance newsletters and so on that have appeared upon conventional web-sites have still had to be sent out to parents via traditional paper methods also, however, anyone in doubt as to the way that technology will force change should reflect upon the instigation of the online School Profile (www.schoolsfinder.direct.gov.uk/about-school-profile) and the demise of the annual Governors' Report to Parents.

Schools who are committed to moving early into online communications with parents should begin that dialogue now. Get parents to opt into email alerts and preferred access to the portal materials and contact all parents, reassuring those that do not currently have access to the Internet that they will continue to receive paper copy as long as this is necessary. Begin to plan for the phased introduction and engage governors within this dialogue. If you have an ICT governor then he or she will be pivotal in supporting your initiative, as there are certain to be reservations amongst the governing body. Remember also that the 2007–08 target is only the first part of the roll out of portal services to parents and that by 2010 all parents should have access to a full managed learning environment.

22nd January

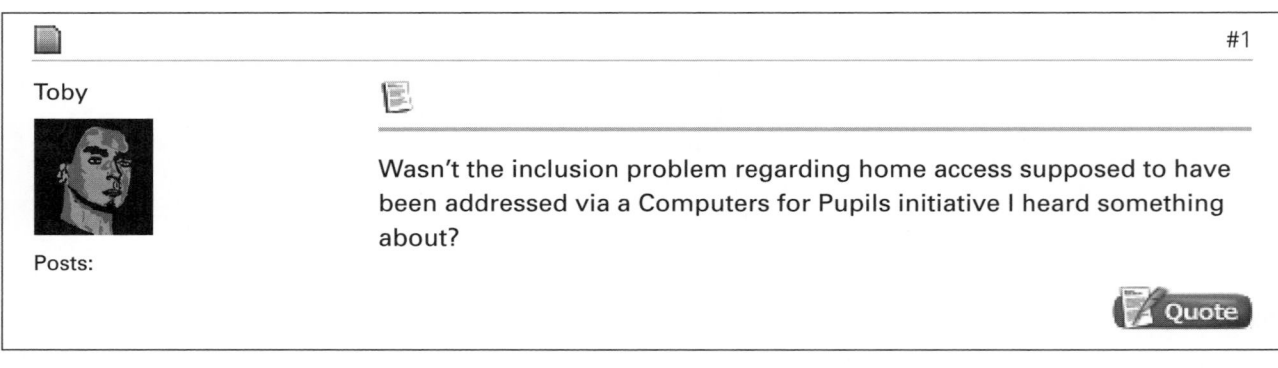

Wasn't the inclusion problem regarding home access supposed to have been addressed via a Computers for Pupils initiative I heard something about?

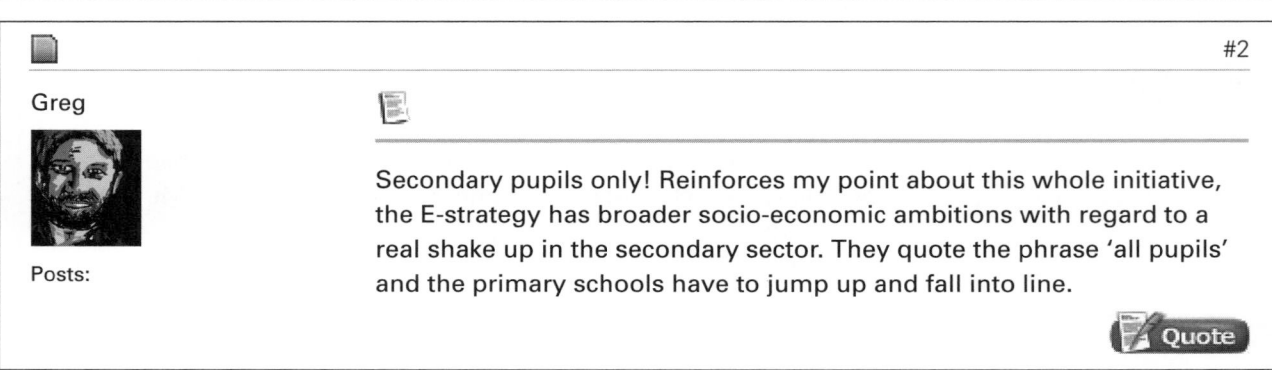

Secondary pupils only! Reinforces my point about this whole initiative, the E-strategy has broader socio-economic ambitions with regard to a real shake up in the secondary sector. They quote the phrase 'all pupils' and the primary schools have to jump up and fall into line.

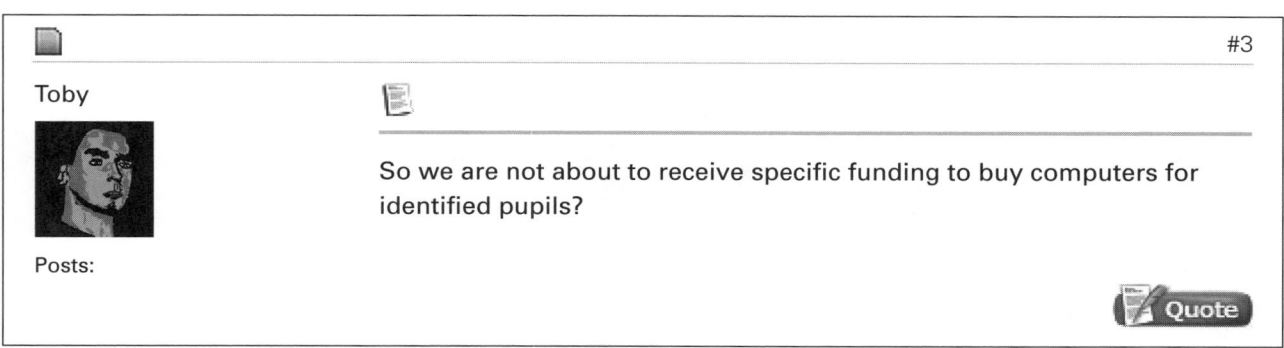

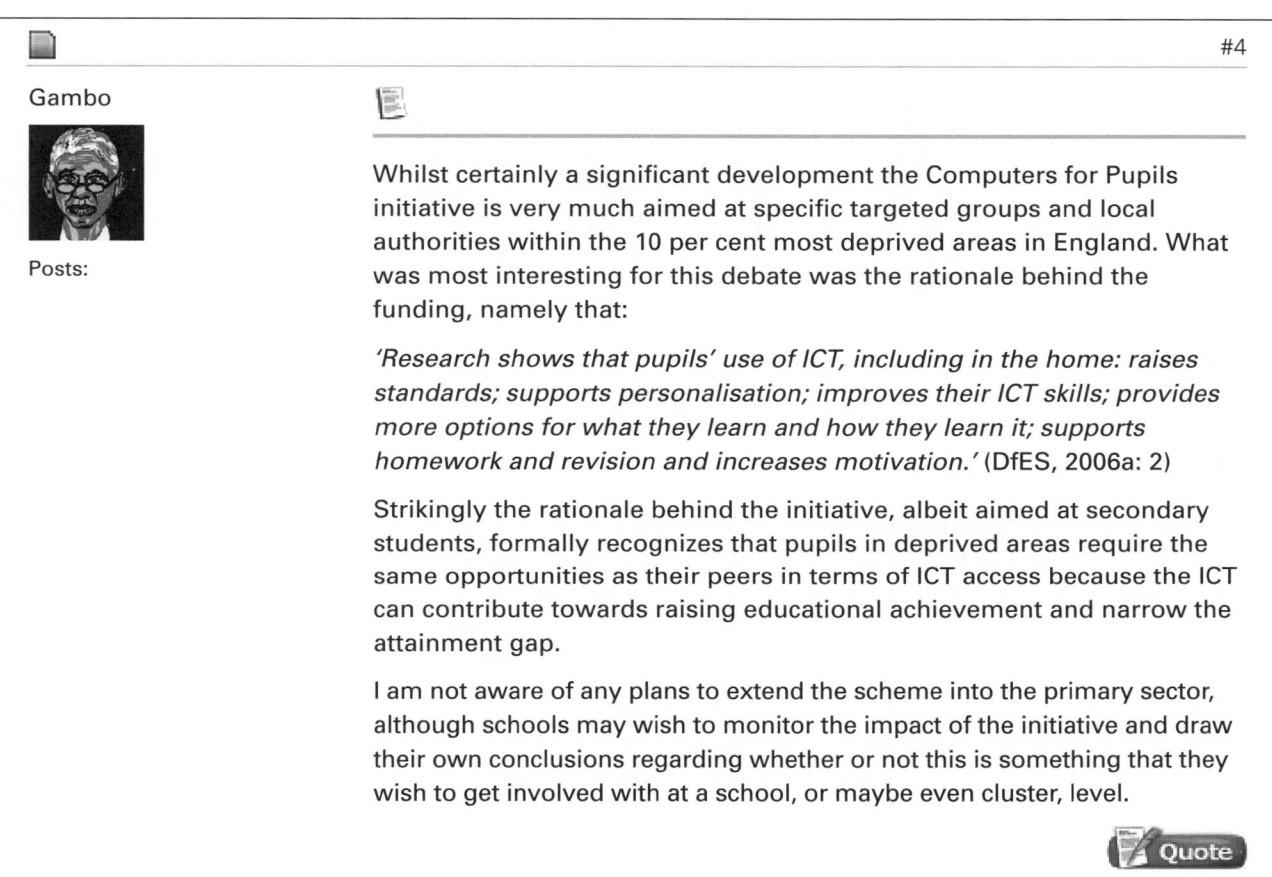

The third focus for the portal will be to provide a pupils' area where children may access resources for learning away from the classroom. This is the area most discussed in terms of ICT breaking down barriers to learning and connecting the home with school. It offers the potential of seamless learning and the promise of engaging pupils out of hours. Clearly, therefore, schools must now work hard to discover which children actually have access to the Internet. This should be every school's primary task at the moment.

The UK National Statistics Omnibus Survey (2006) noted that 57 per cent of British households (around 13.9 million) could access the Internet from home.

Figure 5.2 demonstrates the marked increase in home access to the Internet within the UK in recent years. However, depending upon your locality, it also clearly implies that nearly half of your pupils will not be able to access any resources that are placed within your school portal. Your first action therefore is to establish which pupils have home access to the Internet and then to devise a reasonable strategy for including those that do not within any impending online initiative.

Many schools already survey pupil home use through questionnaires, but this may be an opportunity for an original online activity. The following template may be used or adapted to collect initial data regarding the current preparedness of your school community for such an initiative.

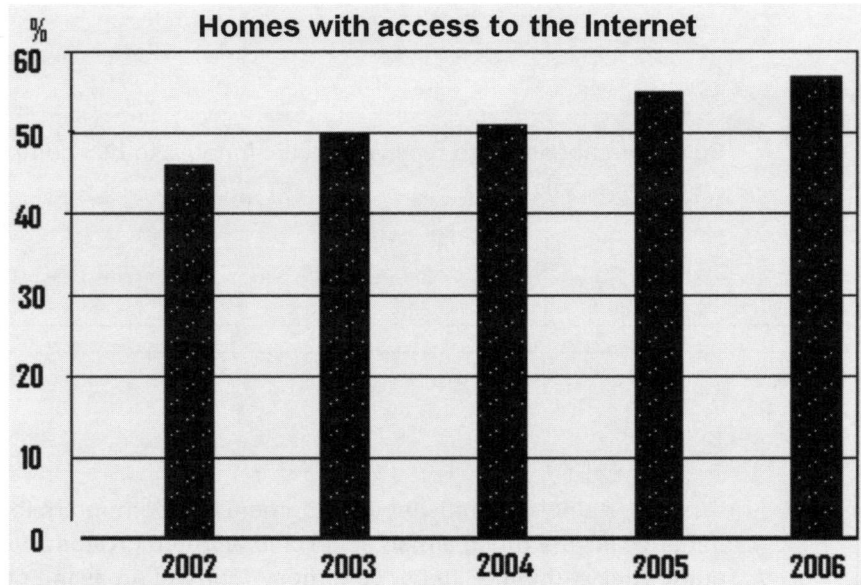

Figure 5.2 Home Internet access

Source: National Statistics Omnibus Survey, Northern Ireland Omnibus Survey and Survey of Internet Service Provider (2006) Available on the net at http://www.james-wright.org

Dear Parent,

Re: School Personal Online Learning Audit

It is the Government's goal to provide every pupil with a personal online learning space by April 2008 in order to access online support when they need it with the potential ultimately to talk online to fellow students or gain online tutorial support when they are not in school. The aim is to make it easier for parents and carers to engage with and support their children's learning by opening up school-based Internet systems, bridging the gap between school and home, making available secure access to pupil information, learning activities and email based communication.

At ...... we are committed to providing our pupils with the best possible learning opportunities and are therefore currently assessing the value of such a scheme to our parents and should very much appreciate your views, comments and participation within the following short survey. All responses will remain anonymous and will only be used by the school to produce overall school or cohort data at this stage. The school may store individual information securely, however this information will only be used to guide school practice and will not be shared with third parties.

I do hope that you feel able to participate it what promises to be an extremely exciting development.

School Personal Online Learning Audit

I support the idea of my child using the online learning portal.   *YES/NO*

I have Internet access at home via broadband to a PC.   *YES/NO*

I have Internet access at home using another method.   *YES/NO*

My child is allowed to access the school website from home.   *YES/NO*

Pupil's Name: _____

Class: _____

Often the most valid data is obtained from online activities and schools may wish to use a web-based quiz in order to collect information about home Internet access.

23rd January

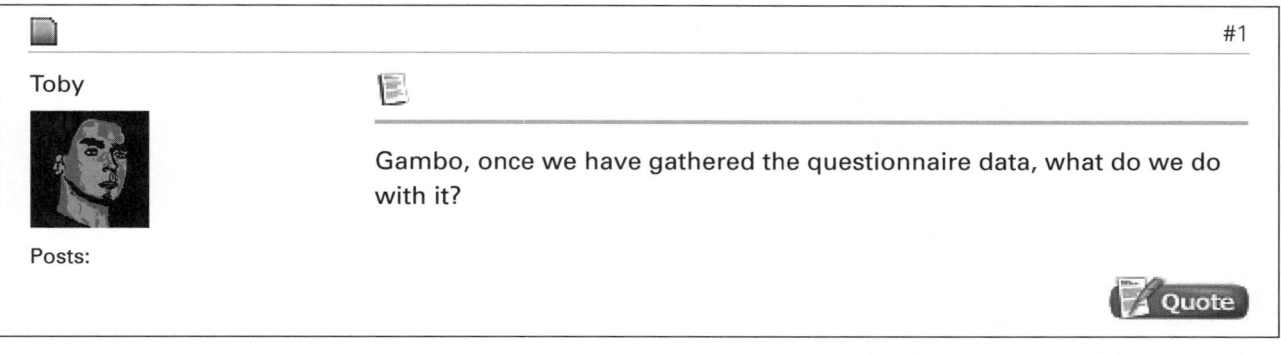

Toby

Posts:

Gambo, once we have gathered the questionnaire data, what do we do with it?

Quote

#1

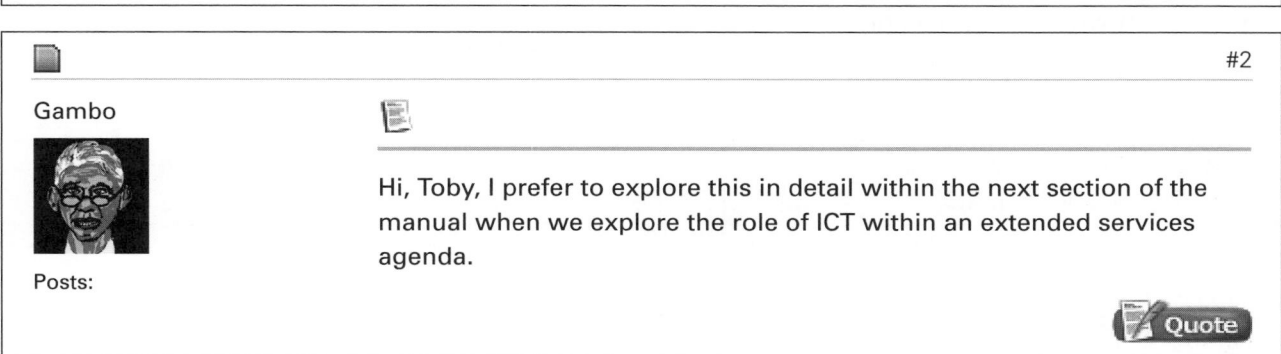

Gambo

Posts:

Hi, Toby, I prefer to explore this in detail within the next section of the manual when we explore the role of ICT within an extended services agenda.

Quote

#2

25th January

Week 20, Task 15 – Extended Learning – the Role of ICT in the Community

The simplest way in which schools can address any potential inequalities arising from the development of virtual learning systems is to ensure that those children who do not currently enjoy home access to the Internet may use the school network out of hours. Schools engaged within the extended services agenda will already have assembled a varied menu of activities and E-learning co-ordinators should aim to ensure that ICT is at the heart of this agenda. Under the auspices of study support, colleagues should cross-reference the learning portal initiative to ensure that ICT access is part of any core offer and that extended services funding is used to provide out-of-hours ICT provision. By 2010, all children should have access to a variety of extended services in or through their school, and these services must be accessible for all irrespective of individual learning needs, as dictated within the 2004 Children Act. Primary schools will also be in receipt of personalization funding through the school standards grant for personalization (SSG(P)) from 2006 onwards and many will participate in the Primary Capital Programme which directly aims to:

'Provide wider access to services for the local community, such as ICT services, sports facilities or adult learning.' (DfES, 2006b: 16)

And to ensure that:

'Every child and family will have access to a primary school in their locality which is a focus for local services, offers ICT facilities after hours, provides parenting support, adult education and healthcare, and provides childcare 8am to 6pm.' (DfES, 2006b: 30)

Schools may already be exploring ways of developing adult use of the network out of school hours. The effective co-ordinator will be able to utilize the linkage between these various initiatives in order to develop clear synergy between the various plans. Ultimately, every school now needs to have a serious plan for the opening up of resources and that plan should in some form directly target students who do not have home access to computers. Given that this will probably lie within a raft of other associated forms of provision including adult learning classes and so on, there are inevitably going to be many E-safety concerns that will need to be addressed. Your final task for this month must therefore be to consider the implications of such measures for your school including logistics and staffing.

Table 5.2 Out-of-hours resource review

Audit	Response	Further action required
Which computers will be available for out-of-hours use?		
Have you considered accessibility taking into account whole-school security?		
What will be the impact upon the overall condition of the equipment?		
Will the initiative financially support the network or detract from it?		
Which peripheral equipment might be made available?		
Is it feasible for the initiative to finance the purchase of specific equipment?		
When will resources be available and to whom?		
Who will staff the identified workshops?		
Will additional staff be required to open and secure the premises?		
Will additional technical support be required?		
Will refreshments be available and what are the logistical implications of such provision?		
What are the overall benefits of such provision for the learners?		
Have you completed a full risk assessment in terms of the overall network security and the school's E-safety policy?		
Which specific times and arrangements will be in place to support access to identified pupils as part of the E-portal initiative?		
Are there any specific training issues related to this initiative?		

Available on the net at http://www.james-wright.org

Table 5.2 provides an initial walk-through audit that might be used either as a stand-alone activity or in conjunction with the 'Extending schooling' section of the BECTA self-review matrix. As an item for discussion by your ICT team, it should highlight any specific difficulties that might lie ahead in meeting the inevitable demand of community initiatives.

26th January

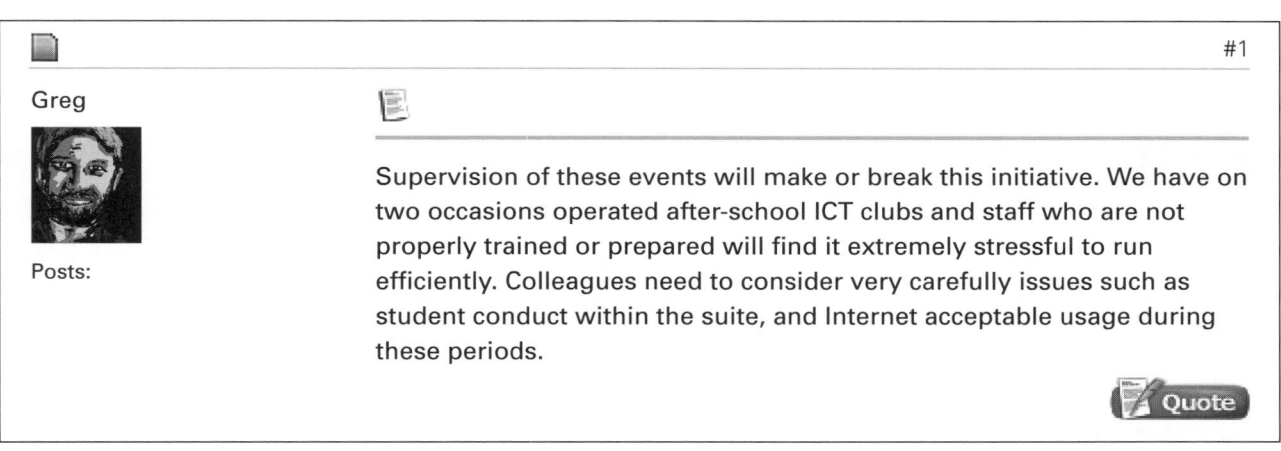

#1

Greg

Posts:

Supervision of these events will make or break this initiative. We have on two occasions operated after-school ICT clubs and staff who are not properly trained or prepared will find it extremely stressful to run efficiently. Colleagues need to consider very carefully issues such as student conduct within the suite, and Internet acceptable usage during these periods.

Quote

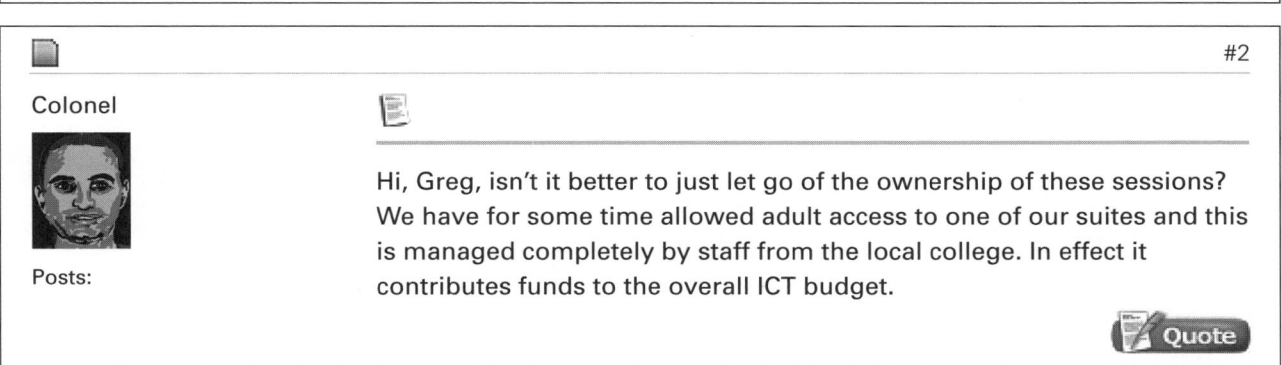

#2

Colonel

Posts:

Hi, Greg, isn't it better to just let go of the ownership of these sessions? We have for some time allowed adult access to one of our suites and this is managed completely by staff from the local college. In effect it contributes funds to the overall ICT budget.

Quote

27th January

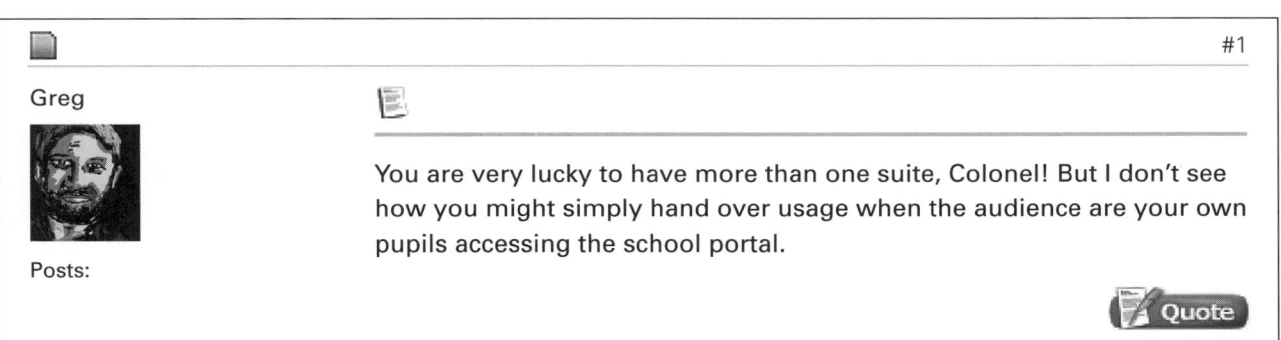

#1

Greg

Posts:

You are very lucky to have more than one suite, Colonel! But I don't see how you might simply hand over usage when the audience are your own pupils accessing the school portal.

Quote

28th January

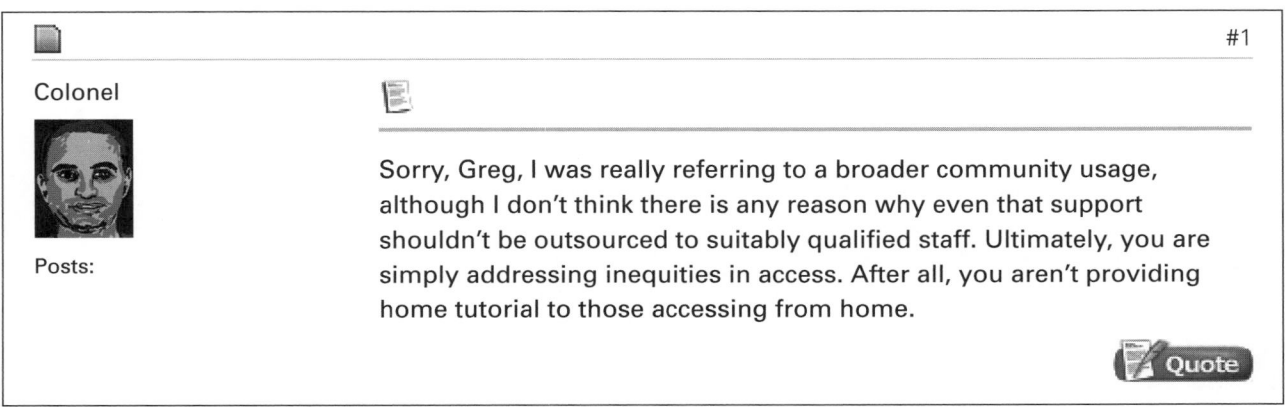

#1

Colonel

Posts:

Sorry, Greg, I was really referring to a broader community usage, although I don't think there is any reason why even that support shouldn't be outsourced to suitably qualified staff. Ultimately, you are simply addressing inequities in access. After all, you aren't providing home tutorial to those accessing from home.

Quote

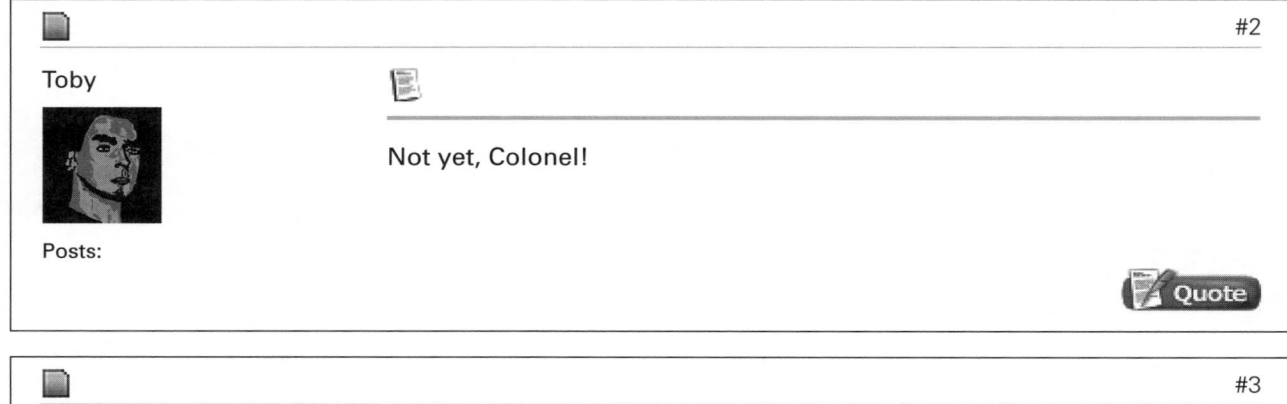

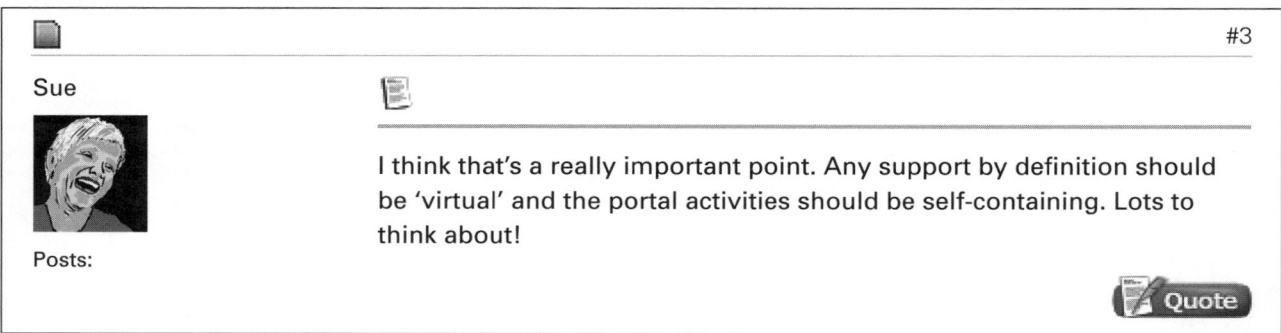

Next month I'd like to broaden our consideration of extended learning to discuss the sorts of extra-curricular opportunities that colleagues are beginning to deliver and suggest some creative alternatives that might be useful. Not unrelated will be our continued look at the development of online learning and the challenges that colleagues face in ensuring that this is fully appropriate for the primary school agenda.

Chapter 6 • *February*

1st February

Week 21, Task 16 – Extended Learning – Extra-Curricular Opportunities 1

Having reviewed the inherent barriers to providing access to ICT resources for extended learning, co-ordinators should now identify precisely what opportunities the school could provide within its extra-curricular provision, over and above any materials that may be accessed by the portal.

Let us consider after-school extra-curricular clubs. Colleagues should look to make the most of the opportunities to extend the curriculum in terms of creativity and collaboration offered by such clubs rather than simply providing raw access, or replication of what is already provided during the core curriculum offer.

This week colleagues should choose a preferred focus for this extra-curricular provision, to adopt a top-down approach to its planning in order for it to fully support existing improvement themes within the schools development.

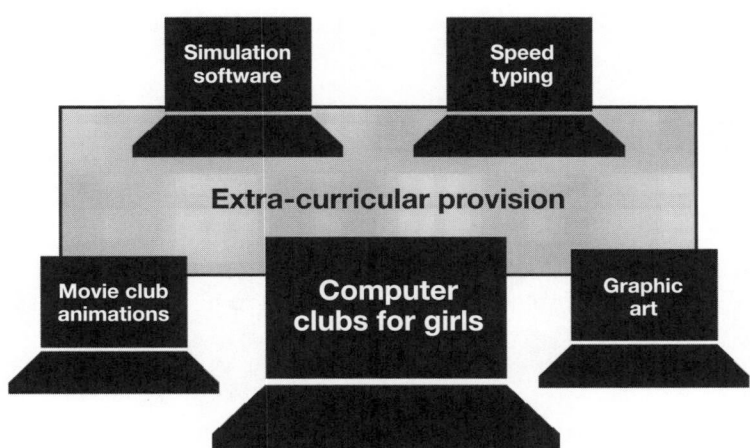

Figure 6.1 Extra curricular provision
Available on the net at http://www.james-wright.org

Figure 6.1 offers a range of themes from which colleagues might choose to direct future clubs. Consider the school's distinctiveness as you select an activity that fits well with your current provision and existing school improvement priorities. Do not be tempted to 'pick and mix'. There is probably a good argument to be made for adopting any or all of the club activities, however your core purpose will be diluted if you do so. Take time to discuss the options with colleagues now before we explore each individual option further.

2nd February

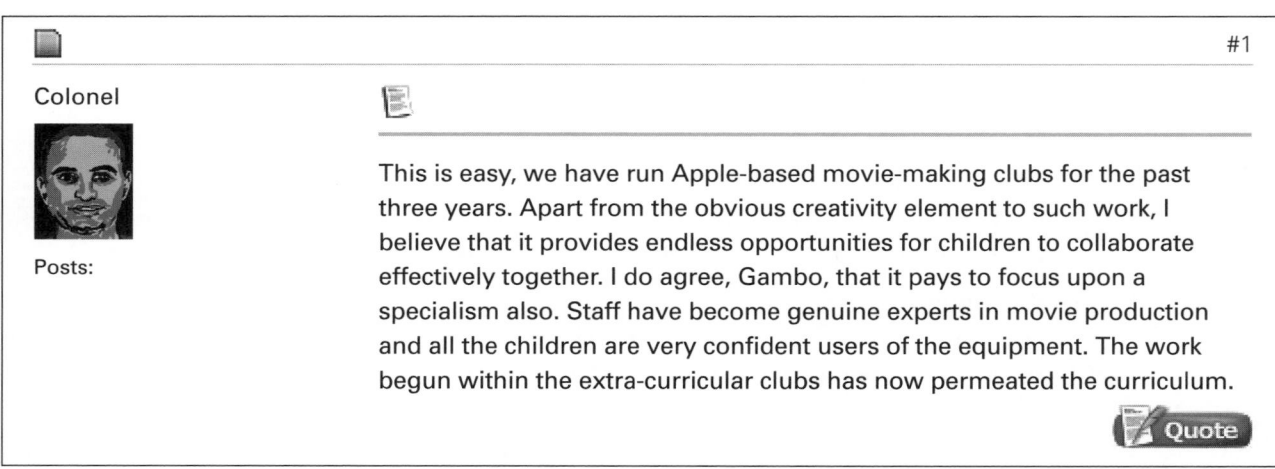

Colonel

Posts:

#1

This is easy, we have run Apple-based movie-making clubs for the past three years. Apart from the obvious creativity element to such work, I believe that it provides endless opportunities for children to collaborate effectively together. I do agree, Gambo, that it pays to focus upon a specialism also. Staff have become genuine experts in movie production and all the children are very confident users of the equipment. The work begun within the extra-curricular clubs has now permeated the curriculum.

Quote

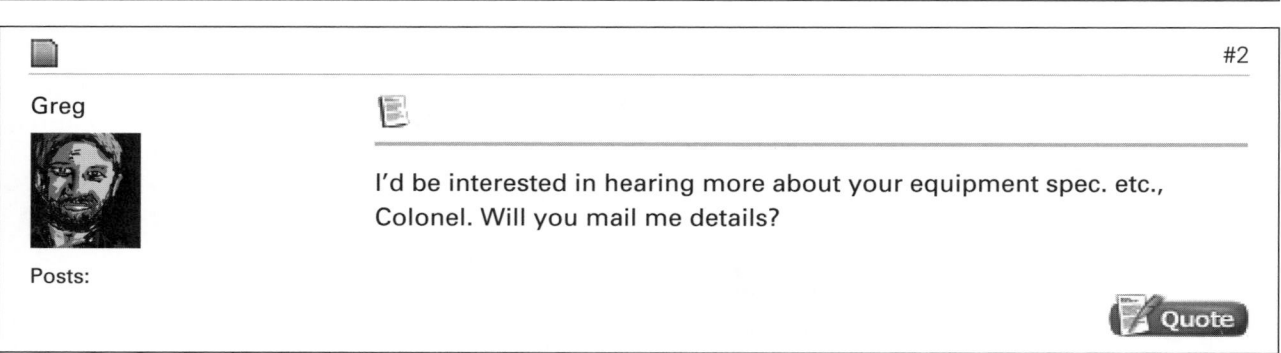

Greg

Posts:

#2

I'd be interested in hearing more about your equipment spec. etc., Colonel. Will you mail me details?

Quote

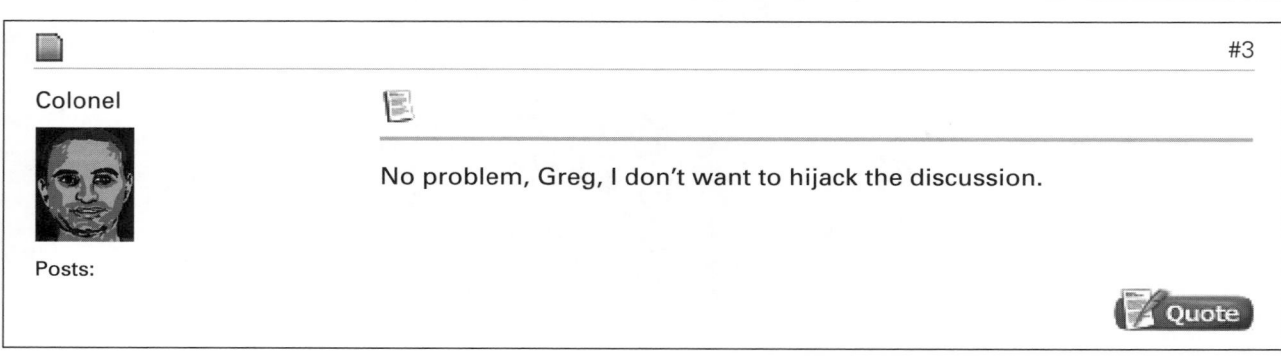

Colonel

Posts:

#3

No problem, Greg, I don't want to hijack the discussion.

Quote

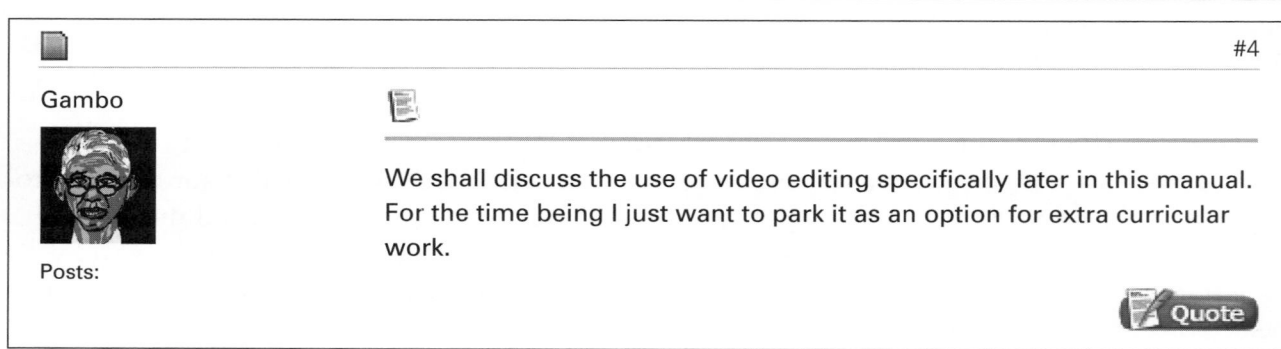

Gambo

Posts:

#4

We shall discuss the use of video editing specifically later in this manual. For the time being I just want to park it as an option for extra curricular work.

Quote

3rd February

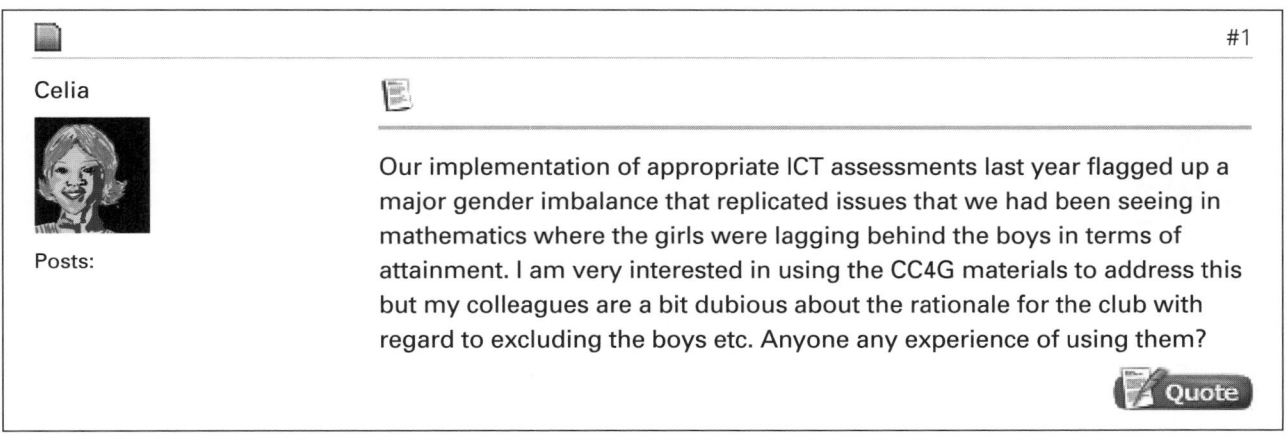

	#1
Celia Posts:	Our implementation of appropriate ICT assessments last year flagged up a major gender imbalance that replicated issues that we had been seeing in mathematics where the girls were lagging behind the boys in terms of attainment. I am very interested in using the CC4G materials to address this but my colleagues are a bit dubious about the rationale for the club with regard to excluding the boys etc. Anyone any experience of using them?

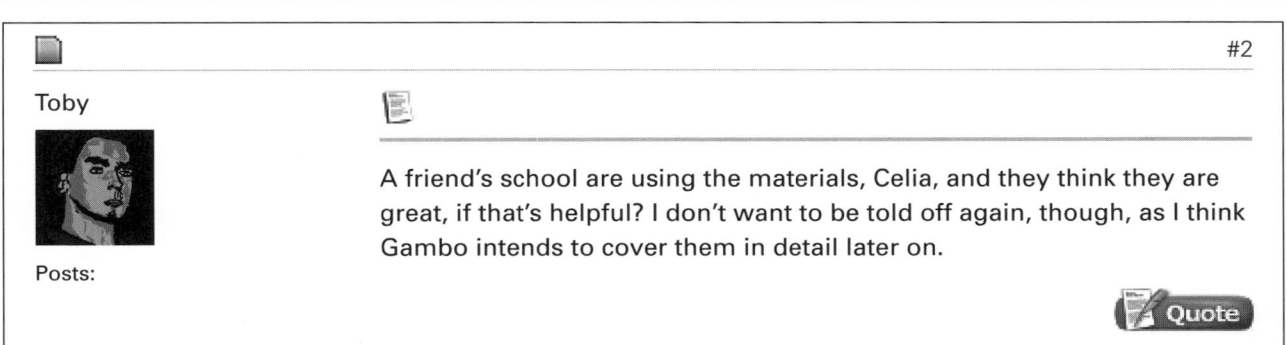

	#2
Toby Posts:	A friend's school are using the materials, Celia, and they think they are great, if that's helpful? I don't want to be told off again, though, as I think Gambo intends to cover them in detail later on.

4th February

This month we are going to give particular consideration to the use of simulation software plus the opportunities that exist for schools to use extra-curricular provision to develop keyboard skills. Consider some of the advantages below.

Simulation software

An after-school club is an ideal opportunity for a school to experiment with the learning potential of state of the art commercial packages. Far and away market leader in this sector is the Sim City series by Electronic Arts Inc. (www.simcity.ea.com). Earlier editions produced by Maxis (www.maxis.com). The possibilities and breadth of learning opportunities are endless, and previous versions of the games such as SimCity 3000 may be acquired extremely cheaply. The city simulator reproduces a virtual world where simulated citizens (Sims) exist and where traffic, commerce, industry, utilities and taxes are graphically reproduced in a stunning format. Pupils learn as they assume the role of mayor managing their creation. Ultimately, insight gained from playing SimCity may be transferred to the real world to support the geography, PSHE and citizenship curricula as well as providing extensive opportunities to exercise mathematics and literacy activities.

Review the usage of the simulation software at Erving Elementary School, Erving, Massachusetts, USA (www.erving.com/simcity2000/index.htm) including lesson plans and advice for implementation. Class teacher Kathleen Bridgewater's philosophy behind the initiative would be well heeded by all colleagues as they embark upon our journey towards embedding E-learning:

'Don't waste students' time ... it's only worthwhile when it helps the children to gain a better sense of the world they inhabit.'

Colleagues looking to develop the use of the Sims resources should also download the educational companion teacher's guide to SimCity 3000 written by Margy Kuntz (2001) and available for free download from the SimCity 3000 website at: www.simcity3000unlimited.ea.com/us/guide/

5th February

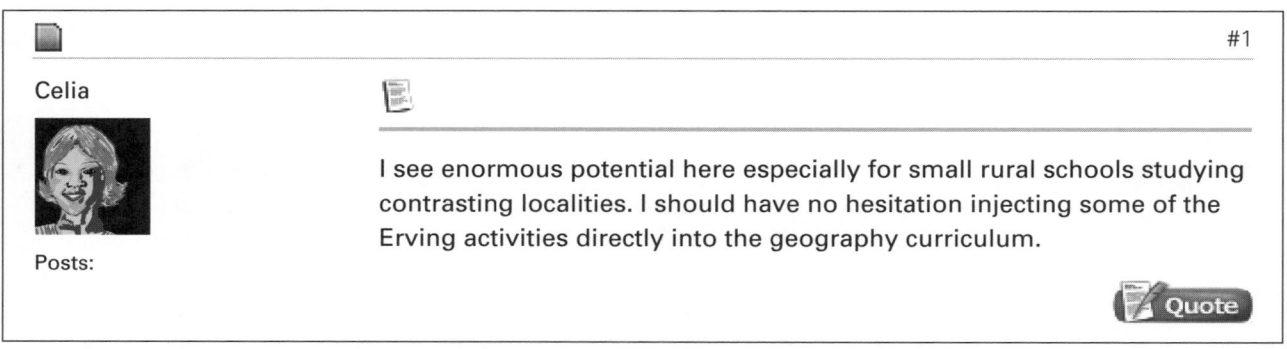

Celia

Posts:

#1

I see enormous potential here especially for small rural schools studying contrasting localities. I should have no hesitation injecting some of the Erving activities directly into the geography curriculum.

Quote

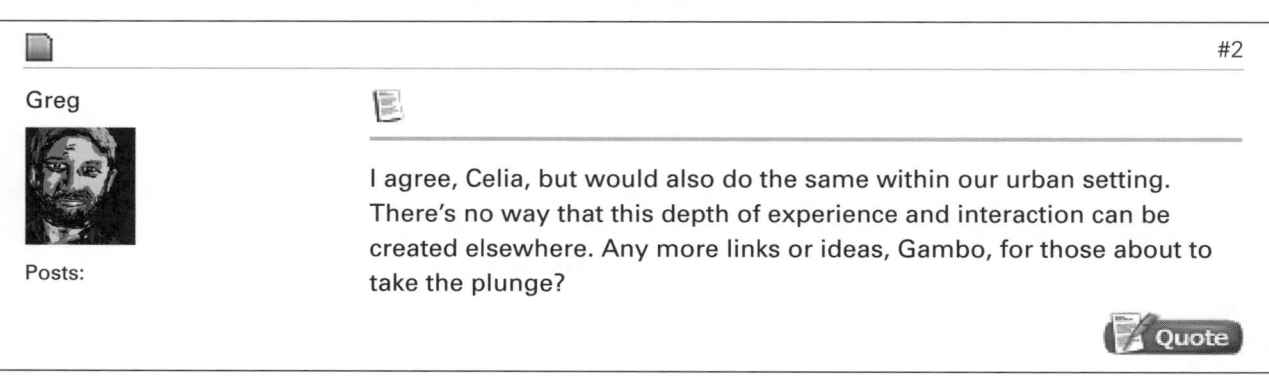

Greg

Posts:

#2

I agree, Celia, but would also do the same within our urban setting. There's no way that this depth of experience and interaction can be created elsewhere. Any more links or ideas, Gambo, for those about to take the plunge?

Quote

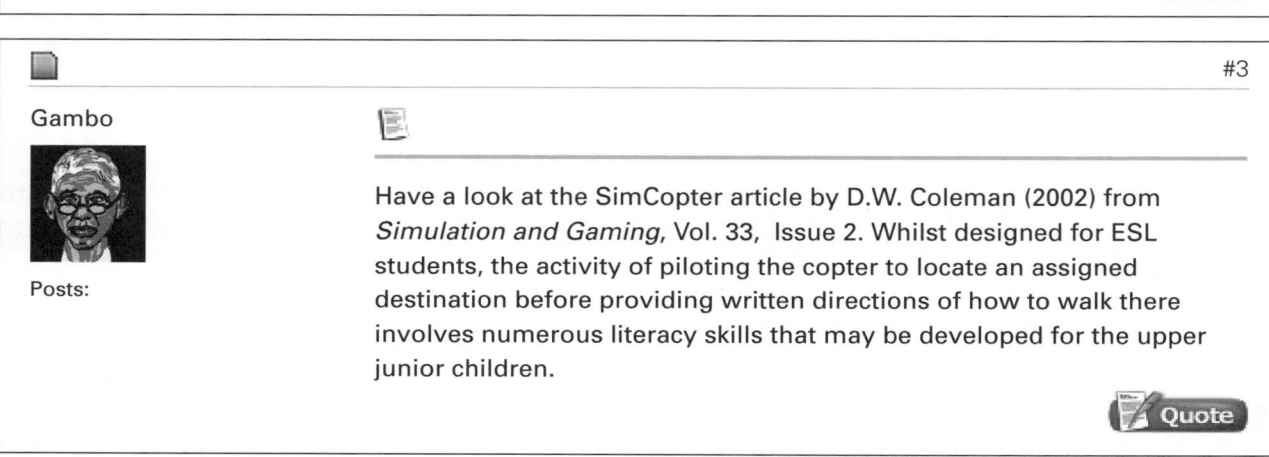

Gambo

Posts:

#3

Have a look at the SimCopter article by D.W. Coleman (2002) from *Simulation and Gaming*, Vol. 33, Issue 2. Whilst designed for ESL students, the activity of piloting the copter to locate an assigned destination before providing written directions of how to walk there involves numerous literacy skills that may be developed for the upper junior children.

Quote

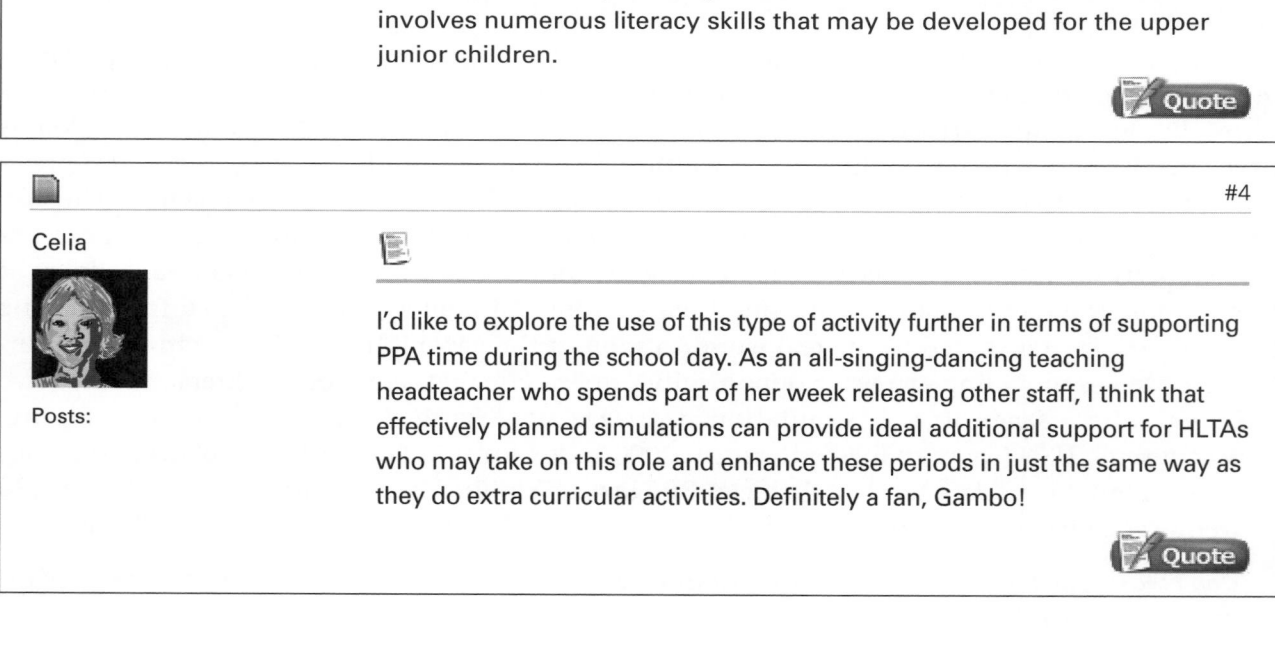

Celia

Posts:

#4

I'd like to explore the use of this type of activity further in terms of supporting PPA time during the school day. As an all-singing-dancing teaching headteacher who spends part of her week releasing other staff, I think that effectively planned simulations can provide ideal additional support for HLTAs who may take on this role and enhance these periods in just the same way as they do extra curricular activities. Definitely a fan, Gambo!

Quote

Keyboard skills

The teaching of keyboard skills is another area not without controversy in primary education. For a number of years teachers have introduced laptop computers into cross-curricular lessons to accommodate replacement activities in which children simply 'typed up' the best copy of their work. Teachers often became frustrated that the children could not type quickly enough and called for ICT lessons to be passed over to speed-typing activities on the basis that if the child could not type effectively then the whole E-learning initiative was fundamentally floored. Hopefully, we have travelled some way since those times and the primary strategy has done a lot of good work in introducing digital literacy and challenging the notion of non-stop word-processing activities with the ubiquitous MS Word.

This may be a good time therefore freed from the historical pedagogical debate to revisit the whole area of keyboard skills as an extra-curricular activity targeting amongst other areas the Every Child Matters (ECM) priority that each child will be able to achieve economic well being.

Whilst the keyboard remains the core access device for most portable computers children will need to acquire prerequisite skills in order to operate one fluently. Most children given appropriate access to ICT will develop their own typing style, however it is undeniable that as these idiosyncratic styles evolve it is frustrating for pupils whose lack of keyboard skills may also impede creative thinking and writing. There is also some debate regarding the relationship between poor keyboard skills and repetitive strain injury (RSI). Colleagues therefore need to assess whether there is a demand within school for structured keyboard practice clubs that will ultimately impact upon curriculum access within the school.

Most 'systems' used in school today are built around commercial software packages which use highly motivational games formats to reinforce 'muscle memory' of basic letter keyboard placements providing repetitive practice of finger positions. Many such systems are available directly via the Internet and therefore lend themselves readily to out-of-school activities. Spend a little time reviewing the materials available from the BBC at www.bbc.co.uk/schools/typing. Also the innovative Free Typing Games website located at www.freetypinggame.net

7th February

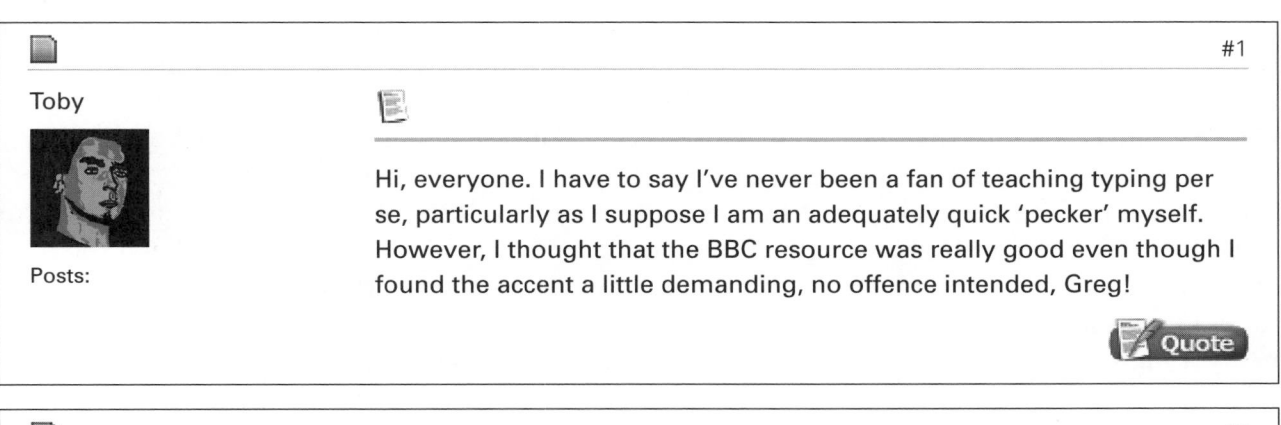

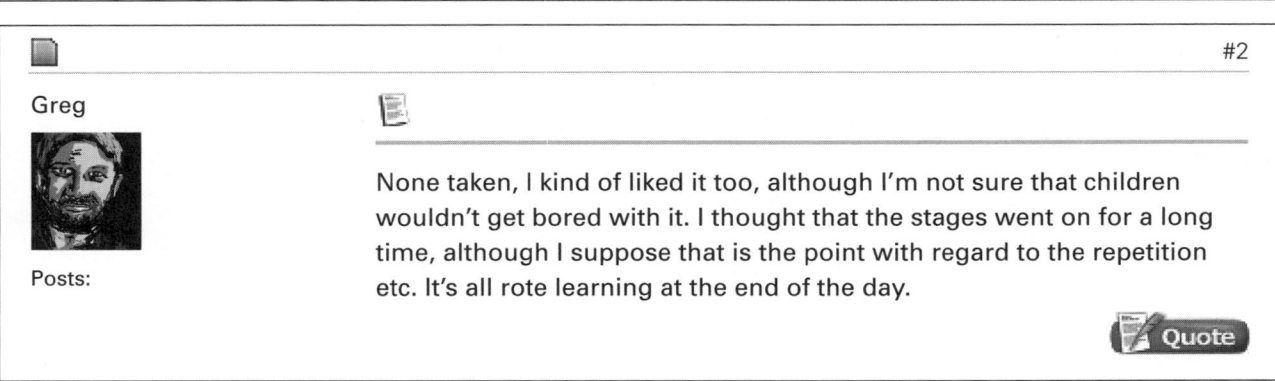

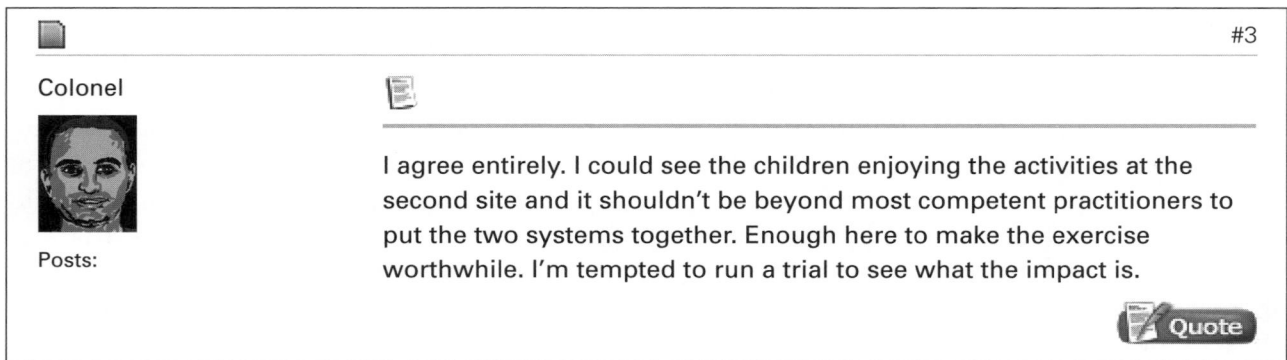

An alternative might be the use of tutor boards representing real keyboards that can therefore be used outside of the ICT suite opening up new opportunities in terms of out of school provision. Many colleagues may be familiar with the Keyboard Crazy concept. This is a freestanding replica QWERTY keyboard into which children slot upper and lower case letter tablets during competitive spelling and grammar activities. In so doing pupils may build up their positional recognition speed as they begin to memorize where each letter sits upon the QUERTY keyboard. Associated software provides reinforcement games similar to those discussed in the previous section. Full details are available from the company's website at www.keyboardcrazy.co.uk where the company offers a variety of trial options.

Next month we will reflect upon two more out-of-school activities, namely, the use of a high-impact graphic art club and a focused review of the DfES sponsored Computer Clubs for Girls initiative.

8th February

Week 23, Task 17 – Online Learning - Developing an Interactive School Website

Last month we reflected upon the challenges of ensuring that online learning initiatives at school remained inclusive and not divisive. Hopefully, colleagues have been able to put into place strategies to take schools forward without penalizing staff, pupils or parents who currently lack online capabilities. For the next two weeks we are going to examine key tenets of a primary model that will address the needs of two of the platform's three core audiences: parents and staff. The third, the pupils, we will examine in March. Within this model I aim to identify key elements within BECTA's core criteria for their Learning Platform Functional Requirements document (2006b) that may confidently be expected to enhance the primary school's learning experience.

Let us begin with some givens. Whichever platform your school adopts should logically fall under some sort of localized umbrella of support. Avoid at all costs being tempted down the road of unilateral experimentation. Do not be tempted by technical support or parental offers to devise something bespoke; invariably this will lead to some unsustainable disaster, as has been learnt by many a high school colleague. If the initiative is planned strategically there should be no technical support issues arising from your learning platform. Ultimately, you will simply have adopted a service that you will pay for and you can then concentrate on establishing the essential outcomes from that service and map them against staff, parent and pupil usage. In particular the extent to which such services facilitate communication between school and staff, school and parent and teacher and pupil.

Staff use of a primary learning platform

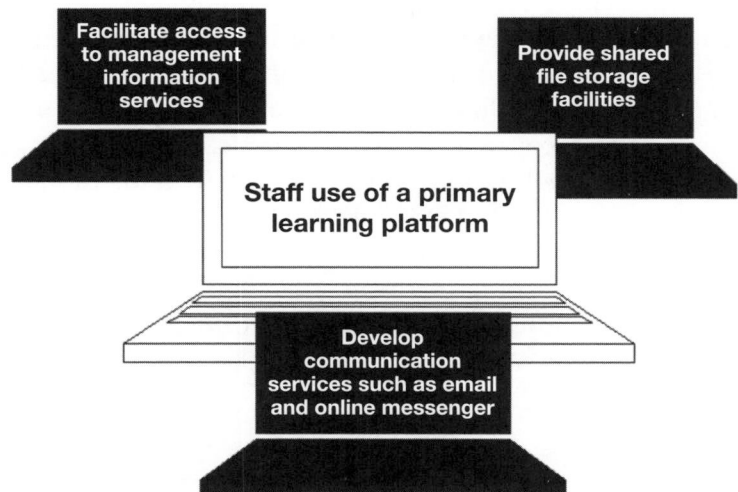

Figure 6.2 Staff use of primary learning platform
Available on the net at http://www.james-wright.org

Figure 6.2 identifies three core areas in which colleagues may anticipate potential gains to be achieved for staff using the portal and which give rise to three essential questions that co-ordinators will wish to resolve this week.

First, are we ready to allow staff greater protected access to information management software in order to improve pupil assessment, record-keeping, tracking and target-setting systems?

Effective schools understand that a core aspect of school self-evaluation is not only the collection of accurate and up-to-date information regarding pupil attainment but, more pertinently, the effective use of that information by staff to produce realistic yet challenging targets for their pupils. Schools may already have effective and secure access to SIMS or similar management software. Colleagues should, however, be aware of the manner in which the learning platform will enable staff to gain greater use of this data and to share it with colleagues. Therefore, in theory the portal could be viewed as a school improvement mechanism that will improve the means by which pupil progress is tracked and resources allocated. Key to the decision to prioritize such usage will be security concerns arising from increased access.

Second, will staff benefit from the provision of always on file-share resources?

Colleagues may already enjoy a server-based planning and activity resource bank that is shared by staff and which over time has begun to noticeably save time by simplifying administrative exercises. Typically these might include whiteboards flip charts and so on as well as core planning resources, although many colleagues will still run their own resource systems operating parallel to the school's. Online file-sharing may be a logical next step that integrates a series of systems and allows teachers to plan and prepare lessons effectively and swiftly either at home or in school. Similarly there is great potential for developing the subject leader role both in terms of collating subject resources and the development of online subject E-portfolios.

In order to move forward in this area, finally (and this list is not intended to be exhaustive but may help to focus discussion), are staff ready to take advantage of the advanced use of email and messenger communication services?

An effective learning platform will provide the school with integrated email, web-boards and live online messenger services as potential means to improve communication across the school. Unless you work within a very large three- to four-form primary it is unlikely that communication is seen as a problem within school. However, briefing notes, memos, and so on can be very effectively absorbed within electronic systems without staff feeling that they are being turned into metronomes and denied basic human interactions. Some schools will, and have, absorbed such systems and quickly accommodated messenger contact groups that simply add an extra dimension to existing systems; however, for many, such moves will be seen as undesirable at the present time.

Colleagues will need to be prepared to 'enforce' email use, should it be adopted, or you will quickly be confronted with chaos should most staff adopt this as a means of communicating memos, briefings and so on, and certain colleagues decide to boycott the system. It is reasonable having established such a system for school leadership to expect staff to log in daily if adequate training is provided and time allocated to do so. Staff will quickly object if this task becomes burdensome.

In conclusion, my own thoughts are that currently staff are unlikely to see their working day transformed by the advent of a learning platform, although over time there are going to be benefits that will become apparent – more of a gradual evolution rather than a revolution at the present time.

12th February

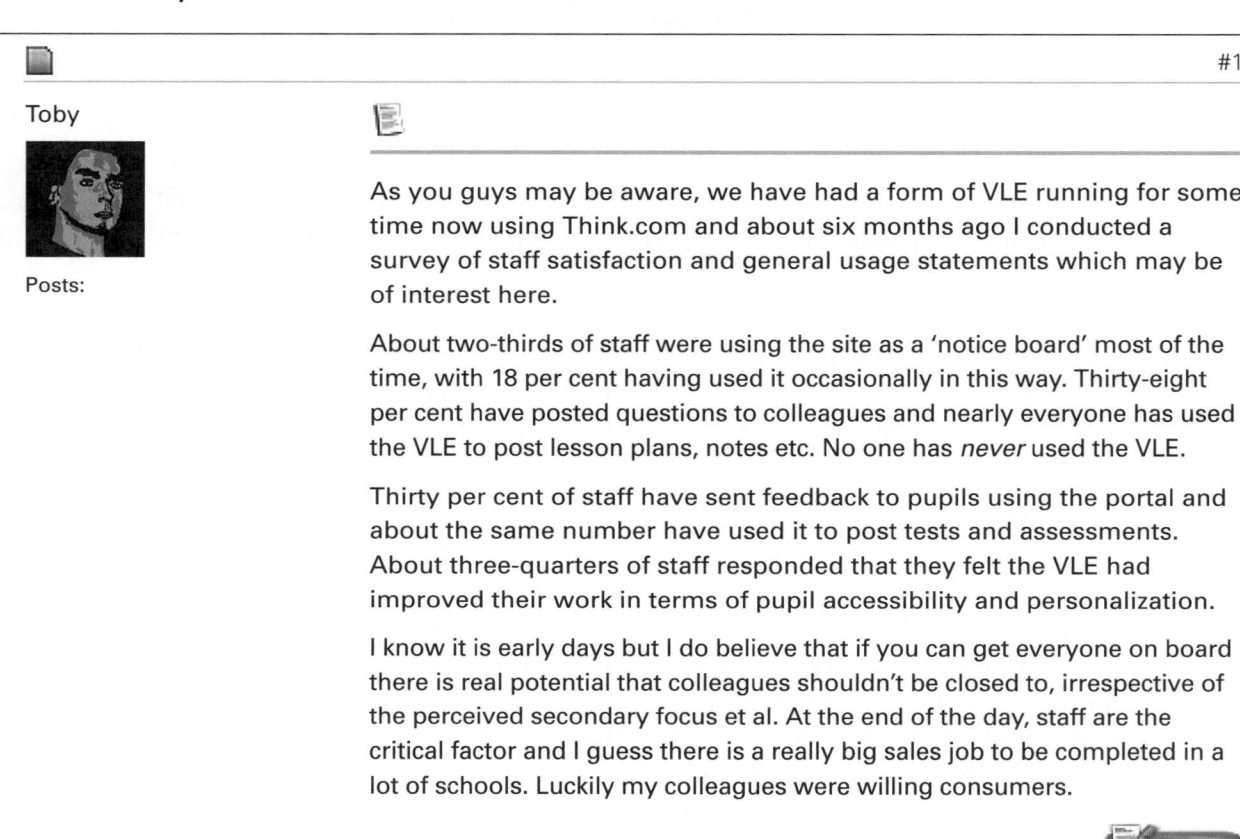

#1

Toby

Posts:

As you guys may be aware, we have had a form of VLE running for some time now using Think.com and about six months ago I conducted a survey of staff satisfaction and general usage statements which may be of interest here.

About two-thirds of staff were using the site as a 'notice board' most of the time, with 18 per cent having used it occasionally in this way. Thirty-eight per cent have posted questions to colleagues and nearly everyone has used the VLE to post lesson plans, notes etc. No one has *never* used the VLE.

Thirty per cent of staff have sent feedback to pupils using the portal and about the same number have used it to post tests and assessments. About three-quarters of staff responded that they felt the VLE had improved their work in terms of pupil accessibility and personalization.

I know it is early days but I do believe that if you can get everyone on board there is real potential that colleagues shouldn't be closed to, irrespective of the perceived secondary focus et al. At the end of the day, staff are the critical factor and I guess there is a really big sales job to be completed in a lot of schools. Luckily my colleagues were willing consumers.

 Quote

#2

Greg

Posts:

Very impressive, Toby! You really are beginning to cut it, I can see now why Gambo asked you to chair the forum. But you are right to recognize that staff aren't all at the same level of readiness. I still believe that we have some base ICT skill levels to address before asking some teachers about advanced ICT usage, however I salute you.

 Quote

14th February

Parental use of a primary learning platform

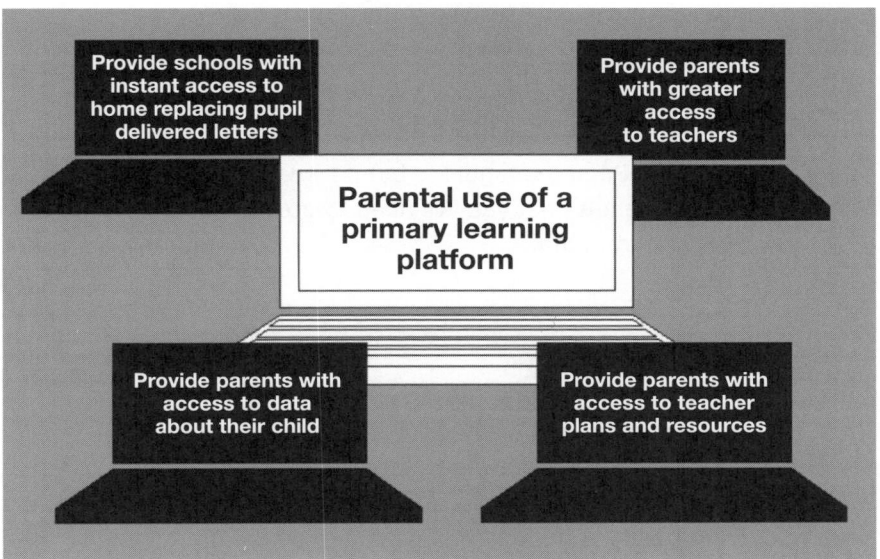

Figure 6.3 Parental use of primary learning platform
Available on the net at http://www.james-wright.org

As with staff usage it is important for colleagues to identify core outcomes that are achievable and desirable in terms of parental usage of any proposed learning platform. Figure 6.3 identifies four clear areas where this might be pertinent for your school.

The first two points I shall deal with together as they are essentially two sides of the same improved communications link. Over a reasonably short period of time it may be expected that many, though not all, parents will choose to receive school communication via email, online postings or text messenger and alerts rather than their children conveying home hard-copy letters. This simply reflects movements in the wider culture such as online banking, utility accounts, and so on. Sceptics nearly always make the mistake of underestimating the extent to which such processes have very rapidly become embedded within the wider society. Notwithstanding the access and inclusion issues raised in the previous chapter, there are obvious savings to be made in terms of environmental impact, time and cost savings through reduced reprographics overheads, and so on. Also, electronic communication is instant and not reliant upon a child to deliver copy nor subject to the bottomless pit of time necessary to chase up and confirm receipt of such letters. Homework reminders and so on will be posted online or emailed to parents and a lot of the current ambiguities with regard to our expectations of homework may be removed. Of course, not all parents will want this sort of service and, in the short term at least, alternative parallel arrangements will need to be maintained. A parents' register will have to be compiled with due regard to data protection, and schools will need to provide clear guidelines for staff on the use of such mail ensuring that agreed procedures are consistently applied and requiring agreement from both staff and governors.

16th February

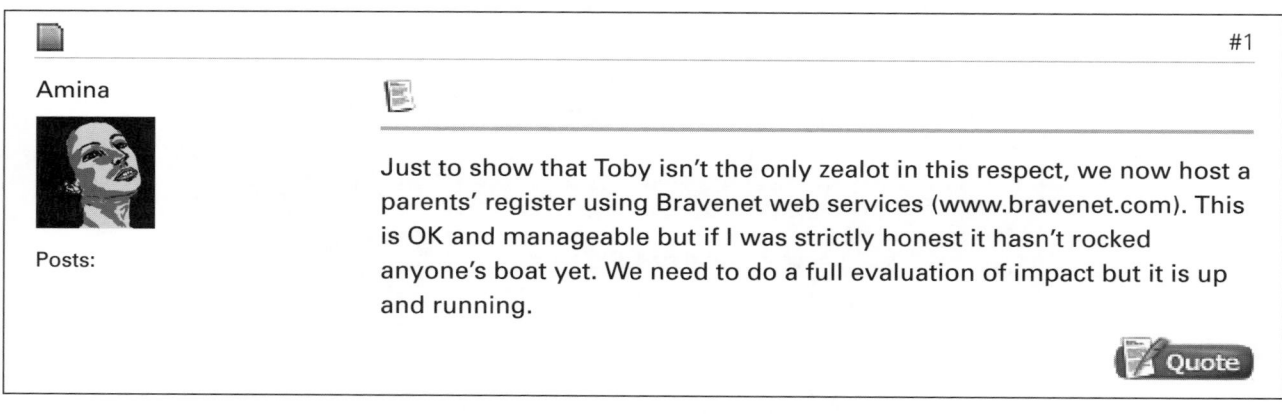

#1

Amina

Posts:

Just to show that Toby isn't the only zealot in this respect, we now host a parents' register using Bravenet web services (www.bravenet.com). This is OK and manageable but if I was strictly honest it hasn't rocked anyone's boat yet. We need to do a full evaluation of impact but it is up and running.

Quote

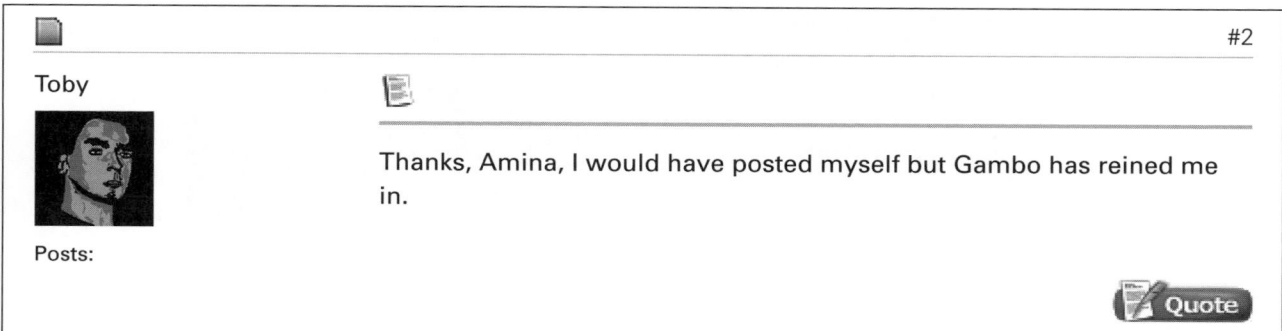

#2

Toby

Posts:

Thanks, Amina, I would have posted myself but Gambo has reined me in.

Quote

18th February

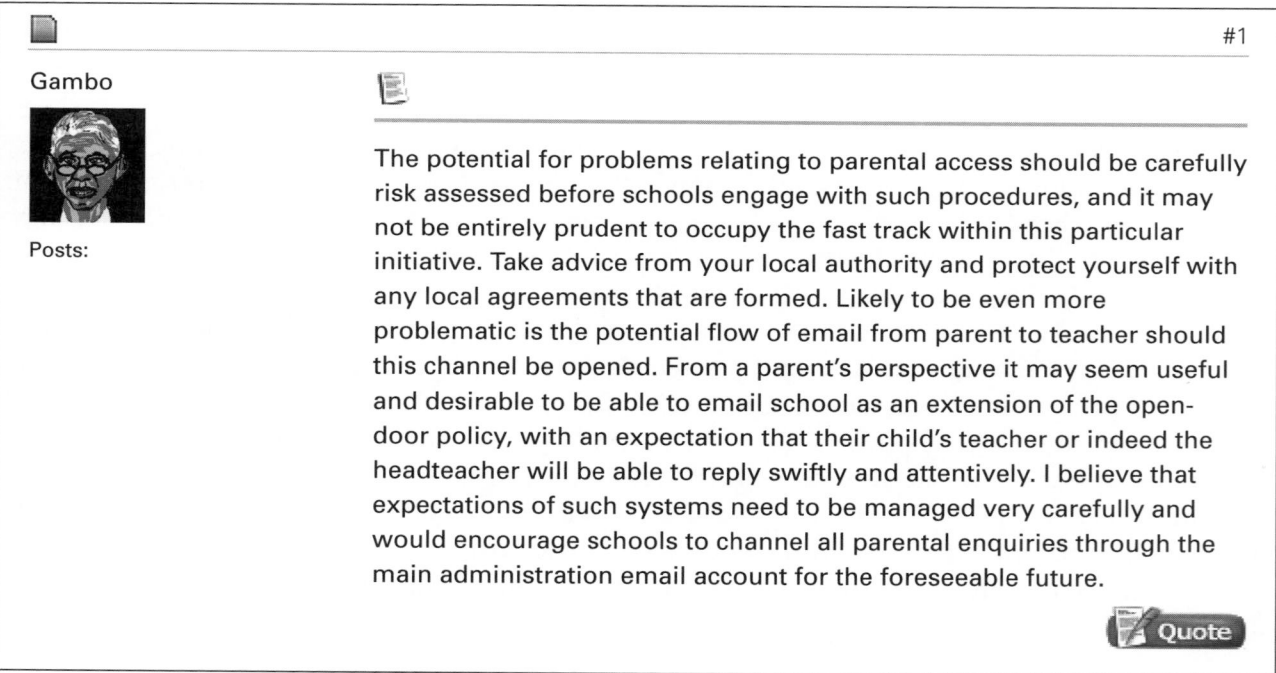

#1

Gambo

Posts:

The potential for problems relating to parental access should be carefully risk assessed before schools engage with such procedures, and it may not be entirely prudent to occupy the fast track within this particular initiative. Take advice from your local authority and protect yourself with any local agreements that are formed. Likely to be even more problematic is the potential flow of email from parent to teacher should this channel be opened. From a parent's perspective it may seem useful and desirable to be able to email school as an extension of the open-door policy, with an expectation that their child's teacher or indeed the headteacher will be able to reply swiftly and attentively. I believe that expectations of such systems need to be managed very carefully and would encourage schools to channel all parental enquiries through the main administration email account for the foreseeable future.

Quote

20th February

I welcome opportunities for any school to improve the manner in which it communicates with its parental body and by 2010 all parents should have access to a managed learning environment. As colleagues plan for this eventuality they should begin to consider the extent to which teachers' plans and digital resources are provided within learning platforms. Carefully consider what is already available via conventional methods, newsletters, topic plans, and so on and how these may be enhanced. Be aware of the big picture, school improvement priorities, subject objectives, and so on all may be shared via the learning portal in a cohesive and organized manner that will improve communication and ultimately personalization as this filters down into class- and pupil-level information.

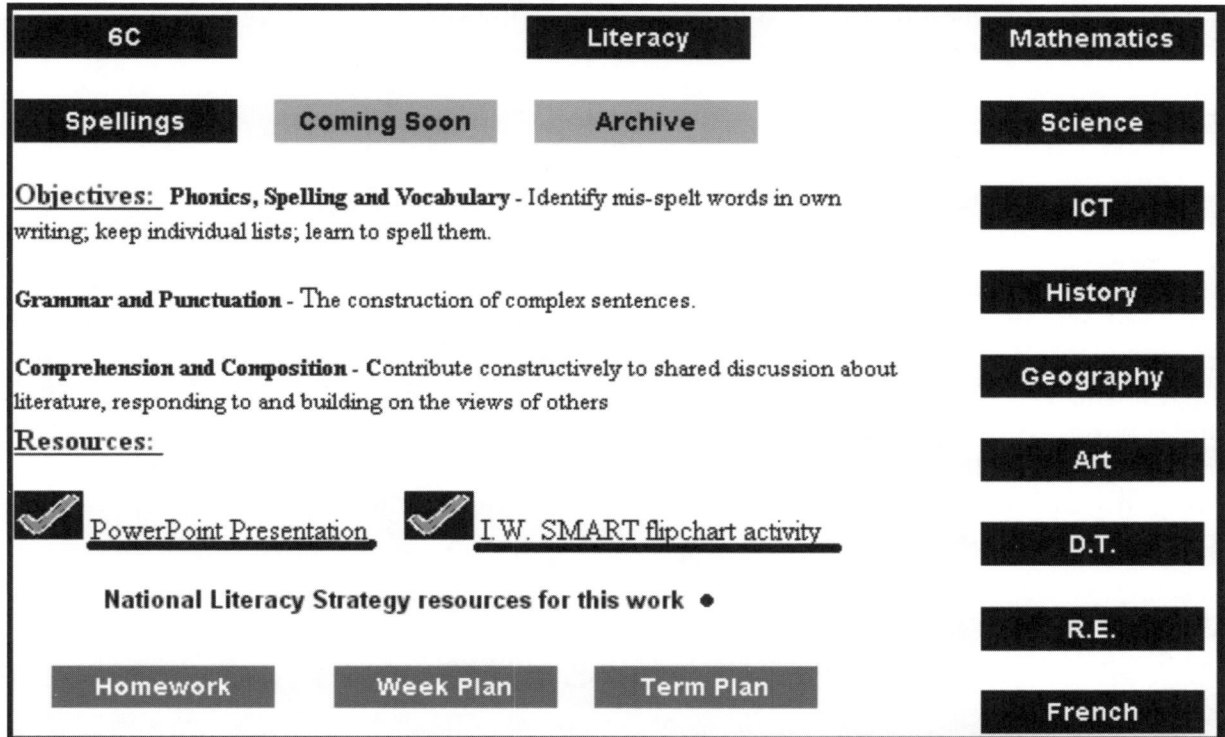

Figure 6.4 Parents' portal
Available on the net at http://www.james-wright.org

Figure 6.4 gives an example of how this may materialize in practice from a parent's perspective. Models will of course vary, and schools may decide that it is actually easier to provide restricted access to areas of the teacher's own resource portal. It is a useful exercise to use the graphic as a starting point or by drawing up your own version as a means of stimulating debate within the school. Colleagues will be only too aware of the staffroom adage that a little knowledge can be a very dangerous thing, and any profession should be cautious about the information that it shares. Some parents will always believe that they can do a better job than staff and too much detail regarding planning and so on may indeed prove to be counterproductive.

21st February

The final element highlighted within Figure 6.3 demonstrated the point that parents will ultimately use the portal to access specific data relating to their own child. In effect this refers to pupil data currently stored upon the school's MIS system, for example attendance data and assessment results. Schools must decide which elements of this data are to be made available to their parental body. Clearly, this is an area where schools need to take very careful heed of local guidance. Products such as Capita's 'Parents' Gateway' (www.parentsgateway.com) will manage this process quite efficiently providing secure web-based access to individual student data directly from a school management system.

'As a personalised website and communication tool Parents' Gateway enables the school to present a consistent image of effective management and one committed to improving student performance.' (www.parentsgateway.com/index.html)

Take a look at the system's website and if you have not already done so, begin to envisage what impact, if any, such structures would have within your school. Which obstacles will need to be overcome and what if any impact upon standards will be offered by such an initiative?

There is an enormous amount for colleagues to consider before we go on next month to look at pupil use of a primary learning platform.

23rd February

Week 24, Task 18 – Able, Gifted and Talented Provision within ICT

The third activity for this month relates to provision for able, gifted and talented children specifically with regard to their ICT abilities. Aware of the amount of material already covered, I am happy for this to be a relatively brief introduction before we look in more detail at some of the cross-curricular usage issues in March. Your first task in this regard is to work with your special needs co-ordinator and review the extent to which the school's register of gifted and talented children includes pupils whose special ability lies in the field of ICT. Do not be too surprised if currently there are no children listed, but do be prepared to open a conversation about identification.

According to the National Curriculum guidance on teaching the gifted and talented, pupils who are gifted in ICT are likely to:

- *Demonstrate ICT capability significantly above that expected for their age*
- *Learn and apply new ICT techniques quickly*
- *Use initiative to exploit the potential of more advanced features of ICT tools*
- *Transfer and apply ICT skills and techniques confidently in new contexts*
- *Explore independently beyond the given breadth of an ICT topic*
- *Initiate ideas and solve problems, use ICT effectively and creatively, develop systems that meet personal needs and interests.* (Source: www.nc.uk.net/gt/ict/index.htm)

When identifying pupils who are gifted in ICT, national guidance also points out that pupils may not be gifted in all aspects of the subject, rather their talents may lie within a specific strand.

Make a judgement with regard to how proactive you have been previously when identifying talents in ICT. Given the extent of home access to computing equipment, it is quite likely that schools underestimate the numbers of pupils capable of exceeding the National Curriculum expectations.

If this area is not something that you currently feel confident in, spend some time reviewing the materials on the QCA site which deals specifically with identification, inclusion issues, teaching strategies including the development of both key skills and thinking skills, exemplar units of work, and provision and monitoring strategies. It would be a very useful exercise if you produced a summary document that reflected your practice, which could be presented to all staff.

28th February

Next month, having developed your own understanding of the key tenets of ICT usage with regard to gifted pupils, we shall discuss how ICT is now being used as a means to develop pupils' talents in different areas of the curriculum.

Chapter 7 • March

1st March

Week 25, Task 19 – Online Learning – Pupil Access to Learning Resources

Having reflected upon the use of online learning resources by staff and parents, it is necessary now to go to the heart of the personalization agenda and to clarify the school's strategy for ensuring that the portal will provide a pupils' area where children may access meaningful resources from home that will enhance and extend their learning experience, notwithstanding the overriding proviso that any initiative does not unnecessarily marginalize pupils without the appropriate home resources to benefit from the initiative.

In setting its priorities schools must be mindful of two powerful factors that will drive the initiative: first, the core criteria that have been set out for any learning platform within BECTA's Learning Platform Functional Requirements document (2006b); second, any regional or authority-wide activities that may deliver some quick wins in this area. Otherwise proceed with caution and anticipate resistance.

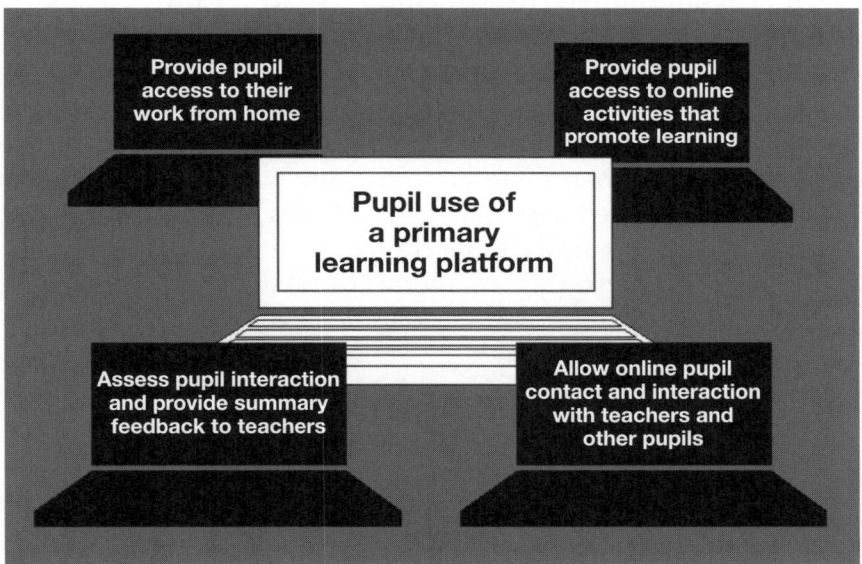

Figure 7.1 Pupil use of a primary learning platform
Available on the net at http://www.james-wright.org

Within Figure 7.1 I have identified four key activities that colleagues may wish to address, all of which relate to areas defined as 'Core Services' by the DfES within their 2005 primary learning platform summary.

The first area to consider and central to the service is the function by which pupils working away from school either at home or at a library or extended service location may use the Internet to safely access their school-based files and folders. Colleagues should consider the access continuum depicted in Figure 7.2

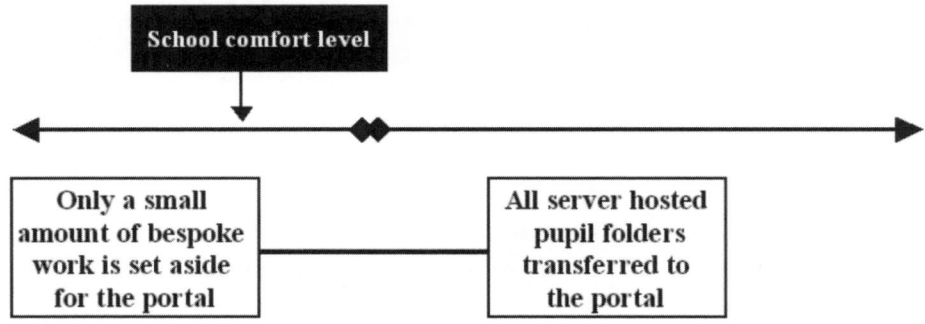

Figure 7.2 Resource access continuum
Available on the net at http://www.james-wright.org

For many schools this challenge will inevitably offer opportunities, for example schools may be able to solve long-standing server problems related to file storage by transferring all pupil folders directly to the Internet and allow access via the portal. Technically this may provide some problems as the Internet in effect becomes a potential bottleneck particularly if there is a shared local authority wide area network (WAN) which can create a logjam at certain peak times. However, that aside, there are clearly advantages to be gained by moving all of the pupils' work currently stored and managed upon the network server to a remotely handled web server. It is clear to see how for many schools this may be perceived as a significant step forward. The main problem, however, is not technical but more related to policy. Do schools want parents to have access to every piece of work that a child stores within their folder? Always best at these times, I think, to move away from the purely theoretical to make direct comparisons to established school practices. Imagine for a moment that, rather than access to ICT files, we were considering a pupil's written work. Schools already have the opportunity to send home all of their books each night for homework to be completed and then returned, providing a continuous loop seamlessly connecting home and school. I have worked with many schools but have yet to encounter such a system, as schools quite rightly prefer homework to be completed in a separate book for obvious reasons. Why should ICT be different? Maybe this is something best left for the blog to consider?

3rd March

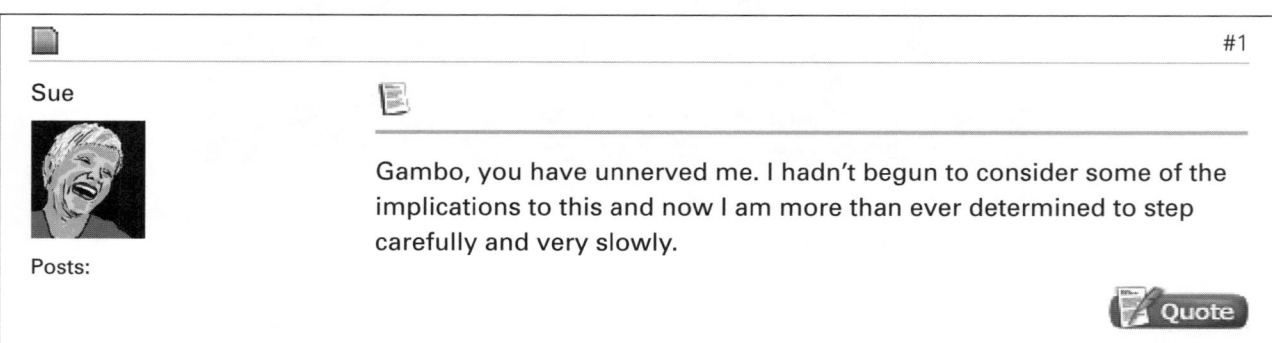

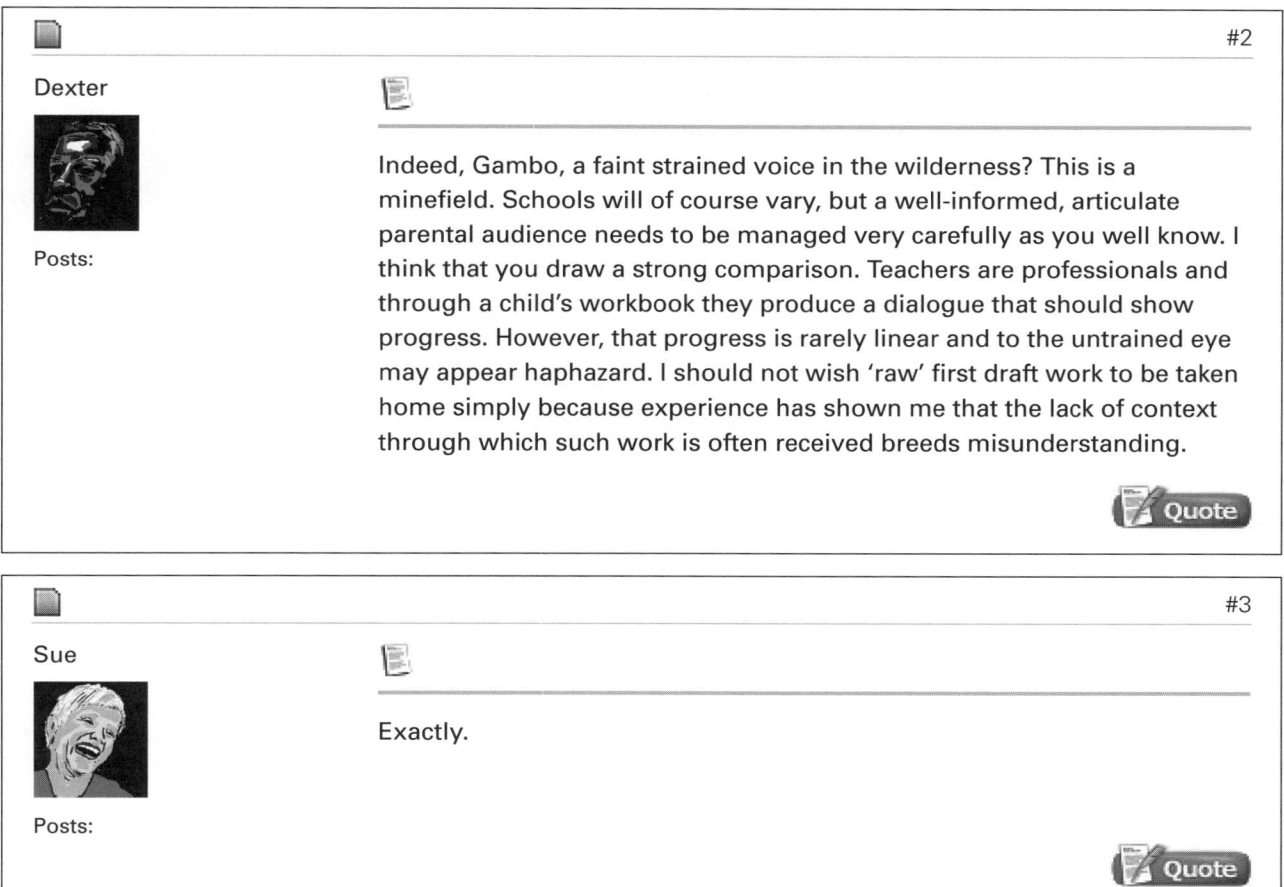

	#2
Dexter Posts:	Indeed, Gambo, a faint strained voice in the wilderness? This is a minefield. Schools will of course vary, but a well-informed, articulate parental audience needs to be managed very carefully as you well know. I think that you draw a strong comparison. Teachers are professionals and through a child's workbook they produce a dialogue that should show progress. However, that progress is rarely linear and to the untrained eye may appear haphazard. I should not wish 'raw' first draft work to be taken home simply because experience has shown me that the lack of context through which such work is often received breeds misunderstanding.

	#3
Sue Posts:	Exactly.

5th March

The potential for problems relating to pupil access should be carefully risk assessed before schools engage with such procedures. Take advice from your local authority and, wherever possible, steer your initiative within a wider context. I should be interested to hear a counter-view if there is one out there. Whatever one's stance there is no doubt that releasing access to all of a child's ICT work is going to raise a number of issues. Strategically it might be a good idea to revisit the audit of folders that you completed last year as part of the assessment and standards work that we reviewed. Were you overwhelmed by the quality and quantity of work within each pupil's folder? Schools may decide that the work which a pupil accesses via the portal is restricted to specific activities, particularly, in the first instance, activities that can be very carefully managed.

The second category deals specifically with the nature and content of the actual out-of-school activities used. This will be a whole-school, cross-curricular initiative involving a broad range of subject areas, indeed when one considers thoroughly the adoption of a learning platform one quickly realizes that a prerequisite to its adoption is an established, mature and evolved use of ICT across the curriculum.

Having accepted following the previous discourse that there are certain architectural issues within a pupil access system, one now needs to consider specifically which if any activities the school is able and willing to deliver to its pupils. One option is for colleagues to approach subject leaders in order for them to identify extension activities, online animated resources and tasks within their subject with which to readily populate the platform. However, it may initially be prudent to focus upon essential core activities. At this point it is also worth deconstructing the popular suggestion that any computer-based activity will inevitably be 'enjoyed' by children.

To a large extent the 'honeymoon period' for computers is over and it is not a given that a PC-based activity will inspire pupils' attention. It would be completely wrong to assume that all activity directed to homes via the learning platform will automatically have children abandoning gaming stations to spend the evening working upon directed activities.

Schools should therefore adopt a core strategy that seeks to support existing homework policy, practices and activities in the initial phase of implementation before evolving new and exciting channels of activities, discussion forum, and so on. This is a whole-school issue and it is for the senior management of the school to decide how the new learning platform services are intended to supplement existing homework strategies. When adopting any learning platform, schools have to make fundamental decisions regarding basic primary pedagogy that lie behind it, and E-learning co-ordinators will by and large be tasked with implementing these fundamental decisions.

Table 7.1 Learning platform content audit

Year group	Current core H/W provision	Subject leader identified priorities	E-learning drivers	Proposal
Reception				
Year 1				
Year 2				
Year 3				
Year 4				
Year 5				
Year 6				

Available on the net at http://www.james-wright.org

Your core activity at this time should be to promote early discussion with regard to what these activities will look like. Take reading, for example, an ever-present link between home and school. What happens to reading programmes once the portal is in place and the key architecture through which homework is managed?

Table 7.1 presents an initial audit of provision that colleagues may wish to introduce as a means to establishing an understanding across the school of where this initiative might ultimately lead and in so doing highlight the major issues prevalent for your school.

8th March

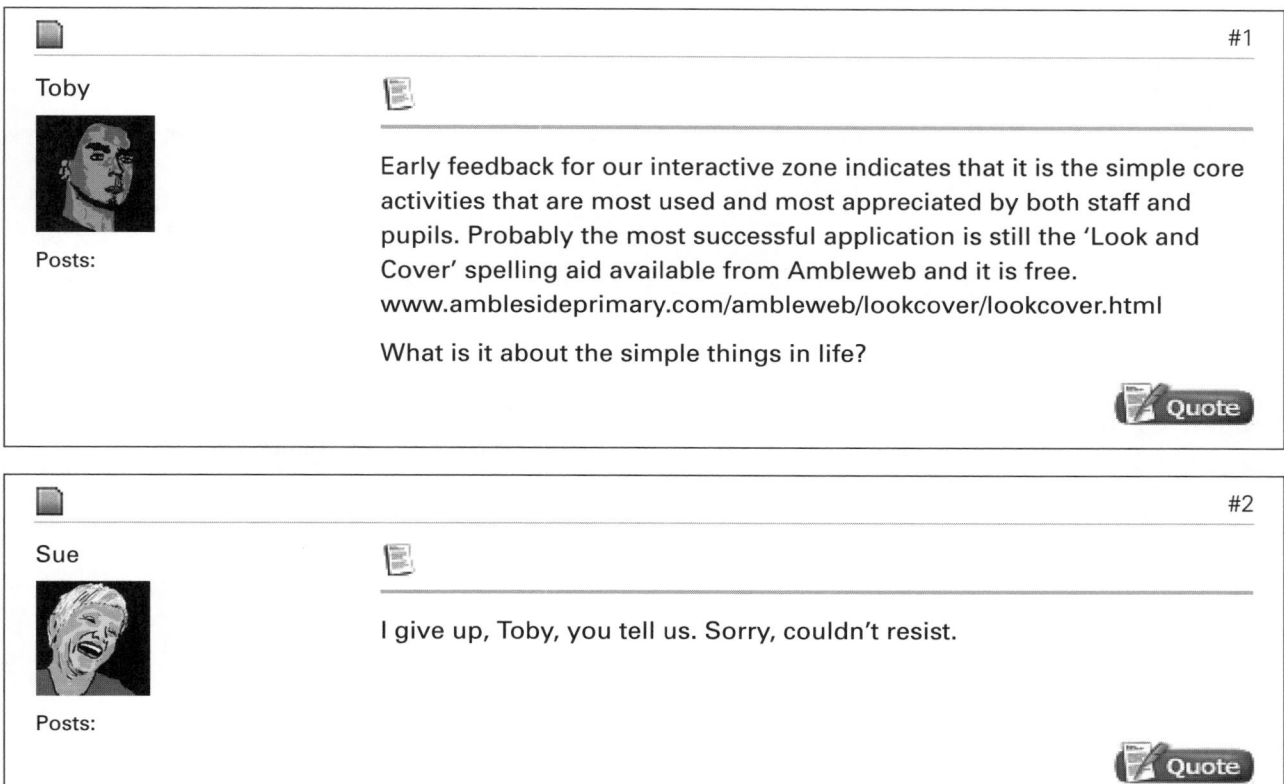

Toby

Posts:

Early feedback for our interactive zone indicates that it is the simple core activities that are most used and most appreciated by both staff and pupils. Probably the most successful application is still the 'Look and Cover' spelling aid available from Ambleweb and it is free. www.amblesideprimary.com/ambleweb/lookcover/lookcover.html

What is it about the simple things in life?

#1

Quote

#2

Sue

Posts:

I give up, Toby, you tell us. Sorry, couldn't resist.

Quote

10th March

The third element that should be planned into provision relates to the outcome of pupil activity and how it is presented to staff. Many teachers are concerned that the only product of any learning platform will be a major increase in marking tasks as a direct result of the additional activity generated. It is essential that work planned into the system utilizes ICT's ability to evaluate, diagnose and summarize outcomes against preset criteria. In effect, an efficient learning platform will manage the activity and take out traditional checking and administrative burdens. Children who do not complete assignments will be immediately highlighted, parents may be notified and fresh tasks assigned automatically without teachers having to scrutinize all tasks or spend vital time and energies interrogating pupils. Summary reports created by the content will form part of teacher assessments and indicate next-steps activities. There is, of course, a challenge here with regard to the provision of learning content and the danger that a learning platform will automate current practice and produce a highly constrained system that children will avoid using. Colleagues need to consider carefully the value of each additional tool that is introduced and not lose sight of the fact that, like any other piece of equipment, the platform is ultimately just another tool to support learning and teaching.

Essentially this is what any learning platform does; it brings together curriculum and tracking systems with an organizational architecture that manages pupil interaction. To many it invokes the archetypal 'sausage factory' approach to learning and may appear increasingly remote from the Web 2.0 Internet world our children are growing up with. Primary schools must not settle into accepting lightly such 'hand-me-down' systems.

12th March

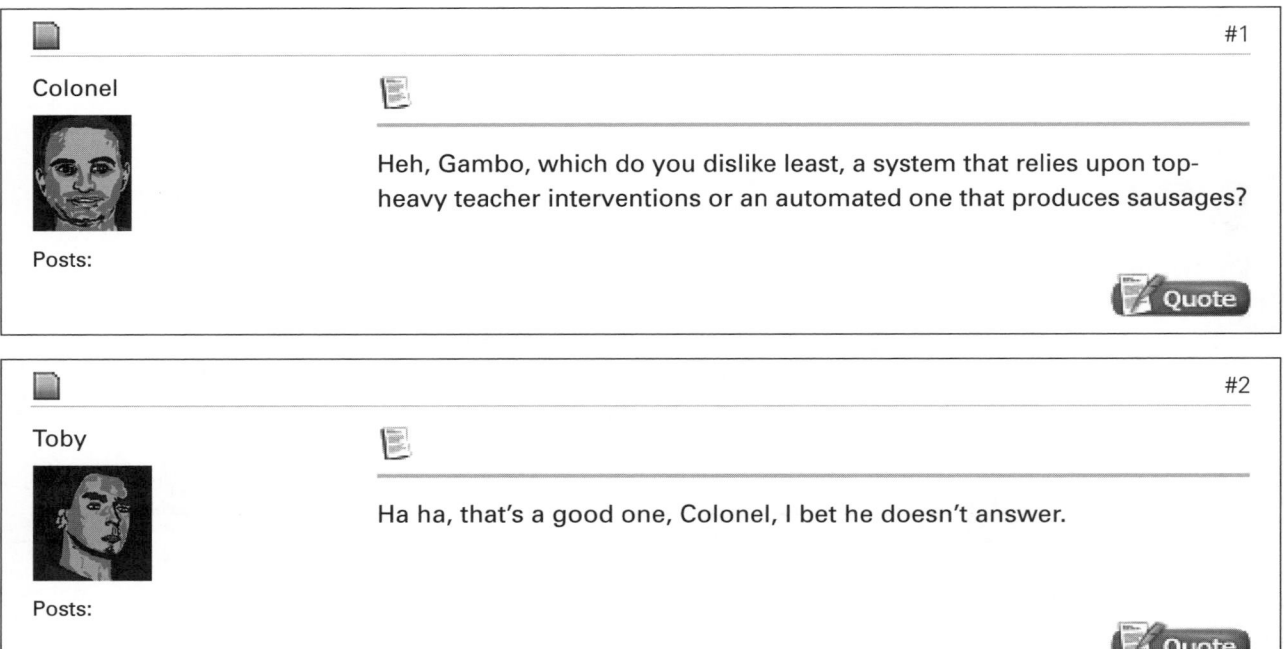

#1

Colonel

Posts:

Heh, Gambo, which do you dislike least, a system that relies upon top-heavy teacher interventions or an automated one that produces sausages?

Quote

#2

Toby

Posts:

Ha ha, that's a good one, Colonel, I bet he doesn't answer.

Quote

13th March

The final aspect to consider, and probably the most radical and innovative component of the learning platform, will be the communication tools that it presents – tools for pupils to communicate with other pupils, with their teacher and with other teachers or tutors from anywhere in the world. This in itself is an enormous area for discussion and will raise again many of the concerns discussed during the E-safety debate. Platforms will provide 'walled gardens' to handle such communications securely but schools will need to manage the wider implications of such tools. Such systems will offer curriculum opportunities during the school day, which colleagues may use to innovate practice, particularly in terms of communicating with pupils from other schools, and so on. However, at this stage you may wish to concentrate upon identifying the core implications of such tools within the home–school extended learning debate. BECTA's functional requirements (2006b) only actually identify one mandatory tool or service in this area, that being the provision of discussion forums for students to post and receive messages (functionality currently available from most standard web sites).

However it does go on to 'Recommend' the following additional services:

- Audio and video-conferencing should be supported.
- Users should be able to create web logs.
- One–one and one–many messaging should be facilitated.
- Knowledge construction tools should be available.
- Users should be able to send messages to individuals and groups of users. (BECTA, 2006: 11)

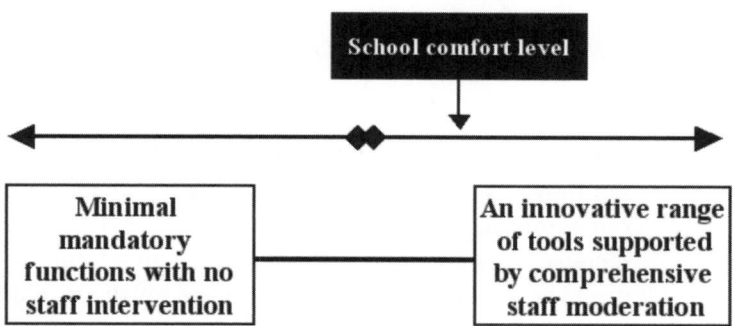

Figure 7.3 Communication continuum
Available on the net at http://www.james-wright.org

Schools should again consider a continuum model as depicted in Figure 7.3 to identify the degree of adoption available. Colleagues may wish to consider the implications of outsourcing out-of-hours online tutorial support through virtual schools possibly brokered by the local authority that will then take on the critical task of E-safety and security responsibility for staff.

Children and young people spend an enormous amount of time chatting and messaging together and it may prove rewarding to allow this function within the security of the school system. There are a number of innovative products that now allow such conversations to be analysed in terms of content, transforming instant conversations to meaningful debate and allowing teachers to configure topics around school activities.

In 2003 I was introduced to the work of Dr Christopher Tan, who was a key speaker at the North West Learning Grid (NWLG) annual conference marking the launch of its preferred learning platform at that time. Dr Tan introduced his Singapore-based 'Knowledge Community' which focused upon a number of projects conducted in primary schools in Hong Kong using Internet-based collaborative project work and specifically 'knowledge construction' through a sophisticated web-based intranet system called Knowledge Community (www.globalkc.net). This portal encourages children to work collaboratively, to think critically, creatively and independently, and to communicate their findings. Use of thinking types and scaffolds provide the teacher with an overview of the entire class contribution to the discussion, and through automatic formatting and highlighting of targeted areas of text can produce an overview of the thinking patterns of each student.

14th March

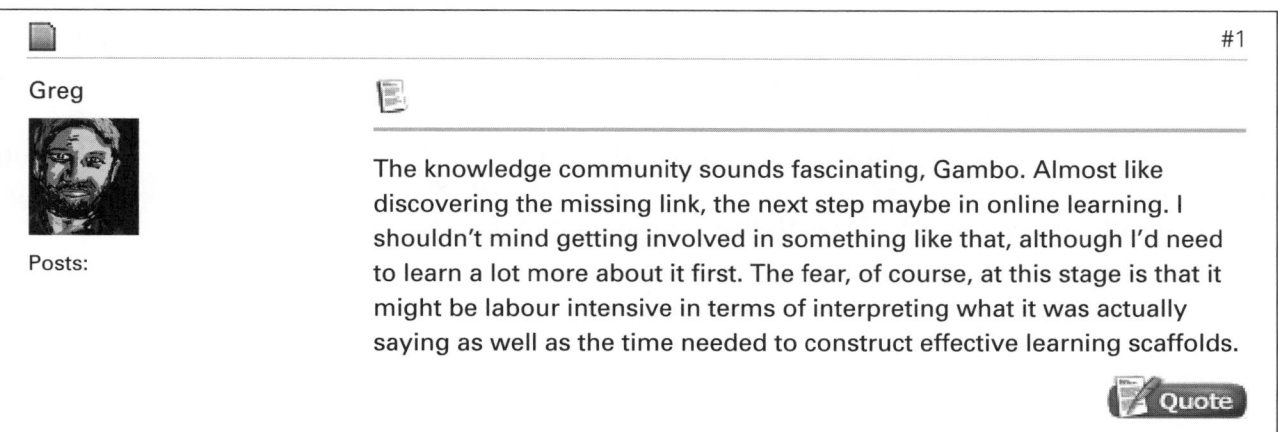

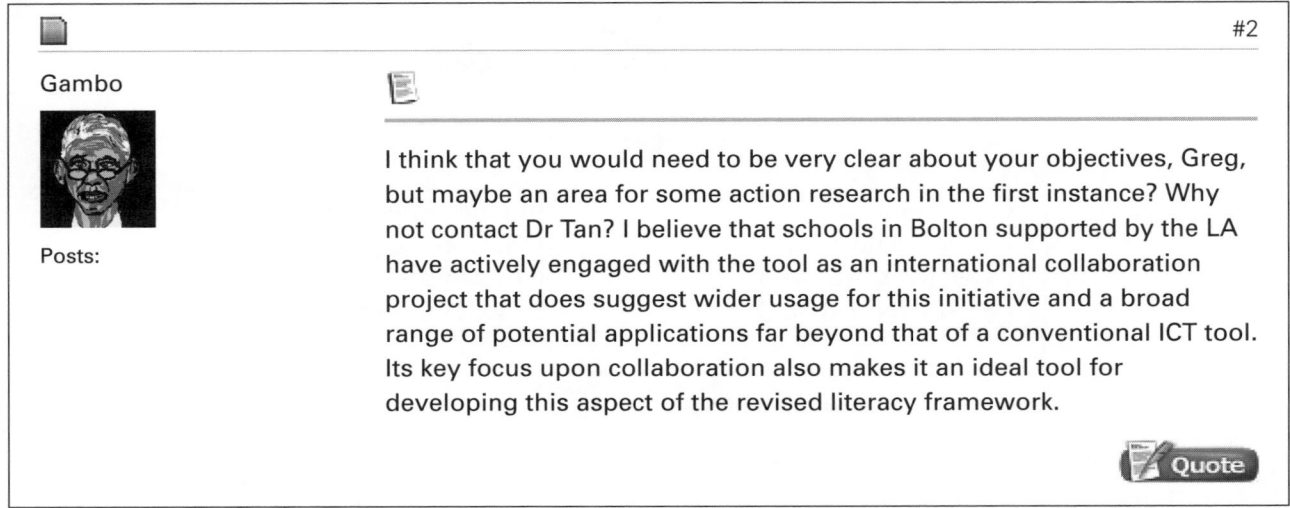

Gambo

Posts:

> I think that you would need to be very clear about your objectives, Greg, but maybe an area for some action research in the first instance? Why not contact Dr Tan? I believe that schools in Bolton supported by the LA have actively engaged with the tool as an international collaboration project that does suggest wider usage for this initiative and a broad range of potential applications far beyond that of a conventional ICT tool. Its key focus upon collaboration also makes it an ideal tool for developing this aspect of the revised literacy framework.

Colleagues should be determined to set clear goals for their learning platform functionality based around their understanding of the schools preparedness for adoption of such advanced communication tools. Collectively decide where to place your school on the communication continuum and begin to develop an adoption strategy accordingly.

15th March

Week 27, Task 20 – Extended Learning – Extra-Curricular Opportunities 2

Last month we began to discuss opportunities to extend the curriculum in terms of creativity and collaboration through ICT-based learning clubs. I introduced a range of themes from which you might consider future clubs in terms of the school's distinctiveness, current provision and school improvement priorities.

As was pointed out during discussion, many schools do exhibit gender differences in terms of ICT outcomes and a disproportionate number of girls go on to choose ICT-related subjects when selecting their options at high school.

In an attempt to address this situation the government introduced the CC4G (Computer Clubs for Girls) initiative, which may be of interest to colleagues. Created by e-skills UK (www.e-skills.com) as a fun way to motivate 10- to 14-year-old girls through ICT after-school clubs, it offers 61 hours of E-learning and 170 hours of offline projects using girl-related themes, such as music, fashion, dance and celebrity, combined with elements of the Key Stages 2 and 3 ICT curricula. Colleagues who wish to pursue this idea with the benefit of what are very high-end 'free' resources should register online at www.cc4g.net and spend some time exploring the website. If this seems the sort of thing that you can engage with then you will need to register your girls and order your club member packs via the website. There are training courses available for the club facilitator, who need not be an experienced ICT professional. The core activities are all provided on the website, www.cc4g.net, through Flash animations supporting downloadable projects.

Table 7.2 CC4G project details

	CC4G Learning Modules
1.	**Campaign**. Running a publicity campaign to raise awareness for a good cause
2.	**Celebrity**. Desktop publishing skills for fanzines, interviews and promotional materials
3.	**Communi-K8**. Digital information, encryption and mobile technology
4.	**DanceM8**. Dance mats, animation and digital dance moves
5.	**Designtime**. Interior and garden design including eco-friendly design
6.	**Fashion**. Data gathering, handling and presentation for a fashion show and catalogue
7.	**Fit4Sport**. Reporting on a team's progress, developing management tools and organizing a school sports event
8.	**Game Girl**. Designing and creating games, from storyboarding to programming
9.	**Investig8**. Analysis and problem solving to investigate a crime scene
10.	**Musicbiz**. Building and using a talent database to search for musicians, and producing show reels, CDs and videos
11.	**Showcase**. The final module, which presents the other topics as different employment roles in a multimedia project
12.	**Soundskool**. Exploring sound to produce radio jingles, audio e-cards and interactive posters.

Source: CC4G® reproduced with permission of e-skills UK, the Sector Skills Council for IT and Telecoms. CC4G is a registered trademark of e-skills UK.
Available on the net at http://www.james-wright.org

16th March

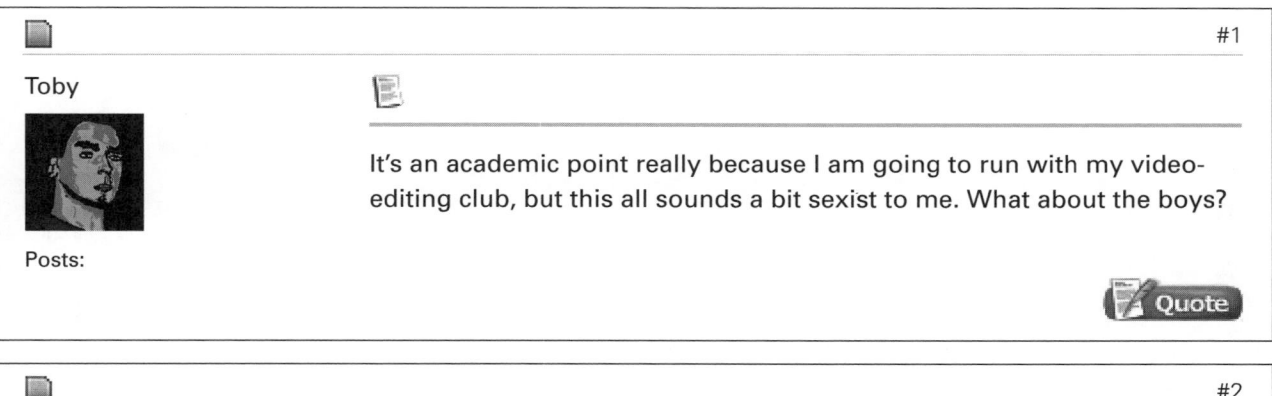

> #1
>
> **Toby**
>
> Posts:
>
> It's an academic point really because I am going to run with my video-editing club, but this all sounds a bit sexist to me. What about the boys?
>
> [Quote]

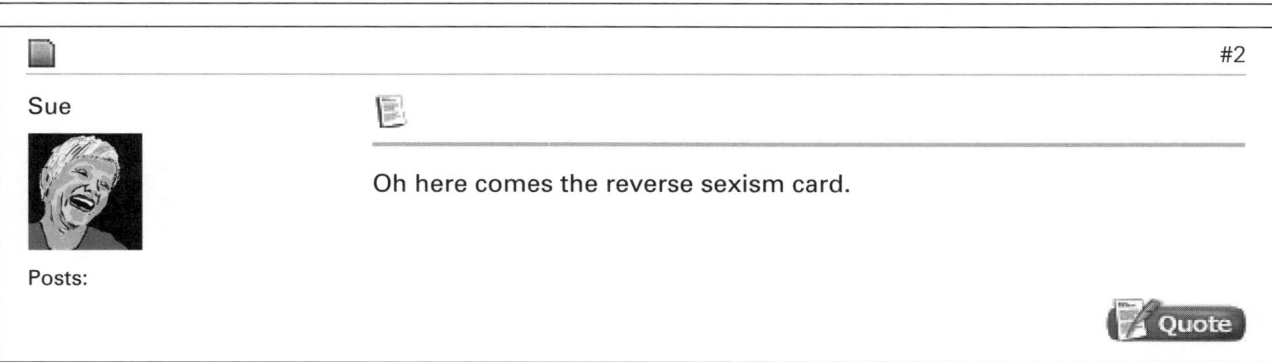

> #2
>
> **Sue**
>
> Posts:
>
> Oh here comes the reverse sexism card.
>
> [Quote]

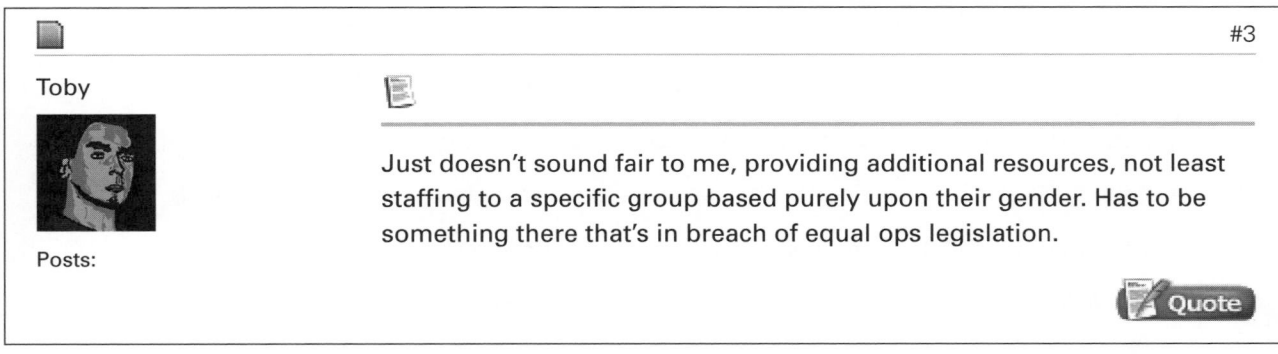

#3

Toby

Posts:

Just doesn't sound fair to me, providing additional resources, not least staffing to a specific group based purely upon their gender. Has to be something there that's in breach of equal ops legislation.

Quote

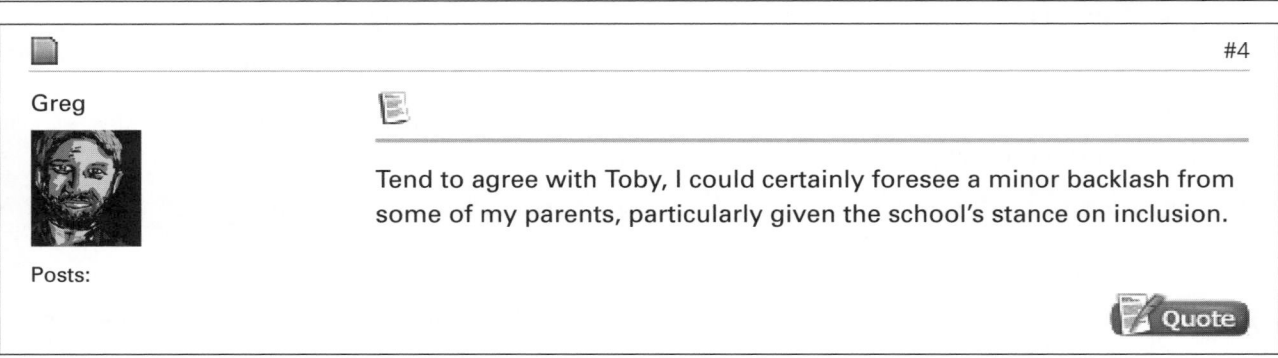

#4

Greg

Posts:

Tend to agree with Toby, I could certainly foresee a minor backlash from some of my parents, particularly given the school's stance on inclusion.

Quote

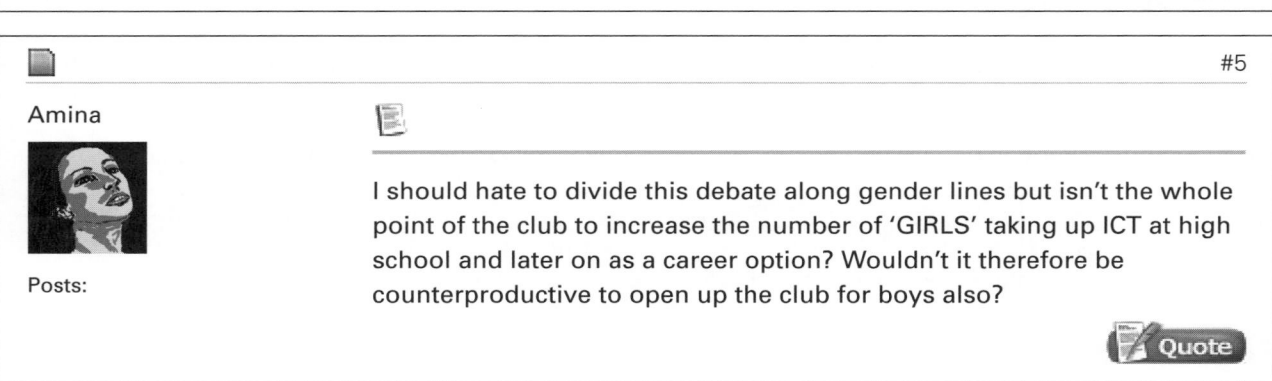

#5

Amina

Posts:

I should hate to divide this debate along gender lines but isn't the whole point of the club to increase the number of 'GIRLS' taking up ICT at high school and later on as a career option? Wouldn't it therefore be counterproductive to open up the club for boys also?

Quote

18th March

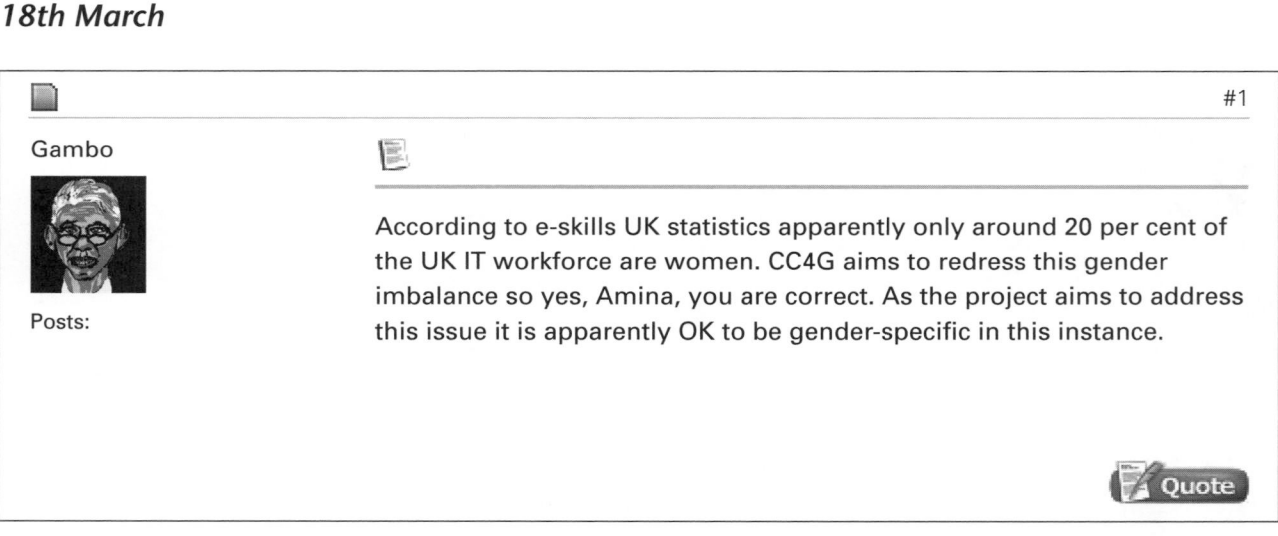

#1

Gambo

Posts:

According to e-skills UK statistics apparently only around 20 per cent of the UK IT workforce are women. CC4G aims to redress this gender imbalance so yes, Amina, you are correct. As the project aims to address this issue it is apparently OK to be gender-specific in this instance.

Quote

Greg

Posts:

#2

Is that legal?

Quote

Gambo

Posts:

#3

CC4G material indicates that the Equal Opportunities Commission advised that the project is covered by Section 47(1) of the Sex Discrimination Act, which supports 'Training or encouragement for particular work where in the previous 12 months one sex has been substantially under-represented'. So there you have it.

Quote

Sue

Posts:

#4

So there! Now that we have put the politics to bed may I say that I love it; my girls will find the resources fabulous! I shall simply set up a parallel activity for the boys, although that probably isn't going to be quite as easy to get past the EOC!

Quote

19th March

Hopefully the final activity for consideration will be a little less politically contentious. Obviously, colleagues will be drawn to reflect their own school's curriculum strengths when considering any extra-curricular provision, however, given the emphasis upon developing creativity within the present primary curriculum, I do think that colleagues should consider how best they might contribute to this arts agenda through the use of technology. Computer graphics add endless new possibilities for teaching right across the curriculum and, in particular, I wanted to reflect a little upon the use of artists' graphics tablets as a means of developing drawing skills in particular, as a cutting-edge twenty-first-century phenomena.

Information and communications technology may contribute to the creative world in much the same manner as it has the literary world and has transformed professions based upon graphic design. There is something incredibly empowering for children when creating or developing and enhancing digital imagery. John Derry, co-author of Corel Painter, writing in 1982, first noted:

'I'll never forget the first time I saw one of my designs glowing on the monitor screen. Some basic thing was forever changed in the way I thought about making images. This was something new and amazing. It was the birth of a medium!' (Derry, 2006)

Once digitized, an enormous raft of techniques are available to the digital artist in terms of manipulation, reproduction and communication of their work. Art-based ICT activities will captivate pupils as they strain to keep pace with the incredible innovations that technology offers, providing new opportunities for children to explore their potential.

For those not familiar with the tablet, it is in effect a computer input device through which hand-drawn images and designs may be digitized and transferred directly to a computer. Designs are made on its surface using a stylus and the image is displayed directly on the computer monitor, where it may be enhanced or manipulated using a range of software.

The use of high-quality graphics tablets and touch-sensitive pens, married to a selection of innovative software, will turn any ICT suite into a digital art studio. Figures 7.4 and 7.5 demonstrate work completed using the Wacom graphics tablet and Painter Software.

Figure 7.4 Self portrait (Reproduced with permission courtesy of Wacom Technology Corp.)
Available on the net at http://www.james-wright.org

Figure 7.5 Still life (Reproduced with permission courtesy of Wacom Technology Corp.)
Available on the net at http://www.james-wright.org

Colleagues eager to develop such a facility may find it useful to examine some of the work in education currently being developed by Japanese manufacturer, Wacom, at www.wacom.com/education.

20th March

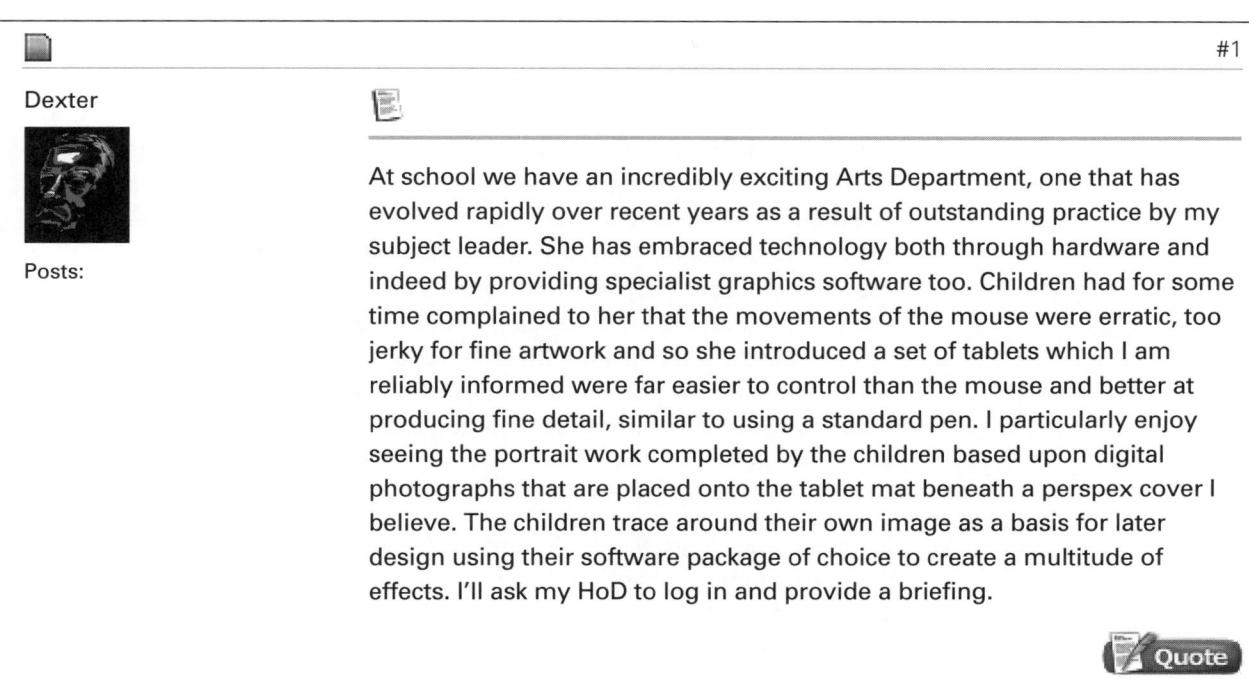

Dexter

Posts:

At school we have an incredibly exciting Arts Department, one that has evolved rapidly over recent years as a result of outstanding practice by my subject leader. She has embraced technology both through hardware and indeed by providing specialist graphics software too. Children had for some time complained to her that the movements of the mouse were erratic, too jerky for fine artwork and so she introduced a set of tablets which I am reliably informed were far easier to control than the mouse and better at producing fine detail, similar to using a standard pen. I particularly enjoy seeing the portrait work completed by the children based upon digital photographs that are placed onto the tablet mat beneath a perspex cover I believe. The children trace around their own image as a basis for later design using their software package of choice to create a multitude of effects. I'll ask my HoD to log in and provide a briefing.

#1

#2

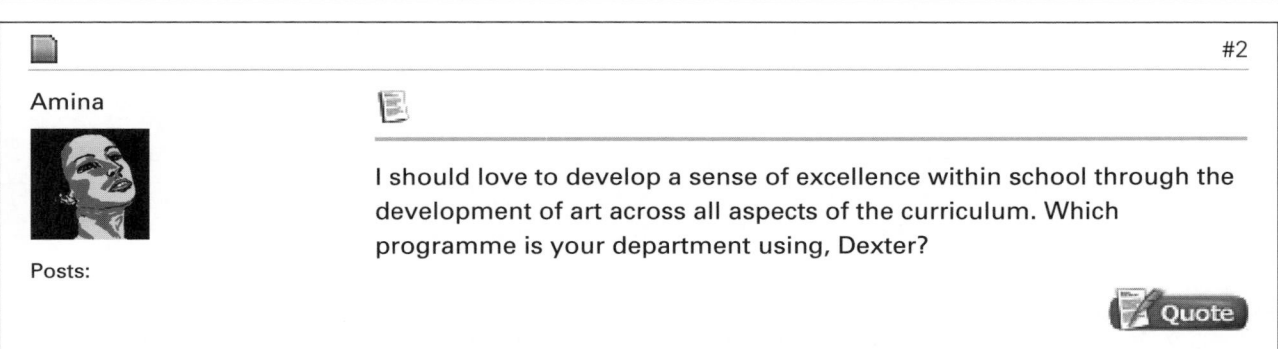

Amina

Posts:

I should love to develop a sense of excellence within school through the development of art across all aspects of the curriculum. Which programme is your department using, Dexter?

21st March

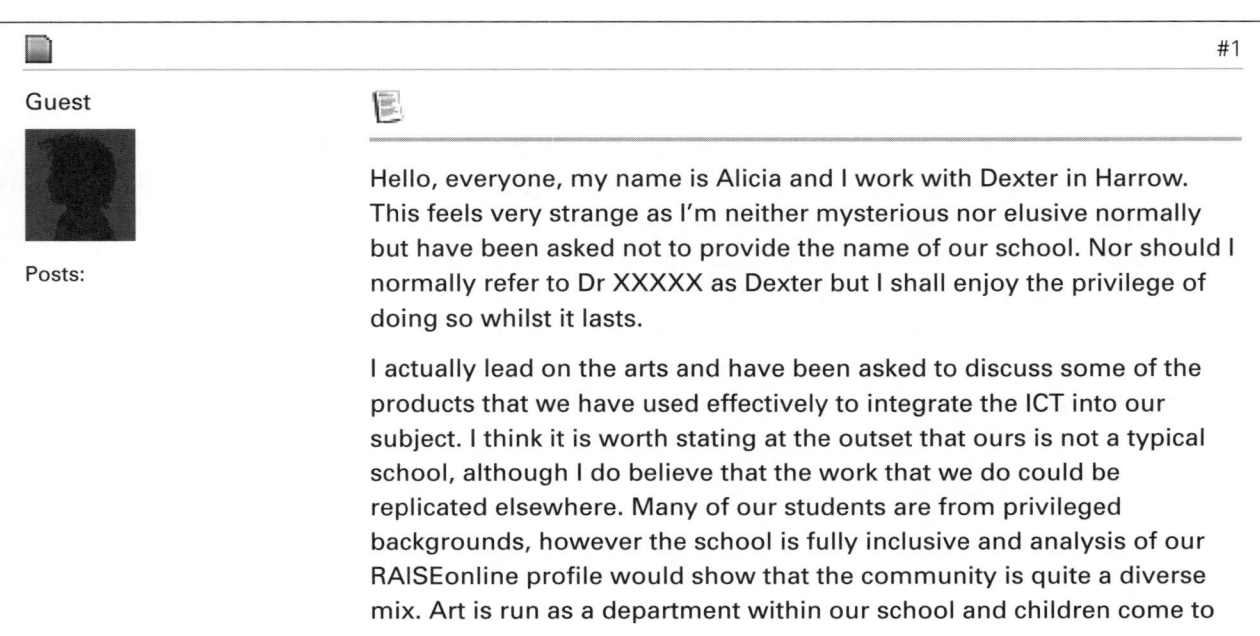

Guest

Posts:

#1

Hello, everyone, my name is Alicia and I work with Dexter in Harrow. This feels very strange as I'm neither mysterious nor elusive normally but have been asked not to provide the name of our school. Nor should I normally refer to Dr XXXXX as Dexter but I shall enjoy the privilege of doing so whilst it lasts.

I actually lead on the arts and have been asked to discuss some of the products that we have used effectively to integrate the ICT into our subject. I think it is worth stating at the outset that ours is not a typical school, although I do believe that the work that we do could be replicated elsewhere. Many of our students are from privileged backgrounds, however the school is fully inclusive and analysis of our RAISEonline profile would show that the community is quite a diverse mix. Art is run as a department within our school and children come to the Art Department in much the same way that they might at a high school where their class teacher is supported by highly skilled assistants, many of whom are artists in their own right. As you may imagine, the department is extremely dynamic and lively. In terms of ICT, children are taught to experiment with image, colour and texture using the PCs. We animate and create abstract designs but also focus upon graphic art, linear drawings and engravings that may be produced digitally prior to subsequent development either on the computers or using other more conventional media. All of our computers now use Revelation Natural Art software, as it does seem to balance the benefits of a professional art studio with that of a child-focused educational package. The variety of tools available, such as the different coloured pens and palette through which the students may modify colour, are selected in the way that artists would choose their own materials, allowing the lesson to remain as a creative not technical session, one through which images evolve and do not instantly appear as with many ICT tools.

Children quickly grow confident using the applications, not least because there are many levels of 'undo' allowing both reflection and experimentation and, so, together with the graphics tablet, this has allowed ICT to become a seamlessly integrated element of the department's provision.

I hope that is of some interest. You can see the RNA software at: www.logo.com/rna/

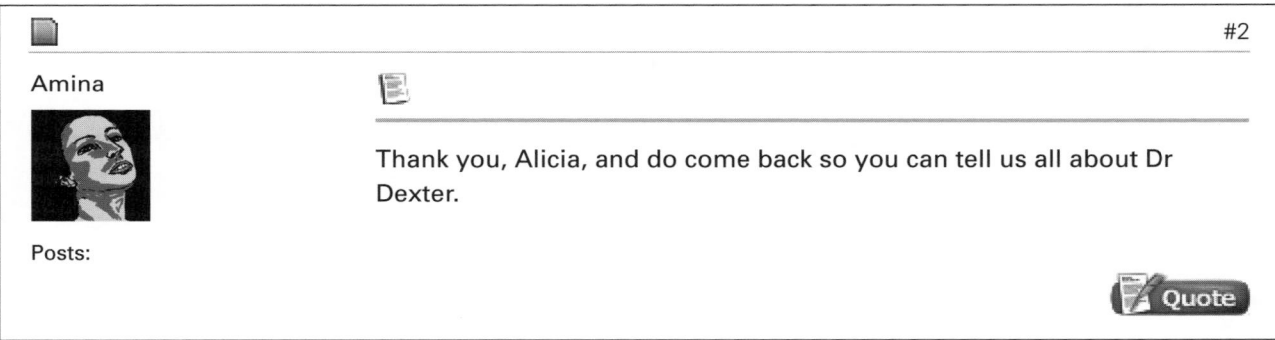

#2

Amina

Thank you, Alicia, and do come back so you can tell us all about Dr Dexter.

Posts:

In conclusion a carefully equipped ICT suite will provide numerous opportunities for children to produce a wide range of artwork, to collaborate creatively and even to animate their work. Colleagues should give careful consideration to staffing and ensure that they provide adequate training for the person who will run the group.

The four activities I have highlighted this month and last were aimed to provide a stimulus for E-learning co-ordinators to help make informed choices about high-impact provision within an extended school agenda. Colleagues will subsequently need to prepare carefully costed proposals that embrace the school's ethos, character and distinctiveness, and provide opportunities for E-learning to lie at the heart of 'Excellence and Enjoyment'.

22nd March

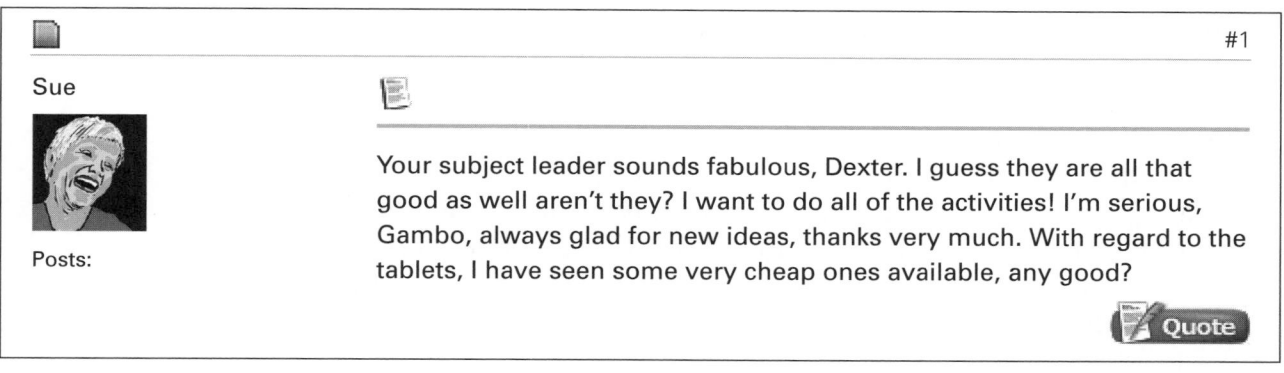

Sue

Posts:

#1

Your subject leader sounds fabulous, Dexter. I guess they are all that good as well aren't they? I want to do all of the activities! I'm serious, Gambo, always glad for new ideas, thanks very much. With regard to the tablets, I have seen some very cheap ones available, any good?

Quote

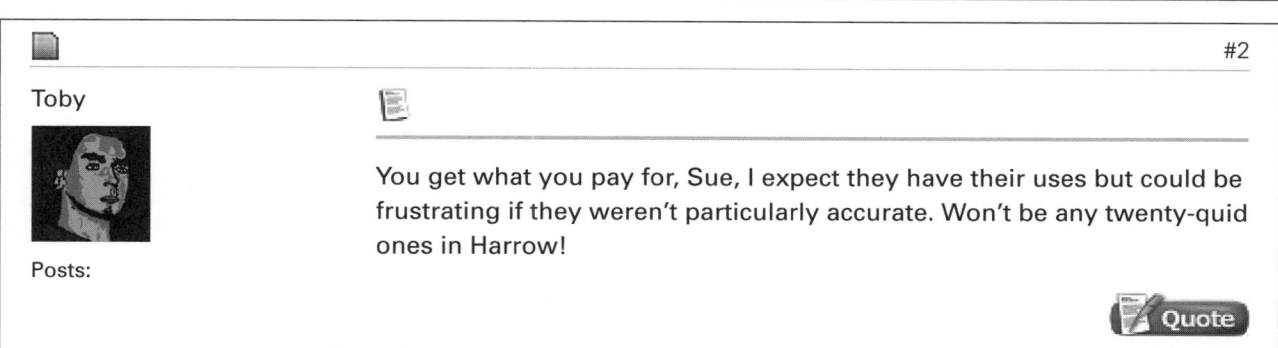

Toby

Posts:

#2

You get what you pay for, Sue, I expect they have their uses but could be frustrating if they weren't particularly accurate. Won't be any twenty-quid ones in Harrow!

Quote

23rd March

Week 28, Task 21 – Able, Gifted and Talented Provision across the Curriculum

Table 7.3 Self-evaluation of ICT for able, gifted and talented pupils

	Planning for ICT as a means of developing provision for *able gifted and talented pupils*
Level 5	No explicit links have been made at whole-school level between ICT and *provision for able, gifted and talented pupils*. Where ICT does aid *provision* this is not identified and shared with other staff.
Level 4	The school's policy for *able, gifted and talented pupils* pays little or no attention to the potential of ICT to enable and extend the learning of different groups of pupils. Examples of ICT *challenging* pupils to *extend* learning are patchy and unplanned
Level 3	The policy for *able, gifted and talented pupils* fully recognizes the role of ICT in enabling and supporting learning. Staff are aware of its potential, but are not always able to fulfil school aims due to lack of training or resource availability
Level 2	Most staff plan appropriately for ICT to support the full range of pupils in enabling or widening their access to learning. The special needs of *able, gifted and talented pupils* are met, at least in part, through the use of ICT.
Level 1	All, or nearly all, staff take a proactive role in identifying how ICT can be used to *extend* access to learning for different groups of pupils. Many good examples of this can be identified and are shared within the school.

Source: Adapted from BECTA Self-review Framework.
Available on the net at http://www.james-wright.org

In February you worked with your special needs co-ordinator (SENCO) to review the extent to which the school's register of gifted and talented children included pupils whose special ability lay in the field of ICT. Having spent some time reflecting upon the development of talented pupils with specific regard to ICT as a discrete subject you should now return to the BECTA self-review framework, in particular Element 3a-2 which identifies progression with regard to inclusion. Table 7.3 is an adaptation of the BECTA inclusion strand and relates specifically to provision for the most able pupils.

Looking at the progression through the maturity model above it suggests that the E-learning co-ordinator probably needs to consider four distinct stages of development that should be reflected within the action plan that you produced from the SRF in the spring term.

First, co-ordinators need to be confident in their own understanding of the issues surrounding work with able, gifted and talented (AG&T) children and in their ability to lead discussions effectively from an ICT perspective. This is the second task to be achieved; then the outcomes of this work should be reflected within the school's planning systems before, finally, staff training is adapted in order to support able children effectively.

Table 7.4 Effective ICT for able, gifted and talented pupils

Effective ICT use	Current school self-evaluation	Resources required
How does ICT facilitate able children working at their own pace through independent, personalized learning?		Personalized learning platform Tablet computer
How is ICT used to develop and accommodate higher-level thinking skills?		Appropriate simulation and programming software, e.g. LOGO
How does ICT enable able pupils to communicate with other learners?		Personalized learning platform Discussion forum Email, messenger
How does ICT provide information resources to support study?		Internet, intranet, personalized learning platform
How does ICT support collaborative working?		Shared assignments, e.g. video-editing, Wiki

Available on the net at http://www.james-wright.org

Complete Table 7.4 as a means of establishing an overview of the role that ICT is currently playing within your school. A few exemplar resources are included that may be a useful starting point. The task may generate some essential criteria that could be added to the school's policy if it is not already incorporated. Consider cross-referencing each of the core elements above within existing document architecture or incorporate a distinct paragraph relating to the use of ICT as a tool to enrich learning amongst able, gifted and talented children.

24th March

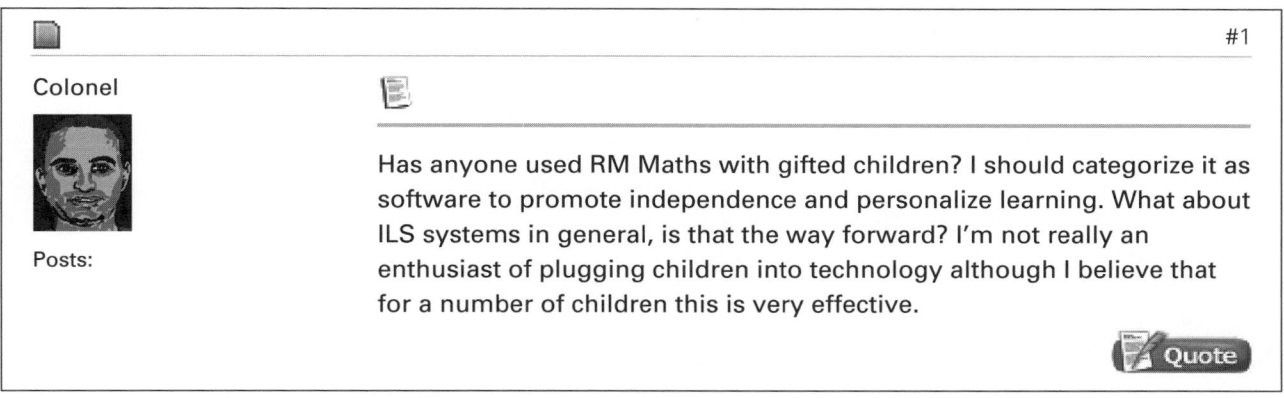

Colonel

Posts:

Has anyone used RM Maths with gifted children? I should categorize it as software to promote independence and personalize learning. What about ILS systems in general, is that the way forward? I'm not really an enthusiast of plugging children into technology although I believe that for a number of children this is very effective.

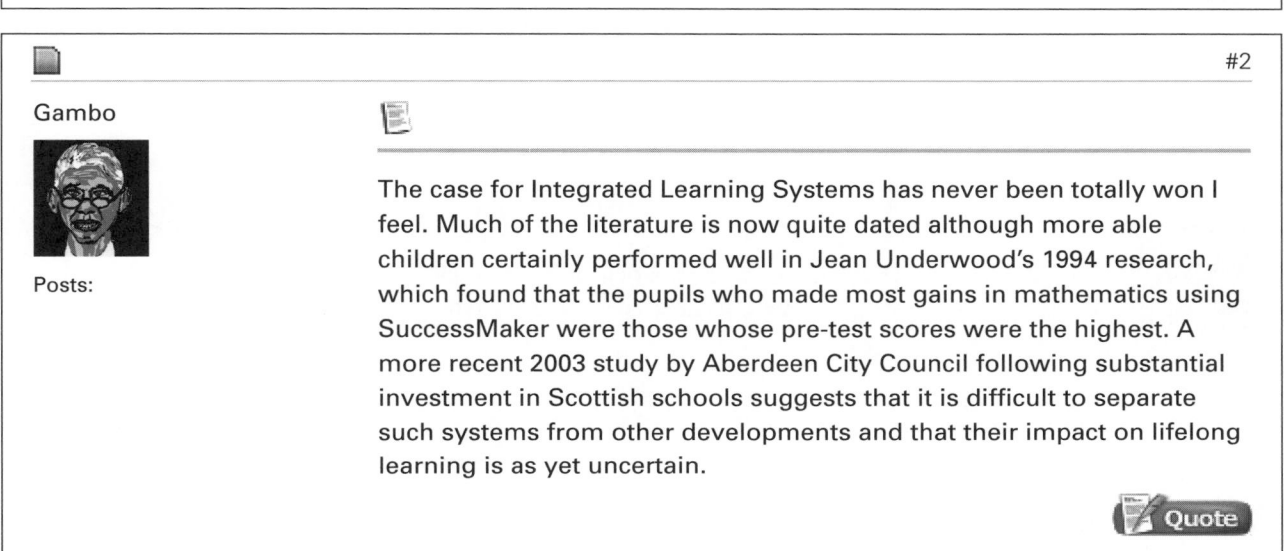

Gambo

Posts:

The case for Integrated Learning Systems has never been totally won I feel. Much of the literature is now quite dated although more able children certainly performed well in Jean Underwood's 1994 research, which found that the pupils who made most gains in mathematics using SuccessMaker were those whose pre-test scores were the highest. A more recent 2003 study by Aberdeen City Council following substantial investment in Scottish schools suggests that it is difficult to separate such systems from other developments and that their impact on lifelong learning is as yet uncertain.

26th March

Next consider opportunities for the use of ICT to feature within lesson plans. Already many schools have adopted a challenge element to planning and are cross-referencing ICT opportunities to extend learning as championed within the revised national frameworks. You will need to develop staff expertise in this area before you can expect then to plan appropriately, which there-fore brings us directly to the fourth stage of implementation with regard to staff CPD. Ensure that ICT elements are built into global AG&T training presented at school and that they incorporate many of the elements highlighted. It is worth noting when considering the development of planned opportunities for ICT to support able children that in essence the discussion is much wider as Richards (2005: 61) notes:

'[T]o effectively integrate ICT in education teachers need to increasingly become designers rather than merely transmitters of learning.'

Therefore colleagues need to be alert to this position when one works to embed ICT particularly with regards to a cutting edge facility to support the development of a personalized curriculum. Cameron Richards (2005: 63) indicated:

'The challenge of ICT integration is as much at the centre of a conflict between old and new pedagogies as it is in terms of how educational values are alternately influenced by institutional imperatives for change and existing social contexts.'

Colleagues will recognize this ultimate recurring theme that lies at the heart of the E-learning agenda. Just as for some colleagues these ideas will be merely abstract discourse, to others they will strike at the heart of their own personal struggles to overcome the resistance of the status quo.

25th March

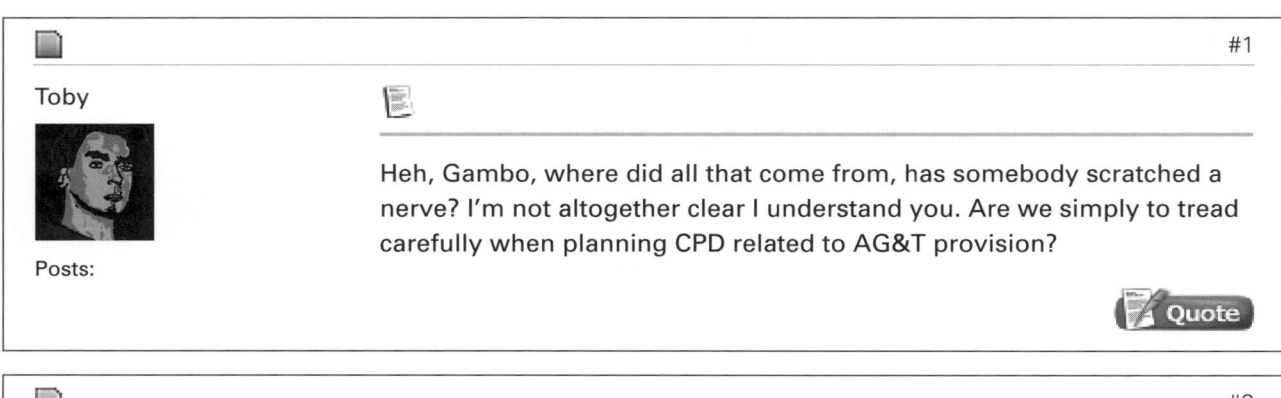

#1

Toby

Posts:

Heh, Gambo, where did all that come from, has somebody scratched a nerve? I'm not altogether clear I understand you. Are we simply to tread carefully when planning CPD related to AG&T provision?

Quote

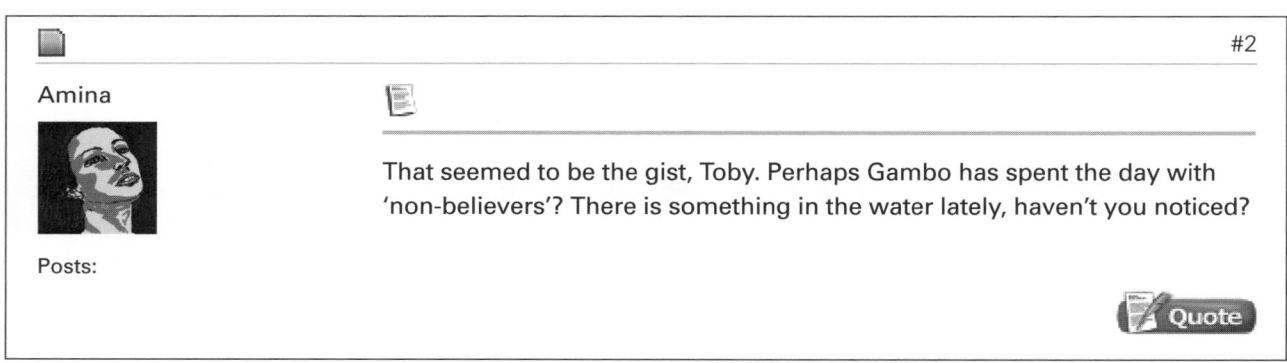

#2

Amina

Posts:

That seemed to be the gist, Toby. Perhaps Gambo has spent the day with 'non-believers'? There is something in the water lately, haven't you noticed?

Quote

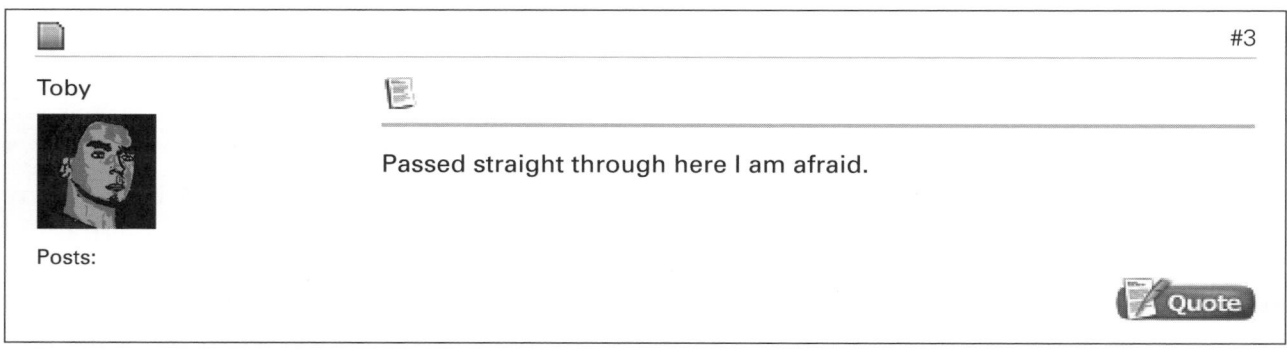

#3

Toby

Posts:

Passed straight through here I am afraid.

Quote

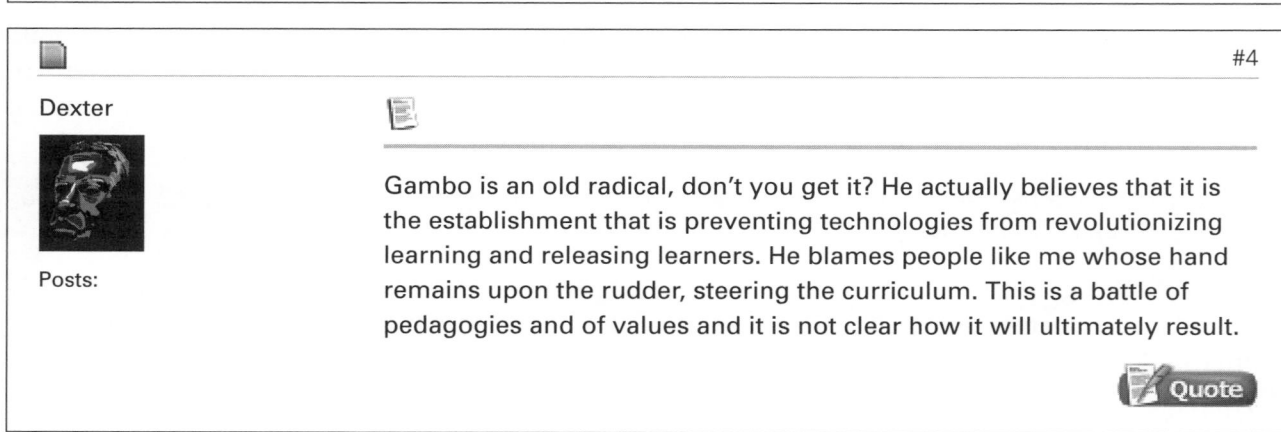

#4

Dexter

Posts:

Gambo is an old radical, don't you get it? He actually believes that it is the establishment that is preventing technologies from revolutionizing learning and releasing learners. He blames people like me whose hand remains upon the rudder, steering the curriculum. This is a battle of pedagogies and of values and it is not clear how it will ultimately result.

Quote

Chapter 8 • *April*

1st April

Week 29, Task 22 – MIS – How ICT Is Supporting School Management Systems

As Easter approaches and colleagues may already be on school closure I have learnt from previous feedback that this is not a great time to invent a host of new tasks, rather a good time to take stock. For the next two weeks we shall examine developments and trends in information management in order to clarify the nature of the initiative within your school and how it relates to your role.

Spend some time this week considering three fundamental questions.

1 What is the role of management information systems with relation to school improvement at my school?
2 To what extent is this perceived as an ICT/E-learning initiative here and therefore to what extent am I responsible for driving the initiative?
3 What is the strategy for developing the use of data systems within my school?

Your task is simply to discuss these within your teams and establish the basis of a data strategy.

6th April

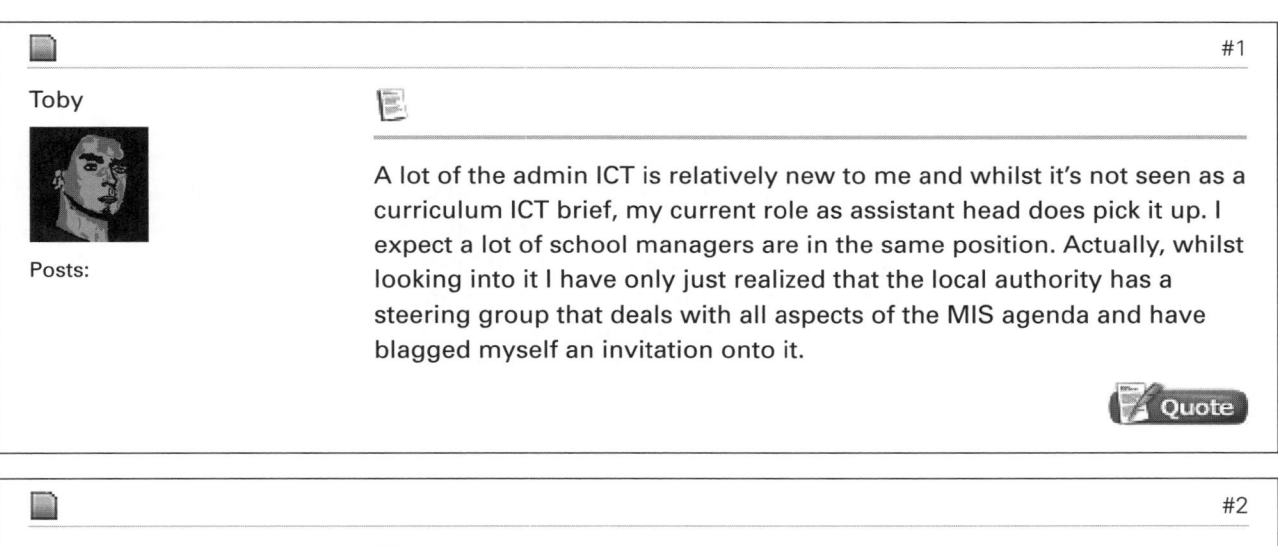

#1

Toby

Posts:

A lot of the admin ICT is relatively new to me and whilst it's not seen as a curriculum ICT brief, my current role as assistant head does pick it up. I expect a lot of school managers are in the same position. Actually, whilst looking into it I have only just realized that the local authority has a steering group that deals with all aspects of the MIS agenda and have blagged myself an invitation onto it.

Quote

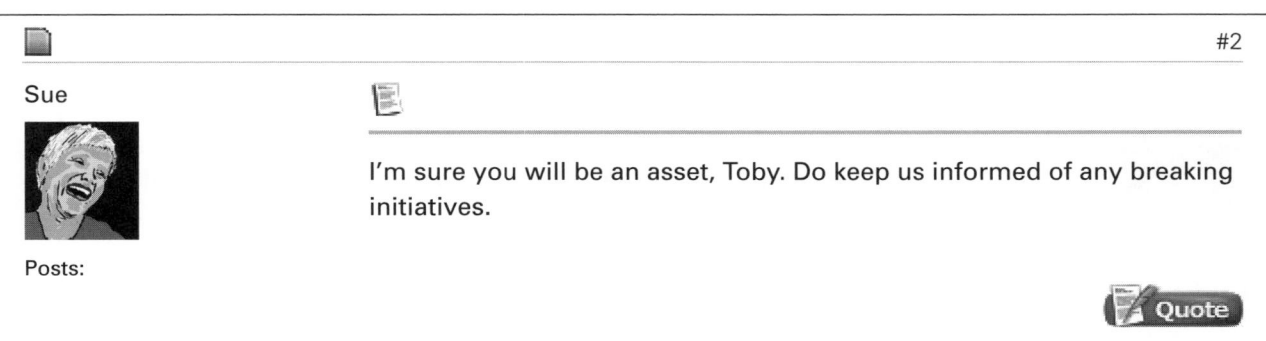

#2

Sue

Posts:

I'm sure you will be an asset, Toby. Do keep us informed of any breaking initiatives.

Quote

7th April

Every school creates, collects, processes and transfers electronic data, which it compiles for central government generally via the local authority. Currently, school data is at the heart of management and accountability and, as self-evaluation has become central to the school improvement agenda, a school's ability to make sense of the flow of government-provided data has become critical and has fundamentally raised the status and importance of school management systems.

Within any individual school colleagues should understand the limits upon their autonomy in deciding a current and future information management strategy. Primary schools require local authority support to set up and operate MIS systems and must understand the relationship between global data management sources such as SIMS and internal class-level tracking systems. As a management tool, full access and administrator's rights to SIMS (or equivalent system) are normally restricted to the school headteacher and administration manager with the co-ordination of assessment data constantly developing to satisfy DfES target-setting requirements. Primary teachers currently access a relatively small amount of information as the need arises, and colleagues may wish to consider broadening this access in the light of the development of managed learning environments (discussed previously) but also to begin to understand how such systems might evolve in the future. In one sense we are currently at the crossroads of developments in the use of data. Plans to develop the UK National Curriculum will require ever more sophisticated tools that respond to changes in what we teach and how we measure what is learned. Colleagues need to be clear about which strategy the school has in place to take account of these changes.

8th April

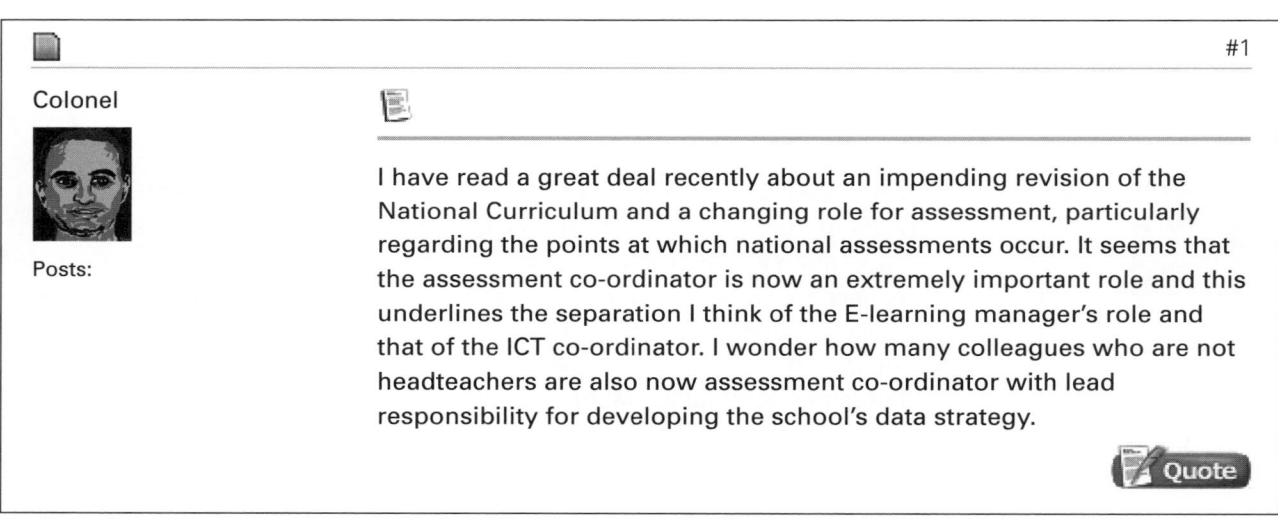

Colonel

Posts:

#1

I have read a great deal recently about an impending revision of the National Curriculum and a changing role for assessment, particularly regarding the points at which national assessments occur. It seems that the assessment co-ordinator is now an extremely important role and this underlines the separation I think of the E-learning manager's role and that of the ICT co-ordinator. I wonder how many colleagues who are not headteachers are also now assessment co-ordinator with lead responsibility for developing the school's data strategy.

Quote

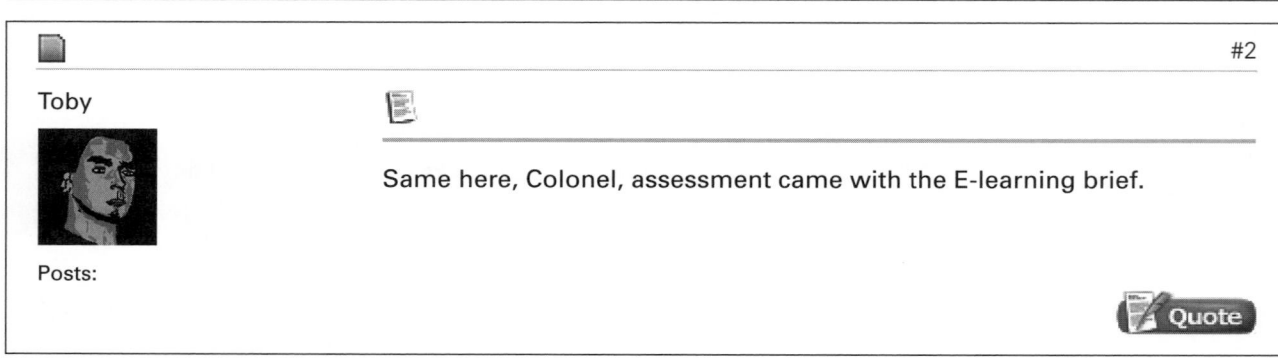

Toby

Posts:

#2

Same here, Colonel, assessment came with the E-learning brief.

Quote

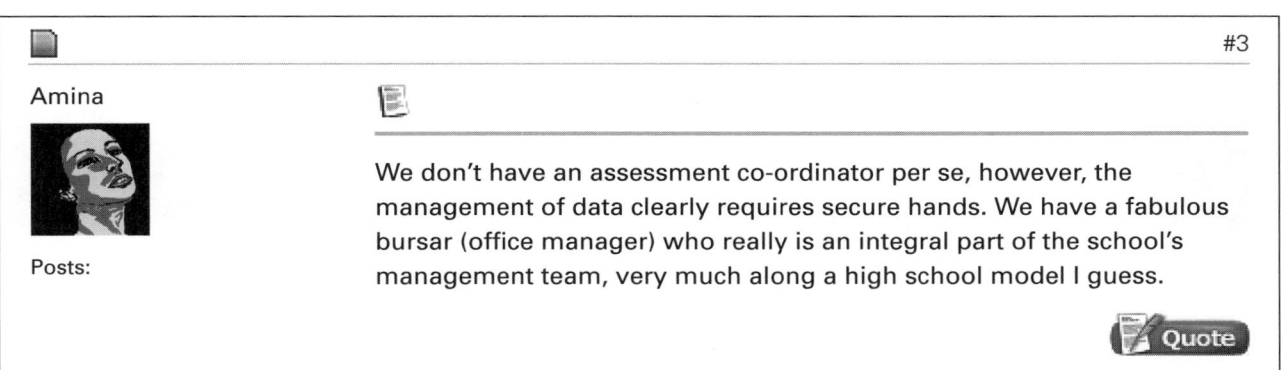

Amina

Posts:

We don't have an assessment co-ordinator per se, however, the management of data clearly requires secure hands. We have a fabulous bursar (office manager) who really is an integral part of the school's management team, very much along a high school model I guess.

10th April

Colleagues should be aware of certain guiding principles to inform future strategy as highlighted within the DfES Information Management Strategy. At its core, data collection and analysis should reduce the teacher's workload and not add to it whilst it provides essential information to aid school improvement. Therefore, unnecessary tasks (and collection of data) must be avoided and energies directed to the effective analysis of essential information. Data transfer should be a straightforward automated process with information stored and transferred electronically. I think that it is of particular importance that schools are able to plan their management of data strategically before they embark on providing parents with access to a full managed learning environment in 2010. In answering the core questions raised earlier this week, colleagues are beginning to juxtaposition themselves in this respect.

Colleagues need to make plans for the maintenance of an efficient learning platform infrastructure that will facilitate interoperability (that is, specifically the ability of two or more systems to communicate with each other) based upon a secure and reliable broadband connection. Apologies for the inclusion of technospeak at this stage, however, the phrase is inescapable within current learning platform discussions as increasingly the whole debate is driven by the determination to avoid the spectre of competing commercial environments proliferating across schools, none of which is able to transfer data to the other.

Similarly, colleagues might want to discuss the notion that information should probably be 'centralized', that is, accessed from a single trusted source which supplies the information needed to support a personalized learning environment and is easily accessible by teachers and, in some instances, parents. It does not really matter where this data is held so long as the host is secure.

12th April

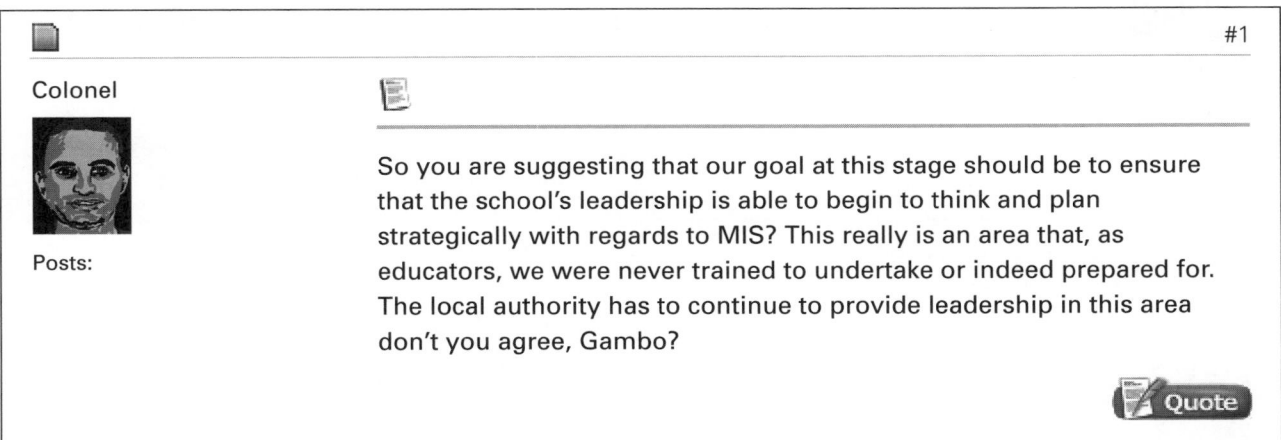

Colonel

Posts:

So you are suggesting that our goal at this stage should be to ensure that the school's leadership is able to begin to think and plan strategically with regards to MIS? This really is an area that, as educators, we were never trained to undertake or indeed prepared for. The local authority has to continue to provide leadership in this area don't you agree, Gambo?

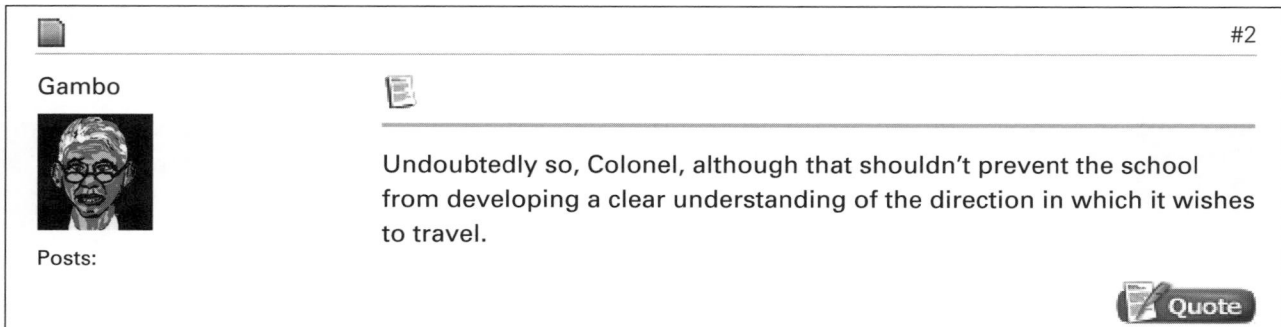

#2

Gambo

Posts:

Undoubtedly so, Colonel, although that shouldn't prevent the school from developing a clear understanding of the direction in which it wishes to travel.

Quote

#3

Dexter

Posts:

As a headteacher I often find myself being directed into uncharted and often dangerous waters. My instinct tells me to seek out all available advice and then to provide leadership. I must say that I agree with Gambo's thrust that, in the absence of in-house expertise, leadership teams must establish clear principles based upon their own school's vision and understanding. When considering the storage of essential secure data I often draw an analogy with financial management and the role of my bank. As companies develop and expand they require expert financial support to safeguard the company's capital, in essence stored and transferred electronically by the bank. Would any medium-sized corporation now attempt to house it's own security vaults on site? Clearly this would be an insane act of megalomania, however, schools' most sensitive and valuable resources still reside locally upon administration servers. Far better, I feel, if the local authority took on this role centrally. Colleagues should lean heavily on their county colleagues for guidance in this area as they define their medium-term strategy.

Quote

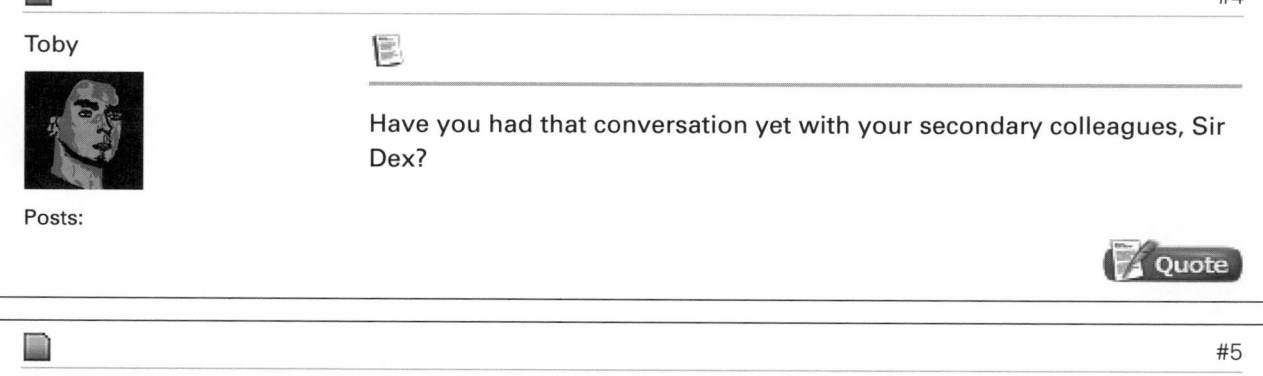

#4

Toby

Posts:

Have you had that conversation yet with your secondary colleagues, Sir Dex?

Quote

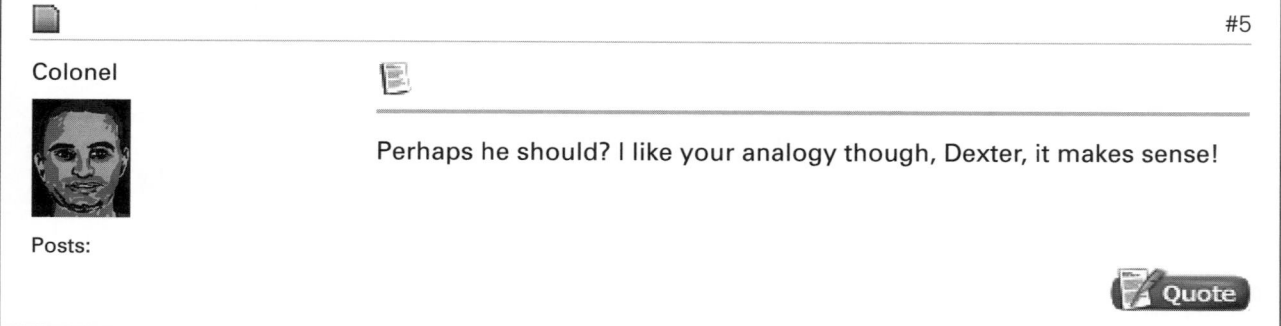

#5

Colonel

Posts:

Perhaps he should? I like your analogy though, Dexter, it makes sense!

Quote

There is no doubt that information has become critical to the improvement of performance in schools and that it needs to be managed extremely carefully. The volume and complexity of data grows each year, as do the possible sources of that information. Schools cannot become information islands and must continue to use this 'intelligence' effectively to support their most vital decision-making processes.

Earlier in the week I introduced the term 'interoperability', which I shall now ally with the concept of convergence. This is a period in which digital systems are coming together and I am indebted to Dexter for eloquently highlighting this point for me via his blog contribution. Each school must be clear about who owns information and who secures it. Who is responsible for keeping it up to date and making it available? Which systems do we trust to manage our information?

As data storage becomes more centralized, structures may be lost and colleagues must therefore be ever mindful of the key outcomes that need to be achieved. Hopefully you will now have answers to the three questions posed at the start of this activity and be able to review your strategy in the light of local and national data agendas.

15th April

Week 31, Task 23 – Provision for Children with Special Educational Needs

As this is a time for reflection I suggest that colleagues model their strategic approach to SEN upon that taken with regard to able, gifted and talented children returning to BECTA's self-review framework, Element 3a-2 on page 117. The same stages of progression are relevant, although co-ordinators must ensure that it is the school's SENCO who leads in this area. E-learning co-ordinators should concentrate on developing their own professional understanding of work in this area from an ICT perspective.

It is essential to establish a strong relationship with your SENCO and to become a useful partner, not someone to be feared. Ensure that ICT has a voice in terms of supporting children with learning difficulties and, in particular, that you are able to work with colleagues in ensuring that ICT provision is embedded within individual education plans when appropriate.

Colleagues should provide lead guidance when supporting the delivery of the ICT curriculum and the use of ICT applications across the curriculum. Initially, therefore spend time this week becoming familiar with the QCA ICT subject-specific guidelines for *Planning, Teaching and Assessing the Curriculum for Pupils with Learning Difficulties* (2001) available for download from the National Curriculum website at www.nc.uk.net/ld/ICT_content.html. As this document clearly points out, the ICT programme of study is entirely relevant to pupils with learning difficulties, therefore, with modification it can provide stimulating and challenging learning opportunities.

Familiarize yourself with the content of Table 8.1 as it provides a useful broad-brush review of provision and entitlement based upon the QCA guidelines.

Table 8.1 SEN learning outcomes at KS1 and KS2

	Key Stage 1	Key Stage 2
Focus of teaching	Provide opportunities to work with a variety of resources which carry information, and to use a range of ICT tools	Provide opportunities to work with information from a variety of sources • To use a range of ICT tools • To understand that everyday devices can be controlled • To produce work using symbols, sounds, pictures and text • To review and evaluate their work.
All pupils with learning difficulties (including those with the most profound disabilities)	Have opportunities to observe, explore and experience a range of ICT tools, and explore and respond to a variety of stimuli	Experience and explore a range of ICT tools. They use information from the environment to make simple choices. They communicate these choices by appropriate means. They learn that they can have an effect on the environment and on other people.
Most pupils with learning difficulties (including those with severe difficulties in learning) who will develop further skills, knowledge and understanding in most aspects of the subject	Explore information from a range of sources, make choices, and communicate them to others by a variety of means	Know that information can be gathered from different sources and that it can be used to help them make simple decisions and choices. They understand that machines can be controlled by instructions and that they can produce work using symbols, sounds, pictures and text.
A few pupils with learning difficulties who will develop further aspects of knowledge, skills and understanding in the subject	Learn that information can be presented in different forms, and that it can be used to help them make choices and to communicate likes and dislikes. They learn that machines and devices can be controlled and used creatively to develop and express ideas	Use ICT to develop their ideas and to present them in different forms. They communicate what they like and dislike about their work.

Source: QCA.
Available on the net at http://www.james-wright.org

18th April

Colleagues should be aware of the common requirement within the National Curriculum statutory orders to use appropriate ICT with pupils with special needs. Schools are therefore legally obliged to put these requirements into practice when planning and delivering lessons to all pupils. It is also worth reminding ourselves that at Key Stage 1 (KS1) there no statutory requirement to teach the use of ICT in the programmes of study for non-core foundation subjects whereas there is for English, Mathematics and Science. At KS2 only Physical Education has no statutory requirement to use ICT.

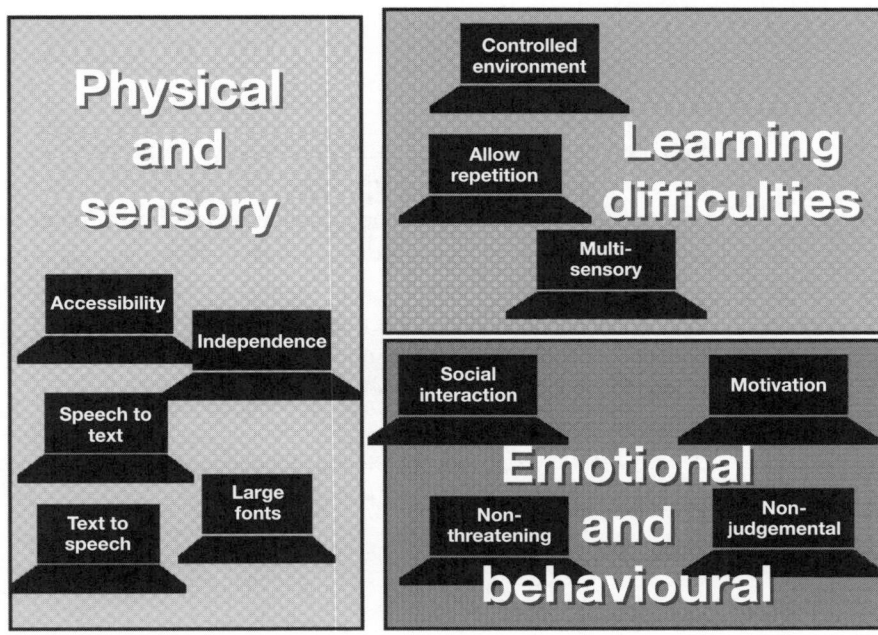

Figure 8.1 ICT support for pupils with SEN
Available on the net at http://www.james-wright.org

Figure 8.1 provides some indication of the manner in which ICT may support children with different types of learning difficulties. Because of the creative and attractive environment produced by software, learners want to learn through the use of computers, and multimedia provides opportunities for different learning styles to become simultaneously engaged. Colleagues should be aware of the different access devices and processes that ICT may offer children with physical and sensory disabilities and so overcome barriers to learning. Likewise the organized, controlled environment that the computer offers is welcomed by children with a range of learning difficulties. Computers may offer focused repetitive tasks that can be carefully matched to an individual pupil's needs allowing them to practise appropriately planned skills. Information and communication technology will facilitate collaboration to support social development amongst pupils with emotional and behavioural difficulties and can provide successful learning opportunities free from the fear of failure.

Work in this field is extremely rewarding and absorbing. Spend time developing your experience, especially if you have the opportunity to work with children to experience the benefits that ICT can bring. If colleagues feel that this is an area they would like to explore further, contact your local authority to arrange an opportunity to visit a special school in your area where there may be some extraordinary work already taking place. Finally, whilst providing a broad scaffold to support understanding of some of the areas within this field, do be aware that by nature children have very individual needs and are likely to require specific support based around expert assessment.

20th April

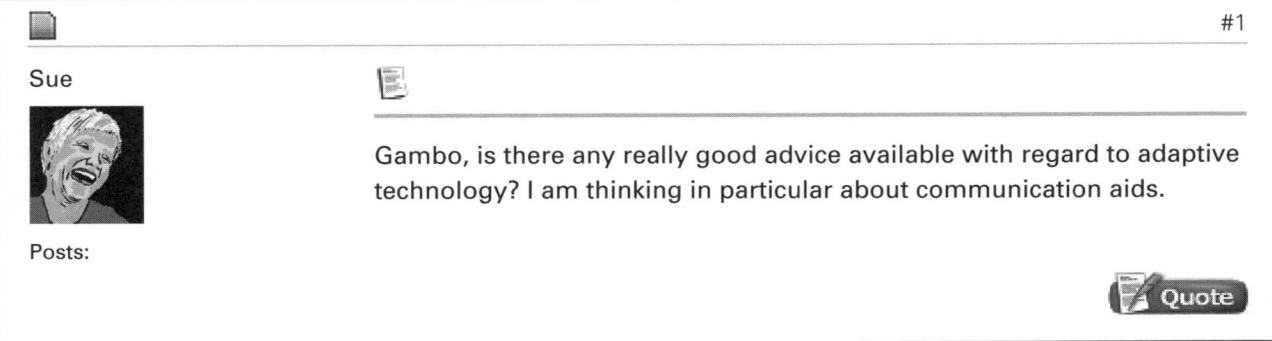

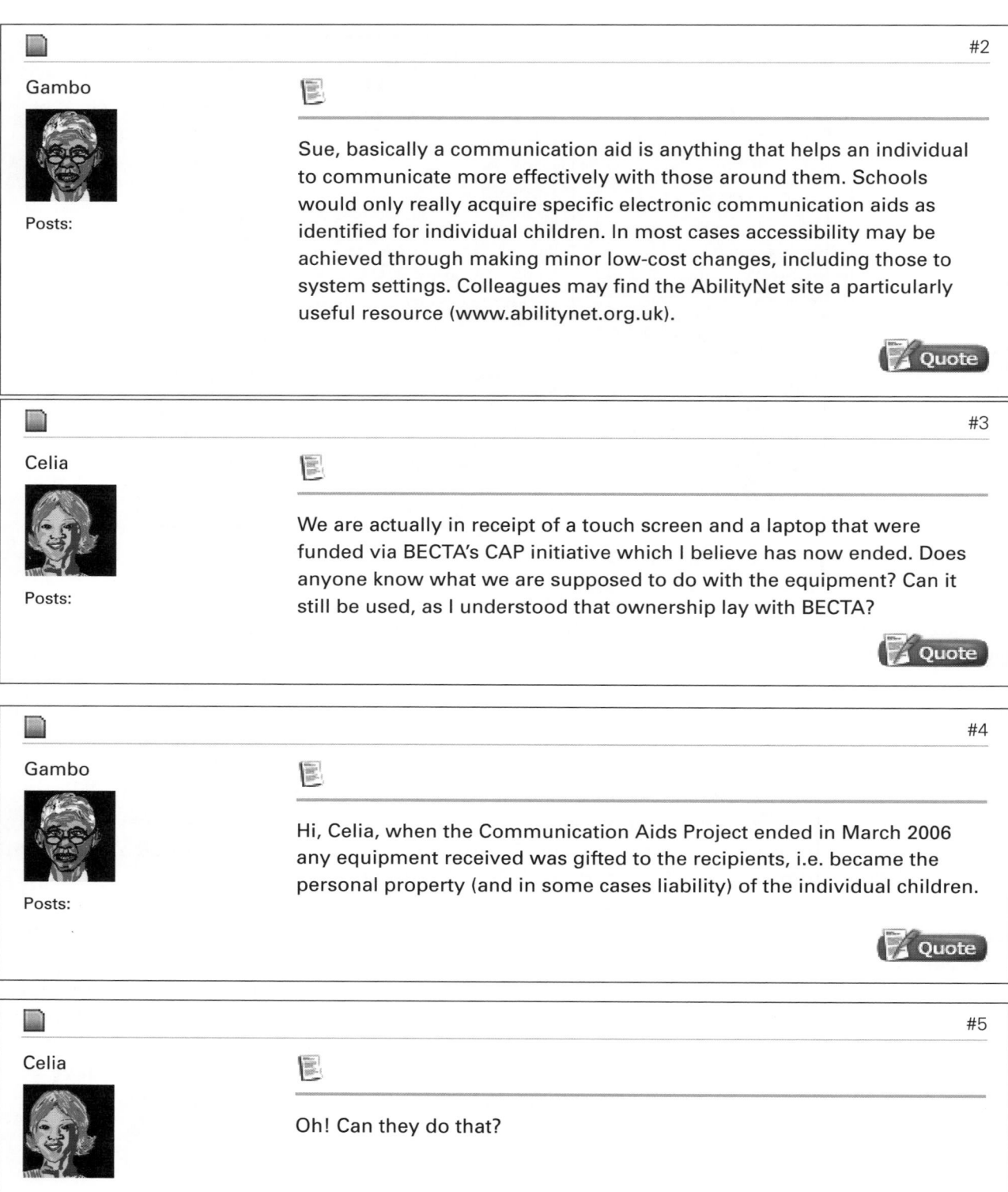

#2

Gambo

Posts:

Sue, basically a communication aid is anything that helps an individual to communicate more effectively with those around them. Schools would only really acquire specific electronic communication aids as identified for individual children. In most cases accessibility may be achieved through making minor low-cost changes, including those to system settings. Colleagues may find the AbilityNet site a particularly useful resource (www.abilitynet.org.uk).

Quote

#3

Celia

Posts:

We are actually in receipt of a touch screen and a laptop that were funded via BECTA's CAP initiative which I believe has now ended. Does anyone know what we are supposed to do with the equipment? Can it still be used, as I understood that ownership lay with BECTA?

Quote

#4

Gambo

Posts:

Hi, Celia, when the Communication Aids Project ended in March 2006 any equipment received was gifted to the recipients, i.e. became the personal property (and in some cases liability) of the individual children.

Quote

#5

Celia

Posts:

Oh! Can they do that?

Quote

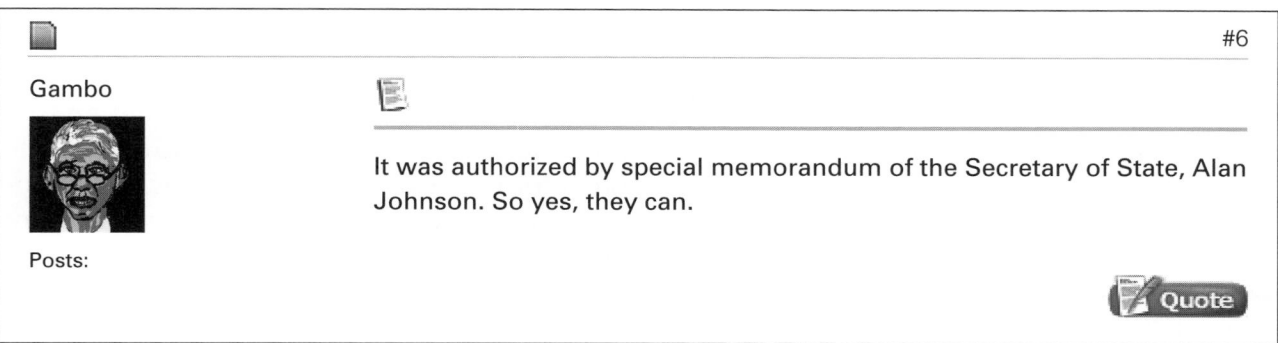

It was authorized by special memorandum of the Secretary of State, Alan Johnson. So yes, they can.

22nd April

Week 32, Task 24 – Curriculum Review and Redesign

As E-learning co-ordinator you need to incorporate within your role a vision of how cutting-edge technology will serve your school both now and in the future. The best co-ordinators and subject leaders understand current priorities because they have the foresight to anticipate how events are likely to evolve. Throughout this year you have invested a lot of time and energy in establishing the E-learning narrative that you and your colleagues have undergone and by this stage yours will be a highly effective E-enabled school with ICT serving the staff, pupils and broader community. Your final task of the spring term (forgive me if you are already enjoying a break) is to look ahead at developing innovations that will put the school at the cutting edge of E-learning. Using BECTA's model of maturity I hope that by this stage your schools are comfortably residing in the ICT-Marked zone, BECTA's Level 2 and now contemplating accession to Level 1. Remember that, typically, Level 2 school systems have been redesigned as a result of ICT and are now secure and embedded. Level 1 schools apply ICT innovatively to create new services and learning experiences that innovate and redefine the learning environment.

This is the subject for your consideration this week, in particular the extent to which the changes that you have overseen now impact upon ICT as a discrete subject and the use of ICT within all aspects of school life. Consider curriculum review and redesign that becomes essential as a result of E-learning developments with regard to the following core questions:

Is progress now being restricted as a result of an adherence to outmoded curriculum design?
Is it still appropriate to teach ICT as a discrete subject?
Is it appropriate to teach other subject areas outside of an ICT suite?
Do portable devices now offer an ideal solution in terms of the evolving role of ICT and E-learning or are they simply some form of negotiated compromise?

Colleagues should engage fully with the global debate surrounding the development in ICT and its likely impact upon education. In his work, *Planning, Forecasting, and Inventing Your Computers-in-Education Future*, (2005), David Moursund, founder of the International Council for Computers in Education (ICCE), describes many of the challenges that the education system will face in the light of increasingly rapid technological change. He cites the increase in storage capacity of computer chips (by a factor of several million over the past 25 years), the evolution of broadband and fibre optic connections as resulting in ICT hardware capabilities doubling every 1.5 to 2 years. He confidently notes that:

> *'Curriculum, instruction, and assessment will take place in an environment in which all students have routine access to very powerful ICT systems and use them routinely much in the manner that students use pencil, paper, and books today.'* (Moursand , 2005: 105)

27th April

Education is changing, one example of the manner in which ICT has altered the world forever being the way in which information is at the fingertips of all manner of learners. From my personal computer a global search of the word 'computer' returns 849,000,000 entries from Google. This has to place demands upon the education system for the development of research skills and understanding of intelligent search criteria as opposed to a traditional focus upon rote learning and the memorizing of facts. In 2003 the DfES published *Fulfilling the Potential: Transforming Teaching and Learning through ICT in Schools*, which identified the following aims for the next stage of development:

'*To ensure that:*

ICT makes a significant contribution to teaching and learning across all subjects and ages, inside and outside the curriculum

ICT is used to improve access to learning for pupils with a diverse range of individual needs, including those with SEN and disabilities

ICT is used as a tool for whole-school improvement

ICT is used to enable learning to take place more easily beyond the bounds of the formal school organization and outside the school day

ICT capabilities are developed as key skills essential for participation in today's society and economy.
(DfES, 2003: 7)

DfES copyright material is reproduced under the terms of HMSO Guidance Note 8.

In his 2006 formative review of current US educational policy, *Rethinking and Redesigning Curriculum*, James Pellegrino questions the ongoing validity of the curriculum, instruction and assessment triad, and argues that existing assessment systems are fundamentally flawed, and that the dominant institutional theories and models simply have not kept pace with knowledge of how people learn. In the USA, as in the UK, the agenda is one towards ever greater personalization. This view is to some extent echoed within the DfES 2007 consultative document, *Making Good Progress* that invites a debate about how best individual progress may be brought to the forefront of the educational agenda and invites a more formative approach to data that adjusts our approaches to classroom assessment for a greater focus upon each individual's progress. I commend both documents to you for study this Easter. In one sense the future is now upon us and fundamental curricular changes with ICT at their heart are about to evolve before our eyes. I sincerely hope that E-learning professionals such as those engaged with these weblogs are actively engaged in these changes. Enjoy Easter!

Chapter 9 • *May*

4th May

The final chapters, what a journey this has been and I hope that you feel that it has been worthwhile and that your pupils and staff have benefited as a result of your contribution. We have two significant enterprises to complete throughout the summer: the first, a revisit to the heart of the matter, successful self-evaluation which we undertake from three different perspectives beginning this month with that of the government's inspection agency, Ofsted. The second major series of activities that we shall review looks at the evolution of a variety of new technologies that have each in turn promised to revolutionize the way that we teach and learn. My intention is to provide a strategic review of each individual technology's potential, beginning this month with a review of the impact of multimedia presentation products with particular regard to digital video, podcast and the potential of pupil's television. Finally, we take three separate reviews of currently pertinent topics in order to complete our 66-activity cycle (Books 1 and 2). The first of these will be a contemporary discussion of our roles and relationships with regard to governors and parents. Table 9.1 provides an organized overview for the entire term.

Once again I have left August empty as a time for reflection. Hopefully by that time my work here will be done.

Week 33, Task 25 – School Self-Evaluation of ICT – an Ofsted Perspective

Colleagues will be aware that in September 2005 a new relationship began between the government and schools, refocusing school improvement emphasis on effective school self-evaluation and embodied within the '*Every Child Matters*', 2005 revised Section 5 Ofsted inspection framework (Ofsted 2005b).

The previous Section 10 framework was effectively scaled back and individual subjects (including ICT) were no longer inspected or reported on within the new framework. (There may, however, be ICT 'subject inspections' during which samples of schools will be inspected within specific regions and reports will provide overviews of themes that would not normally cite individual schools.) From this time onward headteachers have become responsible for applying the framework in-house, requiring a much more rigorous programme of self-evaluation than was necessary prior to the new relationship commencing. From an Ofsted perspective it is the school leadership that now comes under the most intense scrutiny during inspection. This defines the purpose of this section of the manual but also in effect defines the E-learning co-ordinator's role. You have to understand the school's ICT journey inside out and ultimately contribute appropriately to the Ofsted Self-Evaluation Form (SEF) that your headteacher must post online prior to inspection. The SEF marks the end-product of this self-evaluation process.

Your first task this week is to download the following documents from the Ofsted website and begin to familiarize yourself with each of them:

1 '*Every Child Matters' Framework for the Inspection of Schools in England* from September 2005
2 *Conducting the Inspection – Guidance for Inspectors of Schools*
3 *Using the Evaluation Schedule – Guidance for Inspectors of Schools*.

Your task is now to highlight each of the documents with regards to how they apply within your E-learning brief, that is how will you prepare evidence ahead of inspection to meet the requirements of each specific section?

Table 9.1 Summer term plan

SUMMER TERM			
MAY	**JUNE**	**JULY**	**AUGUST**
School Self-evaluation of ICT In which co-ordinators will focus upon successful self-evaluation which we undertake from three different perspectives			A graphical overview of the 33 tasks completed and short discussion of options for coordinators considering next steps
An Ofsted Perspective A thorough examination of the role of ICT within the revised Ofsted Section 5 framework and the E-learning co-ordinator's contribution to the Ofsted Self-evaluation Form (SEF)	**Progress Over Time** A 360-degree self-evaluation is adopted by undertaking a long-term view of developments with specific reference to the previous Section 10 Ofsted report	**Every Child Matters** Identifies core ICT issues set against each of the five ECM priorities and establishes a scaffold upon which to develop the school's E-learning ECM strategy	
New Technologies In which co-ordinators look at the evolution of a variety of new technologies that have each in turn promised to revolutionize the way that we teach and learn			
Video Editing, Podcasts and Pupil TV A review of the impact of multimedia presentation products with particular regard to digital video, podcast and the potential of pupil's television	**Video Conferencing and Mobile Communication** Communication devices that are establishing a foothold in primary education	**Blogs, Wikis and Web 2.0** Impact on schools of second generation Internet applications emphasizing opportunities for online collaboration	
Working with Governors and Parents A discussion of roles and relationships with regard to governors and parents in which we seek out the views of these groups of the school's E-learning development	**The National Digital Curriculum, an Implementation Review** The removal of the BBC 'Jam' resource and a review of the strategic challenge and operational responses available to E-learning co-ordinators	**The ICT Mark and ICT Excellence Awards** Describes the process by which schools may achieve accreditation underlining their status as advanced E-learning schools	

Available on the net at http://www.james-wright.org

7th May

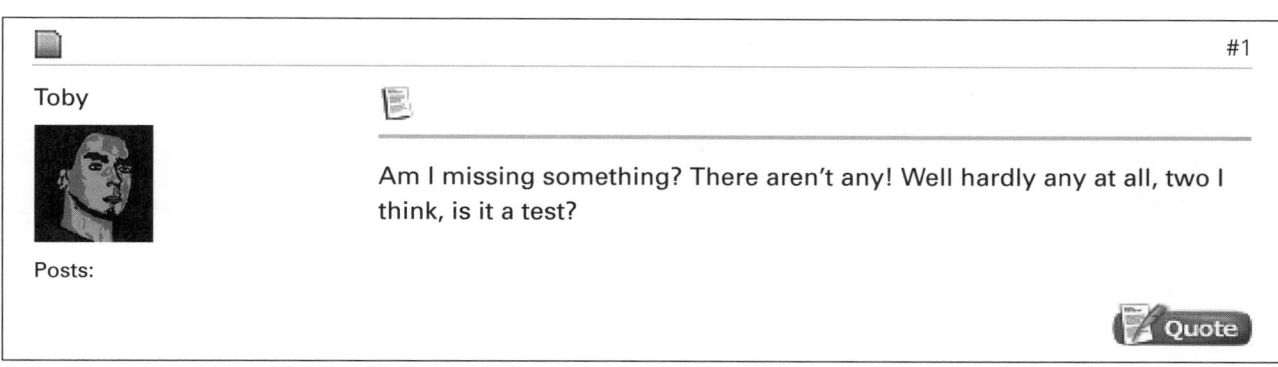

Toby   #1

Posts:

Am I missing something? There aren't any! Well hardly any at all, two I think, is it a test?

Quote

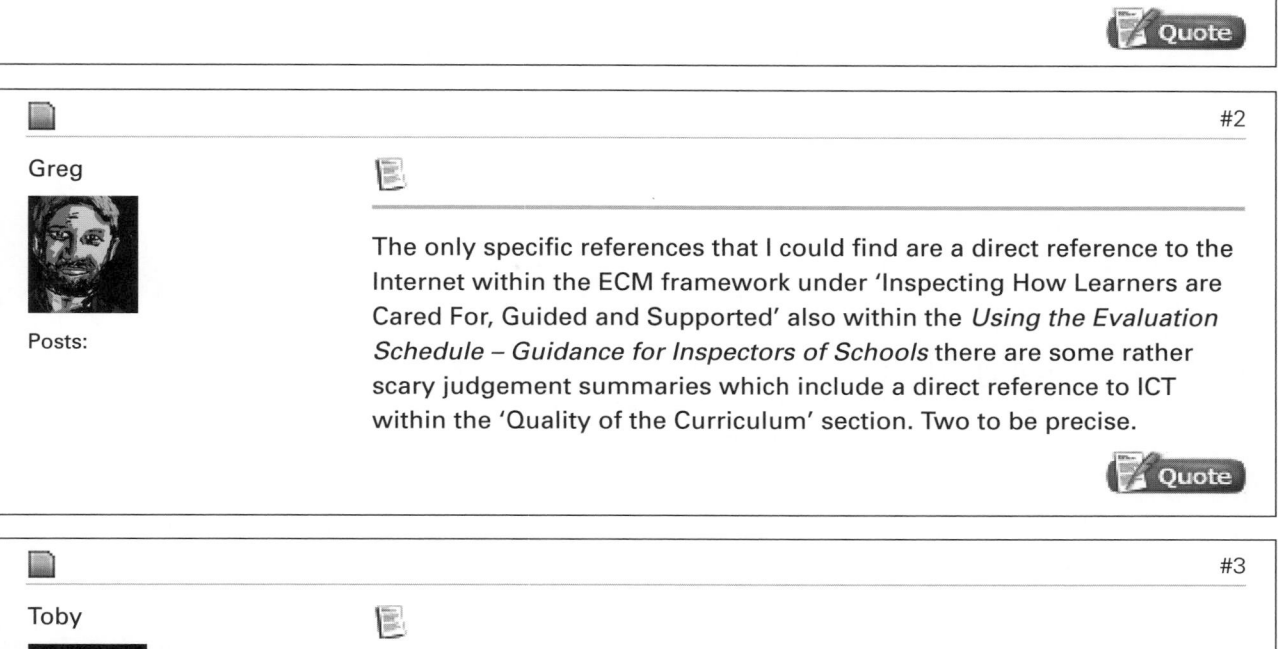

Greg   #2

Posts:

The only specific references that I could find are a direct reference to the Internet within the ECM framework under 'Inspecting How Learners are Cared For, Guided and Supported' also within the *Using the Evaluation Schedule – Guidance for Inspectors of Schools* there are some rather scary judgement summaries which include a direct reference to ICT within the 'Quality of the Curriculum' section. Two to be precise.

Quote

Toby   #3

Posts:

Ditto.

Quote

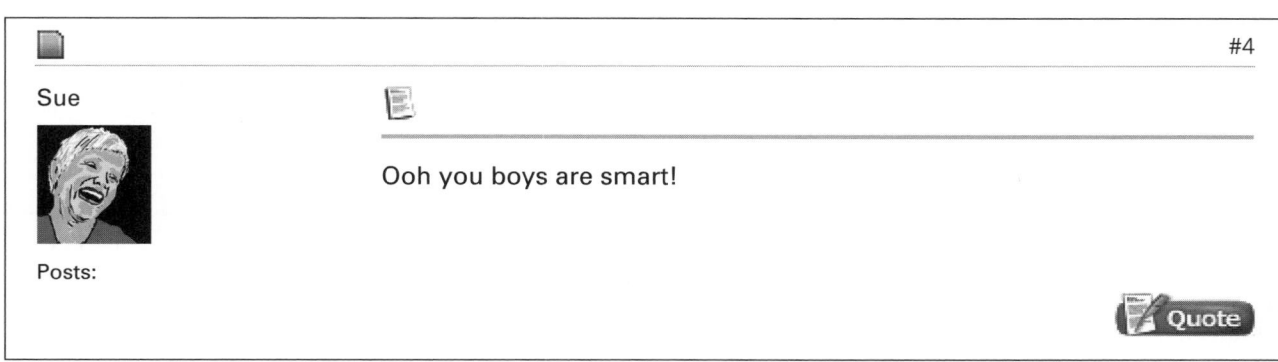

Sue   #4

Posts:

Ooh you boys are smart!

Quote

7th May

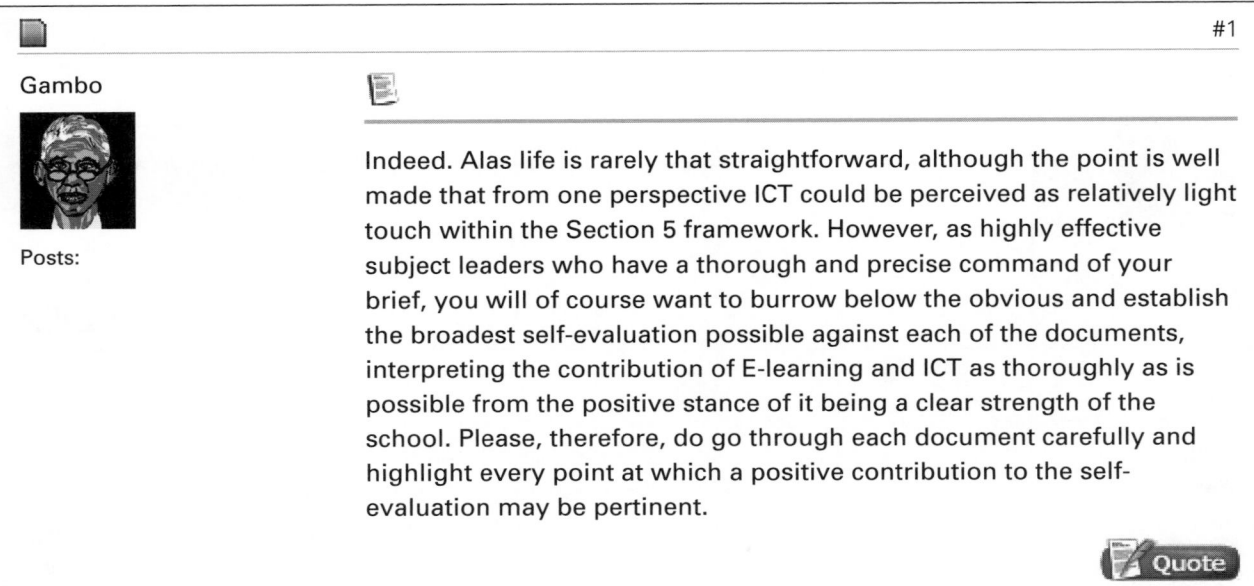

	#1
Gambo Posts:	Indeed. Alas life is rarely that straightforward, although the point is well made that from one perspective ICT could be perceived as relatively light touch within the Section 5 framework. However, as highly effective subject leaders who have a thorough and precise command of your brief, you will of course want to burrow below the obvious and establish the broadest self-evaluation possible against each of the documents, interpreting the contribution of E-learning and ICT as thoroughly as is possible from the positive stance of it being a clear strength of the school. Please, therefore, do go through each document carefully and highlight every point at which a positive contribution to the self-evaluation may be pertinent.

Table 9.2 Ofsted documentation review

Document title	Relevant section	ICT relevant statement
'Every Child Matters' Framework for the Inspection of Schools in England from September 2005	Introduction	Judgements made about *standards and achievement ... quality of the school's provision*
	The inspection system – what is inspected?	the *quality of the education* provided in the school ... meets *the needs of the range of pupils* *standards achieved* *leadership and management* whether the *financial resources* made available to the school are managed efficiently *Well-being* of ... pupils.
	The inspection system – internal school self-evaluation The inspection process – before the Inspection	The school should be encouraged to seek the views of any *significant partners* in the school's work
	The inspection process – onsite inspection	tracking *school processes* analysing *samples of pupils' current and recent work*
	The common inspection schedule	the extent to which ... is meeting the following five outcomes for children and young people *1. Being healthy* *2. Staying safe* *3. Enjoying and achieving* *4. Making a positive contribution* *5. Achieving economic well-being*

	The common inspection schedule – overall effectiveness	the effectiveness of any steps taken to promote *improvement since the last inspection* the effectiveness of *links with other organisations* to promote the well-being of learners
	The common inspection schedule – achievement	the extent to which *learners enjoy their work* (3) the acquisition of *workplace skills* (4, 5) the development of *skills* which contribute to the social and *economic well-being of the learner (2, 4, 5)* the extent to which learners adopt *safe practices* and a *healthy lifestyle* (1, 2, 5)
	The common inspection schedule – quality of provision	*resources promote learning* *curriculum meet external requirements* *enrichment activities ... contribute to learners'* enjoyment and achievement provision contributes to the learners' capacity *to stay safe and healthy* the quality and *accessibility of information*, advice and guidance
	The common inspection schedule – leadership and management	how effectively ... clearly direct improvement and promote the well-being of learners through **high quality care, education and training the adequacy and suitability of staff the adequacy and suitability of specialist equipment, learning resources and accommodation** **how effectively and efficiently resources are deployed**
Conducting the Inspection – Guidance for Inspectors of Schools	The approach to inspection	There is a strong focus on the **well-being of pupils** in the light of the Green Paper *Every Child Matters* and the Children Act 2004 **Individual subjects are not inspected. The quality of the school's leadership and management** ... the school's capacity to improve, are at the heart of this approach to inspection.
	Using the school's Self-Evaluation Form	When compiling the pre-inspection briefing, the lead inspector will evaluate the *school's view of itself as expressed in the SEF Inconsistencies between the SEF's conclusions and the evidence*, and also from significant matters that the *SEF seems to have omitted*
	Inspecting teaching	The basis of the *school's view of the quality of teaching needs to be tested out*. Where, for example, the outcomes are good, the teaching is likely to be good *scrutiny of the school's records of lesson monitoring* a series of *short, focused visits to lessons*

Document title	Relevant section	ICT relevant statement
	Inspecting how well the curriculum meets the needs of the learners	relevant *senior member of staff to explore any issues* should cover the implementation of *national strategies* and the development of *basic skills*. Discussions with learners should indicate how they *experience and enjoy the curriculum*. Where particular elements of the curriculum, such as ... *safe and healthy lifestyles*, are said to be delivered across the curriculum, this can be checked out by talking with staff and learners about these matters and, if necessary, looking through a small *sample of schemes of work*
		The quality of individual education plans The *range and take-up of enrichment activities* The school might well wish to *suggest to inspectors activities that might be observed*.
	Inspecting how learners are cared for, guided and supported	They (pupils) should be asked whether they *feel safe* ... and whether they are aware of risks, for example *FROM THE INTERNET* whether the school does all it can to provide a *safe physical environment*
	Inspecting leadership and management	... selecting two or three *major initiatives and devising inspection trails* to see how effectively they are implemented. The *quality of professional development arrangements*
Using the evaluation schedule – guidance for inspectors of schools	The purpose of inspections	Inspectors must report on: *the quality of the education provided in the school* *how far the education meets the needs of the range of pupils at the school* *the educational standards achieved in the school* *the quality of the leadership in and management of the school, including whether the financial resources made available to the school are managed efficiently*

Ofsted material is Crown Copyright reproduced under the terms of HMSO Guidance Note 5.
Available on the net at http://www.james-wright.org

10th May

Table 9.2 provides a comprehensive overview of each of the documents in terms of direct commentaries that E-learning and ICT might reasonably expect to contribute towards. Of course, the contribution will vary enormously from school to school and no school would wish to cross-reference each of the areas highlighted, however, it should provide direction for subject leaders when bringing together the self-evaluation that they are already completing and directing this appropriately in terms of any future inspection.

Table 9.3 Ofsted judgement summaries

Overall effectiveness	
Outstanding (1)	Exceptional: all or **almost all elements of the school's work.**
Good (2)	Generally strong performance across **all aspects of a school's work.** A school may be good in a variety of ways, and may have **pockets of excellence,**
Satisfactory (3)	The school's work is **inadequate in no major area.**
Inadequate (4)	A school is likely to be inadequate if the standards achieved; learners' personal development and well-being: **overall quality of provision;** or leadership and management is judged to be inadequate.
Achievement & Standards	
Outstanding (1)	
Good (2)	**Most subjects and courses perform well,** and some better than this, with **nothing that is unsatisfactory.**
Satisfactory (3)	
Inadequate (4)	**Performance in a number of subjects and courses is unsatisfactory.**
Personal Development & Well-Being	
Outstanding (1)	Learners' personal development and well-being are at **least good in all or nearly all respects.**
Good (2)	**They feel safe, are safety conscious without being fearful,** and they adopt healthy lifestyles.
Satisfactory (3)	
Inadequate (4)	Learners **do not** engage readily with the community or **make satisfactory progress in the skills and qualities that will equip them for work.**
Quality of Teaching	
Outstanding (1)	Teaching is at least good in all or nearly all respects and is **exemplary in significant elements.**
Good (2)	**The teachers' good subject knowledge** lends confidence to their teaching styles, which engage learners and encourage them to work well independently. **Teaching assistants and other classroom helpers, and resources, are well deployed to support learning.**
Satisfactory (3)	Teaching is **inadequate in no major respect,**
Inadequate (4)	Learners generally, or particular groups of them, do not make adequate progress because the **teaching is unsatisfactory. Teachers' knowledge of the curriculum and the course requirements are inadequate,** and the level of challenge is often wrongly pitched. The **methods used do not sufficiently engage and encourage the learners.**
Quality of the Curriculum	
Outstanding (1)	The curriculum exemplary in significant elements.
Good (2)	**There is good provision for literacy, numeracy and ICT. Education for safety and health is good,** as are the **opportunities for enrichment,** which are varied, have a high take up and are much enjoyed.

Satisfactory (3)	The curriculum is **inadequate in no major respect**, and may be good in some respects.
Inadequate (4)	There is **weak provision for literacy, numeracy or ICT**. There is **inadequate provision for education in safety and health** and work-related learning. **The school has a limited range of enrichment activities** and opportunities for learners to take responsibility in the community, or they do not participate adequately in those that are available.
Care, Guidance & Support	
Outstanding (1)	
Good (2)	**Arrangements for the safeguarding of pupils are robust and regularly reviewed, and risk assessments are carefully attended to.**
Satisfactory (3)	
Inadequate (4)	**Its systems are too weak, or staff are inadequately trained or vigilant, to safeguard or promote learners' safety and health.**
Leadership & Management	
Outstanding (1)	
Good (2)	**The leadership of the school is successfully focused on raising standards and promoting the personal development and well-being of learners. Resources are well used.**
Satisfactory (3)	
Inadequate (4)	Leadership and management have too little effect so that **standards are too low** quality of its **self-evaluation is inadequate** and managers do not have a realistic view of its weaknesses **Resources are not well deployed**, because the school does not have a well-ordered sense of its priorities,

Ofsted material is Crown Copyright reproduced under the terms of HMSO Guidance Note 5.
Available on the net at http://www.james-wright.org

Table 9.3 takes the judgement summaries mentioned previously and again highlights areas for which an E-learning brief may substantially contribute. Spend some time studying each document possibly as a checklist for your own current SEF contribution.

13th May

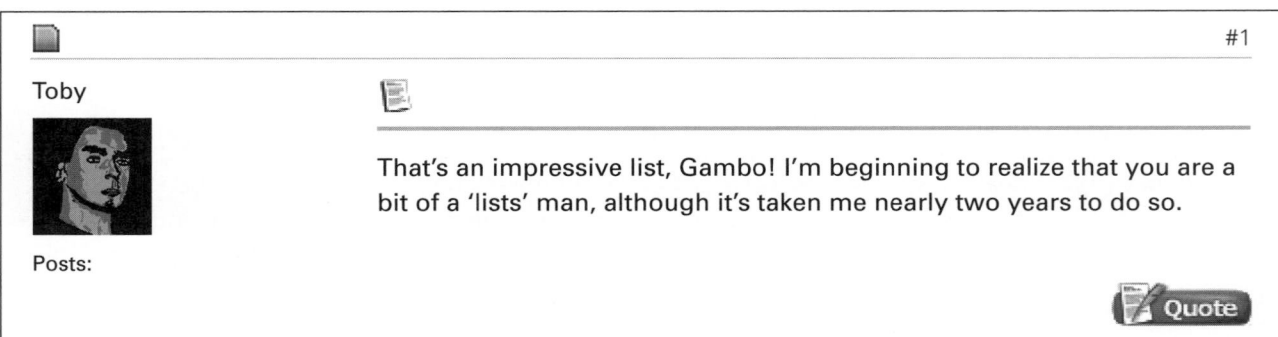

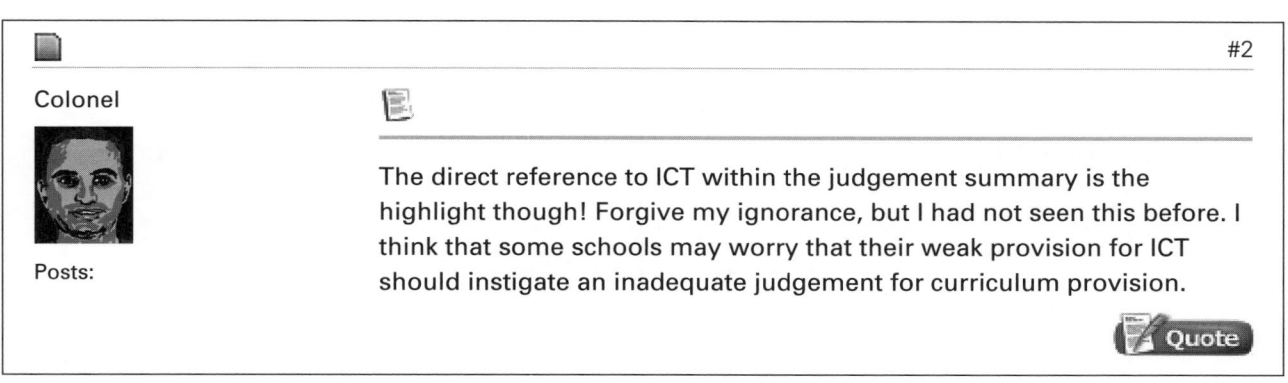

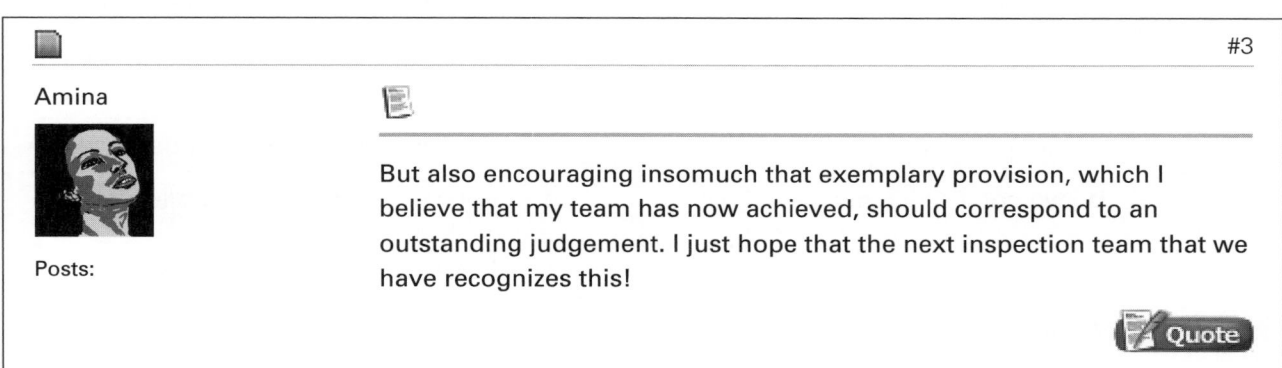

15th May

Summarizing the statements that I highlighted within Tables 9.2 and 9.3, I believe that the following list identifies 11 core elements that colleagues should seek to address through the SEF document.

Bringing it all together – focus of Section 5 Ofsted framework

Standards in ICT – pupil work samples
Provision of equipment and management of resources
Inclusive use of ICT
How well the subject is led and managed (M & E)
Adoption of safe practices
Links with other organizations
Enjoyment – enrichment
A key skill – Economic well-being
Staff confidence and competence – professional development
Accessibility of information
National strategies.

Finally, each of these elements identified within the original Ofsted documentation may be realigned with the core sections of the Self-Evaluation Form (SEF) in order to identify how and in which areas colleagues may most effectively contribute to this document. Table 9.4 indicates how this may best be achieved.

Table 9.4 E-learning contribution to SEF

Core ICT Self-evaluation elements	Relevant section of Ofsted SEF
Standards in ICT – pupil work samples	3 – Achievement & Standards
Provision of equipment and management of resources	5 – Quality of Provision 6 – Leadership & Management
Inclusive use of ICT	7 – Overall Effectiveness & Efficiency
How well the subject is led and managed (M & E)	5 – Quality of Provision 6 – Leadership & Management
Adoption of safe practices	4 – Personal Development & Well-Being 5 – Quality of Provision
Links with other organizations	7 – Overall Effectiveness & Efficiency
Enjoyment – enrichment	4 – Personal Development & Well-Being 5 – Quality of Provision 6 – Leadership & Management
A key skill – economic well-being	3 – Achievement & Standards 4 – Personal Development & Well-Being
Staff confidence and competence – professional development	5 – Quality of Provision 6 – Leadership & Management
Accessibility of information	5 – Quality of Provision
National strategies	6 – Leadership & Management

Available on the net at http://www.james-wright.org

Colleagues may wish to re-draft their own contribution to the school's Self-Evaluation Form in order to have materials available to submit for senior management team (SMT) review as part of the ongoing school improvement cycle.

16th May

Celia

Posts:

#1

Would it be possible to request sample SEF extracts from colleagues? Traditionally our SEF has been very light on ICT, anorexic in fact. I'd really appreciate seeing some strong examples.

Quote

#2

Colonel

Posts:

Here is the relevant contribution for Section 3a from our updated Self-Evaluation Form.

What are learners' achievement and standards in their work?
Assessment for learning is fully embedded at ****** and all subjects are carefully assessed and moderated using the online portfolios viewable from the school website. Recent subject leader moderation of standards in ICT, validated by local authority support indicated that standards were above average for all strands of the ICT curriculum with 84% of pupils attaining Level 4 or above by the end of Year 6. The priority that was placed upon developing core skills in ICT over recent years is now enabling pupils to develop their learning in all areas of the curriculum supported by the purchase of mobile laptop equipment which provides greater access to ICT across the curriculum.

#3

Greg

Posts:

We have just updated section 4, Personal Development & Well-Being to account for the contribution of ICT to the Every Child Matters agenda. I am happy for colleagues to let me know what they think.

4b – To what extent do learners feel safe and adopt safe practices?
Children at XXXXX are intelligent and safe users of the Internet as reported via the annual pupil survey. We have instigated an E-safety scheme of work so that all children are taught of the potential dangers of the Internet and in September we shall host our first parents information evening in order for pupils to share with their families the lessons they have learnt. The Acceptable Internet Use policy was updated in 2006 to account for developments in technology and in line with BECTA guidelines.

4c – How much do learners enjoy their education?
ICT enriches the curriculum through the use of innovative technologies that allow all learners to excel. For example each year-group produces its own termly podcast which is downloaded by parents from the school website. Feedback obtained by the school council highlighted the popularity of this initiative with children of all ages.

4e – How well do learners prepare for their future economic well-being?
We provide each pupil with comprehensive access to ICT facilities both as a discrete national curriculum subject and as a key skill across each subject area. By the end of Year 6 pupils are expected to achieve the regional passport in ICT skills which equates to Level 4 of the national curriculum and which is recognized and developed through our transition work into Y7 with the cluster high school.

17th May

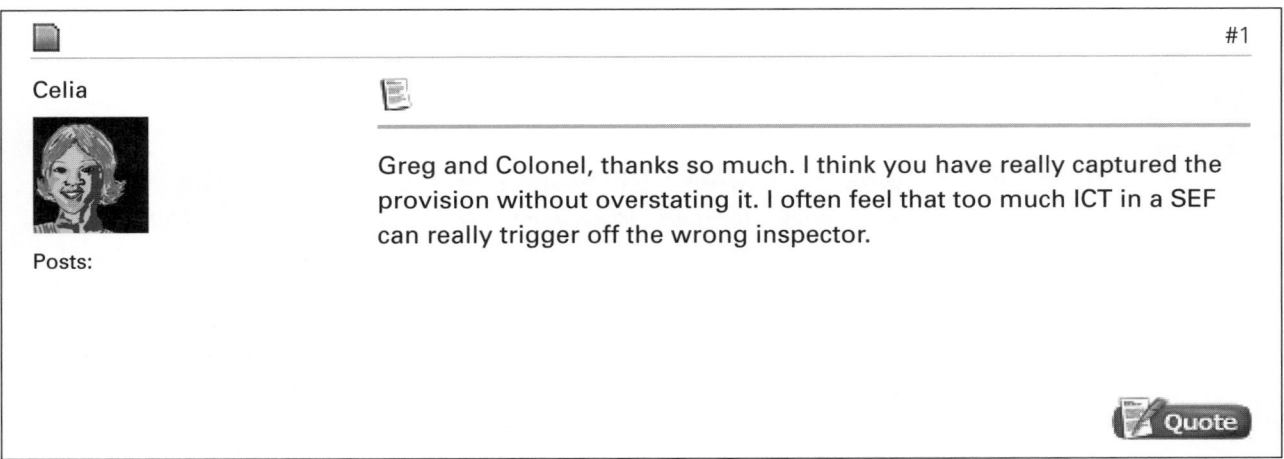

#1

Celia

Posts:

Greg and Colonel, thanks so much. I think you have really captured the provision without overstating it. I often feel that too much ICT in a SEF can really trigger off the wrong inspector.

Quote

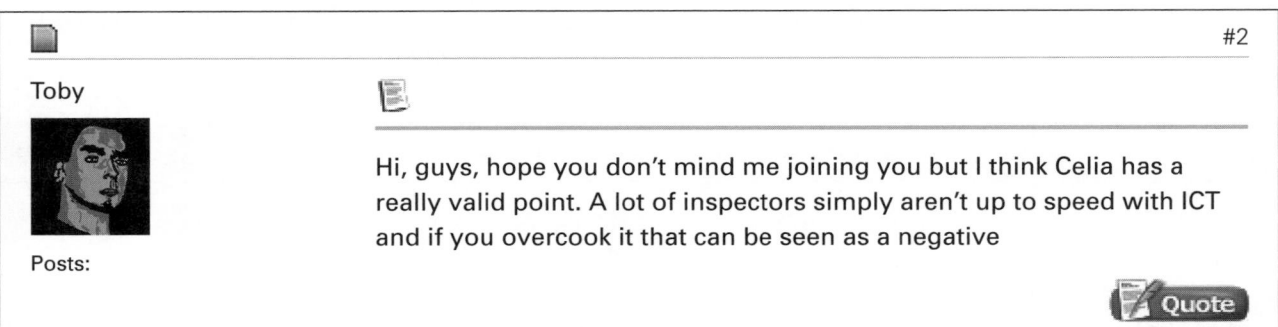

#2

Toby

Posts:

Hi, guys, hope you don't mind me joining you but I think Celia has a really valid point. A lot of inspectors simply aren't up to speed with ICT and if you overcook it that can be seen as a negative

Quote

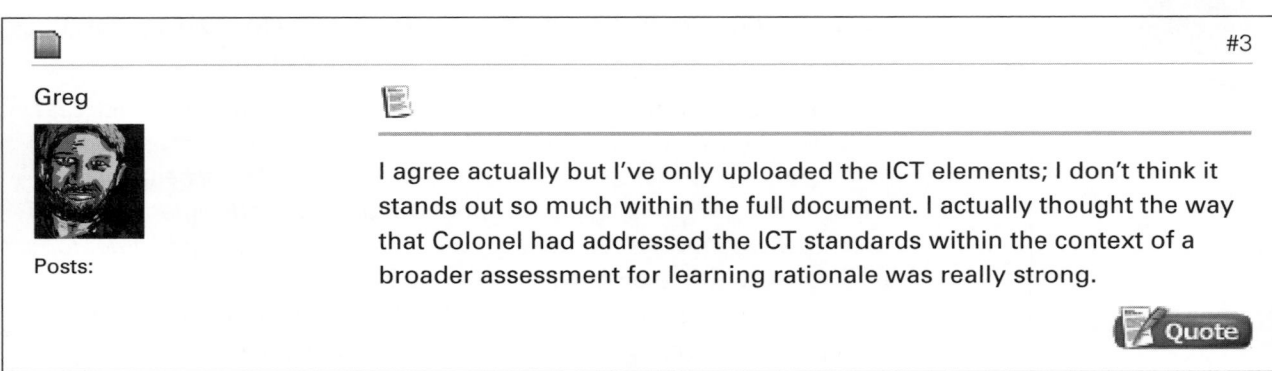

#3

Greg

Posts:

I agree actually but I've only uploaded the ICT elements; I don't think it stands out so much within the full document. I actually thought the way that Colonel had addressed the ICT standards within the context of a broader assessment for learning rationale was really strong.

Quote

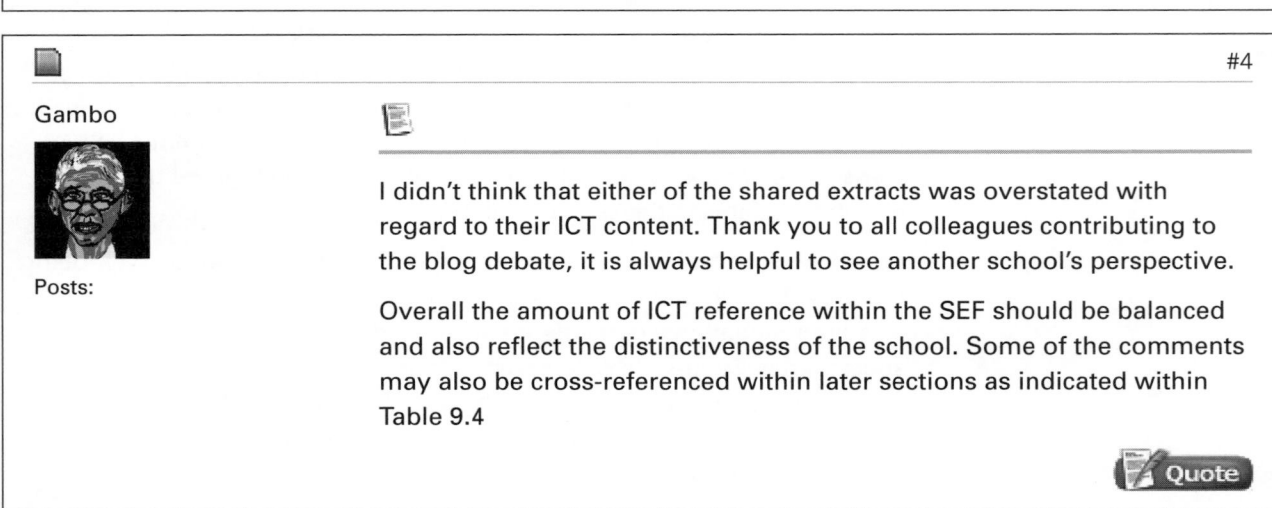

#4

Gambo

Posts:

I didn't think that either of the shared extracts was overstated with regard to their ICT content. Thank you to all colleagues contributing to the blog debate, it is always helpful to see another school's perspective.

Overall the amount of ICT reference within the SEF should be balanced and also reflect the distinctiveness of the school. Some of the comments may also be cross-referenced within later sections as indicated within Table 9.4

Quote

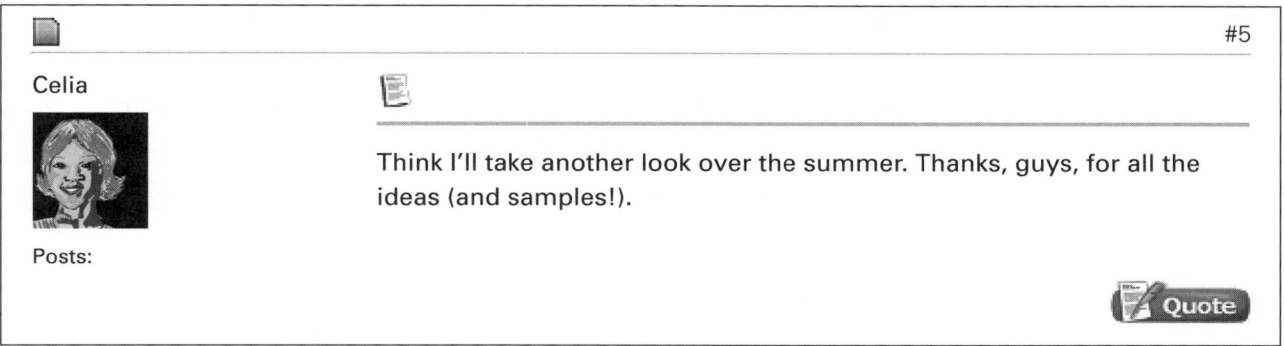

Celia

Posts:

Think I'll take another look over the summer. Thanks, guys, for all the ideas (and samples!).

Quote

18th May

Week 34, Task 26 – New Technologies, Video-Editing, Podcasts and Pupil TV

Colleagues need not only to be proactive when introducing new technologies as they become available and relevant for a school, but also should constantly evaluate the impact of such initiatives. This term colleagues will be asked to evaluate the impact of three groups of technologies using a standard evaluation template, beginning this week with a group of broadcast or presentational use of multimedia. Each activity set allows teachers and pupils opportunities to combine media in order to present the outcome of their work in a rich, contemporary highly motivating form. Colleagues should be aware of the impact potential of each technology and to decide how to prioritize each one within the school's particular circumstances. Remember that it is unlikely that any school will be using all new technologies effectively and may seek to prioritize investment based upon particular circumstances.

Digital media is used in primary schools because of its unique ability to meet the needs of different types of learner; to develop speaking and listening skills and support the use of drama; to facilitate collaboration and to introduce creativity within an enriched curriculum. Group projects provide a variety of exciting roles and responsibilities demanding different types of knowledge and skills.

Within the Revised Primary Strategy literacy framework (www.standards.dfes.gov.uk/primary frameworks/literacy) one of the 12 strands of learning focuses specifically upon group discussion and interaction. Consider specifically how any of the highlighted forms of media can be used to address this strand against the following DfES criteria.

'Foundation stage – Interact with others, negotiating plans and activities and taking turns in conversation Use talk to organise, sequence and clarify thinking, ideas, feelings and events.

Year 1 – Take turns to speak, listen to each other's suggestions and talk about what they are going to do; ask and answer questions, make relevant contributions, offer suggestions and take turns; explain their views to others in a small group; decide how to report the group's views to the class.

Year 2 – Ensure that everyone contributes, allocate tasks, and consider alternatives and reach agreement; work effectively in groups by ensuring that each group member takes a turn challenging, supporting and moving on; listen to each other's views and preferences, agree the next steps to take and identify contributions by each group member.

Year 3 – Use talk to organise roles and action; actively include and respond to all members of the group; use the language of possibility to investigate and reflect on feelings, behaviour or relationships.

Year 4 – Take different roles in groups and use the language appropriate to them, including the roles of leader, reporter, scribe and mentor; use time, resources and group members efficiently by distributing tasks, checking progress and making back-up plans; identify the main points of each speaker; compare their arguments and how they are presented.

Year 5 – Plan and manage a group task over time using different levels of planning; understand different ways to take the lead and support others in groups; understand the process of decision-making.

Year 6 – Consider examples of conflict and resolution, exploring the language used; understand and use a variety of ways to criticise constructively and respond to criticism.'

DfES copyright material is reproduced under the terms of HMSO Guidance Note 8.

Digital video

Digital video should be a prominent feature within your school as a key learning tool. The traditional high cost, 'expert' categorization of movie-making in schools has now subsided and the use of digital video has become a mainstream tool for creative teachers. As well as its enormous acknowledged motivational appeal, digital video projects naturally facilitate meaningful group work in a range of cross-curricular settings as well as providing unique innovative learning opportunities that are suited to a range of different learning styles. There is also an increasing realization that schools need to be innovative in the way that they develop pupils' digital literacy. Producing, editing and manipulating digital video provides a unique opportunity for children to experience concepts such as media bias, propaganda, persuasion and point of view. Digital video is the most important cultural medium that exists. Consider the use of social collaboration websites such as YouTube and MySpace and you begin to understand the real relevance and influence of video. Finally, and perhaps most persuasively, is the shift from teacher to learner when producing and editing digital video. Unlike many innovations such as the proliferation of the interactive whiteboard that have fundamentally impacted upon teaching, these media focus directly on the learner and, as such, potentially are a much more powerful factor in contributing to achievement.

20th May

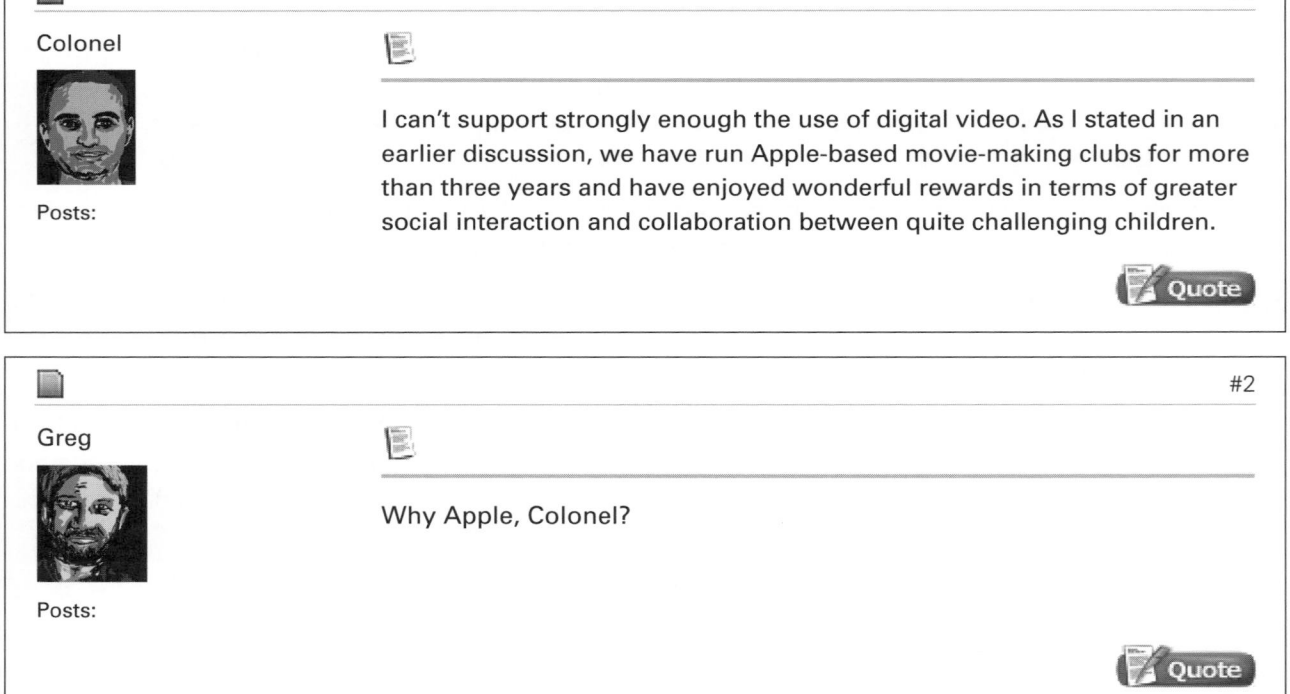

	#1
Colonel	
Posts:	I can't support strongly enough the use of digital video. As I stated in an earlier discussion, we have run Apple-based movie-making clubs for more than three years and have enjoyed wonderful rewards in terms of greater social interaction and collaboration between quite challenging children.

	#2
Greg	
Posts:	Why Apple, Colonel?

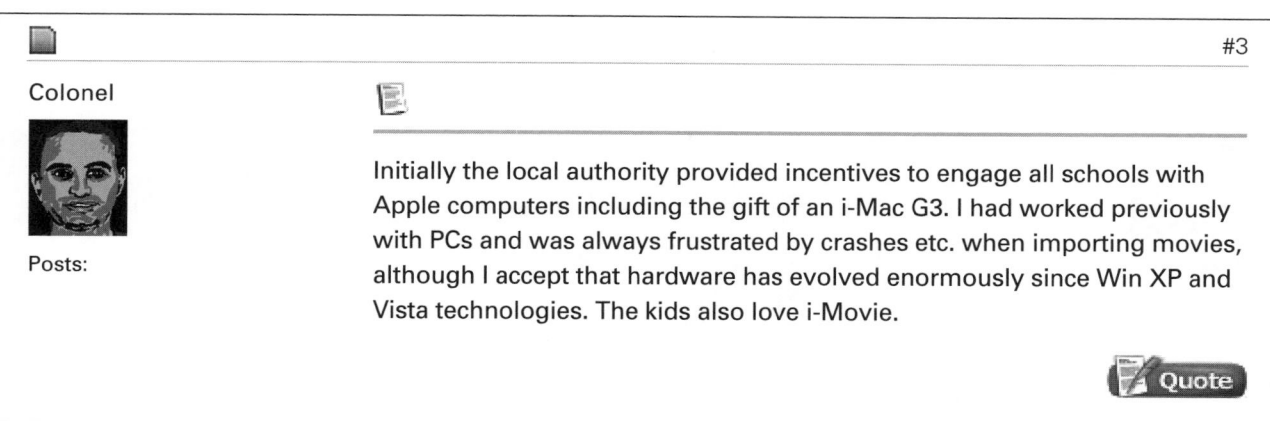

Colonel

Posts:

#3

Initially the local authority provided incentives to engage all schools with Apple computers including the gift of an i-Mac G3. I had worked previously with PCs and was always frustrated by crashes etc. when importing movies, although I accept that hardware has evolved enormously since Win XP and Vista technologies. The kids also love i-Movie.

Quote

21st May

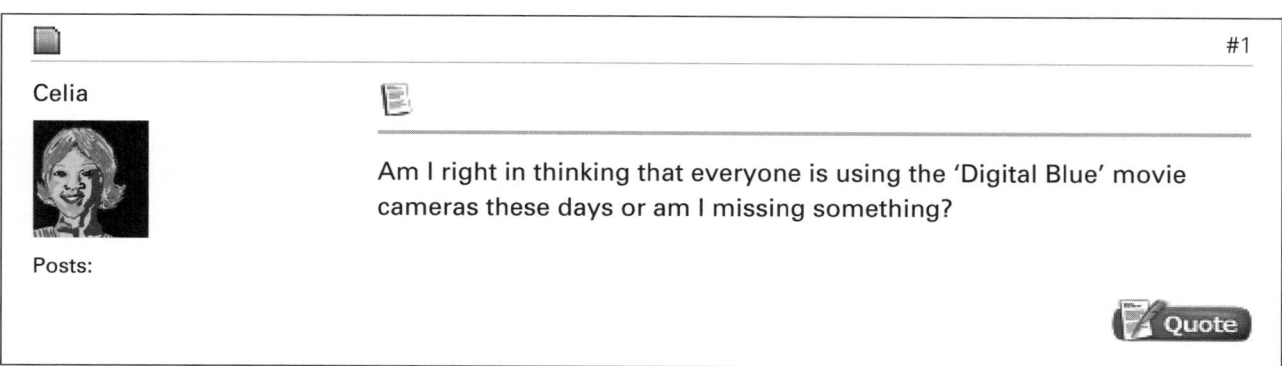

Celia

Posts:

#1

Am I right in thinking that everyone is using the 'Digital Blue' movie cameras these days or am I missing something?

Quote

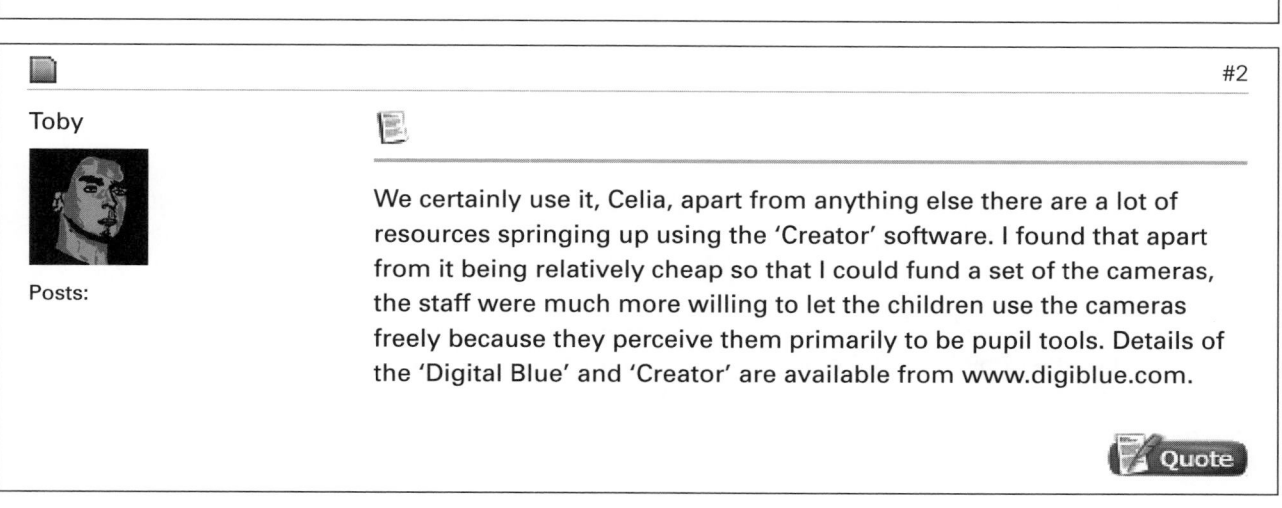

Toby

Posts:

#2

We certainly use it, Celia, apart from anything else there are a lot of resources springing up using the 'Creator' software. I found that apart from it being relatively cheap so that I could fund a set of the cameras, the staff were much more willing to let the children use the cameras freely because they perceive them primarily to be pupil tools. Details of the 'Digital Blue' and 'Creator' are available from www.digiblue.com.

Quote

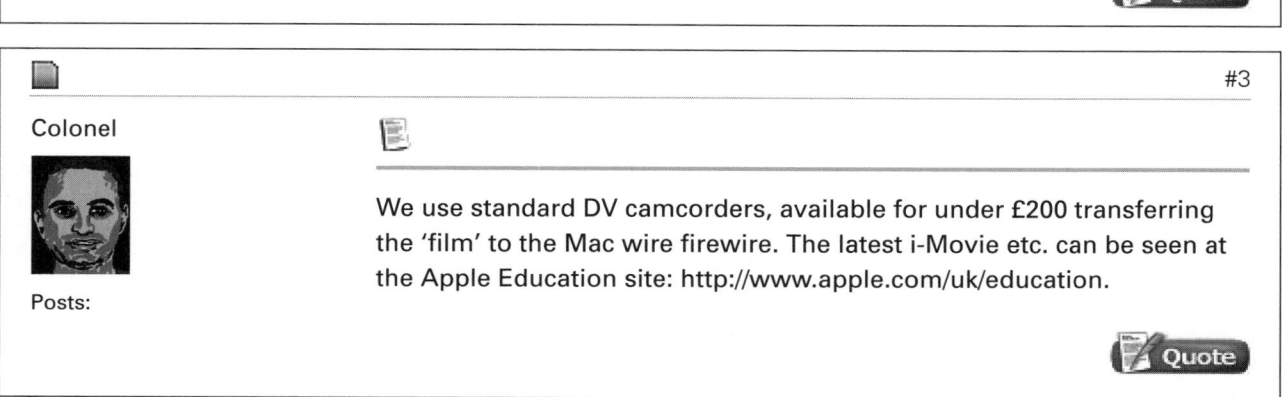

Colonel

Posts:

#3

We use standard DV camcorders, available for under £200 transferring the 'film' to the Mac wire firewire. The latest i-Movie etc. can be seen at the Apple Education site: http://www.apple.com/uk/education.

Quote

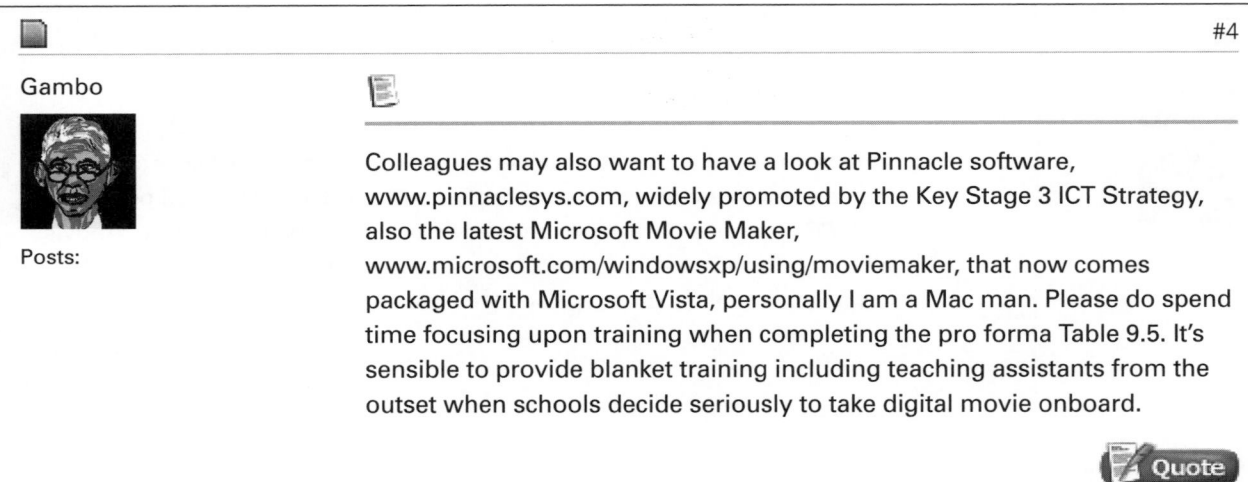

#4

Gambo

Posts:

Colleagues may also want to have a look at Pinnacle software, www.pinnaclesys.com, widely promoted by the Key Stage 3 ICT Strategy, also the latest Microsoft Movie Maker, www.microsoft.com/windowsxp/using/moviemaker, that now comes packaged with Microsoft Vista, personally I am a Mac man. Please do spend time focusing upon training when completing the pro forma Table 9.5. It's sensible to provide blanket training including teaching assistants from the outset when schools decide seriously to take digital movie onboard.

Quote

21st May

Table 9.5 New technology review, Part 1.

Type of technology	Video-editing	Podcasting	Pupil TV
Perceived benefits	Highly motivational Meet the needs of different types of learners Develop speaking and listening skills Multiple cross-curricular opportunities Facilitate collaboration Introduce creativity High medium relevance Focus upon the Learner Develops digital literacy	Highly motivational Develop speaking and listening skills Multiple cross-curricular opportunities Facilitate collaboration Introduce creativity Focus upon the Learner Develops digital literacy	Highly motivational Meet the needs of different types of learners Develop speaking and listening skills Multiple cross-curricular opportunities Facilitate collaboration Introduce creativity High medium relevance Focus upon the Learner Develops digital literacy
Potential drawbacks	Teacher training requirements Moderately expensive medium	Teacher training requirements E-safety concerns	Teacher training requirements E-safety concerns Highly expensive medium Labour intensive
Current school position			
Strategic goals			
Key actions needed			
Costs			

Available on the net at http://www.james-wright.org

Table 9.5 affords colleagues the opportunity to reflect upon how various broadcast presentational technologies might impact within their school. Direct some time this week to completing the template in order to assimilate each initiative within the school's overall ICT development plan, reflecting upon potential obstacles that might need to be overcome. Most initiatives that take off do so because the seeds of success are already present within school.

Podcasts

As with digital video, podcasting has become a popular, achievable activity within primary schools that have rapidly adopted technology initiated within popular culture. The emergence of Apple's iPod as 'must-have' iconic 'kit' used primarily for music downloads has created a huge market for portable digital audio devices, which in turn has developed an industry exploring new ways of using the proliferated hardware, thus the rising popularity in the distribution of audio files across the Internet. Schools wishing to adopt this 'in-house' radio broadcast facility have seized the opportunity to develop audio activities in much the same way as they have with digital video but have the added benefit of streaming the end product across the Internet using RSS syndication feeds obtained either commercially or, in many cases, by the local authority. Client software 'reads' the media files enabling automatic download.

22nd May

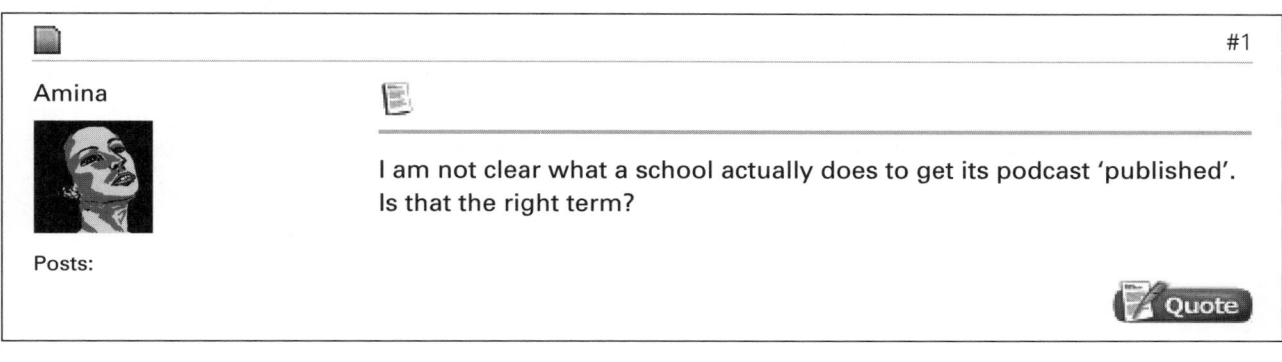

#1

Amina

Posts:

I am not clear what a school actually does to get its podcast 'published'. Is that the right term?

Quote

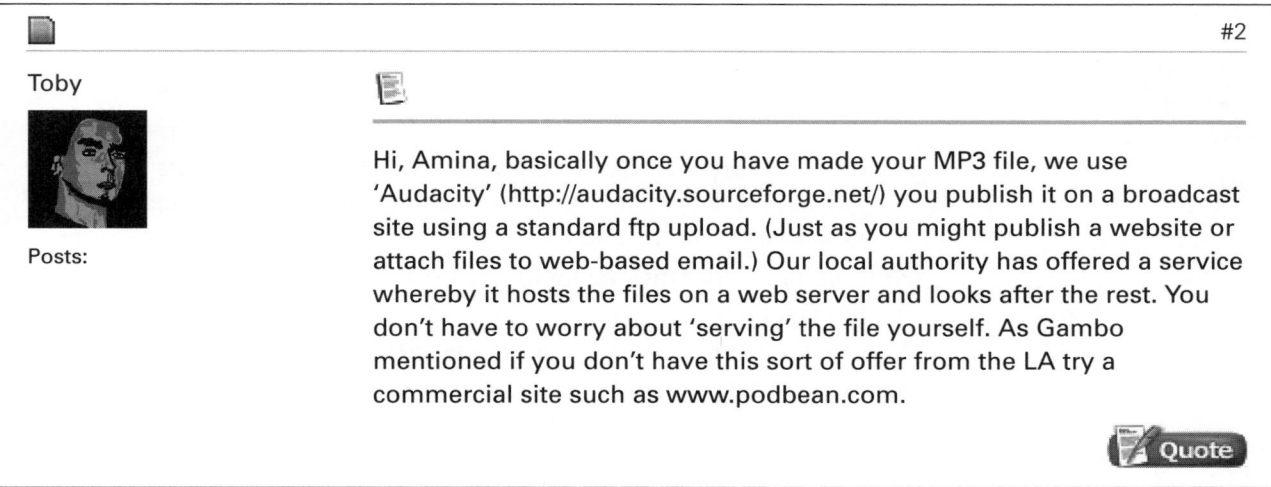

#2

Toby

Posts:

Hi, Amina, basically once you have made your MP3 file, we use 'Audacity' (http://audacity.sourceforge.net/) you publish it on a broadcast site using a standard ftp upload. (Just as you might publish a website or attach files to web-based email.) Our local authority has offered a service whereby it hosts the files on a web server and looks after the rest. You don't have to worry about 'serving' the file yourself. As Gambo mentioned if you don't have this sort of offer from the LA try a commercial site such as www.podbean.com.

Quote

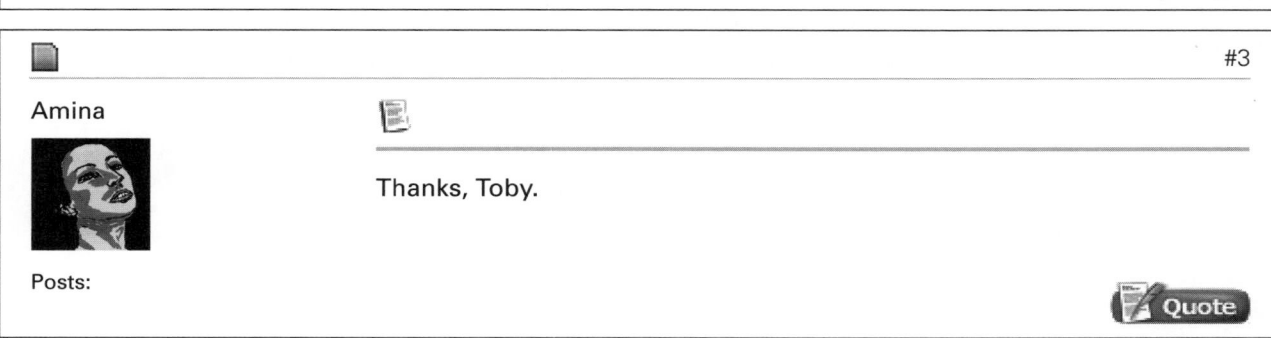

#3

Amina

Posts:

Thanks, Toby.

Quote

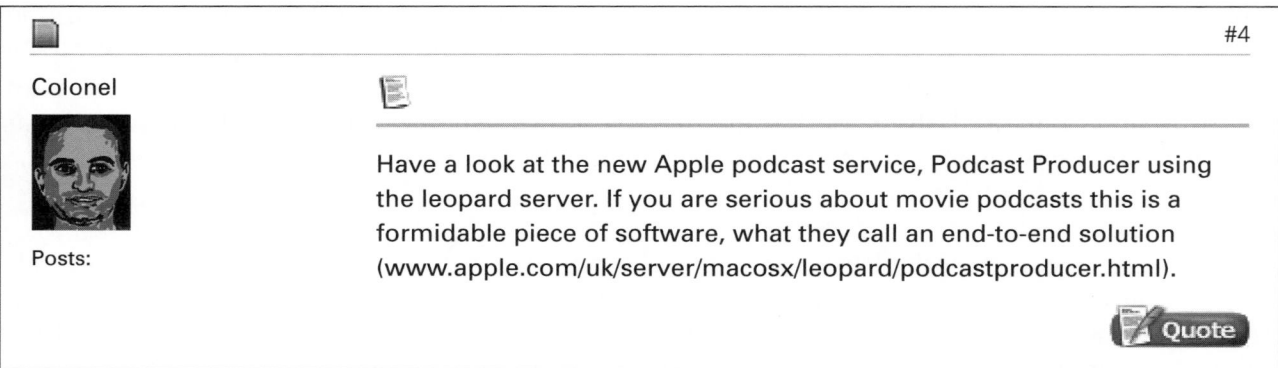

Podcasts enable pupils and staff to share information with anyone in real time. Consider the potential for lessons to be downloaded at home by absent pupils within the context of our discussions regarding the development of learning platforms. In terms of equipment this is a relatively inexpensive activity given that most PCs are equipped with sound-recording equipment and there is a variety of free 'mixing' software available. Schools that develop podcast initiatives will generally invest in some medium-quality digital sound recorders and tend to use MP3 players and iPods rather than the computer for portability when listening to other podcasts.

Colleagues should aim to quickly get beyond the technology and focus upon the 'production' editing elements of the practice where the real learning benefits lie. As was the case with the digital video work, it is the opportunity to plan, create and collaborate that brought about the strongest learning opportunities. The technology provides communication and audience for a high-quality end-product. It might be worth stating that podcasts may also incorporate video, although when broadcasting video files the E-safety concerns are increased proportionally.

23rd May

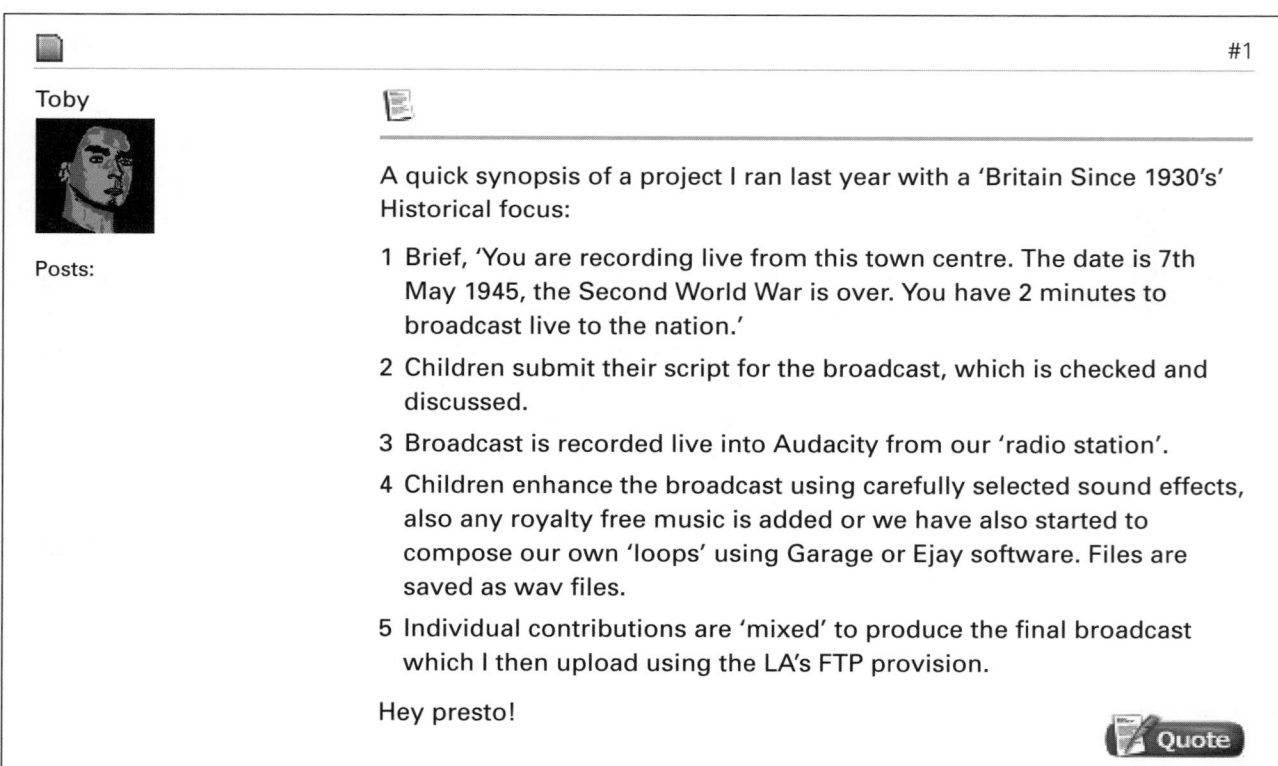

24th May

Pupils TV

The ultimate extension of multimedia activity for the aficionado is the creation of live pupils television and daily web broadcasts. At present there is not an enormous amount of activity from commercial organizations to market these services although a few small 'cottage' in-house arrangements do prosper. The 'behind scenes' work in maintaining such a studio is enormous, involving the maintenance of permanently manned 'crews', however the learning potential to establish a school on the E-learning map are also enormous. Colleagues interested in pursuing this avenue may want to look at some of the work of the incredible New Zealand school, Marina View (www.marinav.school.nz) where daily in-house television forms just part of an astonishing array of technology at the children's daily disposal.

Ultimately colleagues may need to carefully consider their own school's readiness to take on any such initiatives not simply in terms of technical infrastructure or even staff competence in maintaining services. Ultimately we are encountering the cutting edge of the curriculum review that we examined in April, and schools such as Marina View are redefining their core purpose in the light of the opportunities that the broadcast technologies are providing. E-learning co-ordinators have to be confident that they can take their school's senior management, its governors and the wider community with them on such a journey. This is the focus for our final study for this month.

25th May

Week 35, Task 27 – Working with Governors and Parents

Throughout the summer my eye was drawn to the battle of school fingerprinting that unfolded on the web during 2006. At the heart of the controversy was a school's use of biometrics to identify pupils for a variety of registration purposes. Colleagues may quickly brief themselves on the detail of the debate by Googling 'fingerprinting primary children', to learn about the can of worms opened up in terms of parental consent, consultation and the management of public relations in relation to the school's use of technology. A nucleus of parents appalled by the 'Big Brother' connotations of this activity skilfully used the Internet to describe the 'assault' on children's hands by teachers holding them down to fingerprint them and of their minds for assuring them that this was all right. Far be it from me to get involved in such a heated controversy here, however, it does serve as a cautionary tale for all colleagues engaging in state-of-the art practice which ultimately involves the lives of relatively young children. At the heart of every truly E-enabled school will be the intelligent informed support of its parents and governing body (so often the best sounding board for the more vociferous elements of the community served by the school).

I therefore ask two questions:

What is your governors' view of the E-learning development of the school?
What are parents' views about the E-learning development of the school?

Colleagues will no doubt have an immediate, almost intuitive, response to these questions but, as we approach the end of May, I recommend that you think carefully about how this view has been formed, the evidence that supports it and how you might go forward to challenge and test the views of the bodies that you serve.

26th May

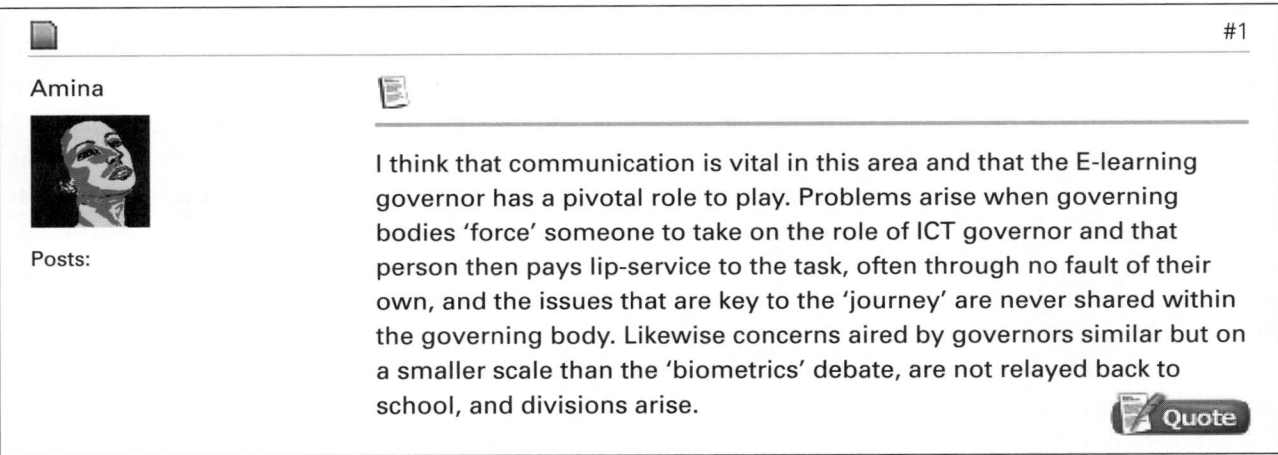

#1

Amina

Posts:

I think that communication is vital in this area and that the E-learning governor has a pivotal role to play. Problems arise when governing bodies 'force' someone to take on the role of ICT governor and that person then pays lip-service to the task, often through no fault of their own, and the issues that are key to the 'journey' are never shared within the governing body. Likewise concerns aired by governors similar but on a smaller scale than the 'biometrics' debate, are not relayed back to school, and divisions arise.

Quote

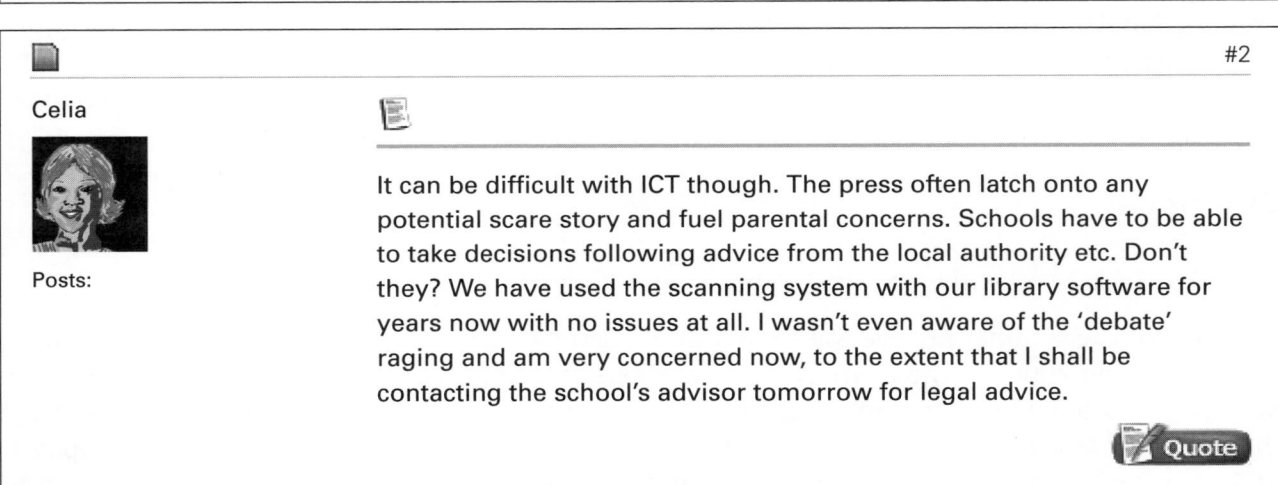

#2

Celia

Posts:

It can be difficult with ICT though. The press often latch onto any potential scare story and fuel parental concerns. Schools have to be able to take decisions following advice from the local authority etc. Don't they? We have used the scanning system with our library software for years now with no issues at all. I wasn't even aware of the 'debate' raging and am very concerned now, to the extent that I shall be contacting the school's advisor tomorrow for legal advice.

Quote

27th May

Transparency is a very important concept within our work. An E-confident school should wear its badge proudly and the core tenets of its vision should be integral to the school's broader aims. This is a concept that I have tried to contextualize within all of our work and which lies at the heart of the narrative that you drew up within the ICT team earlier this year. Governors and parents need to be comfortable with the school's ambitions, and confident that the school listens to their concerns. Your activity for this week is to discuss these issues within the E-learning/ICT team. Put it on the agenda at this term's group strategy meeting, giving the ICT governor plenty of advance notice so that, if there is anything in the shadows, they have fair opportunity to voice their concerns. Discuss the two questions that I posed at the beginning of the week and identify where the evidence base lies. For example, are parents' views about E-learning incorporated within the annual parental survey? If so, what is done with the information when it is harvested? How is information regarding developments related to E-learning shared with parents?

During our E-safety discussion we flagged up the notion of an Internet safety event or information evening. Similar activities could be planned annually or any parental event could have an E-learning dimension. I can think of very few initiatives that do not have an ICT element, and the objective is to build up over time the perception of the school as being one that is forward looking in terms of technology. Access to the local press should be developed so that major initiatives are applauded again allowing colleagues to manage the public perception of the overall strategy.

Finally ensure that your governors are well informed of the national ICT agenda and that it does not therefore become associated with just your school or, worse, with yourself. BECTA produces a range of extremely useful information bulletins for governors under their *ICT – Essential Guides for School Governors* publications, which cover ten different themes covering a variety of topics and available free from BECTA or for download as PDF. If governors have not already had access to these it may be useful to encourage them to do so.

Next month we return to our self-evaluation review as you reflect upon the school's progress since its last Ofsted inspection. We directly relate our E-journey to the national ICT benchmark and consider where we are each heading,

Chapter 10 • *June*

1st June

Week 37, Task 28 – School Self-Evaluation of ICT – Progress over Time

Following on from our examination of Ofsted's current position with regard to ICT, colleagues should continue to adopt a 360-degree rounded self-evaluation by undertaking a long-term review of developments. Co-ordinators must understand what the school's progress over time looks like from an external perspective and the evidence base from which this is derived.

To begin colleagues should seek out their previous Section 10 Ofsted inspection report (pre-2005) and re-familiarize themselves with the school therein described in terms of ICT. At this stage highlight all references to ICT both as a subject and as a cross-curricular tool and prepare to summarize the report to your ICT leadership team.

5th June

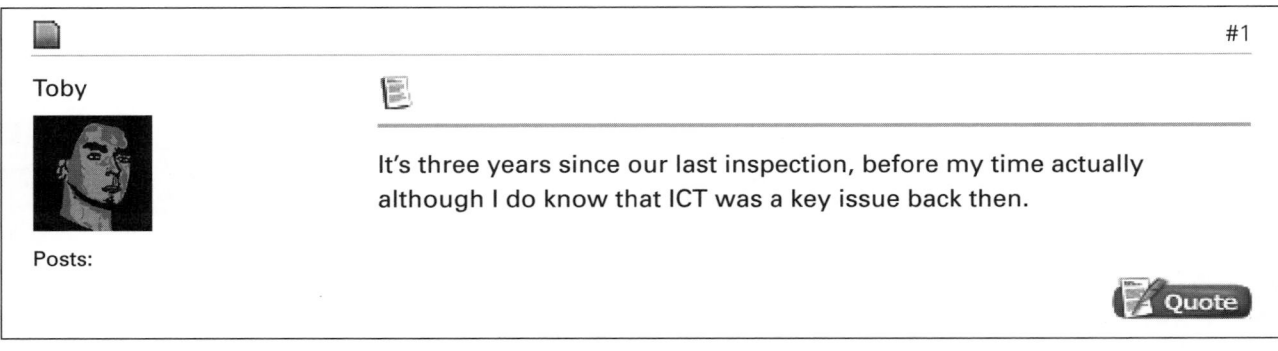

#1

Toby

Posts:

It's three years since our last inspection, before my time actually although I do know that ICT was a key issue back then.

Quote

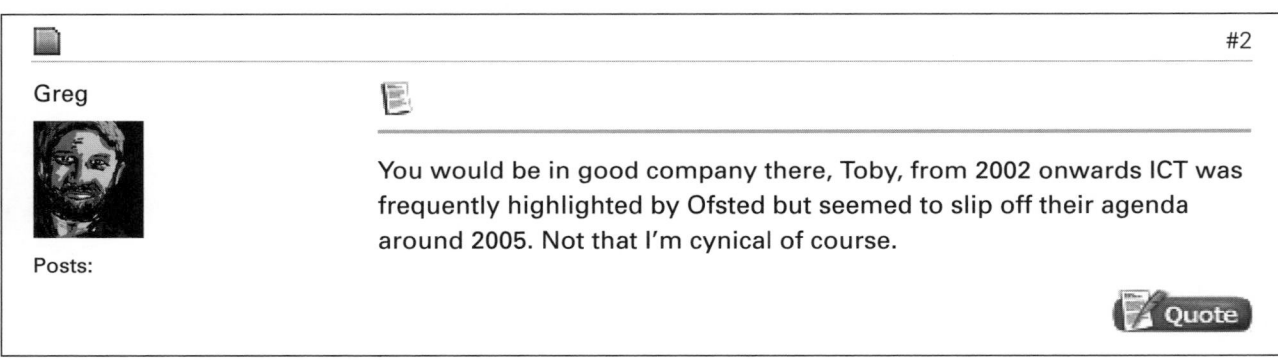

#2

Greg

Posts:

You would be in good company there, Toby, from 2002 onwards ICT was frequently highlighted by Ofsted but seemed to slip off their agenda around 2005. Not that I'm cynical of course.

Quote

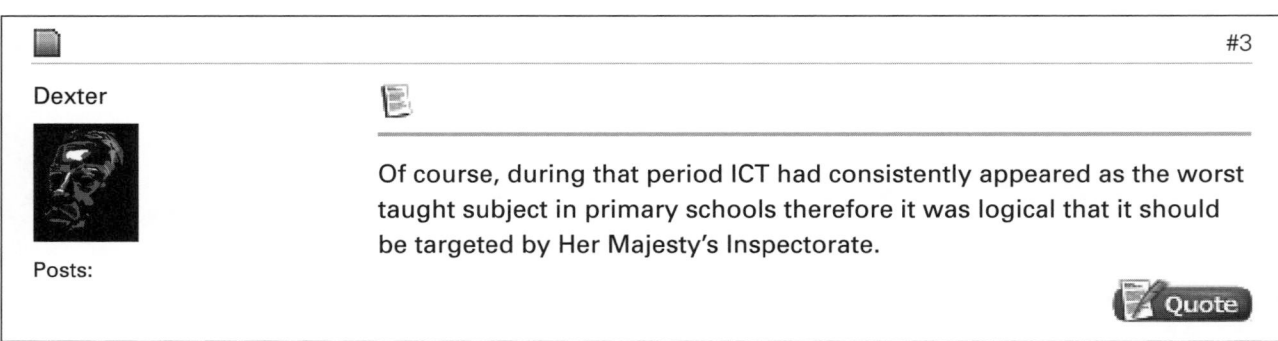

#3

Dexter

Posts:

Of course, during that period ICT had consistently appeared as the worst taught subject in primary schools therefore it was logical that it should be targeted by Her Majesty's Inspectorate.

Quote

6th June

Table 10.1 Section 10 Ofsted report ICT references

ICT extracts from Section 10 Ofsted report for XXXXXXXXX School 5th June 2004	
STANDARDS ACHIEVED BY PUPILS Pupils are not given sufficient opportunities to apply their competent basic skills in information and communication technology (ICT) to other subjects.	**QUALITY OF EDUCATION PROVIDED BY THE SCHOOL** TEACHING AND LEARNING **Main strengths and weaknesses** Teachers do not make enough use of information and communication technology (ICT) in other subjects. Whilst teachers generally demonstrate a confident approach to the teaching of ICT, it is not being used well to support learning across the curriculum.
THE CURRICULUM **Main strengths and weaknesses** Not enough use is made of ICT across the curriculum. The use of ICT across the curriculum is also underdeveloped.	
	LEADERSHIP AND MANAGEMENT The teachers are now much more confident and skilled in teaching ICT.
AREAS OF LEARNING IN THE FOUNDATION STAGE KNOWLEDGE AND UNDERSTANDING OF THE WORLD There are well used resources for ICT. A good start has been made to introducing young pupils to ICT. Both nursery and reception children can log in and are developing satisfactory skills in the use of the mouse. Subsequently they use learning programs well on the classroom computers, some of which have touch screens.	**MATHEMATICS** Insufficient use is made of ICT in the classroom.
	SCIENCE Little use is made of ICT to support learning in the subject. However, not enough use is made of ICT to enhance provision. A new coordinator has taken over the subject ... knows that teachers need to plan more opportunities for pupils to use ICT in science.
GEOGRAPHY AND HISTORY **Main strengths and weaknesses** The use of ICT is not widely used. The use of ICT in recording is not high.	**MUSIC** **Main strengths and weaknesses** The use of ICT is not well developed.

(Cont. over)

INFORMATION AND COMMUNICATION TECHNOLOGY

Provision for information and communication technology (ICT) is **good**.

Main strengths and weaknesses

The school benefits from a new state of the art ICT suite with interactive whiteboard.

Good subject leadership by the co-ordinator.

The contribution the subject makes to the way that pupils work with each other is good.

Confident teaching.

There is not enough use of computers in other subjects.

Commentary

Standards in all areas of ICT match those expected nationally. Pupils take part in lessons in the new ICT suite, which is having a positive effect in raising standards. By the end of Year 2 pupils use the mouse and keyboard well. They log on and select a program confidently. Their word processing skills are good and they edit text and save their work prior to logging off. By Year 6, most pupils use computers confidently and competently.

They use spreadsheets well to investigate data, and sift out unwanted information carefully. Pupils in Year 6 use their ICT skills to prepare PowerPoint presentations. Pupils make good progress in developing their basic skills, and their achievement is good.

Since the previous inspection teachers have received further training and most now teach the subject with confidence. Teaching in all the lessons observed was good. Lessons are well planned and teachers are developing satisfactory skills in the use of the interactive whiteboard to make their explanations clear. Teachers achieve a good balance between formal instruction and giving time to allow pupils to practise skills. They make lessons interesting and tasks challenging with the result that pupils enjoy the activities. Pupils' enthusiasm for the subject is good and they maintain a good level of concentration when working at a computer. They work well individually and in pairs, more competent pupils readily giving help and advice to their peers.

The subject co-ordinator has considerable expertise that she uses to good effect in supporting other staff and in helping them to gain confidence.

INFORMATION AND COMMUNICATION TECHNOLOGY ACROSS THE CURRICULUM

As pupils become more confident they are beginning to use computers in other subjects. For example, the Year 2 pupils used their skills to cut and paste and alter the size of images well before creating a photomontage of buildings in the area. This linked very well with their artwork on the local building site when every pupil had taken at least two photographs of the site with the school's digital camera. In general the use of computers across the curriculum is not well developed. Some use is made of ICT in English to produce written work but little use was made of computers in most of the lessons observed.

Available on the net at http://www.james-wright.org

The example report (see Table 10.1) indicates that at this stage in June 2004, this school had achieved a great deal in terms of ICT particularly as a discrete subject but provides clear indicators of what the school should do next, identifying core areas where improvements were required.

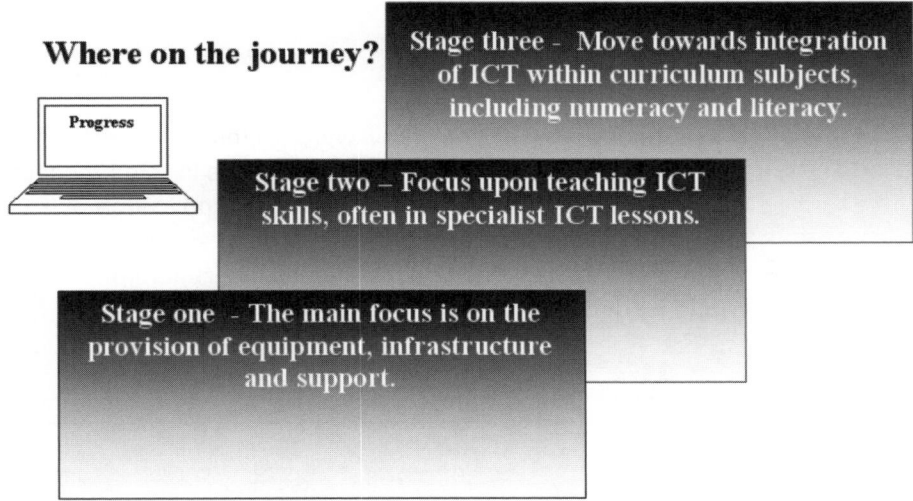

Figure 10.1 Progress over time, core focus
Available on the net at http://www.james-wright.org

Figure 10.1 provides a crude means for grouping schools in terms of their ICT maturity and E-learning development. From this perspective 'XXXXXXXXX School' may be perceived as having reached stage two of its E-learning development by 2004. Its co-ordinator should identify clearly how it has moved forward since this time against core indicators such as current computer pupil ratios, or the amount of time allocated to ICT. Co-ordinators need to be clear about the extent to which teachers' confidence in teaching and assessing ICT has progressed since the time of the previous inspection and whether or not all staff are now using ICT confidently.

Try to incorporate this type of summary data within your ongoing review from the BECTA SRF in order to create a single coherent picture for any future inspection that complements and agrees with the school's internal self-evaluation.

7th June

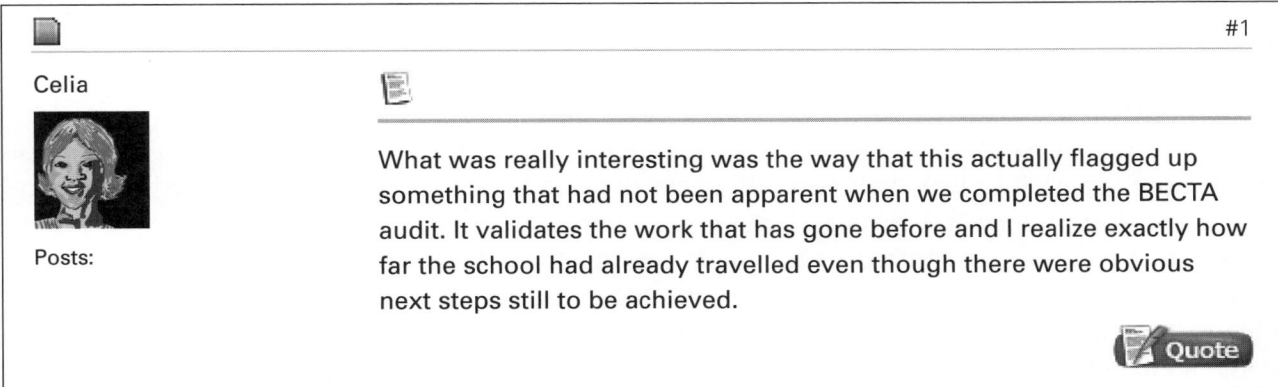

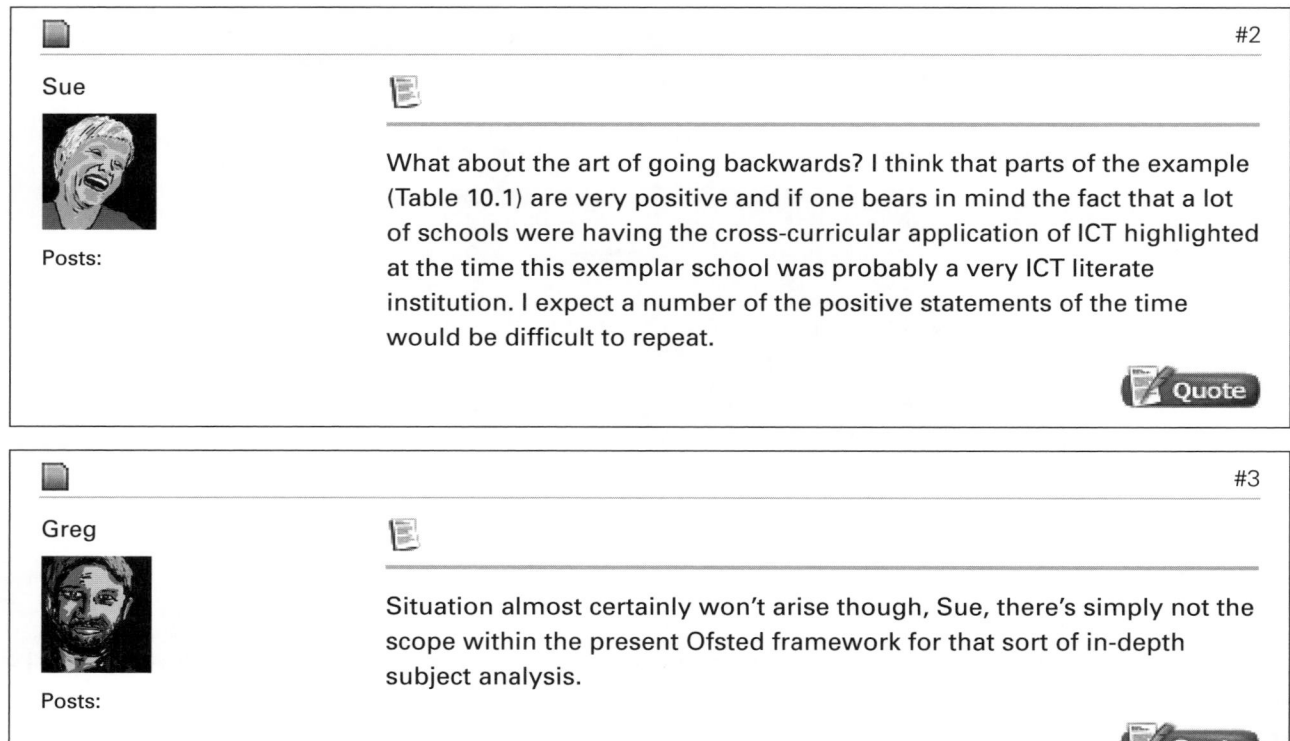

#2

Sue

Posts:

What about the art of going backwards? I think that parts of the example (Table 10.1) are very positive and if one bears in mind the fact that a lot of schools were having the cross-curricular application of ICT highlighted at the time this exemplar school was probably a very ICT literate institution. I expect a number of the positive statements of the time would be difficult to repeat.

Quote

#3

Greg

Posts:

Situation almost certainly won't arise though, Sue, there's simply not the scope within the present Ofsted framework for that sort of in-depth subject analysis.

Quote

8th June

Week 39, Task 29 – New Technologies, Videoconferencing and Mobile Communications

Following on from the review of multimedia presentation devices in May our second analysis of new technologies involves communication devices that are establishing a foothold in primary education but have not yet in the widest sense developed beyond niche usage. Remember that our main concern as E-learning managers is to be evaluative and clear about the impact of initiatives such as these. I have therefore again provided a review template for this purpose based upon the one used last month.

Videoconferencing

The first thing to accept with regard to videoconferencing is that this is no longer 'new' technology. School capacity to link 'live' initially over telephone lines and now using cabled broadband has been around for several years and as a result there is an established community of professionals within education committed to the exploitation of this form of ICT as a key cross-curricular tool. Likewise there is a large body of opinion that remains quite sceptical of its value. Videoconferencing (VC) has 'come of age' due to advances primarily in the network bandwidth available to schools and the resolution of earlier security protocols by which local authorities in particular and regional consortia allow VC 'traffic' to traverse their wide area networks. Up to this point only very specific initiatives supported by ring-fenced funding have driven forward VC projects and developed the expertise required for them to flourish, making it difficult for schools to engage unilaterally. Colleagues who now wish to develop their awareness of the range of practical applications available in this direction should first confirm the status of local connectivity and in particular review their regional consortium capability with regard to any existing conference activities. All national consortia are listed below.

Regional broadband consortia
Cumbria & Lancashire Education Online
http://www.cleo.net.uk/
East of England Broadband Network (E2BN)
http://www.e2bn.org/
East Midlands Broadband Consortium (EMBC)
http://www.embc.org.uk/home/default.asp
London Grid for Learning (LGfL)
http://cms.lgfl.net/lgfl/web/homepage
Northern Grid for Learning (NGfL)
http://www.portal.northerngrid.org/
South East Grid for Learning (SEGfL)
http://www.segfl.org.uk/
North West Learning Grid (NWLG)
http://www.nwlg.org/
West Midlands RBC (WMNet)
http://www.wmnet.org.uk/
South West Grid for Learning (SWGFL)
http://www.swgfl.org.uk/
Yorkshire Humber Grid for Learning (SWGFL)
http://www.yhgfl.net/

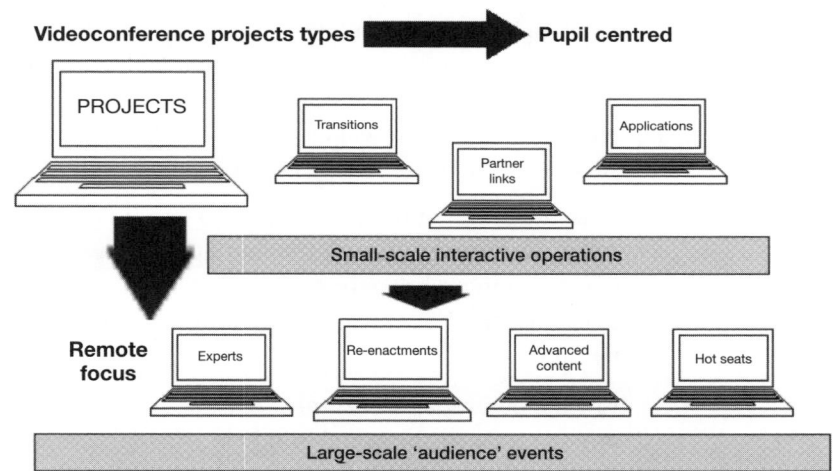

Figure 10.2 Video conference project overview
Available on the net at http://www.james-wright.org

Figure 10.2 provides an overview of the range of activities that schools currently enjoy using secure videoconference facilities. I tend to view these 'projects' in two broad spheres: first, those that are inherently small scale but highly interactive in terms of pupil participation; second and conversely, activities that predominantly aim to bring some form of expertise into the classroom which the pupils 'receive' often in quite a passive manner. Figure 10.2 further subdivides each of these activity groups.

Within the first group, activities essentially link children with other schools either locally or globally, although time differences may be a significant consideration when planning such events.

Within the applications category I include activities that involve the sharing of key tools by pupils connected using the VC service. Virtual whiteboards or shared software applications, including chat facilities, would fall into these categories. The second set involves schools using the live link facility to bring expertise into the classroom. Activity genres include the incorporation of dramatic re-enactment services similar to those that have traditionally visited schools and access to advanced curricular resources, often a favourite amongst high schools providing transition links to science laboratories and so on. Figure 10.2 will hopefully provide a theoretical scaffold to help colleagues decide what is pertinent to their own situation at the present time.

10th June

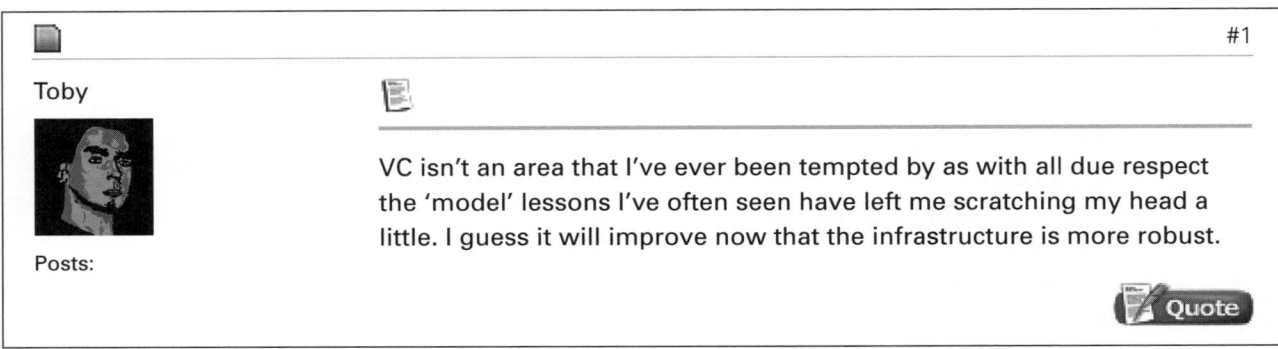

#1

Toby

Posts:

VC isn't an area that I've ever been tempted by as with all due respect the 'model' lessons I've often seen have left me scratching my head a little. I guess it will improve now that the infrastructure is more robust.

Quote

#2

Sue

Posts:

Oh I am a fan, Toby! I guess it's really tailor-made for small-school usage, anything that can extend the school community has particular appeal for small schools. Plus videoconferencing isn't the technical headache many people imagine it to be, our support is remote and immediate and all staff are very confident in using the system. I guess we are lucky to have had a supportive environment from the local authority for some time now.

Here are some of the things that no one pointed out to me before I started out on videoconferencing but that I would have certainly found helpful. Apologies to those experienced in using VC, as I'm not trying to teach anyone how to suck eggs. They are seemingly obvious but really helpful rules.

Always be prepared. Connect early to iron out any gremlins and have things ready to show including visual aids. Likewise write down what you want to say beforehand. Make sure that the children understand the rules of conversation, that they listen carefully and speak slowly but clearly, avoiding talking when they need to be listening. (Which, incidentally, is useful when developing listening partners in school anyway.) Typing questions etc. into the simultaneous chat window is a very useful tip, as is having something onscreen that the other children recognize, which brings the whole experience to life. Finally, I would suggest using plain simple backgrounds as they transfer much better as indeed do plain clothes. Oh, and avoid sudden unnecessary movements!

Quote

15th June

Table 10.2 New technology review, Part 2

Type of technology	Videoconferencing	Mobile technology
Perceived benefits	Highly motivational Develop speaking and listening skills Multiple cross-curricular opportunities Facilitate collaboration Develops school's teaching profile Key transition tool	Highly motivational Increased opportunities for curriculum development Multiple cross-curricular opportunities Facilitate collaboration Develops digital literacy
Potential drawbacks	Teacher training requirements Technical Infrastructure needed Expensive medium 'Event' level organization required Potential learner passivity	Teacher training requirements Considerable E-safety concerns Relatively expensive medium with regard to high impact coverage
Current school position		
Strategic goals		
Key actions needed		
Costs		

Available on the net at http://www.james-wright.org

Table 10.2 should be completed by colleagues reviewing the appropriateness of videoconferencing within the school's overall ICT development goals.

Ultimately the quality of your conference will as with most things rely upon good teaching, effective and comprehensive preparation and secure planning based upon appropriate learning objectives. I do believe that the continued development of videoconferencing as a key E-learning tool within the primary school is going to be seriously tested and may ultimately be compromised by the changes in ICT funding that have seen many initiatives falter, not least those that require significant capital outlay and have not yet become embedded within the primary school landscape. Outside of education, videoconferencing has not really had the cultural impact of many of its technological contemporaries, albeit a very cheap and readily available 'gadget' for home use. By this I mean in comparison to the use of MSN messenger chat, mobile phone text messages or the sharing of online digital video using websites such as YouTube the existence of cheap videoconference functionality using, first, Netmeeting and, subsequently, MSN Messenger, Yahoo and AOL Messenger systems and, ultimately, Skype have failed to capture the public's imagination largely because the 'relevant generation' largely finds them to be dull.

Maybe the advent of modern foreign languages within the primary curriculum will finally establish a unique niche for videoconferencing. Appearance consciousness in particular has been a significant cultural 'turn-off' to the adoption of systems by the general public who appear to prefer to use the telephone, chat room or text.

There are some major players within the videoconference arena, such as NASA's Digital Learning Network (http://nasadln.nmsu.edu/dln), that offer exciting conference links, which colleagues should aim to incorporate within any plans that they develop.

Finally, no discussion of the current videoconferencing landscape would be complete without appropriate reference to Global-Leap (www.global-leap.com) a not-for-profit organization, established to provide help, support and develop and extend content for videoconferencing in the classroom. Since its inception by the DfES in 2001 Global-Leap has established itself as the primary UK hub and champion of school-based videoconferencing; however, following the cessation of government funding, the transfer of its business base to school subscriptions currently provides a real test of schools' appetite for videoconferencing. Writing in the *Guardian* in January 2006, Mike Griffith, Director of Global-Leap identifies a lack of funding within the key areas of content and practical support as the key contributors to the failure of videoconferencing to become embedded within the schools sector.

18th June

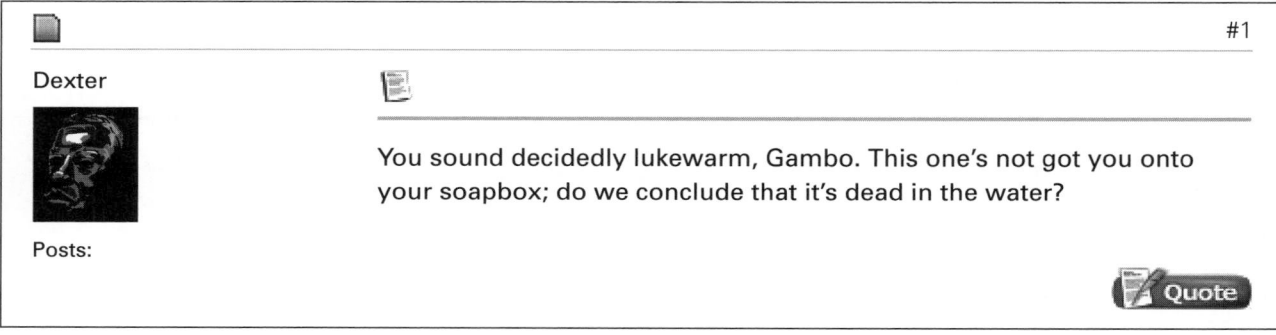

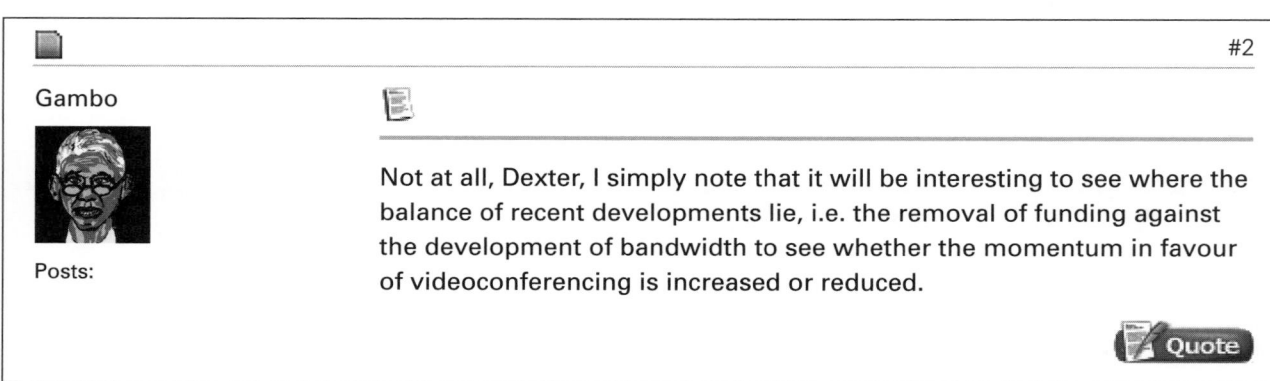

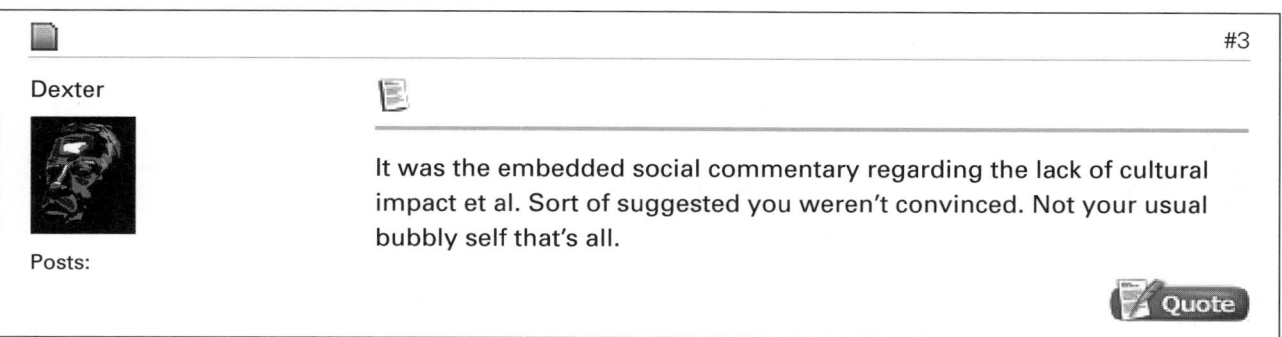

Dexter

Posts:

#3

It was the embedded social commentary regarding the lack of cultural impact et al. Sort of suggested you weren't convinced. Not your usual bubbly self that's all.

Quote

19th June

Mobile Communications

The attraction of 'mobile' devices, personal digital assistants (PDAs) and mobile phones is the idea that they allow teachers and pupils to have increased access to ICT. In effect, educators who support the use of such devices understand that coverage may be increased using cheaper hardware that is not fixed to a specific location and thereby provides the user with personalization of the technology. The Pocket PC has for some time offered a low-cost computer platform to users that a variety of national pilots have investigated due to its versatility and portability based around wireless connections that can genuinely take the technology to the learning and provide each pupil with their own computer at an affordable cost. A number of local authority funded initiatives in recent years have therefore attempted to evaluate the impact of presenting classes of children with portable devices in order to develop personalized, collaborative learning. Personal digital assistants have presented fresh opportunities to improve standards in literacy, for example, by promoting reading using e-books delivered to the devices in MS Reader. A number of online digital libraries such as the highly commendable Project Gutenberg resource (www.gutenberg.org) have made a vast array of texts available. Alternatively, proactive local authority grids for learning offer bespoke resources such as those available from the Birmingham Grid for Learning (www.bgfl.org/ebooklibrary).

Learners allowed to take home PDAs respond most positively to initiatives and reportedly enjoyed reading the E-books especially allied to the fact that the PDA was a personal device that contained only their work not shared with other children. Reports suggest that able students make the best use of the devices, whereas less able students can find them difficult to use. Handwriting recognition packages have also been helpful, particularly with regard to motivating boys to write and to share their work using the device's infrared connectivity.

19th June

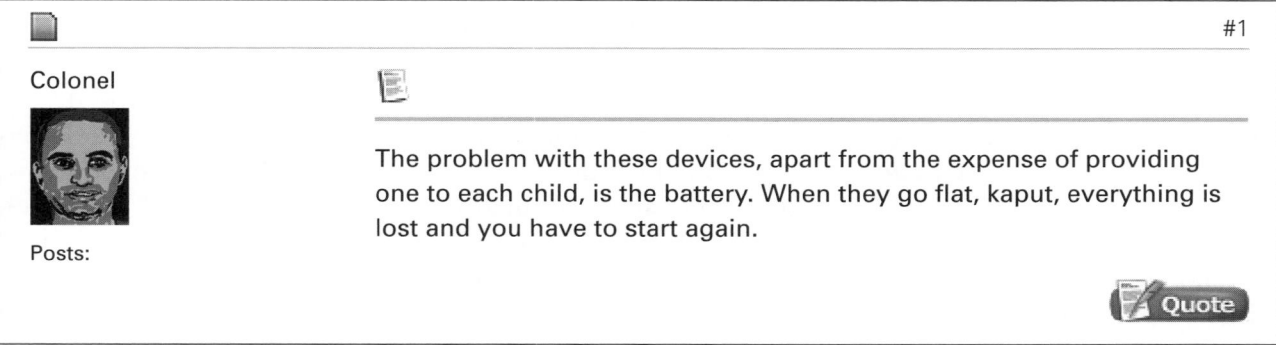

Colonel

Posts:

#1

The problem with these devices, apart from the expense of providing one to each child, is the battery. When they go flat, kaput, everything is lost and you have to start again.

Quote

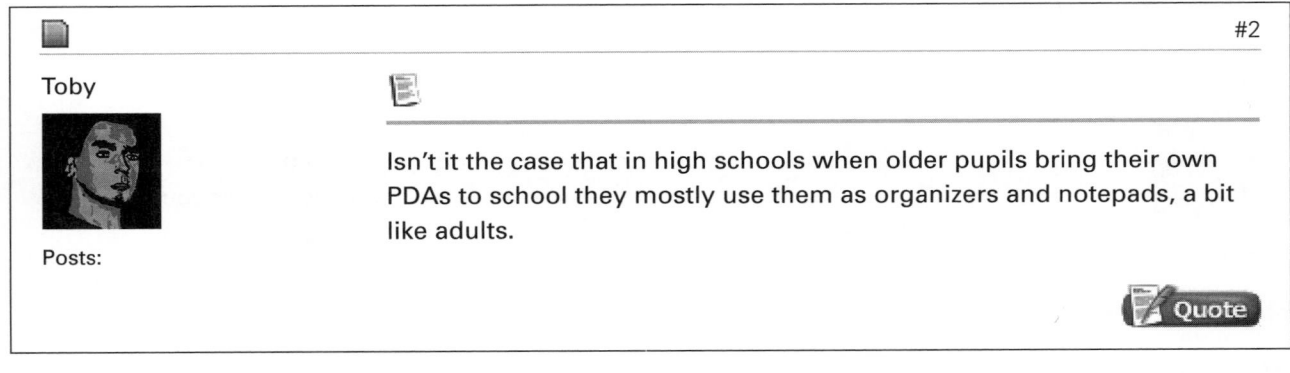

Toby

Posts:

Isn't it the case that in high schools when older pupils bring their own PDAs to school they mostly use them as organizers and notepads, a bit like adults.

#2

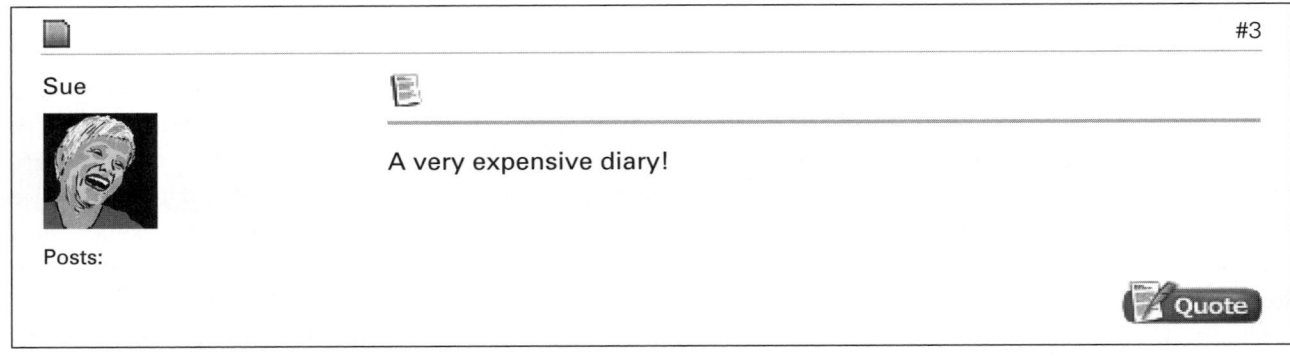

Sue

Posts:

A very expensive diary!

#3

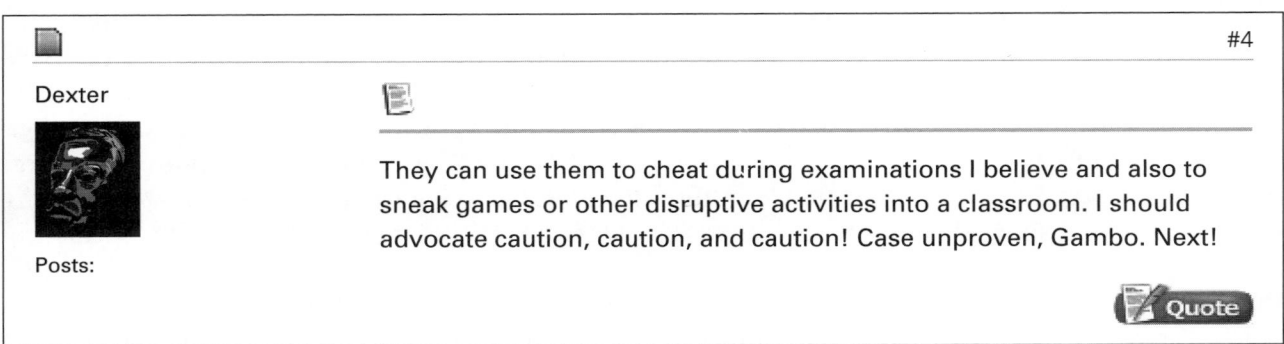

Dexter

Posts:

They can use them to cheat during examinations I believe and also to sneak games or other disruptive activities into a classroom. I should advocate caution, caution, and caution! Case unproven, Gambo. Next!

#4

20th June

The rapid development of mobile phone technology has questioned the role of the PDA as the champion of portability within the primary school. Certainly within the broader non-educational sphere sales of mobile phones have far outstripped those of PDAs, whilst to some extent the technology has converged.

Mobile phone technology is an extremely exciting, rapidly moving and controversial field that may potentially transform ICT in schools and towards which colleagues must carefully consider their approach, protocols and strategy with regard to its adoption. Indeed, by the time you are reading this it will certainly be irreversibly out of date due to the speed at which the commercial industry is adapting and evolving. Do not underestimate the profile that the mobile phone has established for itself based upon its development from simple communication device into a powerful miniature computer, which now seamlessly manipulates multimedia content. If colleagues are startled by the relentless progress of the mobile telephone and the possible consequences that it could create within schools, they should take small comfort from the fact that like many other cutting-edge technologies the chalk face lies with their high school colleagues. The personalized virtual learning environment will undoubtedly provide a fertile testing ground for this technology, not least because of the ease with which security and identity are handled by mobile phones as opposed to the complex world of user names and passwords required by the Internet. However, my cause here is not to speculate as to where exactly the mobile phone will lead us in terms of overall ICT provision but to consider it as a logical alternative to a PDA as a mobile primary device, that is, a relatively cheap piece of equipment that allows the functionality of the computer to be permanently attached to the user.

21st June

Toby

Posts:

#1

I appreciate the potential of using mobile phones but even I would need a lot of convincing, Gambo, in the present climate.

Quote

Sue

Posts:

#2

I agree, Toby. I also think that some of the issues we discussed last month regarding parents' views should be right at the forefront of this discussion. Not to mention the teachers' unions who would gladly impose a blanket ban on their use.

Quote

Greg

Posts:

#3

We already ban children from bringing mobiles into school. Some parents opposed that but our position was carefully explained. I agree that this is mainly an issue for high schools at the present time, and they are welcome to grapple with it.

Quote

22nd June

There are disadvantages when considering the mobile telephone as a substitute computer. Inevitably the display screen is small, limiting its usage to displaying text in particular and at present all use of network services would incur significant costs. The advantages of Bluetooth technology, that is, the ability to send files via radio waves between a mobile phone and other Bluetooth-enabled devices is still very limited in terms of the workable distance (around 10m on average) across which they can be used.

There are of course concerns that were alluded to within the log discussion and any use of this medium within schools would have to be governed and policed very tightly in terms of clear unambiguous protocols. Colleagues will be familiar with the 'happy slapping' phenomena and the Internet is currently the home to quite scandalous videos of teachers being humiliated by the covert use of cameras within mobile phones which are later posted on file share sites. These are major considerations for colleagues when completing the appropriate section of Table 10.1.

23rd June

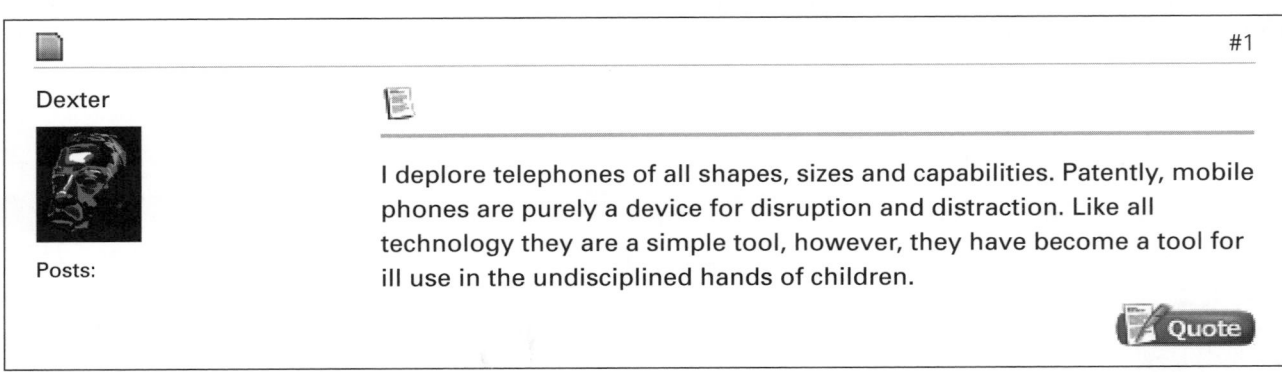

Dexter

Posts:

I deplore telephones of all shapes, sizes and capabilities. Patently, mobile phones are purely a device for disruption and distraction. Like all technology they are a simple tool, however, they have become a tool for ill use in the undisciplined hands of children.

#1

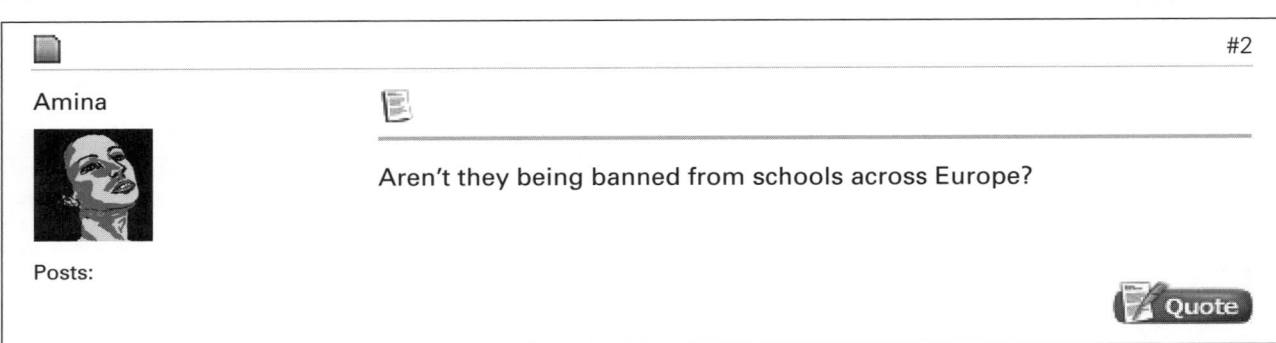

Amina

Posts:

Aren't they being banned from schools across Europe?

#2

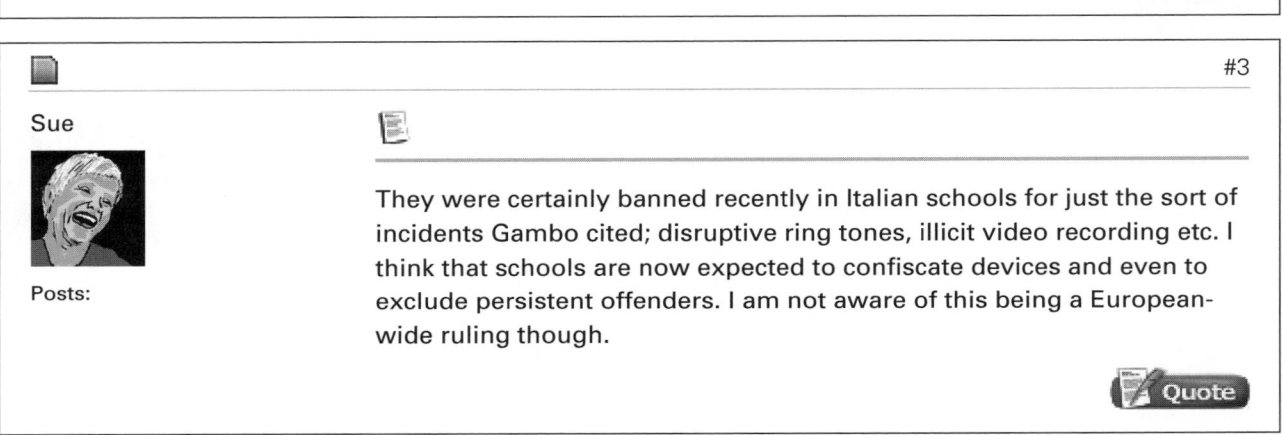

Sue

Posts:

They were certainly banned recently in Italian schools for just the sort of incidents Gambo cited; disruptive ring tones, illicit video recording etc. I think that schools are now expected to confiscate devices and even to exclude persistent offenders. I am not aware of this being a European-wide ruling though.

#3

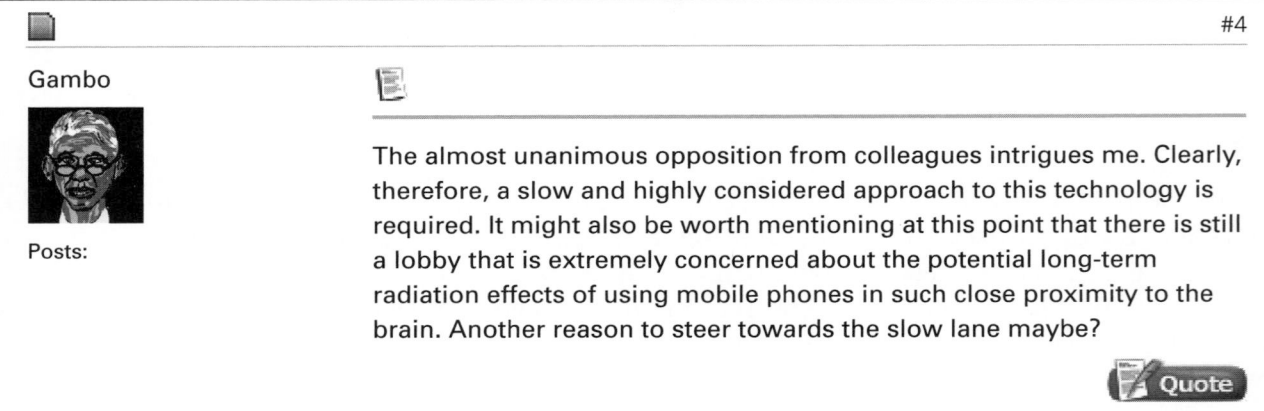

Gambo

Posts:

The almost unanimous opposition from colleagues intrigues me. Clearly, therefore, a slow and highly considered approach to this technology is required. It might also be worth mentioning at this point that there is still a lobby that is extremely concerned about the potential long-term radiation effects of using mobile phones in such close proximity to the brain. Another reason to steer towards the slow lane maybe?

#4

25th June

Week 40, Task 30 – The National Digital Curriculum – an Implementation Review

The recent history of BBC 'Jam' otherwise referred to as the Digital Curriculum is a salient lesson to all working in E-learning and there are clear lessons for colleagues to heed regarding its recent demise. BBC Jam came offline on the 20th March 2007 after the BBC Trust responded to complaints to the European Commission by commercial rivals and returned to the drawing board in terms of their proposals for a replacement online education service. This follows tireless efforts to undermine the project by those who saw their core business threatened by a 'free' national platform. Around only 10 per cent of the planned 'Jam' content was actually available and the BBC now reflects upon how best to meet its brief of promoting formal education in the context of school-age children.

Colleagues will be aware of the focus I placed upon the initiative within Book 1 and I still assert that colleagues have to respond appropriately to a national framework for digital content and need to redefine that strategy if the core system does not re-emerge at some point in the future. It does not seem possible for the independent commercial sector to deliver such a product that will be relevant to schools in the coming years without anticipating further enormous government provision of ring fenced E-learning credits.

The final activity of this month will therefore be for colleagues to review the strategic decisions made last year with regard to adoption of the digital curriculum and if at all possible to follow the example of the trustees at the BBC and 'suspend' the adoption of the project for the time being. Now may be a time to 'wait and see'.

25th June

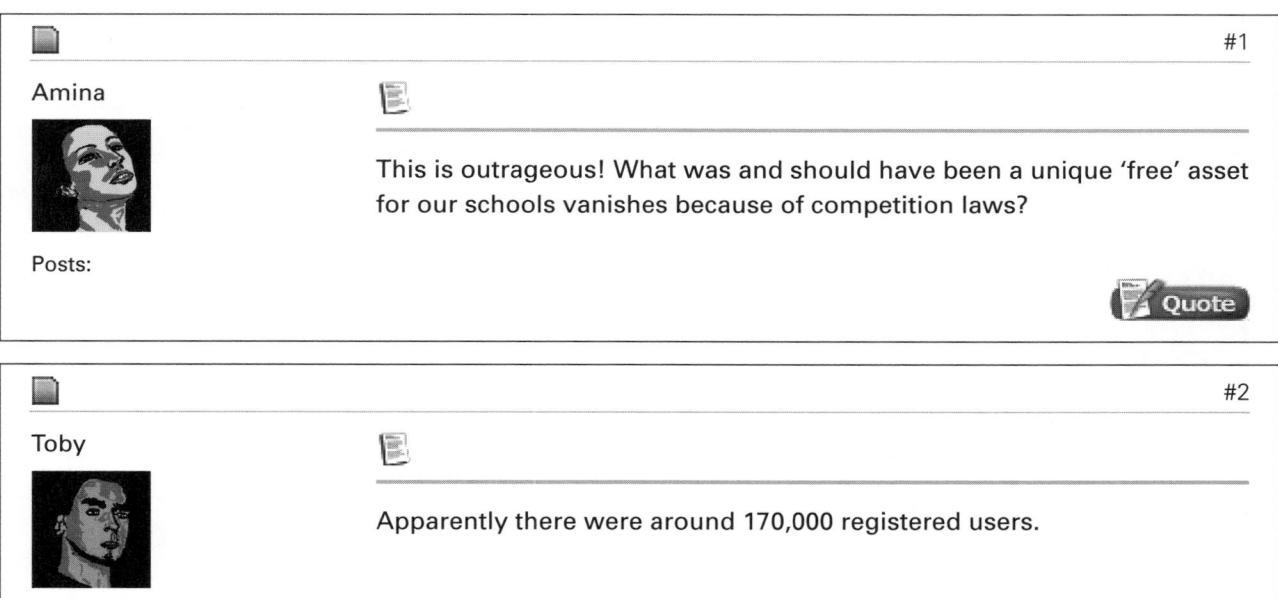

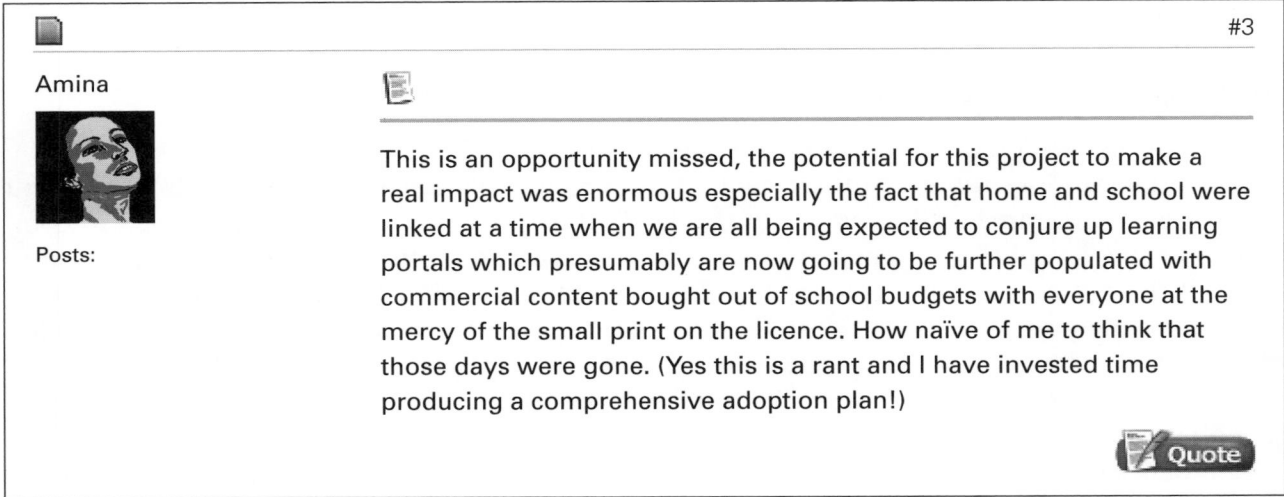

Amina

Posts:

#3

This is an opportunity missed, the potential for this project to make a real impact was enormous especially the fact that home and school were linked at a time when we are all being expected to conjure up learning portals which presumably are now going to be further populated with commercial content bought out of school budgets with everyone at the mercy of the small print on the licence. How naïve of me to think that those days were gone. (Yes this is a rant and I have invested time producing a comprehensive adoption plan!)

Quote

26th June

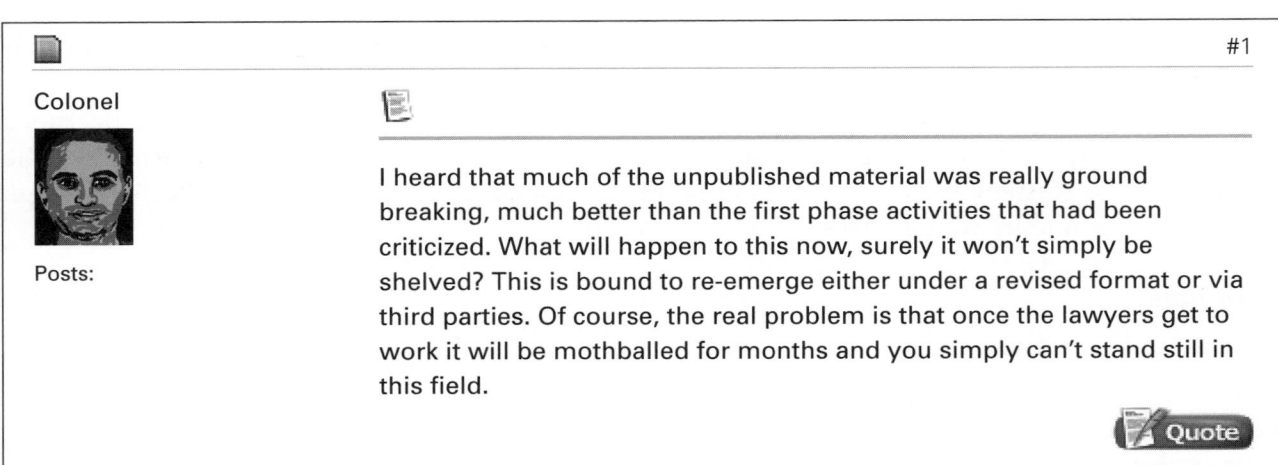

Colonel

Posts:

#1

I heard that much of the unpublished material was really ground breaking, much better than the first phase activities that had been criticized. What will happen to this now, surely it won't simply be shelved? This is bound to re-emerge either under a revised format or via third parties. Of course, the real problem is that once the lawyers get to work it will be mothballed for months and you simply can't stand still in this field.

Quote

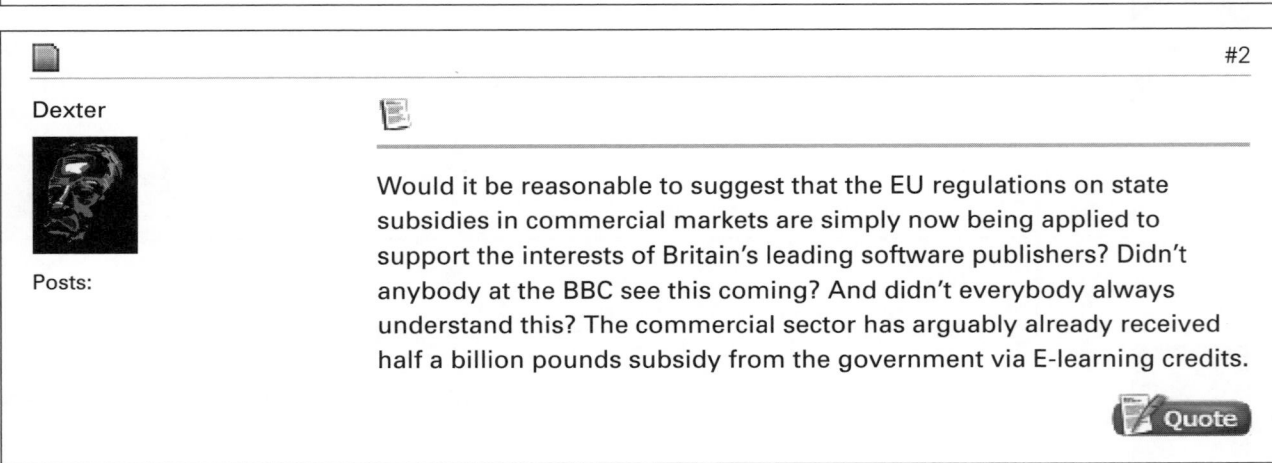

Dexter

Posts:

#2

Would it be reasonable to suggest that the EU regulations on state subsidies in commercial markets are simply now being applied to support the interests of Britain's leading software publishers? Didn't anybody at the BBC see this coming? And didn't everybody always understand this? The commercial sector has arguably already received half a billion pounds subsidy from the government via E-learning credits.

Quote

27th June

The main criticism directed at the BBC from the commercial software makers appears to be that the 'Jam' materials were insufficiently 'distinctive and complementary' to teaching materials already in the marketplace. BBC Jam was always intended as a pupil resource, a learning tool rather than teaching software aimed at the independent learner. It is reasonable from this to deduce that any 'Son of Jam' will be very explicitly aimed at home usage and that colleagues will need to plan and budget for school content provision for some time to come.

Chapter 11 ● *July*

2nd July

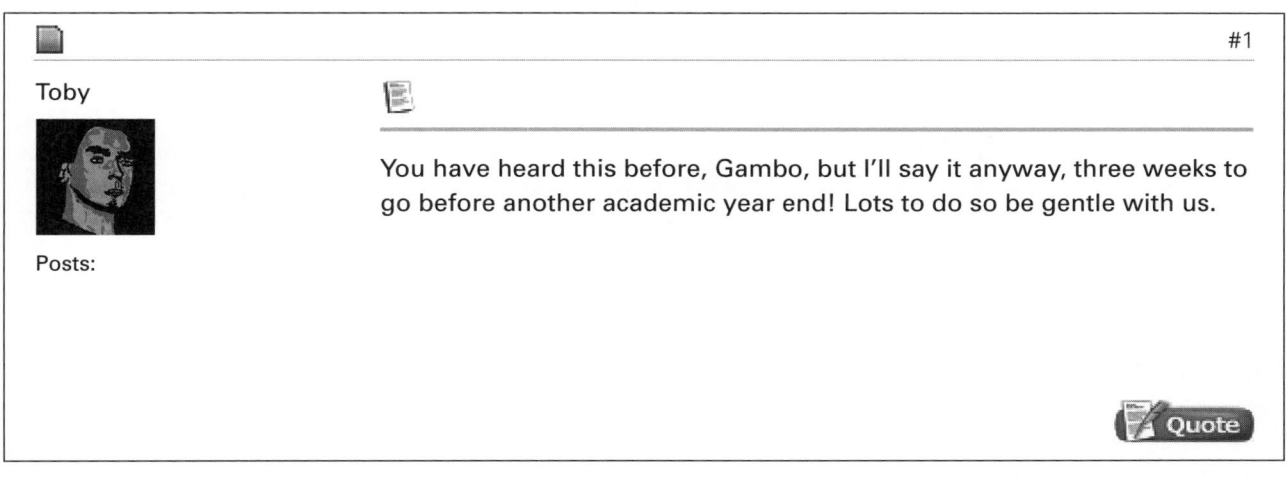

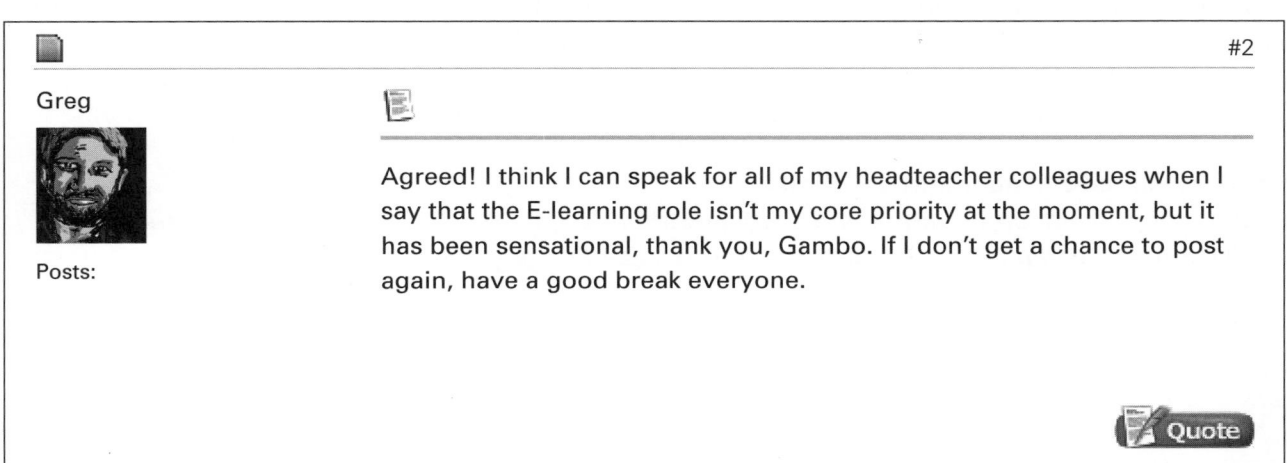

2nd July

Week 41, Task 31 – School Self-Evaluation of ICT – Every Child Matters

I do not need to remind colleagues of the status that the Every Child Matters Education Act (2005) has established at the heart of the UK education agenda, nor that the manner in which the five core outcomes for children and young people, namely, to be healthy, to stay safe, to enjoy and achieve, to make a positive contribution and to achieve economic well-being, are addressed is central to the self-evaluation of ICT. Schools have to identify situations where children are potentially at risk and to investigate all avenues of co-operation with outside agencies when supporting their development. For colleagues working within ICT the ECM agenda has catapulted E-safety to the pinnacle of the E-learning brief. At a time when the role of ICT and its associated funding has appeared to be submerged beneath other competing priorities, it is E-safety that has retained the attention of headteachers and local authority lead officers across the country, requiring the closest scrutiny. An element of this I feel has been reflected throughout this manual. However, colleagues should aim to address the full range of issues that arise for ICT from the ECM agenda.

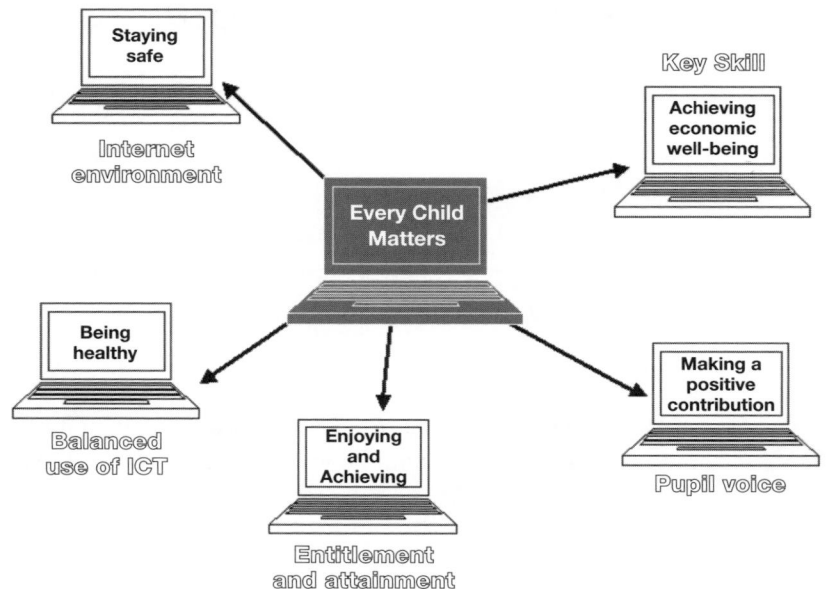

Figure 11.1 Every Child Matters overview
Available on the net at http://www.james-wright.org

Figure 11.1 provides a simple scaffold through which to identify the ICT core issues set against each of the five priorities. Colleagues should ensure that they have a good understanding of each broad area of concern and its relationship with the Ofsted SEF proposed, changes to which will explicitly incorporate core cross-referenced items between ICT and Every Child Matters, namely:

Section 3a (achievement and standards)
The extent to which information and communication technology (ICT) capability and other key skills enable learners to improve the quality of their work and make progress.

Section 4b (personal development, safe practices)
The extent to which learners adopt safe and responsible practices in using new technologies, including the Internet.

Section 4e (personal development, economic well-being)
Through the development of literacy, numeracy, information and communication technology, enterprise capability, economic and business understanding and financial capability.

5th July

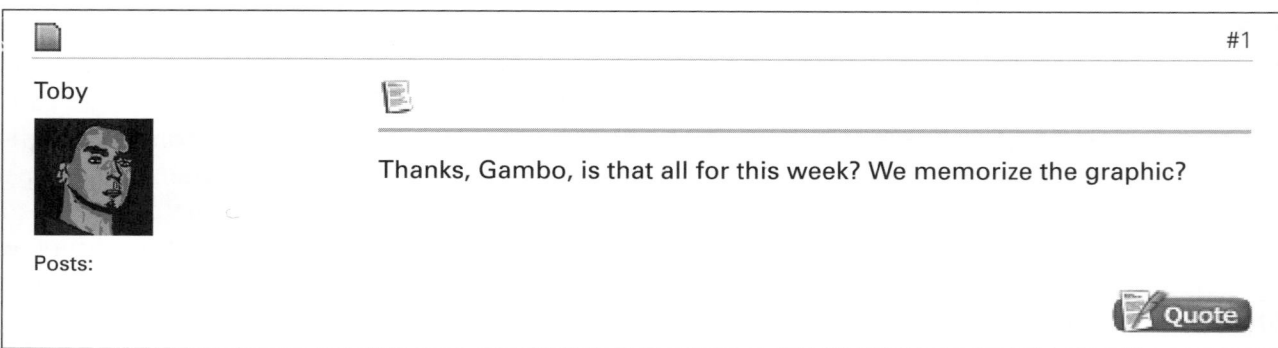

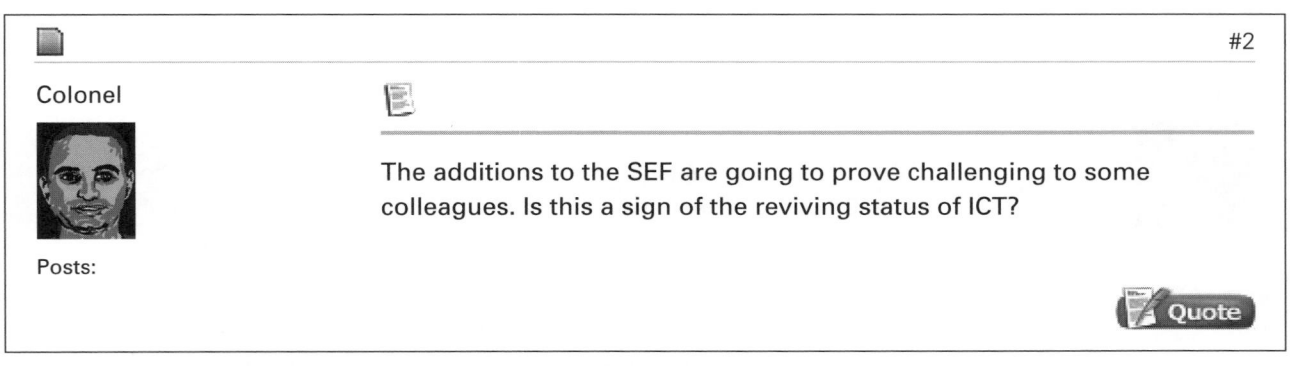

Colonel

Posts:

The additions to the SEF are going to prove challenging to some colleagues. Is this a sign of the reviving status of ICT?

#2

Quote

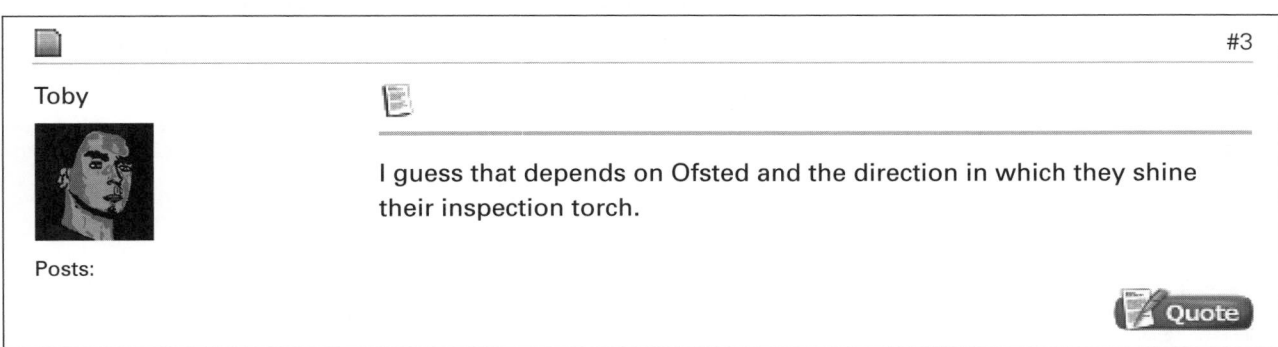

Toby

Posts:

I guess that depends on Ofsted and the direction in which they shine their inspection torch.

#3

Quote

6th July

To consolidate your command of this area I recommend to you Terry Friedman's excellent overview, *Every Child Matters, What It Means for the ICT Teacher* (2005) available for free download as a PDF from Terry's website (www.terry-friedman.org.uk) This document provides a comprehensive discussion brief for activities against each of the priorities most of which retain relevance within a primary school setting. Use the document as a basis for review, highlighting areas that are pertinent for you at this time and which may promote activities within your development plan linked to your ongoing self-review.

8th July

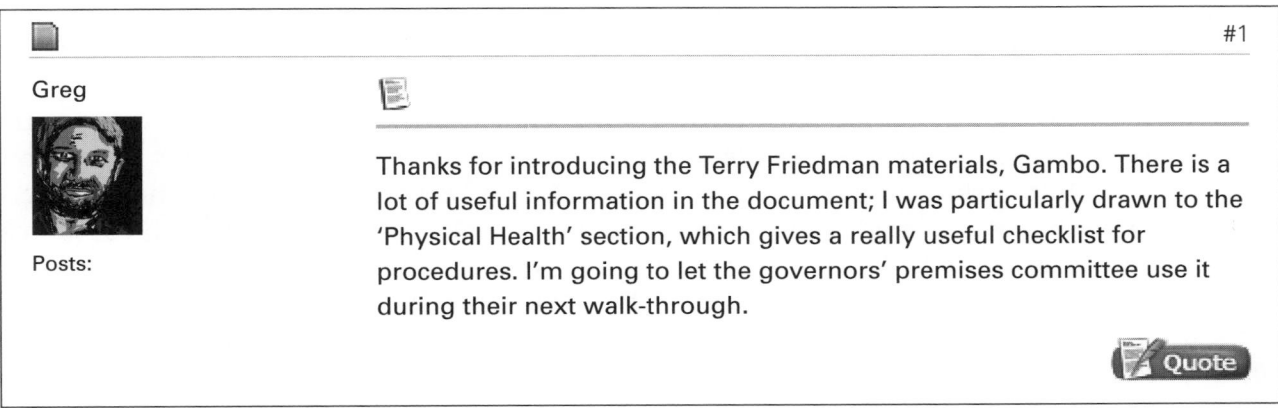

Greg

Posts:

Thanks for introducing the Terry Friedman materials, Gambo. There is a lot of useful information in the document; I was particularly drawn to the 'Physical Health' section, which gives a really useful checklist for procedures. I'm going to let the governors' premises committee use it during their next walk-through.

#1

Quote

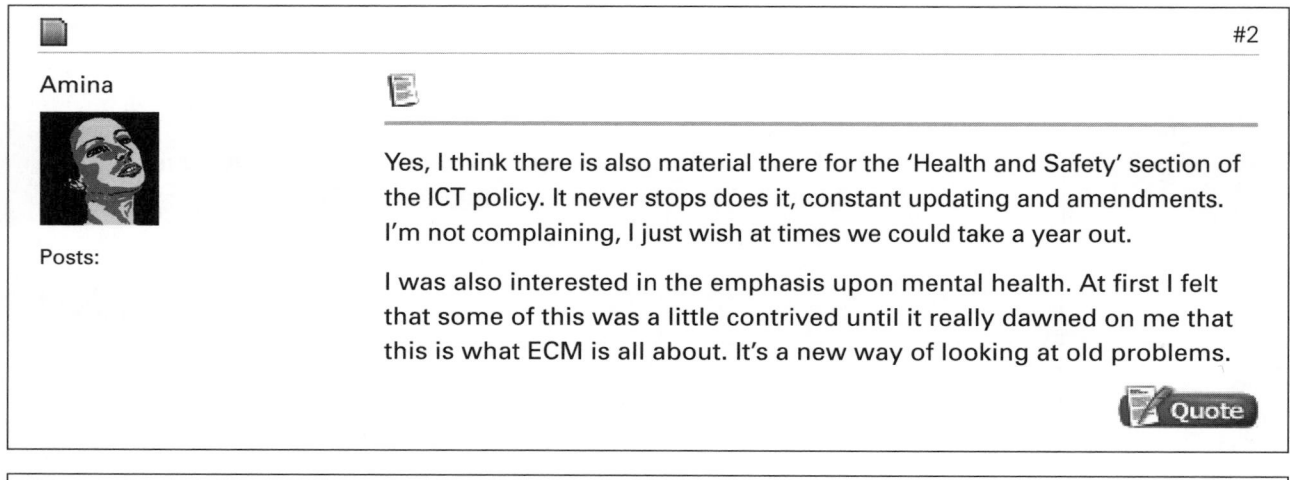

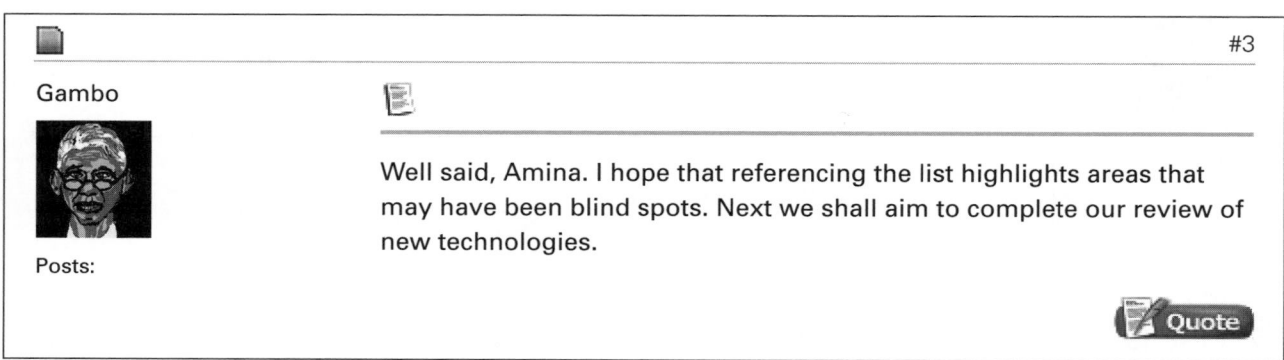

9th July

Week 42, Task 32 – New Technologies – Blogs, Wikis and Web 2.0

The final innovations review and your penultimate activity as E-learning co-ordinator for this year relates to the phenomenal development upon the Internet of that which has become known as Web 2.0 or Read/Write Web. This implied second-generation Internet emphasizes online collaboration and sharing, and marks a shift for the web from being primarily a tool of reference to one of collaboration. In some sectors educators have seized upon this shift as transformational technology. Colleagues should carefully consider the potential of the new omnipresent social collaboration tools, web logs and wikis, and attempt to identify their immediate relevance for the primary classroom.

Compared with traditional websites Web 2.0 characteristically involves a broad democratic ownership of content, which is contributed to and controlled by the site's users. This interaction is implicit within the site's architecture and facilitated by its applications. Whilst there are certainly many examples that grade more highly in terms of social collaboration I often use global auction house eBay as the best example of such a site given its daily almost organic development that occurs independent of its owners and authors. Ultimately it is user generated with a series of innovative tools and applications that enable users to interact and to develop their own presence within the system.

Interviewed by the BBC in 2005 Sir Tim Berners-Lee, creator of the first website in 1991 noted that:

'For years I had been trying to address the fact that the web for most people wasn't a creative space; there were other editors, but editing web pages became difficult and complicated for people. What happened with blogs and with wikis, these editable web spaces, was that they became much more simple. When you write a blog, you don't write complicated hypertext, you just write text, so I'm very, very happy to see that now it's gone in the direction of becoming more of a creative medium.' (BBC News, 8th September 2005, http://news.bbc.co.uk/1/hi/technology/4132752.stm)

As colleagues attempt to soft land the government's learning platform initiative via the use of a virtual learning environment (VLE), it is worth considering whether such an expensive often awkward higher education model structured around courses, timetables and testing is actually appropriate for the primary school environment or whether the evolution of a 'small pieces, loosely joined' approach as depicted by David Weinberger in his text of that name (2002) is a more appropriate means to develop collaborative learning using a set of unrelated yet cohesive web services including blogs and wikis.

Our perspective remains a strategic one and therefore your role is to steer the school's plans to incorporate the technologies as and when they become relevant to your wider goals. Once again there is a review template that may be useful in framing your evaluation.

Blogging

Blogging has quickly gained a foothold in some schools as it potentially offers effective educational learning tools, primarily because it introduces a new method of communicating, and a new context for writing. Specifically and almost uniquely blogging has taken over where early web authoring began in terms of allowing pupils to discover a voice. Children use blogs to write about personal events, ideas, and topics relevant to themselves. Blogging dilutes the prospect of failure by removing restrictions and rules and innovative teachers are beginning to use blogs to empower children to create exciting new learning opportunities. In particular, I find that the possibility for children to provide feedback upon each other's writing via blogs is quite an exciting innovation that has the potential to support writers' growing self-confidence and ability to express and publish their ideas to a real audience. They allow young writers opportunities to keep track of their ideas as they develop over time reinventing the age old charm and attraction of a diary but incorporating feedback and comments from others.

If colleagues are not familiar with blogging then part of this week's activity will be to accept the five-minute challenge from Blogger and to try it out for free (www2.blogger.com).

12th July

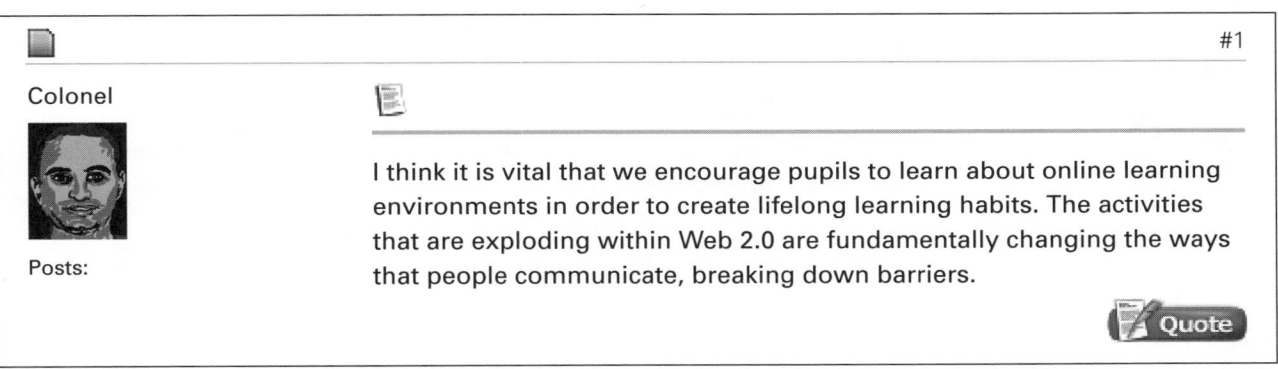

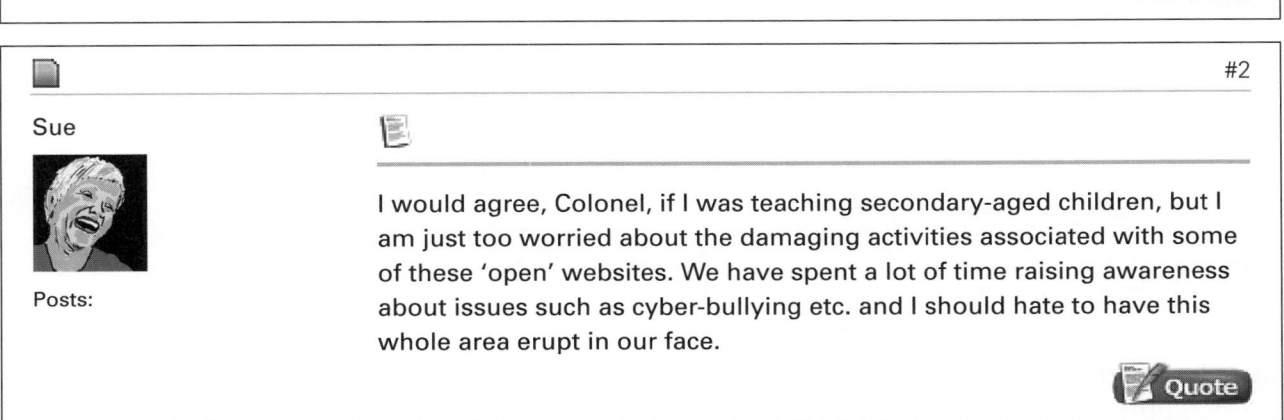

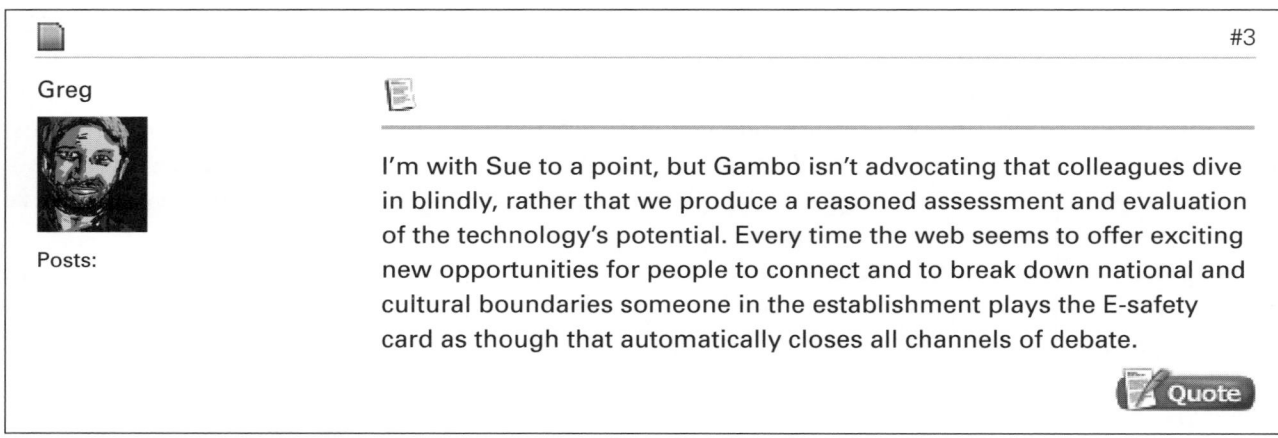

Greg

Posts:

I'm with Sue to a point, but Gambo isn't advocating that colleagues dive in blindly, rather that we produce a reasoned assessment and evaluation of the technology's potential. Every time the web seems to offer exciting new opportunities for people to connect and to break down national and cultural boundaries someone in the establishment plays the E-safety card as though that automatically closes all channels of debate.

#3

Quote

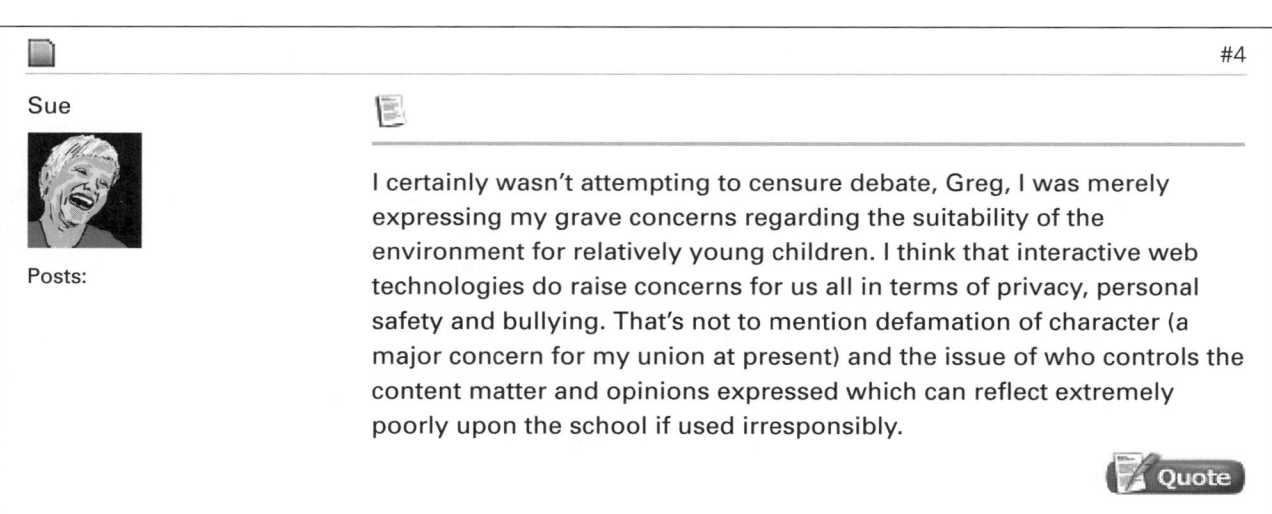

Sue

Posts:

I certainly wasn't attempting to censure debate, Greg, I was merely expressing my grave concerns regarding the suitability of the environment for relatively young children. I think that interactive web technologies do raise concerns for us all in terms of privacy, personal safety and bullying. That's not to mention defamation of character (a major concern for my union at present) and the issue of who controls the content matter and opinions expressed which can reflect extremely poorly upon the school if used irresponsibly.

#4

Quote

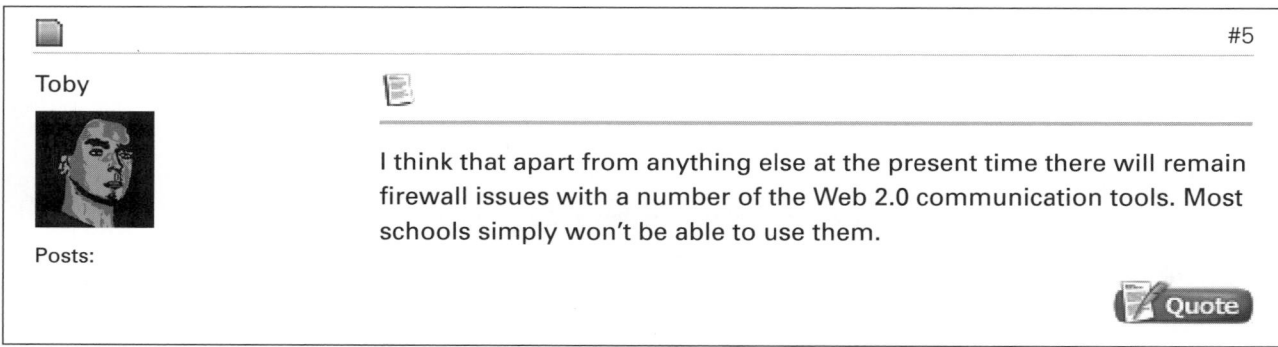

Toby

Posts:

I think that apart from anything else at the present time there will remain firewall issues with a number of the Web 2.0 communication tools. Most schools simply won't be able to use them.

#5

Quote

13th July

Wikis

There can be few Hawaiian terms that have impacted upon the global vernacular as quickly as the term 'wiki-wiki' meaning fast and which describes the modern web phenomena that is the wiki. This powerful server software enables users to create and edit web page content using any web browser and specifically allows users to edit or correct the work of others facilitating group collaboration and contributions to websites. Often registration itself is not required in order to participate.

By far the best known example of a wiki is of course Wikipedia (www.en.wikipedia.org), the free online encyclopedia designed around the core principle that those who use it are also those who create it and that the knowledge of the group is greater than that of any individual. One feature of wikis is that there is no review before modifications are accepted, symptomatic of the zeitgeist that lies behind much of Web 2.0 philosophies. This ease of interaction and operation makes a wiki an effective tool for mass collaborative authoring within the school setting but raises considerable concern and unrest amongst orthodoxy. How do schools assimilate the 'soft security' that marshals wikis and leaves them open to virtual vandalism? Not all online editors are well meaning and it would be very easy for children to sabotage other pupils' work from within collaborative writing projects. Some say that such damage can easily be undone, indeed this has been a feature often noted with regard to Wikipedia, that is, the manner in which other collaborators have quickly reported and corrected malicious editing. However, in educational terms it may well prove to be insurmountably problematic.

In her research on behalf of Futurelab into the use of wikis in schools, Lyndsay Grant (2006) concluded that:

'The social and cultural practices of collaborative working that need to accompany the use of the software in order to take advantage of the functional affordances of the tool were not in the students' repertoire of shared practices.'

One student within the study responding to another pupil's access to their work noted that;

'There should be locks on it. Because they could write rubbish stuff and then you'd get told off for it.' (Mary)

Table 11.1 New technology review, Part 3

Type of technology	Blogs	Wikis
Perceived benefits	Highly motivational Multiple cross-curricular opportunities Facilitate collaboration Develops digital literacy Transition tool Provide pupils with voice Raise self-esteem	Highly motivational Multiple cross-curricular opportunities Facilitate collaboration Develops digital literacy Transition tool
Perceived drawbacks	Some teacher training requirements Considerable E-safety concerns 'Event'-level organization required Pedagogical divisions	Some teacher training requirements Considerable E-safety concerns 'Event'-level organization required Pedagogical divisions
Current school position		
Strategic goals		
Key actions needed		
Costs		

Available on the net at http://www.james-wright.org

Colleagues will clearly have their own views and philosophy relating to the role that these new 'democratic' collaboration tools have within the primary school setting. It is clearly important that the wider ICT team and school articulate this view within the school vision. Table 11.1 may be a useful starting point within this debate.

14th July

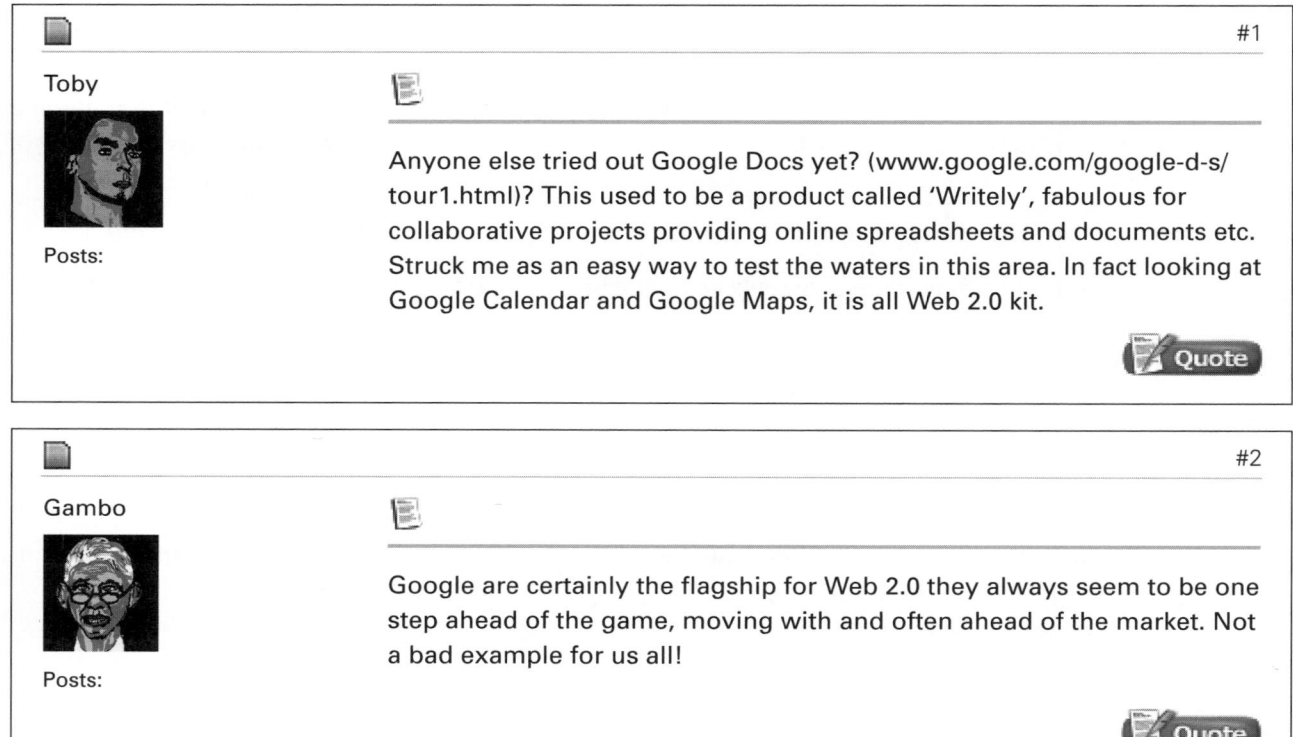

Toby

Posts:

Anyone else tried out Google Docs yet? (www.google.com/google-d-s/tour1.html)? This used to be a product called 'Writely', fabulous for collaborative projects providing online spreadsheets and documents etc. Struck me as an easy way to test the waters in this area. In fact looking at Google Calendar and Google Maps, it is all Web 2.0 kit.

#1

Quote

Gambo

Posts:

Google are certainly the flagship for Web 2.0 they always seem to be one step ahead of the game, moving with and often ahead of the market. Not a bad example for us all!

#2

Quote

16th July

Week 43, Task 33 – The ICT Mark and ICT Excellence Awards

The final task for this term, and indeed this academic year, is to consider application for ICT Mark accreditation for your school. Given the time and effort directed towards the strategic development of ICT and E-learning by yourself and your school's leadership team over the last two years, this should be a formality.

Colleagues will have ascertained from the SRF (http://matrix.becta.org.uk/selfreview) that the school has reached the desired threshold in all aspects of the review and is ready to register for assessment. Prior to doing so, agree within the ICT team both how the assessment is going to be managed and what the school hopes to gain from accreditation, and what comes next?

Schools seeking accreditation will need to provide evidence relating to an appropriate level of attainment from within the framework, either in the form of documentation, pupil portfolios, displays or feedback from colleagues who may be interviewed during the assessment. Schools applying for accreditation will need to populate the matrix with reference to available evidence using the 'commentary' box available within the matrix action planner, incorporating annotations and indicating where appropriate evidence may be scrutinized.

18th July:

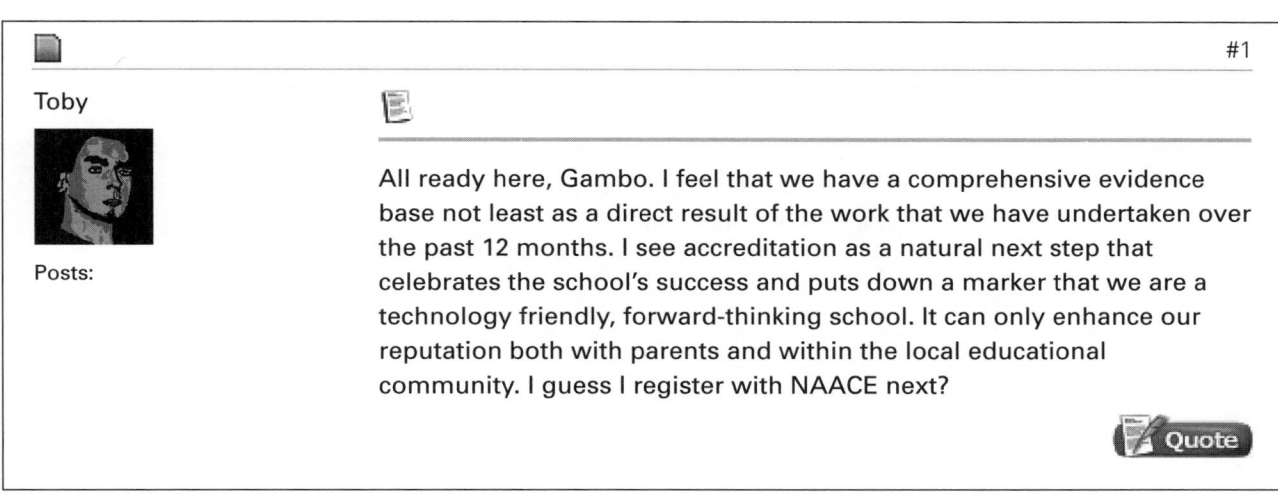

Toby

Posts:

#1

All ready here, Gambo. I feel that we have a comprehensive evidence base not least as a direct result of the work that we have undertaken over the past 12 months. I see accreditation as a natural next step that celebrates the school's success and puts down a marker that we are a technology friendly, forward-thinking school. It can only enhance our reputation both with parents and within the local educational community. I guess I register with NAACE next?

Quote

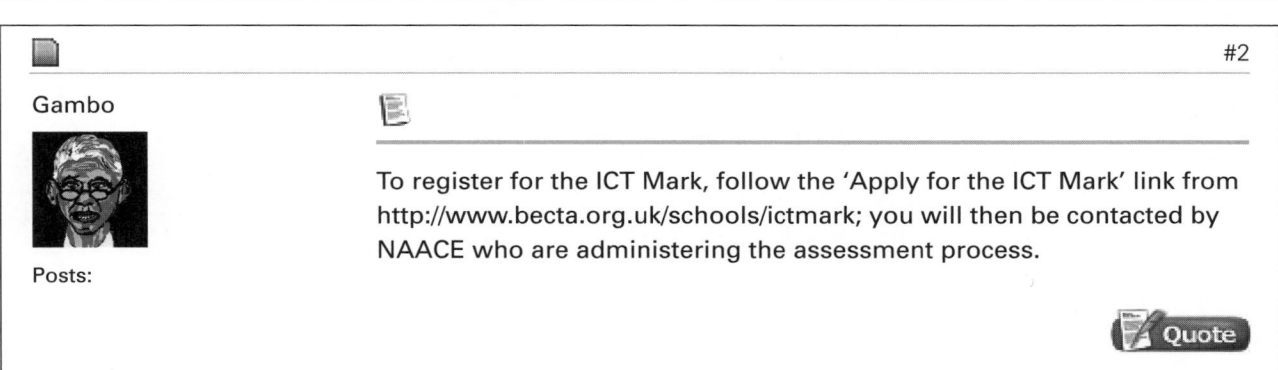

Gambo

Posts:

#2

To register for the ICT Mark, follow the 'Apply for the ICT Mark' link from http://www.becta.org.uk/schools/ictmark; you will then be contacted by NAACE who are administering the assessment process.

Quote

20th July

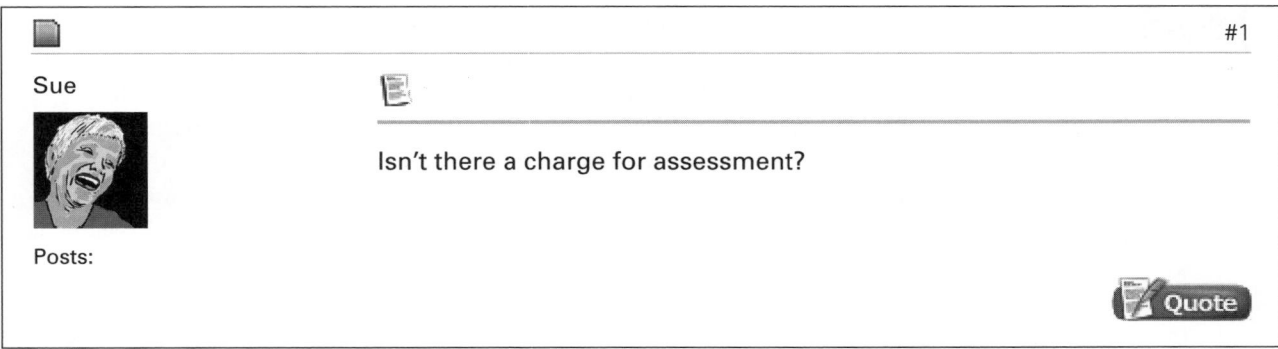

Sue

Posts:

#1

Isn't there a charge for assessment?

Quote

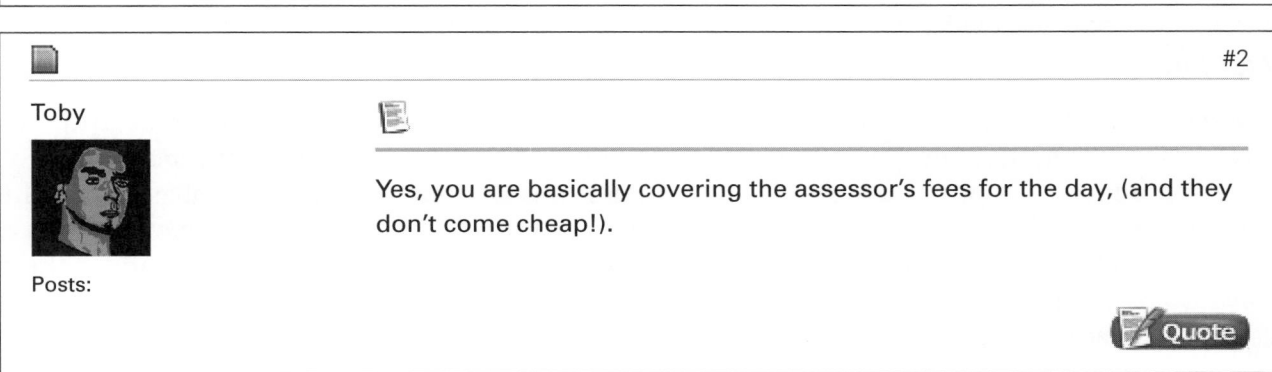

Toby

Posts:

#2

Yes, you are basically covering the assessor's fees for the day, (and they don't come cheap!).

Quote

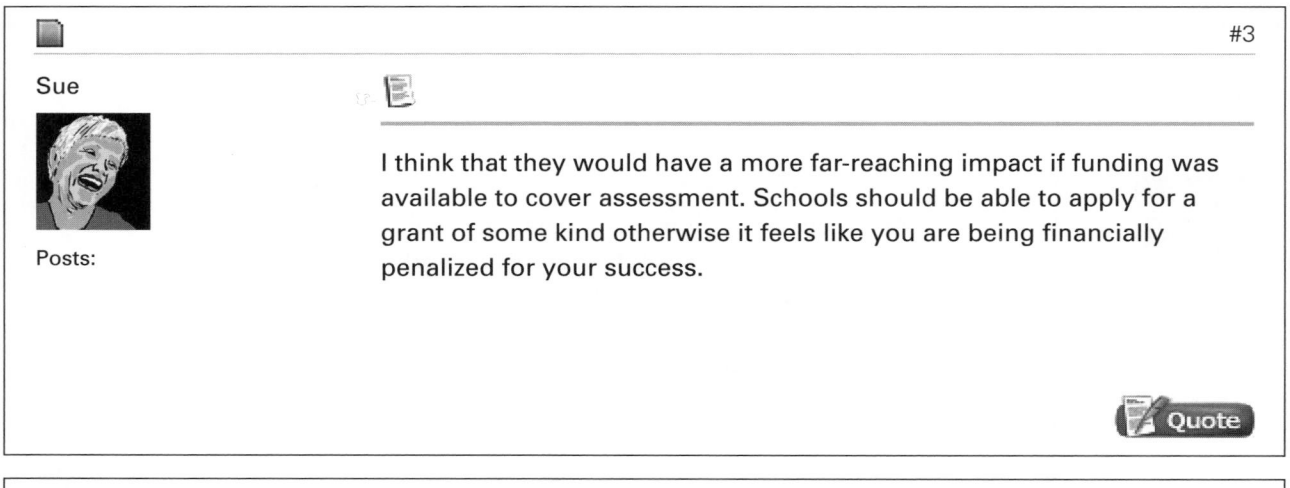

Sue

Posts:

I think that they would have a more far-reaching impact if funding was available to cover assessment. Schools should be able to apply for a grant of some kind otherwise it feels like you are being financially penalized for your success.

#3

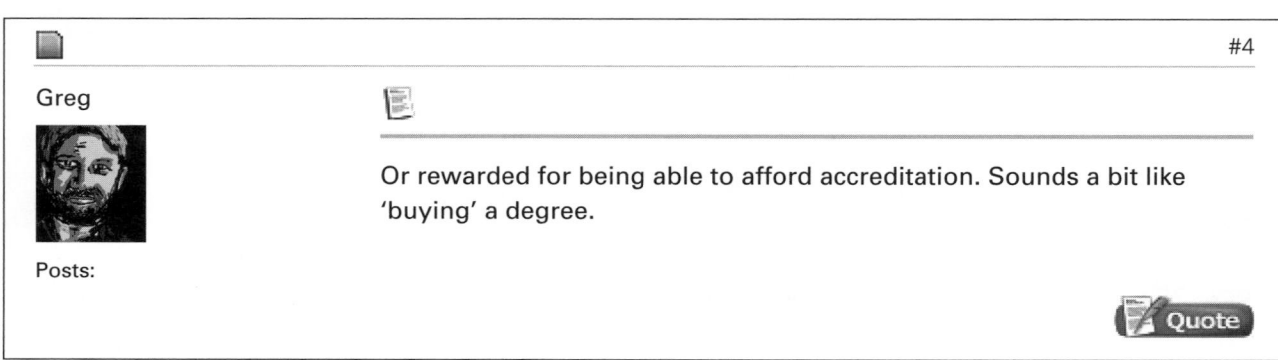

Greg

Posts:

Or rewarded for being able to afford accreditation. Sounds a bit like 'buying' a degree.

#4

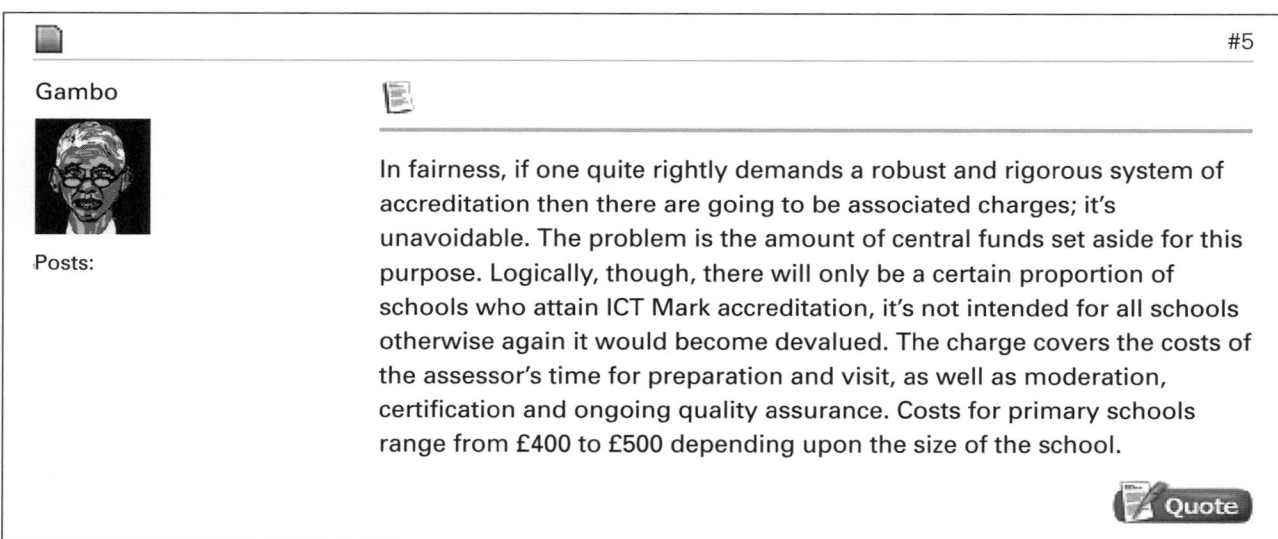

Gambo

Posts:

In fairness, if one quite rightly demands a robust and rigorous system of accreditation then there are going to be associated charges; it's unavoidable. The problem is the amount of central funds set aside for this purpose. Logically, though, there will only be a certain proportion of schools who attain ICT Mark accreditation, it's not intended for all schools otherwise again it would become devalued. The charge covers the costs of the assessor's time for preparation and visit, as well as moderation, certification and ongoing quality assurance. Costs for primary schools range from £400 to £500 depending upon the size of the school.

#5

21st July

Registration will trigger an external process through which NAACE (National Association of Advisors for Computers in Education) will check your SRF and send you a bill for the process. They will allocate you an assessor unless you prefer to select one from their database using the pen portraits at behind the 'Choose an assessor' link at http://www.becta.org.uk/schools/ictmark. Do check that your local authority has not got a scheme in place to support accreditation, there may also be funding available. NAACE and BECTA are working closely with a number of authorities to mobilize support.

21st July

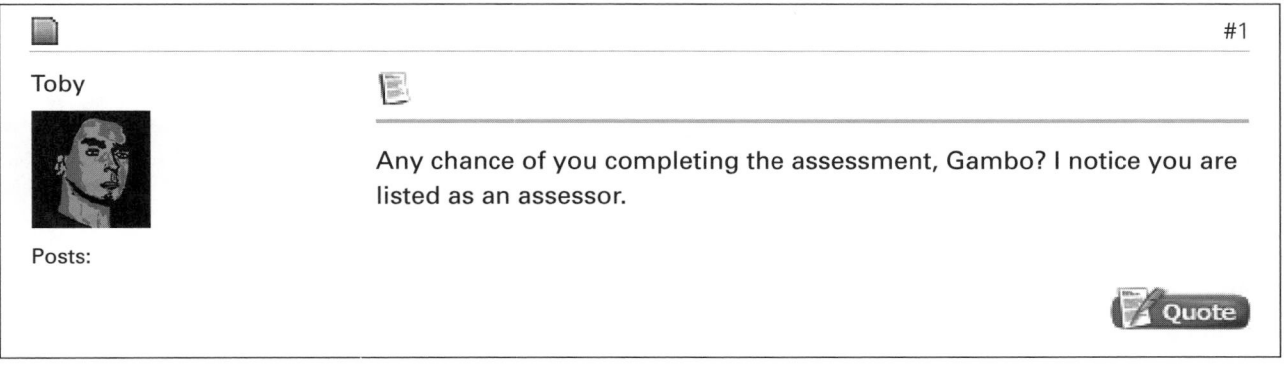

Toby

Posts:

Any chance of you completing the assessment, Gambo? I notice you are listed as an assessor.

#1

Quote

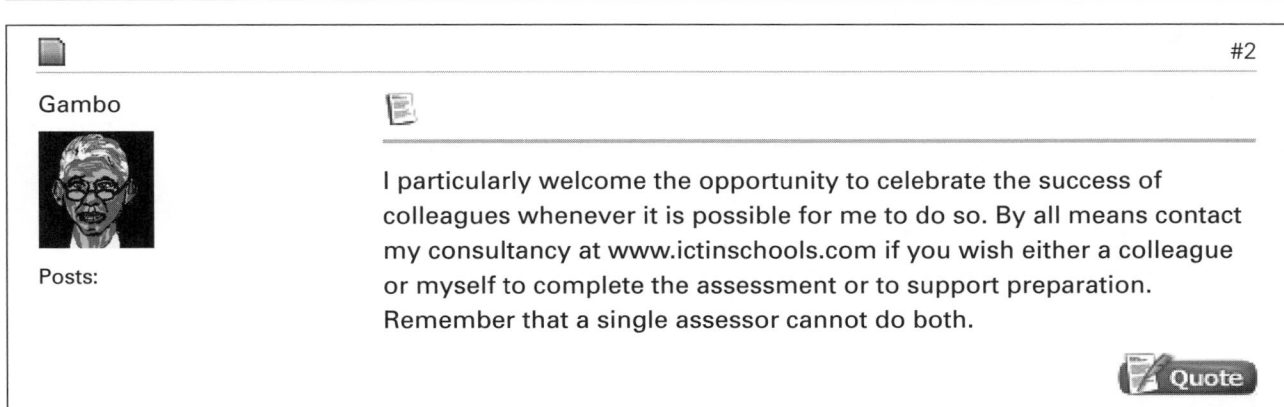

Gambo

Posts:

I particularly welcome the opportunity to celebrate the success of colleagues whenever it is possible for me to do so. By all means contact my consultancy at www.ictinschools.com if you wish either a colleague or myself to complete the assessment or to support preparation. Remember that a single assessor cannot do both.

#2

Quote

22nd July

The assessor will evaluate the SRF and prepare an inspection trail based on the information provided that they will test during their visit to the school. This will normally take half a day. You will know in advance which elements they wish to look at as there will not be time to go through every statement. Two or three elements will be scrutinized in depth to validate the school's self-evaluation, and a typical assessment agenda might include some documentation review but also qualitative data-gathering procedures including interviews and observations. Colleagues familiar with the NaaceMark process will certainly appreciate that this is a much broader, dare I say 'New Ofsted' procedure. It is vital, therefore, that colleagues have internal processes planned to parallel those that the assessor brings. Preparation and ownership of the agreed agenda will facilitate a rewarding accreditation process. Remember that the whole point is to validate the school's own judgement. If you do not think that you are ready yet then delay application and work within your team to gather together sufficiently robust evidence to make the whole process celebratory rather than inquisitorial.

23rd July

The ICT Excellence Awards

Finally, colleagues may wish to consider application for the BECTA 'ICT Excellence Awards' for next year if completion of the SRF has indicated specific areas where the school has outstanding and innovative practice. The award recognizes whole-school best practice whilst focusing on key individuals responsible for that change. I should anticipate that many of you would be eligible. Categories currently available are best whole school, assessment, curriculum, extending learning opportunities, inclusion, leadership and management, and learning and teaching. Schools may win up to £6000 in prize money if successful. Always good to have something new to strive for.

Chapter 12 • *August*

6th August

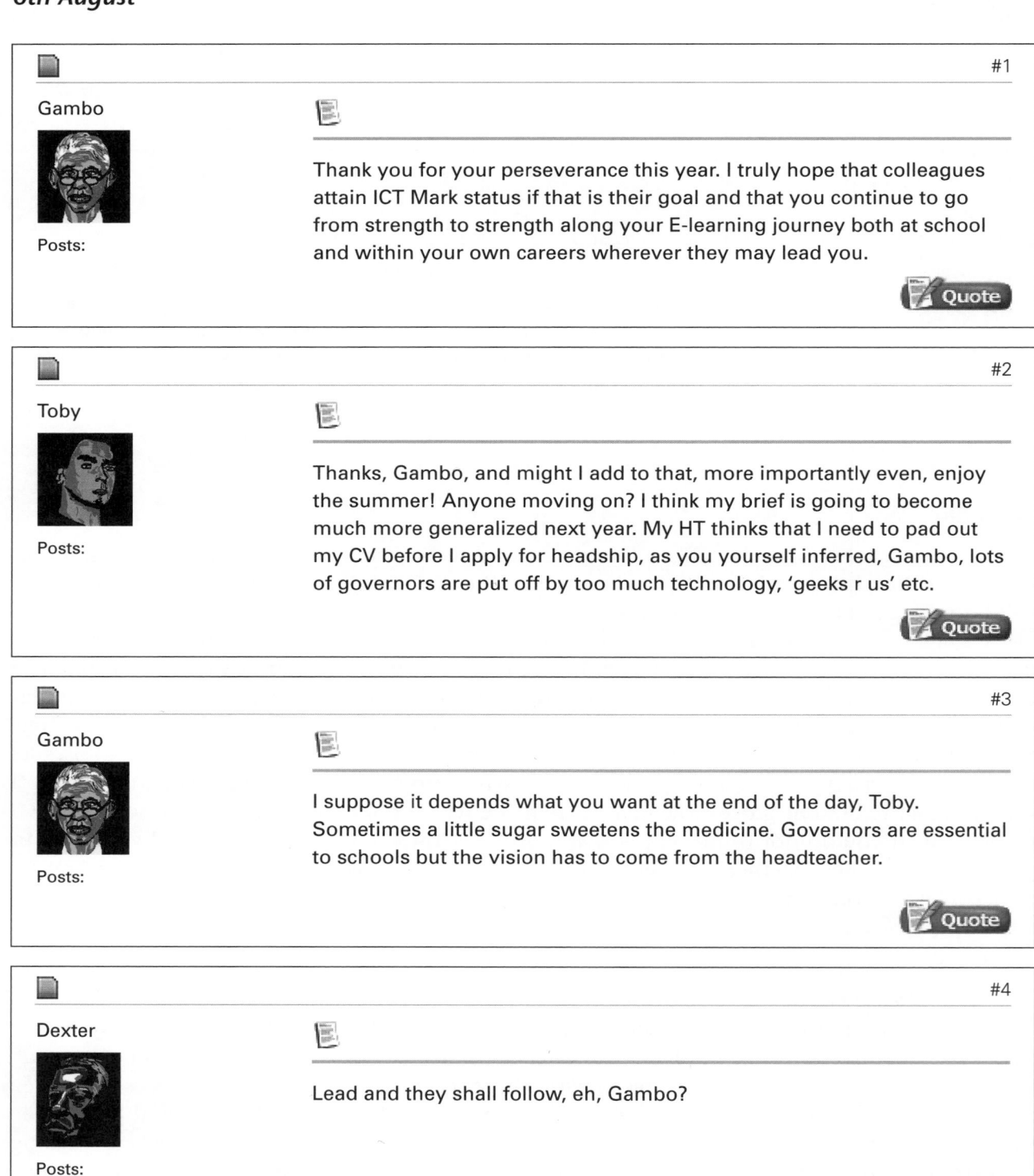

#1

Gambo

Posts:

Thank you for your perseverance this year. I truly hope that colleagues attain ICT Mark status if that is their goal and that you continue to go from strength to strength along your E-learning journey both at school and within your own careers wherever they may lead you.

Quote

#2

Toby

Posts:

Thanks, Gambo, and might I add to that, more importantly even, enjoy the summer! Anyone moving on? I think my brief is going to become much more generalized next year. My HT thinks that I need to pad out my CV before I apply for headship, as you yourself inferred, Gambo, lots of governors are put off by too much technology, 'geeks r us' etc.

Quote

#3

Gambo

Posts:

I suppose it depends what you want at the end of the day, Toby. Sometimes a little sugar sweetens the medicine. Governors are essential to schools but the vision has to come from the headteacher.

Quote

#4

Dexter

Posts:

Lead and they shall follow, eh, Gambo?

Quote

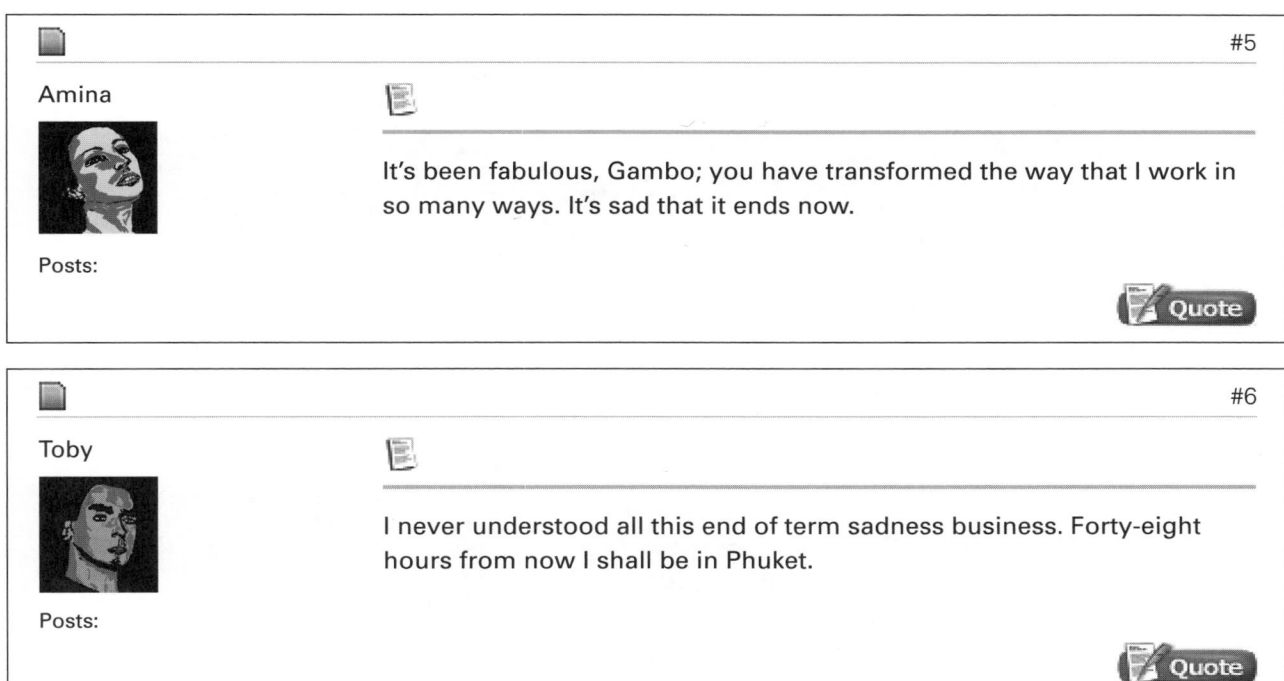

Amina

Posts:

It's been fabulous, Gambo; you have transformed the way that I work in so many ways. It's sad that it ends now.

#5

Quote

Toby

Posts:

I never understood all this end of term sadness business. Forty-eight hours from now I shall be in Phuket.

#6

Quote

Having completed this year's programme any school leader will now have a comprehensive command of the school-wide E-learning agenda. Now may therefore be a very good time to take a look at what has been achieved this year.

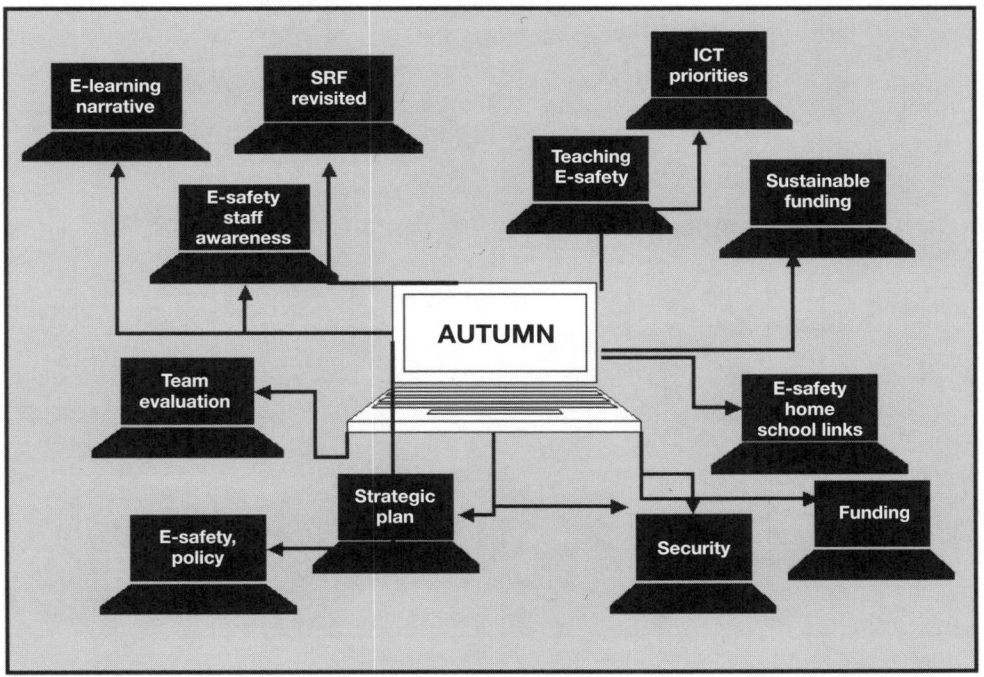

Figure 12.1 Autumn overview
Available on the net at http://www.james-wright.org

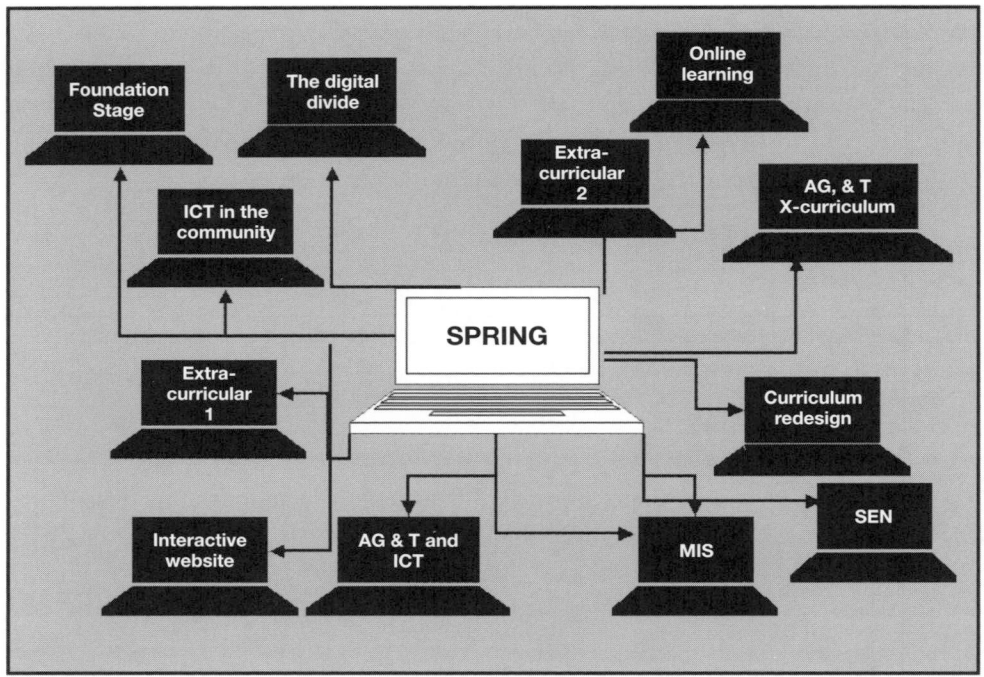

Figure 12.2 Spring overview
Available on the net at http://www.james-wright.org

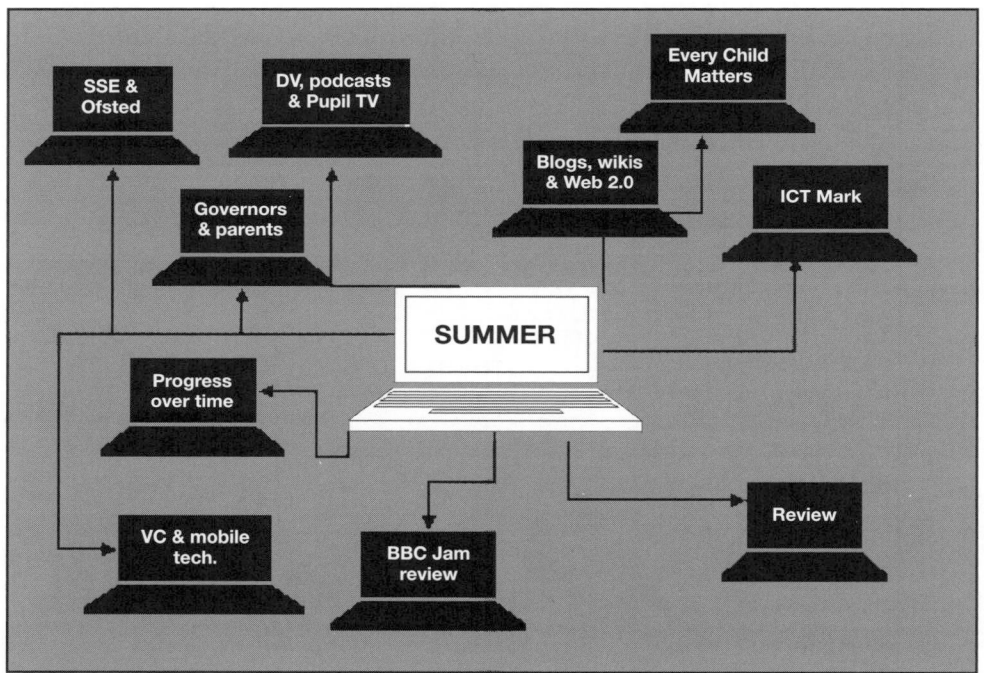

Figure 12.3 Summer overview
Available on the net at http://www.james-wright.org

Figures 12.1, 12.2 and 12.3 provide an overview of all 33 tasks covered this year. Of course the structure is not set in stone and you may wish to revisit specific sections on a needs must basis.

7th August

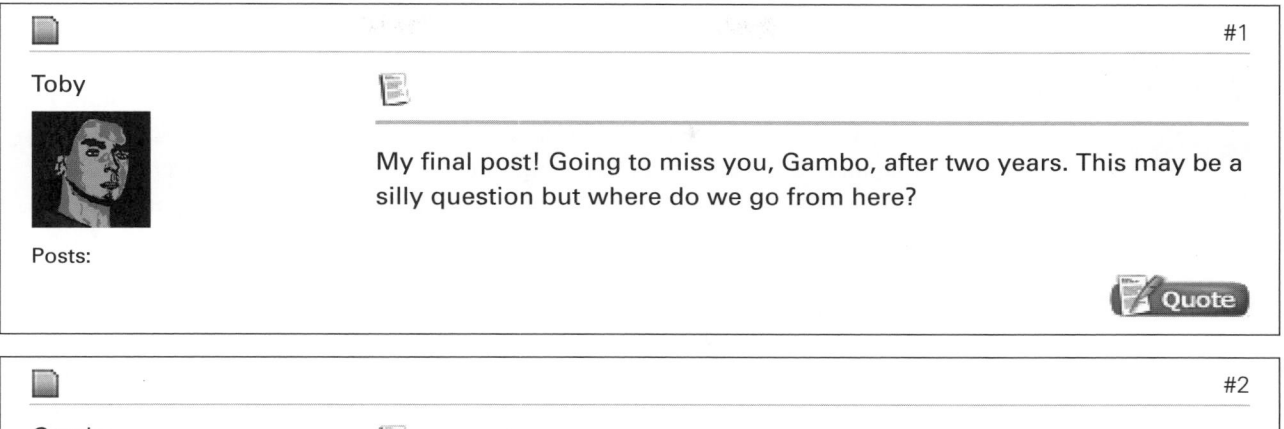

Toby

Posts:

#1

My final post! Going to miss you, Gambo, after two years. This may be a silly question but where do we go from here?

Quote

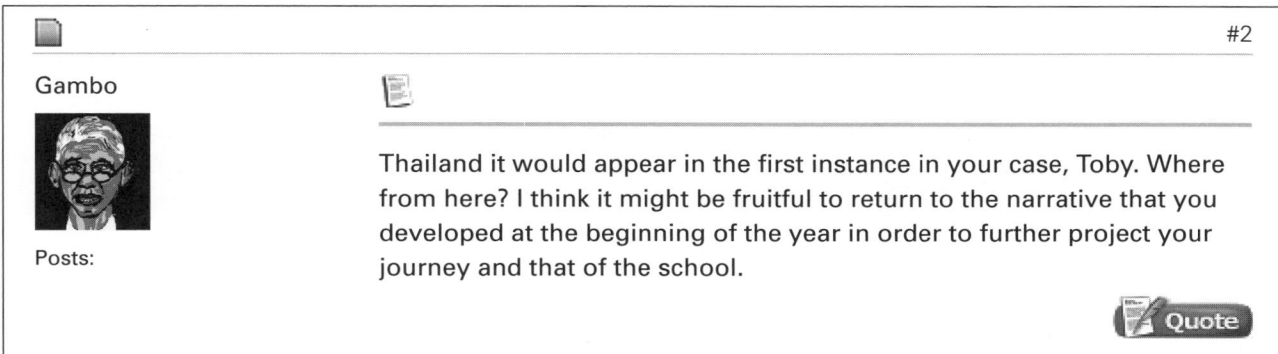

Gambo

Posts:

#2

Thailand it would appear in the first instance in your case, Toby. Where from here? I think it might be fruitful to return to the narrative that you developed at the beginning of the year in order to further project your journey and that of the school.

Quote

8th August

For the E-confident school the challenge is to maintain the systems, staff and structures that lay behind the success. Sustainability is the key, particularly in the light of changes to key personnel. How does any school absorb the loss of a visionary subject leader? Make sure that the structures are sound and that over-reliance and dependence upon individuals is minimized. Likewise financial stability is a key prerequisite; as networks have evolved so has the need for carefully budgeted maintenance and replacement plans.

In recent months we have examined a series of new technologies that will increasingly become synonymous with effective world-class schools, and colleagues will know where their own interests lie in order to develop cutting-edge technologies to further enhance opportunities for all children and to contribute to the national collection of excellence. Similarly, schools may champion changes to the current school curriculum and will wish to be at the forefront of the personalization agenda.

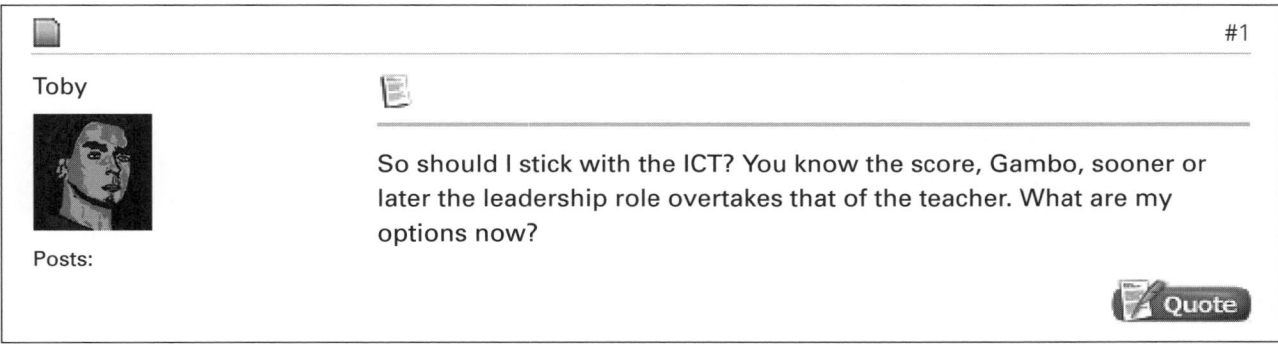

Toby

Posts:

#1

So should I stick with the ICT? You know the score, Gambo, sooner or later the leadership role overtakes that of the teacher. What are my options now?

Quote

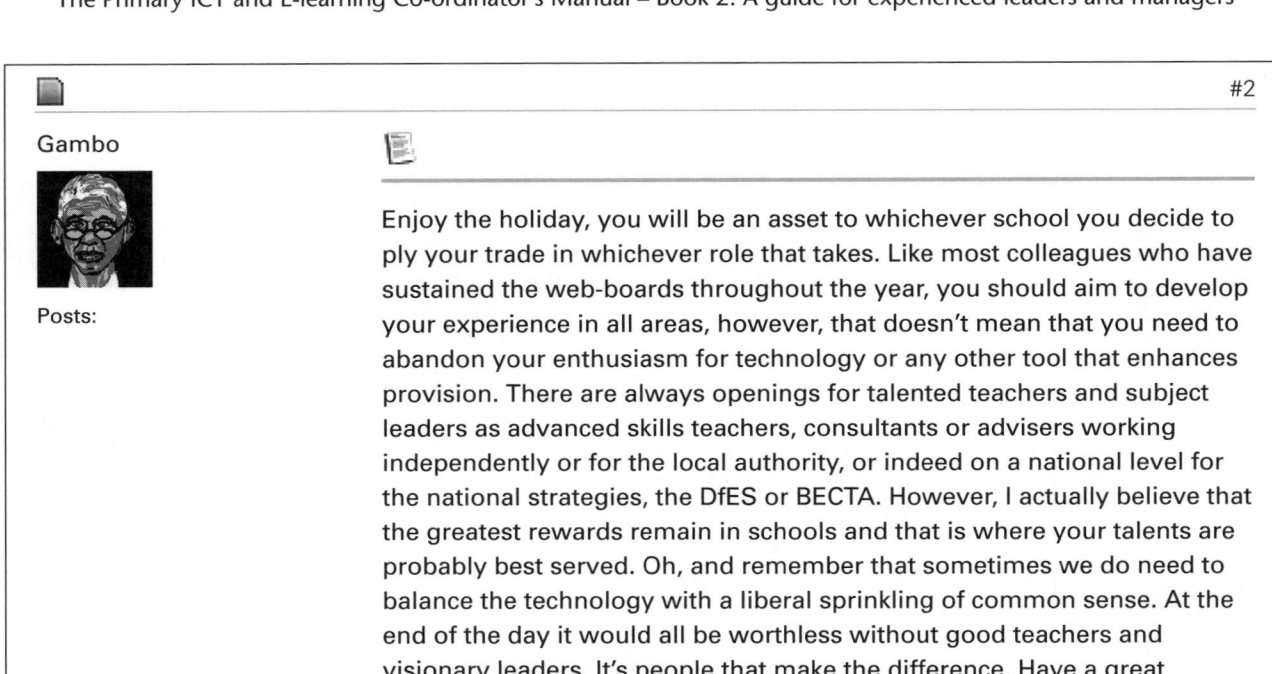

#2

Gambo

Posts:

Enjoy the holiday, you will be an asset to whichever school you decide to ply your trade in whichever role that takes. Like most colleagues who have sustained the web-boards throughout the year, you should aim to develop your experience in all areas, however, that doesn't mean that you need to abandon your enthusiasm for technology or any other tool that enhances provision. There are always openings for talented teachers and subject leaders as advanced skills teachers, consultants or advisers working independently or for the local authority, or indeed on a national level for the national strategies, the DfES or BECTA. However, I actually believe that the greatest rewards remain in schools and that is where your talents are probably best served. Oh, and remember that sometimes we do need to balance the technology with a liberal sprinkling of common sense. At the end of the day it would all be worthless without good teachers and visionary leaders. It's people that make the difference. Have a great summer. I've a feeling we'll be chatting again.

Quote

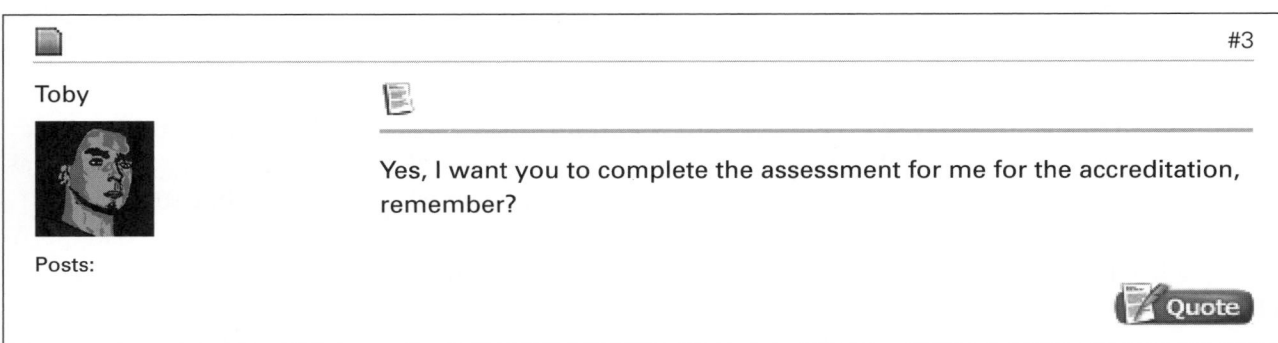

#3

Toby

Posts:

Yes, I want you to complete the assessment for me for the accreditation, remember?

Quote

9th August

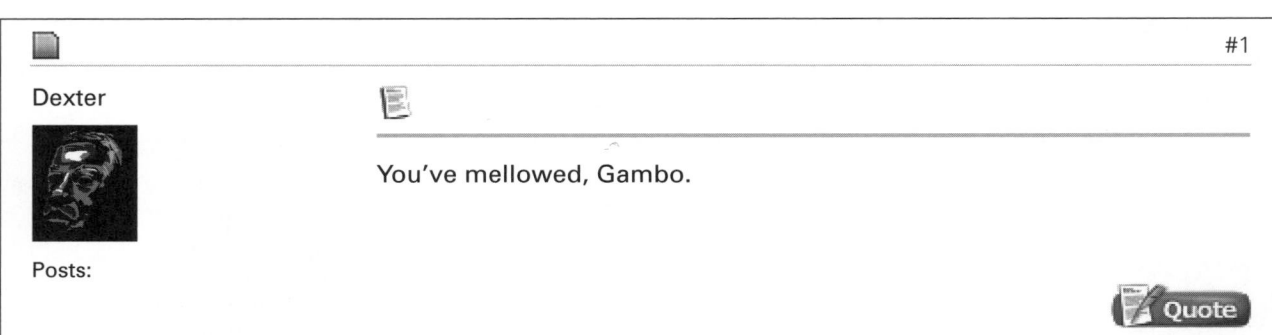

#1

Dexter

Posts:

You've mellowed, Gambo.

Quote

11th August

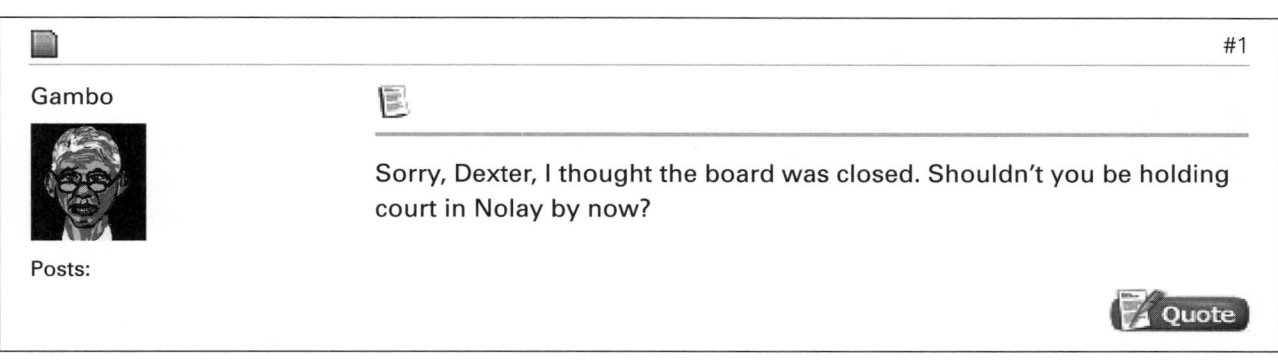

Gambo

Posts:

#1

Sorry, Dexter, I thought the board was closed. Shouldn't you be holding court in Nolay by now?

Quote

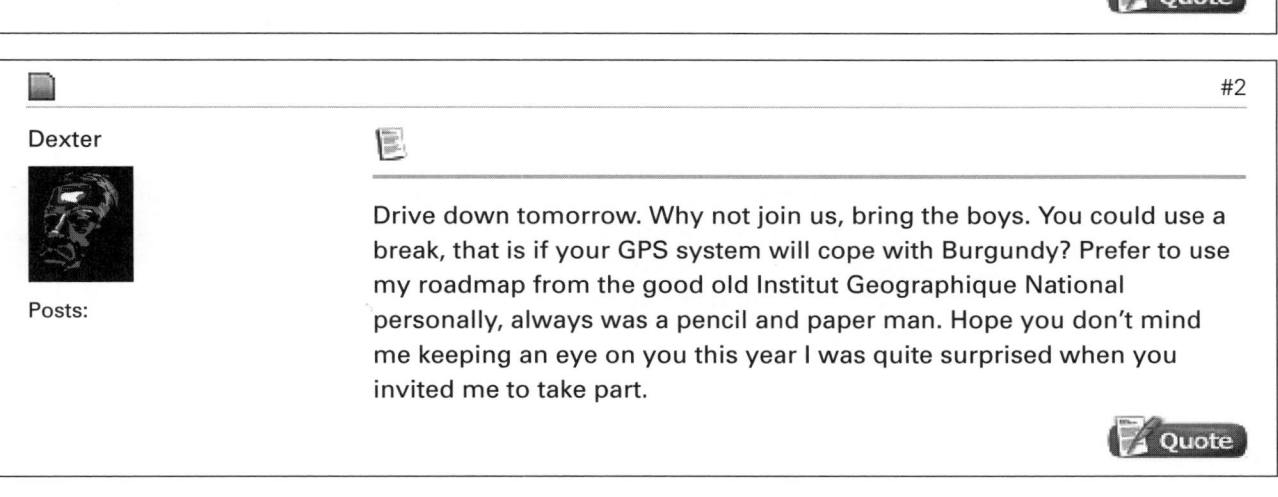

Dexter

Posts:

#2

Drive down tomorrow. Why not join us, bring the boys. You could use a break, that is if your GPS system will cope with Burgundy? Prefer to use my roadmap from the good old Institut Geographique National personally, always was a pencil and paper man. Hope you don't mind me keeping an eye on you this year I was quite surprised when you invited me to take part.

Quote

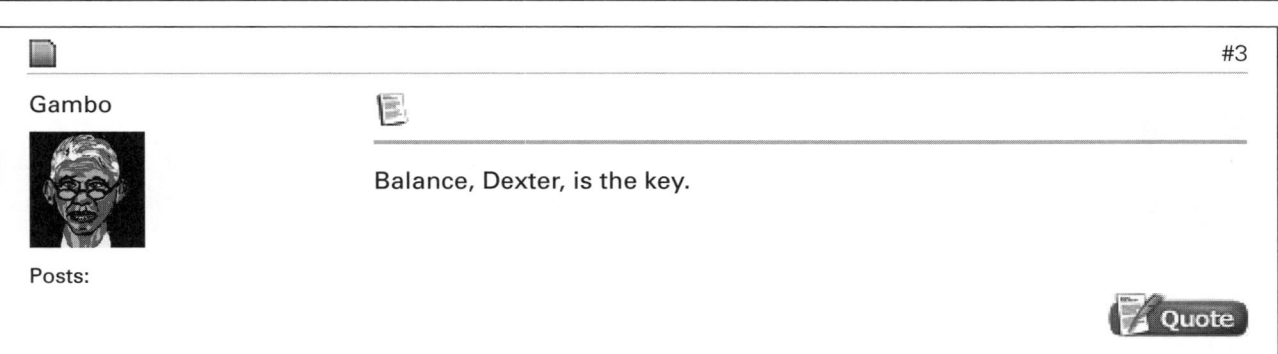

Gambo

Posts:

#3

Balance, Dexter, is the key.

Quote

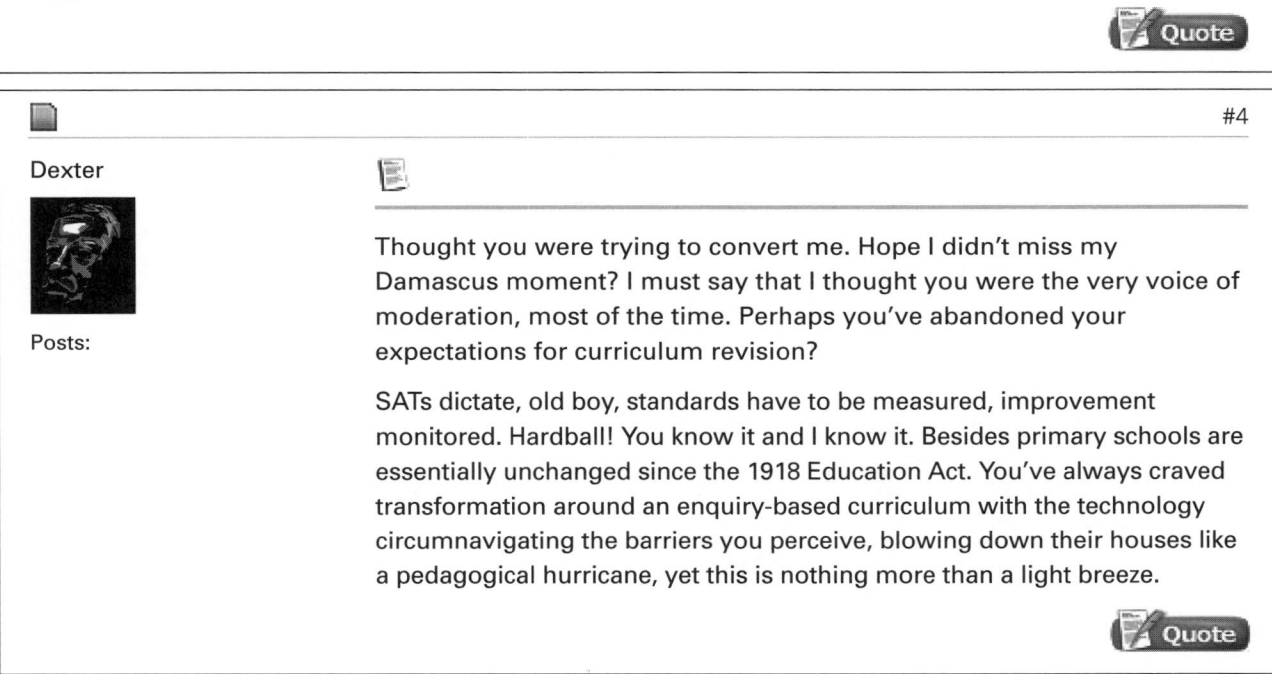

Dexter

Posts:

#4

Thought you were trying to convert me. Hope I didn't miss my Damascus moment? I must say that I thought you were the very voice of moderation, most of the time. Perhaps you've abandoned your expectations for curriculum revision?

SATs dictate, old boy, standards have to be measured, improvement monitored. Hardball! You know it and I know it. Besides primary schools are essentially unchanged since the 1918 Education Act. You've always craved transformation around an enquiry-based curriculum with the technology circumnavigating the barriers you perceive, blowing down their houses like a pedagogical hurricane, yet this is nothing more than a light breeze.

Quote

#5

Gambo

Posts:

But at least you are listening, Dexter. School leaders have to take on board what is happening with regard to the E-learning agenda and in particular how the wider world outside our schools is been reshaped. ECM couldn't have been more explicit about the role of ICT and the need for every child to develop their core skills with regard to economic well-being. Have you not revised your SEF recently? Anyway, it is not about pedagogy it's about life chances and that is why you are here. Even you realize that you can only keep your head in the sand for so long. Ask any teacher who's had an interactive whiteboard installed in their classroom to resort to chalk and talk again and they'll be horrified. It is now time to refocus on the learners and to champion relevance.

Schools are changing, Dexter; you can't seriously quote legislation that's nearly a century old anymore. There is a gale blowing through schools up and down the country and you know it. I'm not talking about hardware. I'm referring to opportunity and the manner in which learners from all sections of society are realizing that they have a voice, within school and beyond.

#6

Dexter

Posts:

I'm heading for France, Gambo. Join me, turn off your PC or Mac or whatever it is you are currently championing. I'm ready for a break, besides I need to speak to you, properly not virtually. I need your advice, call me!

References

Aberdeen schools ILS Investigation (2003), http://www.miice.org.uk/miscellaneousEA.html.

AbilityNet, national charity helping disabled adults and children use computers and the Internet, www.abilitynet.org.uk.

Ambleweb, Ambleside School website, Look and Cover spelling application, www.amblesideprimary.com/ambleweb/lookcover/lookcover.html.

Apple 'i-Movie' movie software, http://www.apple.com/uk/education.

Apple 'Podcast Producer' http://www.apple.co./uk/servewr/macosx/leopard/podcastproducer.html.

Ask for Kids, Internet search engine, www.askforkids.com.

Audacity sound editing software, http://audacity.sourceforge.net/.

BBC, Dance mat typing, www.bbc.co.uk/schools/typing.

BBC News 8th September 2005, Sir Tim Berners Lees Interview, http://news.bbc.co.uk/1/hi/1technology/4132752.sth.

BBC, Online News Report 'Schools mark thieves with water' 24 July 2006, http://news.bbc.co.uk/2/hi/uk_news/england/west_yorkshire/5210888.stm.

BECTA, 'Apply for the ICT Mark', http://www.becta.org.uk/schools/ictmark.

BECTA, 'Choose and Assessor', http://www.becta.org.uk/schools/ictmark.

BECTA, *ICT – Essential Guides for School Governors:*
 1 http://publications.becta.org.uk/display.cfm?resID=25895
 2 http://publications.becta.org.uk/display.cfm?resID=25896
 3 http://publications.becta.org.uk/display.cfm?resID=25898
 4 http://publications.becta.org.uk/display.cfm?resID=25899
 5 http://publications.becta.org.uk/display.cfm?resID=25900
 6 http://publications.becta.org.uk/display.cfm?resID=25901
 7 http://publications.becta.org.uk/display.cfm?resID=25902
 8 http://publications.becta.org.uk/display.cfm?resID=25903
 9 http://publications.becta.org.uk/display.cfm?resID=25904
10 http://publications.becta.org.uk/display.cfm?resID=25905

BECTA, *ICT Investment Planner*, http://schools.becta.org.uk/downloads/ICT%20Investment%20Planner%20-%20v.1.04.xls.

BECTA, *Self-Review Framework Matrix*, http://matrix.becta.org.uk/selfreview.

BECTA, *Ways to Use the Self-review Framework*, http://becta.org.uk/corporate/publications/index.cfm.

BECTA (2005), *E-safety, Developing a Whole-School Approach to Internet Safety*, Ref: 15327

BECTA (2006a), *E-safety, Developing Whole-School Policies to Support Effective Practice*, Ref. BEC1-15402

BECTA (2006b), *Learning Platform Functional Requirements*, http://schools.becta.org.uk/upload-dir/downloads/functional_req_learning_platforms_v1.1.pdf.

Belsey, B. (2004), *Cyberbullying: An Emerging Threat to the 'Always On' Generation*, www.cyberbullying.ca.

BGfL, Birmingham Grid for Learning, eBooks resource library, www.bgfl.org/ebooklibrary.

Blogger, weblog publishing site, http://www2.blogger.com/.

Bravenet online web services, www.bravenet.com.

Child Safe, Internet safety software, www.webroot.com.

CLEO, Cumbria & Lancashire Education Online, regional broadband consortium, http://www.cleo.net.uk/.

Coleman, D.W. (2002), 'On foot in SIM CITY: using SIM COPTER as the basis for an ESL writing assignment, *Simulation and Gaming*, 33 (2): 217–30.

Collins, J. (1992), *Beyond Entrepreneurship*, New York: Prentice Hall.

Computer Clubs for Girls (CC4G), e-skills UK , www.cc4g.net, www.e-skills.com.

Cyberquoll, online Internet safety materials, Net Alert, the Australian Internet Safety Advisory Body, www.cyberquoll.com.au.

Cyber Patrol, Internet safety software, www.cyberpatrol.com.

Cyber Sentinal, Internet safety software, www.cybersentinel.com.

CYBERsitter, Internet safety software, www.cybersitter.com.

Derry, J. (2006), digital artist, Wacom interview, www.wacom-asia.com/community/procorner/interview/johnderry.php.

DfES, *Every Child Matters*, guidance on local safeguarding children boards, www.everychildmatters.gov.uk/lscb.

DfES, Primary Framework for literacy and mathematics, www.standards.dfes.gov.uk/primary frameworks.

DfES, (2003), *Fulfilling the Potential: Transforming Teaching and Learning through ICT in Schools*. DfES/0265/2003.

DfES, (2005a), *Harnessing Technology: Transforming Learning and Children's Services*, www.dfes.gov.uk/publications/e-strategy.

DfES, (2005b), *Learning Platforms: Primary, Making IT Personal – Primary Version*, Ref. 2101–2005DBW-EN.

DfES, (2006a), *Computer for Pupils 2006–08 Guidance for LAs and Schools*, http://www.teachernet.gov.uk/docbank/index.cfm?id=10284.

DfES, (2006b) *Every Child Matters: Primary Capital Programme, Building Primary Schools at the Heart of the Community*, DFES/0287/2006.

DfES, (2007), *Making Good Progress*, Ref. 00030-2007DOM-EN.

Digital Blue 'Creator' movie software, http://www.digiblue.com.

E2BN, East of England Broadband Network, regional broadband consortium, http://www.e2bn.org/.

Egan, G. (1998), *The Skilled Helper*, Belmont, CA: Wadsworth.

EMBC, East Midlands Broadband Consortium, regional broadband consortium, http://www.embc.org.uk/home/default.asp.

ePALS, online pupil email, www.epals.com.

Erving Elementary School, Erving, Massachusetts, USA, www.erving.com/simcity2000/index.htm.

FilterPak, Internet safety software, www.familyconnect.com.

Free Typing Games, free typing games, www.freetypinggame.net.

Friedman, T. (2005), *Every Child Matters, What It Means for the ICT teacher'*, www.ictineducation.org.

Global-Leap, interactive videoconferencing resource, www.global-leap.com.

Google Docs Online Fileshare Service, www.google.com/google-d-s/tour1.html.

Grant, L. (2006), *Using Wikis in Schools: A Case Study*. Futurelab, http://www.futurelab.org.uk/research/disc_papers.htm.

GRID CLUB, Internet proficiency scheme, www.gridclub.com/freearea/tasters/cybercafe/base.htm.

Habbo Hotel, virtual online community, www.habbo.co.uk.

Haugland, S. (2000), 'Early childhood classrooms in the 21st century: using computers to maximize learning, *Young Children*, 55(1): 12–18.

Hector's World, *online Internet safety materials*, Netsafe, New Zealand's Internet safety group, www.hectorsworld.com.

Homerton Nursery School and Early Excellence Centre, http://foundation.e2bn.net.

James Wright Organisation, Primary schools ICT services, www.james-wright.org, www.ictinschools.com.

Keyboard Crazy, *Concept keyboard*, www.keyboardcrazy.co.uk.

Kuntz. M. (2001), *SimCity 3000 Companion Teacher's Guide*, www.simcity3000unlimited.ea.com/us/guide/.

LGfL, London Grid for Learning, regional broadband consortium, http://cms.lgfl.net/lgfl/web/homepage.

Marina View School, New Zealand primary school website, www.marinav.school.nz.

McAfee Parental Controls, Internet safety software, www.McAfee.co.uk.

Microsoft 'Move Maker' movie software, http://www.microsoft.com/windowsxp/using/moviemaker.

Moursund, D. (2005), *Planning, Forecasting, and Inventing Your Computers-in-Education Future*, Eugene, OR: D. Moursund.

Myspace, social networking website, www.myspace.com.

NASA, digital learning network, http://nasadln.nmsu.edu/dln/.

NetNanny, Internet safety software, www.netnanny.com.

Netty's World, Online Internet safety materials, Net Alert, the Australian Internet safety advisory body, www.nettysworld.com.au.

NGfL, Northern Grid for Learning, regional broadband consortium, http://www.portal.northerngrid.org.

Norton Parental Controls, Internet safety software, www.symantec.com.

NWLG, North West Learning Grid, regional broadband consortium, http://www.nwlg.org.

Ofsted (2005a), *Conducting the Inspection – Guidance for Inspectors of Schools*, HMI Ref. 20070007, www.ofsted.gov.uk/publications/20070007.

Ofsted (2005b), *'Every Child Matters' Framework for the Inspection of Schools in England*, HMI Ref. 2435, www.ofsted.gov.uk/publications/2435.

Ofsted (2005c), *Using the Evaluation Schedule – Guidance for Inspectors of Schools*, HMI Ref. 20070014, www.ofsted.gov.uk/publications/20070014.

Parents' Gateway, online MIS parents portal, www.parentsgateway.com.

Pellegrino, J.W. (2006), *Rethinking and Redesigning Curriculum: Instruction And Assessment: What Contemporary Research and Theory Suggests*, National Centre on Education and the Economy for the New Commission on the Skills of the American Workforce.

Pinnacle 'Studio' Movie software, http://www.pinnaclesys.com.

Podbean podcast hosting, http://www.podbean.com.

Project Gutenberg, online digital library, www.gutenberg.org.

QCA, *Guidance on Teaching the Gifted and Talented*, (ICT), www.nc.uk.net/gt/ict/index.htm.

QCA, (2001), *Planning, Teaching and Assessing the Curriculum for Pupils with Learning Difficulties*, www.nc.uk.net/ld/ICT_content.html

Revelation Natural Art, educational art software suite, Logotron, www.logo.com/rna/.

Richards, C. (2005), 'The design of effective ICT-supported learning activities: exemplary models, changing requirements, and new possibilities', *Language Learning & Technology*, 9(1): 60–79.

RM Maths, curriculum software, www.rm.com/Primary/Products/Product.asp?cref=PD2381.

School Profile, www.schoolsfinder.direct.gov.uk/about-school-profile.

Secondlife, virtual online community, www.secondlife.com.

SEGfL, South East Grid for Learning, regional broadband consortium, http://www.segfl.org.uk.

Sim City, simulation software by Electronic Arts Inc., www.simcity.ea.com.

Sim City, simulation software (early editions) by Maxis Inc., www.maxis.com.

Sir Robert Hitcham's Primary School, http://www.hitchams.suffolk.sch.uk/foundation/index.htm.

Smartwater, security marking system, www.smartwater.com.

Stephen, C. and Plowman, L. (2002), *ICT in Pre-school, a Benign Addition? A Review of the Literature on ICT in Pre-school Settings*, Glasgow: Learning and Teaching Scotland.

Stephen, C. and Plowman, L. (2003), *Come Back in Two Years. A Study of the Use of ICT in Pre-school Settings*, Glasgow: Learning and Teaching Scotland.

Surfswell, online Internet safety materials, *The Disney Group*, www.disney.go.com/surfswell.

SWGfL, South West Grid for Learning, regional broadband consortium, http://www.swgfl.org.uk/.

Tan, C. (2003), *E-Mentoring Through Knowledge Community*, www.globalkc.net.

The *Guardian*, 10th January 2006, Mike Griffith interview, http://education.guardian.co.uk/print/0,,5370203-108699,00.html.

Think.com, an online community for learning, www.think.com.

UK National Statistics Omnibus Survey (2006) 'National Statistics Omnibus Survey, Northern Ireland Omnibus Survey and Survey of Internet Service Providers', http://www.statistics.gov.uk/cci/nugget.asp?id=8.

Underwood, J. Cavendish, S., Dowling, S., Fogelman, K. and Lawson, T. (1994), *Integrated Learning Systems in UK Schools*, Coventry: NCET.

Wacom, graphics tablets educational resources, www.wacom.com/education.

Weinberger, D. (2002), *Small Pieces Loosely Joined*, New York: Perseus Books.

Wikipedia, online wiki collaborative encyclopedia, http://www.en.wikipedia.org/.

WMNet, West Midlands RBC, regional broadband consortium, http://www.wmnet.org.uk/.

Yahooligans, Internet search engine, www.yahooligans.yahoo.com.

Yelland, N. (1999), 'Reconceptualizing schooling with technology for the 21st century', *Information Technology in Childhood Education Annual*, pp. 39–59.

YHGfL, Yorkshire Humber Grid for Learning, regional broadband consortium, http://www.yhgfl.net/.

YouTube, video share website, www.youtube.com.

Index